The Adolescent Views Himself

A PSYCHOLOGY OF ADOLESCENCE

The Adolescent Views Himself

A PSYCHOLOGY OF ADOLESCENCE

by Ruth Strang

PROFESSOR OF EDUCATION
TEACHERS COLLEGE
COLUMBIA UNIVERSITY

Drawings by
Sally Donaldson

McGRAW-HILL BOOK COMPANY, INC.

1957　　　New York　　　Toronto　　　London

THE ADOLESCENT VIEWS HIMSELF

Library of Congress Catalog Card Number 57–9437

v

Preface

In spite of the numerous authoritative and comprehensive books on adolescence, one most important area of adolescence has been neglected: the ways in which adolescents perceive themselves and their world. This is so important because the concepts which adolescents form of themselves and of the world in relation to themselves exert a strong influence on their behavior. Even if an adolescent's perception is faulty, i.e., does not accord with the way adults perceive him, it is nonetheless real; it produces real results. Individuals respond to the situation-as-they-perceive-it.

The extensive original data in this book consist of adolescents' own statements of their attitudes and values, their activities and relationships, their problems of growing up. These detailed original descriptions and comments show how adolescents perceive themselves, the world in which they live, the future, and other matters related to their development. They serve as convincing evidence of individuality; they represent the thoughts and feelings of many individual adolescents. These original data are supplemented and interpreted by information gained from previous research and by insights from psychological literature. Against this background, the uniqueness of each adolescent, as he perceives himself, as well as common characteristics, becomes evident.

The organization of a book on adolescents presents a serious dilemma for the author. Since growth is a continuous process, and there is a wide range in the rate of development and age of maturing of normal boys and girls, one hesitates to divide the book into sections covering certain "stages" in growth. Since there are actually no typical adolescents, one is cautious about discussing common characteristics. Since all aspects of development are interrelated, one might give the wrong impression by writing separate chapters on its physical, social, emotional, intellectual, and academic facets. Since adolescent behavior may be interpreted as an attempt to meet certain needs, as a response to the way adolescents perceive themselves and their environment, one cannot merely present the results of overt behavior.

Accordingly, the focus of this book is on the manifold ways in which adolescents perceive themselves in the psychological, social, and physical setting in which they are growing up. In other words, this book attempts to describe the unique transitional stage between childhood and adulthood largely through the eyes of young people themselves: how they view themselves and their world, the developmental tasks to be accomplished during this period, and the kind of learning conditions and guidance they would like to have.

There are many people whom I would like to thank for the insights and illustrations which constitute so much of this book. First of these are the thousands of teen-agers who, during the past ten years in which I have been gathering this material, have written spontaneously and frankly on the way they feel about the many aspects of growing up.

Second, I am grateful to the hundreds of teachers, administrators, and counselors in my graduate classes who have shared with me their observations of adolescents. Obviously it is impossible to mention them all, but among those who have collected compositions with notable skill, or who have made especially insightful interpretations of their observations of adolescents, are the following: Romona C. Beard, Rose Berman, Betty Kay Bone, James A. De Sonne, Harold E. Dietzel, Helen M. Dunn, Joan Dygert, Lois Eldridge, Sally M. Feulner, George M. Frank, Julia Furman, John F. Gardephe, Wayne Graham, Lloyd Y. S. Kim, John Kozak, Jean A. Land, Robert R. Leeper, Samuel J. Levitt, Edith Elizabeth Lott, Charles McDowell, George Melton, Elizabeth C. Milner, Thomas J. Quinn, Thomas Ragoulates, Robert

Lee Randolph, John Francis Ryan, Charles McDowell Thompson, Dorothy M. Webber, Evelyn E. Wilson, and Richard F. Wollin. In addition, larger numbers of compositions were obtained by Dr. Glyn Morris, Director of Guidance, Lewis County, New York, from adolescents in rural communities; by Miss Catherine Beachley, Supervisor of Guidance and Research, Board of Education of Washington County, Hagerstown, Maryland, who not only obtained hundreds of compositions but also gave additional information about the intelligence quotients and reading-grade levels of these students; and by Dr. Ethlyne Phelps, teacher of English and remedial reading and counselor in charge of testing, Normandy Senior High School, St. Louis, Missouri. It has also been an inspiration to hear about Dr. Mary Holman's work with adolescents, individually and in groups, during her many years as director of guidance in the public schools of Orange, New Jersey; Miss Florence Myers' contacts with this age group as administrative assistant and dean of girls in George Washington High School, New York City; Miss Amelia Melnik's points of view based on her intimate understanding of adolescents; Dr. Virginia Bailard's program of counseling and psychological services in the Long Beach, California, city schools; and to have been associated in my Teachers College classes in counseling and group activities with Dr. Frances M. Wilson, Director of Guidance, New York City schools.

To Dr. Warren Roome, Professor of Mathematics at Radford College, Radford, Virginia, I am especially indebted for the tabulation and statistical treatment of many large groups of compositions and for his critical reading of parts of the manuscript, and to Mrs. Alma Fogarty for her expert typing of the manuscript.

Third, I would acknowledge my indebtedness to the multidiscipline writings on the physical, social, intellectual, and emotional aspects of adolescent development.

The sketches by Miss Sally Donaldson and the photographs call attention to certain common characteristics and further emphasize individual differences in adolescents.

From all of these sources I have attempted to compose a realistic view of the development of adolescents, with the focus on the inner world of adolescents—how their world looks to them, and how they feel about it. Such a picture should give teachers, counselors, parents, and young people themselves a keener understanding of how it feels to be an adolescent. This kind of understanding should evoke more informed and vigorous efforts to provide the experiences which adolescents need for their best development.

Ruth Strang

How to Read this Book

Since this is a practical rather than a theoretical book, the reader's purpose will be to extract from it ideas, impressions, facts, and descriptions of procedures which he can use in some way.

First consider what would be helpful for you to know about that "in-between period," adolescence. What sympathy and understanding do you want to gain? What specific questions do you need to answer? What procedures and programs for working with adolescents individually or in groups do you want to improve?

Then read the preface to ascertain the author's intent. Survey the table of contents to gain an idea of the scope of the book. Decide whether to read it as a whole or to select certain chapters of immediate interest and value to you. Whichever you do, it will be well to read each chapter in the following way:

1. Read the chapter title. Recall what you already know about this topic—what you have learned from your own experience, introspection, observation, and reading. What content would you include if you were writing the chapter?

2. Skim the chapter to get a sense of its over-all structure—What is the author trying to do? What questions will the chapter answer? What insights into adolescent needs and development may it afford? How can you relate the ideas you will obtain to your work with adolescents? Supplement and reinforce your own questions by studying those at the end of the chapter.

3. Read the chapter thoughtfully and imaginatively to answer the questions you have raised and to gain other ideas of importance to you.

4. Review to be sure you have obtained the information you want in the form you want it.

5. Apply what you have learned, and incorporate it into your total background of knowledge about adolescents.

6. Check your present knowledge against occasional observation and study of adolescents whom you know.

7. Select from the bibliography books and articles of special interest and value to you, and read them.

Contents

xi

PART THREE
FAVORABLE CONDITIONS

The Adolescent Views Himself

A PSYCHOLOGY OF ADOLESCENCE

CHAPTER 1

Sources of Understanding

We want to understand adolescents for several reasons: so that we can help them to understand themselves better and handle life situations more effectively; so that we can guide them in the use of their resources and provide conditions each individual needs for his best development; so that we shall not mistake normal difficulties of growing up for pathological problems; so that we shall not hurry them through any stage of their development or expect too little or too much of them at any given time.

TWO KINDS OF ERRORS

In the study of adolescents we tend to fall into two kinds of errors. The first is to focus attention on the hypothetical "average adolescent." But actually, "the normal is an ideal. It is a picture that one fabricates of the average characteristics of men, and to find them all in a single man is hardly to be expected. It is . . . [a] false picture." [1] Every time we write a statement about "the adolescent" we can think of some adolescent to whom it does not apply. Adolescents show a wide variation in physique, in physiological maturing, in aptitudes, attitudes, and behavior. As we observe individual adolescents, we are impressed with the infinite variety of biological make-up and cultural background with its varied opportunities for self-realization. There is also a third

[1] W. Somerset Maugham, *The Summing Up*, pp. 68–69, International Collectors' Library ed. New York: Doubleday & Company, Inc., 1954.

dimension of diversity—the manifold ways in which they view themselves and their world. They vary enormously in their concepts of themselves and their hopes for the future. However, we often tend merely to give lip service to the statement made by Tryon and Henry:

> We accept as axiomatic that there are no two persons in the world alike. So, while as psychologists and sociologists we have come to discern common patterns of adjustment, we also realize that each person has his own unique version of these common patterns. Such uniqueness is grounded partly in our genetic inheritance, partly in the long array of successes and failures in making adjustments in the past.[2]

A second common error, highlighted in Luigi Pirandello's play, *Six Characters in Search of an Author,* is that of generalizing and jumping to conclusions from specific incidents. When we hear of one adolescent's escapade, we tend to conclude that "all adolescents are like that." Fritz Redl warns against falling in with "the newspaper stereotypes of youth"—as immature and irresponsible and needing constant supervision.

KINDS OF UNDERSTANDING NEEDED

Two kinds of understanding are needed: (1) an understanding of the many-sided aspects of adolescent development in various environments, and (2) an understanding of the individual adolescents with whom we are in contact. Understanding of adolescent development in general alerts us to behavior, attitudes, and other aspects of development that we might otherwise fail to notice or whose significance we might overlook. Knowing the common sequences and patterns of development, we shall have some idea of how far an individual youngster has progressed toward completing his total growth pattern. We will, as Lawrence K. Frank has so well said, help him to live most fully in

---

[2] Caroline Tryon and William E. Henry, "How Children Learn Personal and Social Adjustment," *Learning and Instruction,* Forty-ninth Yearbook of the National Society for the Study of Education, part I, p. 157. Chicago: University of Chicago Press, 1950.

each stage as it occurs.[3] Knowledge of recurring patterns and common characteristics is helpful when used as a background for the study of the individual. Such understanding may be gained from research and clinical studies.

We can best understand adolescents as individuals if we observe and study them directly and listen to them, without being biased by preconceptions about the "typical adolescent." Without this awareness of individual differences and without an understanding of the individuality of adolescents, we cannot adequately help them to cope with life situations realistically, in accordance with their potentialities and limitations.

Objective measures of various aspects of adolescent development are not enough: we must know what the changes the individual is experiencing mean to him. Reading "the language of behavior," as Dr. James J. Plant used to say, is difficult. There is no blueprint that a psychologist or psychiatrist can give teachers to explain a particular adolescent's behavior. It may have many meanings, depending on the way in which he perceives the situation. We need to know how he feels about growing up. To understand adolescents, we must view them and their world through their eyes. We cannot depend on our recollections of how we felt in *our* teens. Times have changed. The principle of "the obliviscence of the disagreeable" is also likely to operate; we tend to forget the unpleasant.

ACCENT ON PERCEPTION

Psychologists have increasingly emphasized the importance of studying the way an individual perceives a situation. Many recent trends, such as that toward concern with the self-concept and "self-consistency," focus on this emphasis. The way the person perceives himself in relation to the situation largely determines how he behaves and what he learns. In the phraseology of gestalt psychology, a person responds to the "situation-as-per-

[3] Lawrence K. Frank, "Remedial Guidance," in *Yearbook of Education, 1955* (Robert King Hall and J. A. Lauwerys, eds.), p. 471. London: Evans Brothers, Ltd., 1955.

ceived." His perception, in turn, depends on his ability and background, the immediate time and place, the interpersonal relations involved, his unconscious motivation, his previous experience.

In client-centered counseling the individual is helped to gain an understanding of himself and his relationships. In education, too, teachers are urged to look beneath the child's surface behavior to its causes and the meaning which the behavior has for him. When teachers or parents get a glimpse of what a given situation means to a youngster, his actions begin to make sense. And then, when the teacher or parent begins to view young people in a new light, he treats them differently because of his different perception of them.

WAYS OF GAINING UNDERSTANDING

There are many ways of understanding pupils: observing them all during the day; listening sympathetically to them; keeping dated samples of their work; reading their compositions about themselves and their relations with others; engaging them in informal discussions of pictures and case stories; asking them to write their three wishes; studying their spontaneous drawings and paintings, responses to incomplete sentences and stories, and other projective productions. Most of the teacher's understanding of his pupils is thus gained as an intrinsic part of teaching, not as an "extra" added to an already heavy program.[4]

More formal methods are used by counselors, psychologists, and research workers. Beginning with unstructured compositions, recorded group discussions, systematic observations, and scheduled interviews, the student of adolescence may also use various tests and inventories, precise measures of bodily growth, and projective techniques. The results of all methods used may be synthesized in a case study to gain the most complete understanding of an individual.

There are individual differences in the ways youngsters re-

[4] Ruth Strang, "How Children and Adolescents View Their World," *Mental Hygiene*, vol. 38 (January, 1954), p. 28.

spond to various techniques. Some adolescents are stimulated to think freely in a group discussion; others respond best in a face-to-face interview; still others welcome the opportunity to express their thoughts and feelings in anonymous compositions. Some adolescents are far more suggestible than others and are therefore more influenced by the presence of certain items on a check list or by the wording of specific questions.

Combination of Methods

To see the interrelations within total growth and thus to gain the most adequate understanding of adolescents, one should consider a variety of evidence. Frank and his associates [5] used a combination of projective methods with the same individuals to obtain a wealth of deeper understanding of the personality of adolescents. Gesell and his associates recognized the importance of personal documents when they said, "Near the brink of adolescence, we must begin to take children more completely into our confidence." [6]

More [7] made a most intensive study of the relations among the physical, emotional, and social development of thirty-three adolescents—sixteen males and seventeen females—tested over a period between the ages of eleven and seventeen. He selected his subjects from what seemed to be a "typical" Middle Western community and obtained a wealth of data on each subject: intelligence-test scores on the Binet, Wechsler-Bellevue, or Primary Mental Abilities tests; religious affiliation; data on height, weight, chest and hip diameters; ratings on pubic and axillary hair growth for boys, and report of first menstruation of girls. Social data were obtained from interviews with parents and siblings: observations and anecdotal records; reports of participa-

[5] Lawrence K. Frank et al., *Personality Development in Adolescent Girls*. New Orleans: Child Development Publications, 1953.

[6] Arnold Gesell, Frances L. Ilg, and Louise Bates Ames, *Youth, the Years from Ten to Sixteen*. New York: Harper & Brothers, 1956.

[7] Douglas M. More, *Developmental Concordance and Discordance during Puberty and Early Adolescence*, Monograph of the Society for Research in Child Development, Inc., ser. 56, vol. 18, no. 1, 1953. Champaign, Ill.: University of Illinois, Child Development Publications, 1955.

tion in the school and community; sociometric measures and "Guess Who" tests with questions such as, "Who are the ones who are always trying to run things? Who try to tell others what to do?" Deeper psychological data were obtained from a series of ratings made in a clinical case conference, from compositions, from the Rorschach test, and from the Thematic Apperception Test administered three times at intervals. Such a study yields insight into the many-sided aspects of adolescent development, although it does not warrant the drawing of conclusions about adolescents in general.

Unstructured or Slightly Structured Compositions

When youngsters turn an appraising eye upon themselves some of the insights they come up with are startlingly clear, some of the judgments surprisingly hard. . . . In many classrooms today, and in a few camps with leaders skilled in child guidance, youngsters are invited to take a long look at themselves and write down—if they choose—their self-evaluations. The results are as varied as the children themselves—rigidly condemning, realistically balanced, or so self-satisfied as almost to seem a kind of whistling in the dark.[8]

How Obtained. Freely written compositions are easily obtained as a regular part of an English class. They may also be written in other classes or in homeroom or guidance periods.

The following are some of the topics on which compositions for this book were obtained:

The teachers who have helped me most
What I like or dislike about teachers
How I feel when I take home my report card and what my parents do about it
How I feel about growing up, or what growing up means to me
What makes studying hard (or easy) for me
Why it is sometimes hard to get along with parents
What help or guidance persons of my age want from adults
Times when I have felt at a loss, "all at sea," or disturbed
What causes juvenile delinquency
How I feel when I am punished for something wrong I have done

[8] Dorothy Barclay, "What Children Think of Themselves," *New York Times Magazine* (July 31, 1955), p. 36.

The kind of person I think I am; the kind of person others think
I am; the kind of person I would like to become

My reading autobiography

My educational autobiography

How the world looks to me at present

What gives me most satisfaction—what makes me happy or unhappy

What makes me tick

What life means to me

In writing these compositions, the students were encouraged
to focus on content rather than on wording, spelling, and other
details of form, and to write freely about themselves. Except for
one set of compositions, which was later studied with reference
to intelligence and reading ability, the compositions were anonymous. The data yielded by this approach may be quite different
from those yielded in response to specific direct questions or to a
check list.

Despite the authoritarian aura of some classrooms and the human tendency to put one's best foot forward, almost all of these
relatively unstructured compositions seem sincere. They indicate
that adolescents have an interest in writing frankly about themselves. A few show remarkable insights. Many of them, varying,
of course, with the student-teacher relations, give glimpses into
adolescents' inner world of feeling and meaning. Gillespie and
Allport reported in their study of personal documents written
by American university students "a high degree of frankness, individuality, and straightforward reporting. There seems to be
little reticence, little posing, little striving for literary effects." [9]

The following directions for writing one of these compositions
were given to the teacher and students. Similar approaches were
used with others.

To the teacher:

Present the project so as to get the interest and cooperation of the
pupils. The compositions are of no value unless this is achieved. The

[9] James M. Gillespie and Gordon W. Allport, *Youth's Outlook on the
Future, A Cross-national Study*, p. 13. New York: Doubleday & Company,
Inc., 1955.

following approach has been used with high school pupils in presenting one problem. It can be modified for the presenting of other problems.

Directions for pupils:

Everyone feels disturbed, "all at sea," "at a loss," or gets "in a jam" sometimes. It may happen at home, at school, in a club meeting, at social affairs, when you are trying to make plans for the future, such as going to college or getting a job, or in other situations. For your composition this period, think of one time recently when you have felt disturbed, "at a loss," or have had to face some difficult situation. Describe the situation and what you did—picture it so vividly that the reader will see clearly what the difficulty was, what you did, what happened as a result, and whether the result was satisfactory or unsatisfactory.

Put your age, grade, and section at the top of the paper. Also tell whether you are a boy or a girl. Do not sign your name; then you will feel freer to write frankly. As you will not be marked on these papers, you can give your full attention to getting down a true account of real-life uncertainties or troubles.

The teacher was also asked to give the average intelligence of the class and their intelligence range (if available), as well as a brief description of their socio-economic background, and to specify the subject and grade in which the composition was written.

Examples of Compositions. The following are examples of the compositions obtained for two of the topics on which adolescents were asked to write. The wording, spelling, and punctuation are unchanged, because these give some understanding of the students' verbal ability and logical thinking.

The first example was written by a boy fifteen years old, in the seventh grade. It expresses poignantly and sincerely, despite the very bad spelling, the mixed feelings of inadequacy and hopefulness characteristic of many a retarded young adolescent.

When I think of the world a heard I whold like too be a lectrishion. but Im not very smart. and dont get good marks on report cards. I worry a little about geting a job, latter on in life. Id like to get in the servise. but I might not make it. I like school and try my best. Id like to have a faimly later in life. but it might not be possible. At sixteen Id like to go to trade school and make something of myself. and work myself too be a ful flegd lectrishion. my Sunday school teacher takes me up to his house and I help him. he say it will help me later in life. My father say exprence is the best teacher, and I go a long with that. people asked what do you gain by staying back, and I said more frends.

Quite different is the composition of a bright sixteen-year-old boy on the topic, "How it feels to be growing up."

Just how does it feel to be growing up? That question comes into our minds quite often. Really we don't feel any different, but changes are taking place all the time.

Our parents are a little more lenient with "do's" and "don't's"; we don't get whippings any more but a good talking to or punishment in some other way.

Our parents give us the privilege of driving the family car after we have acquired our drivers' license. We are allowed to take trips when our friends drive and not have to have a grown-up in the car. They (the parents) let us drive longer distances with them in the car.

Decisions are left to us also; we have to decide for ourselves without the help of others, things that bother us. Money matters are left up to us also. We have to choose wisely and learn the hard way what is right and what is wrong and how to be thrifty.

I really haven't had a strong feeling of growing up, but I know that I have when I meet people who say they knew me when I was "so high."

Between these extremes, the compositions cover a great variety of subjects with a wide range of expressiveness.

A still less structured type of composition was described by John Glass, a high school English teacher, who used what he called a "stream of consciousness" technique. This gives students an opportunity "to write about what they think rather than thinking about what they write." The directions given were simply:

Write about anything that comes into your mind as you are sitting here. While you are writing, your mind will probably shift from one thing to another. You don't have to stick to one subject. Shift subjects as your mind shifts. Just write your thoughts as they occur to you. I am the only one who will see these papers, so feel free to put down whatever you want.

Some pupils can write about matters which they might be hesitant to mention in a face-to-face situation. One boy in this class, who wrote on his antagonism toward his stepmother, said after class, "I don't mind writing like that. It was fun." Later he talked more freely about other problems.

Favorable Conditions. If the teacher has established a relationship of mutual trust and respect, he will gain much understanding of his group from their freely written responses. A favorable atmosphere is essential to success with any kind of free-response method.

Personal documents should not be requested too frequently. Students get bored if they are asked to write too many subjective compositions. Said one gifted ninth-grader in a class where the teacher had asked the pupils several times to write about adolescent problems: "Miss B., if I have to write another composition about adolescence, I'll scream." The teacher should also be careful never to identify an individual pupil's statements, or to laugh about them with other teachers in the school. Common problems revealed in the compositions, however, can be discussed in class, and students should be encouraged to take their serious personal problems to the school counselor.

Under favorable conditions, in an atmosphere of mutual respect and trust, one rarely gets a facetious response. The compositions themselves show evidences of sincerity. Although adolescents often conceal their feelings when they are with others, they welcome the opportunity to write confidentially about themselves and to express their real feelings. Doing this often helps them to clarify their relations, understand their feelings, and gain perspective. A ninth-grade science teacher in a private school said, "Most of the students entered into the writing of the compositions heartily and did not feel that their privacy was being invaded. For the first time I realized how strong was their desire to express and communicate personal feeling."

Value to Students. The experience of writing this kind of composition seems to have therapeutic value for some students. Many seemed to welcome the opportunity to express pent-up feelings. As one student said, "I feel a sense of relief after getting this out of my system. I've wanted to do this for a long time." A teacher was of the same opinion: "It is apparent from reading the compositions that many of the students welcomed the opportunity to get something off their chests." The "writing-out technique" may help adolescents to objectify their problems; it gives them a chance to release tensions.

The problems which adolescents encounter in growing up—their conflicts with the culture, their need for educational and vocational guidance, their resourcefulness in meeting their problems—all are revealed in these frankly written accounts. A few of the writers go deep into their own wells of loneliness and distress. Some of the compositions are filled with a tension, anxiety, and desperation that indicate that these individuals are writing from the reality of their own lives. Only the individual knows how he thinks and feels and what experiences mean to him.

To write in this way takes effort; introspection is not easy. One student expressed the difficulty in this way: "I hope you don't think this is 'real gone,' but it is hard to put on paper what we think ourself."

Value to Adults. Reading these compositions is a rewarding experience. Teachers, supervisors, administrators, and personnel workers who have cooperated in obtaining and studying these compositions make comments such as the following:

I feel that I have made a visit to that strange world in which adolescents live.

From these compositions on "What help or guidance persons of my age want from adults" I found out many things about my class. It is well worth my time. It gave me firsthand information and insight into what my pupils expect of me.

The students' papers gave me greater insight into the social and economic backgrounds of my pupils, into their interests and needs.

Other teachers said that these frankly written compositions influenced their teaching and guidance practices:

The insight which I have gained will help me immeasurably in guidance work with my classes.

Since I've read my students' compositions I have made my guidance work more concrete and can cite instances, stimulated by students' remarks in these compositions, which have resulted in the students' social maturation and self-guidance.

Even an experienced counselor can profit by reading anonymous personal documents in which reticent youngsters may reveal their feelings more fully than in a face-to-face interview.

Through reading this kind of personal writing, "The teacher may become less concerned with split infinitives and more concerned with split personality; unity and coherence in the paragraph may become subordinate to unity and coherence in the self." [10] Unstructured compositions on almost any subject afford the teacher access to students' real feelings and attitudes, and increase his awareness of the manifold variations and relative prevalence of many problems. According to Allport,[11] "the direct

[10] David H. Russell and Caroline Shrodes, "Contributions of Research in Bibliotherapy to the Language-arts Program," vol. 58, *School Review* (September-October, 1950), p. 418.

[11] Gordon W. Allport, "The Trend in Motivational Theory," in *The Self Explorations in Personal Growth* (Clark E. Moustakas, ed.), p. 30. New York: Harper & Brothers, 1956.

responses of the psychoneurotic cannot be taken at their face value," but the responses of normal people can.

The psychological insights expressed by the adolescents have the authenticity of personal experience, the direct thinking characteristic of childhood and youth, and a certain sensitivity which has not been blurred by facile verbalization. These youngsters have not learned to substitute labels for understanding.

Limitations. The limitations of introspective reports must, of course, be recognized. It has often been said that adolescents cover up their real feelings. In many face-to-face situations, this may be true. But whatever an adolescent writes is valuable as indicating his point of view at a particular moment regarding something that he is willing to communicate. This may be considered a "psychological fact." Even though his moods change and he might not report the same incident in the same way at another time, and even though the feelings he expresses may not be consistent with his total behavior, is not this inconsistency a characteristic of adolescence? Is not any statement that represents the adolescent's genuine feeling at the moment, in a given situation, psychologically "true" for him?

Treatment of Adolescents' Free Responses. To give a vivid impression of individuality, a large number of verbatim records are included in this book. These frank, sincere statements by adolescents highlight the uniqueness of each individual, show the presence of mixed feelings within the same person, and make us aware of certain ideas and feelings that are prevalent among adolescents.

In general, the opinions, feelings, and viewpoints that have been quoted are corroborated by other statements in the adolescent's composition. Unclear statements and statements invalidated by contextual evidence have been omitted. This does not mean that ambivalence has been eliminated. In some of the compositions a clear statement of a particular point of view or feeling may be followed by an equally clear expression of an opposite viewpoint or feeling.

Some of the statements are "typical" in the sense that they are expressed in many compositions. However, some compositions contain unique responses, unusually vivid statements, and insights that are psychologically astute.

There seems to be a relation between the adolescent's use of first, second, or third person and the degree to which he is freely expressing his own feelings, interests, and viewpoints. In general, use of the first person ("I think," "I feel"), considered in connection with other internal evidence, seems to be associated with the most genuine kind of expression. The third person ("Adolescents feel . . . ," "Boys and girls often think . . . ," etc.) seems to be associated with a measure of reluctance to reveal one's own feelings. The second person, when used, seems generally to be employed in a hortatory sense ("You should . . .") by those who appear to be merely repeating lessons that they have learned from parents, teachers, and other adults.

In only one sample—sample 3 in Chapter 4—were the students asked to sign their names. In the other samples, though they were told not to sign their names, a few of the writers did so. It may be that the unsolicited signature indicates a desire to gain approval by expressing acceptable opinions, whereas the anonymous composition corresponds more closely to the person's actual opinion.

The method of content analysis has been applied to the original data from some sets of compositions. From a reading of the compositions, certain common categories emerged. The frequency of statements classifiable under each of these categories was then tabulated. The agreement between two workers was over 90 per cent for the majority of items. There were a few items, however, which were more difficult to classify. These were of low frequency of mention and were not included in quantitative form.

By tabulating a substantial number of compositions and comparing the results with additional samples from the same situation, we found a correspondence sufficiently close to make further tabulation of compositions from that situation unnecessary. For example, there was a rank order correlation of .86 for twenty-five response categories between two sets of compositions on "How it feels to be growing up." The reading of many additional compositions reinforced the conclusions derived from the tabulations.

Frequency of mention indicates the prevalence of certain responses among certain groups of adolescents, but it does not necessarily indicate the importance of an item. An observation or insight expressed by only one adolescent may be more psychologically significant than some statements that are frequently repeated.

The qualitative treatment presents typical responses, idiosyncratic responses, and vivid pictures of how individuals perceive certain situations such as receiving a poor school report, having divorced parents, not getting a date. These direct quotations make *adolescents* come alive. Here the reader sees the individuality of adolescents; individual differences unfold as he reads.

Under each topic the various points of view are arranged, so far as possible, on a continuum or a number of continuums. For example, with respect to report cards, feelings ranging from extreme fear to elation are expressed. Parents' responses to their children's reports of progress can be similarly arranged on a scale with unjust punishment at one end and uncritical approval at the other. Thus we become aware of the wide range of possible responses and viewpoints.

Group Discussion

Some adolescents prefer to talk rather than to write. They respond freely in a discussion group where they are stimulated by the contributions of others, where they trust the adults involved, and where they feel they are either getting the attention of adults or helping them. For example, one teen-age boy who took part in a panel discussion before a graduate class in education said afterward with great satisfaction: "This is the first time I ever had a chance to teach teachers."

The way adolescents tell about their problems and needs is convincing. Panel discussions in which youngsters feel free to speak frankly are among the most popular features of educational meetings. Teachers and administrators are impressed by the comments and insights of young people.

Wire or tape recordings made of various panel discussions capture a wide range of adolescent responses. For example, one record made by an adult who mingled with teen-age gangs and won their confidence revealed what seemed to be a habitual use of shocking language among them. They spoke in the most vulgar terms imaginable. In their value system clever crooks were admired, girls were regarded only as objects of sex desire, stealing was expected and acceptable behavior, and none of them seemed to experience remorse, sympathy, or altruism.

In marked contrast was the recording of a junior high school class discussion, which gave a wealth of insights into the kind of counseling that adolescents want. The following excerpts from that discussion illustrate the value of informal discussion methods:

CHARLOTTE: One of the most important things for a person to do is to get to know himself. And a guidance teacher should help.

LEADER: How would a guidance person go about helping you do that, Charlotte?

CHARLOTTE: The first thing would be to get to know you. As it stands now, I would not call teachers guiders. I do not think they even attempt to guide people. To be a guider, I think you have to know the person you are guiding outside the classroom. You have to know him personally. Many teachers do not have a chance to get to know the pupils because they do not have time; they have to correct so many tests and do other stupid things. In many cases, the pupil doesn't know whether they can trust the guider or not. Before you can have guidance, I think the teacher will have to know her pupils better, and make them feel that they can trust her.

JOHN: Some of the teachers don't teach you the subjects you should know, and when you try to get into the various high schools you cannot get in because you do not have the courses they require in the high schools.

DAVID: Sometimes the relationship with your father and mother or brothers and sisters is not good. Many of the problems that arise in the home cannot be solved in the home situation. They need to be solved outside; you need another person outside of your family to help you solve your problems.

PETER: In most cases, when guidance teachers are interviewing a child, they only scratch the surface. They ask you why you are bad, but do not get down to the more basic reasons, the under-lying reasons of why you are bad.

DAVID: It isn't the guidance teacher that does the guidance, but peo-ple in your own age group that help you solve your problems. A person helps you when he helps you see how it should be done, not in a direct way at all—that is what guidance should do—help you see the best ways out, not tell you what to do.

ROBIN: Some people think counselors should go into personal prob-lems. After all, the home should do that. Perhaps if it doesn't, the counselors could take care of it, but they have a job just directing you scholastically. I think personal problems should be taken care of at home.

This class is one that had needed, and received, the benefits of counseling. When young people discuss topics relating to themselves, they speak from the vantage point of their own first-hand experiences. Their views on the subject often show much insight. Panels of gifted children have given keen insight into school procedures that bore or frustrate them; they present a sound blueprint of the kind of education they want and need. Juvenile delinquents tell us about blighting conditions in their lives and give us glimpses of their need for attention, respect, and responsibility. Panels of high school students who have reading difficulties make a plea for understanding and for more effective instruction and meaningful reading material. In short, panel discussion, when conducted by a person who conveys sincerity in wanting to know how adolescents are thinking and feeling so he may help them make desirable changes in themselves and their environment, will yield much understanding of this transition period of life.

Observation of Adolescents

It is also important to see how adolescents present themselves to others—how they impress other people. The problem here is twofold: (1) to look at the young people themselves, directly and objectively, not through the haze of our own anxieties and preconceptions; and (2) to keep our snapshots of their behavior separate from the general impression they make on us.

We should learn to look for overt behavior that may be of possible significance for the adolescent's development. This gives us factual knowledge about the individual in a variety of situations. But it is also desirable to be a participant observer—one who looks below the surface behavior and tries to understand the reasons for it and to explain the underlying motives. To do this, the participant observer needs to recognize common human feelings. But he must be careful not to project his own feelings on the person being observed and let his feelings affect his perception of the situation. The fact that this combination of objectivity and empathy is so difficult explains why no two people see exactly the same thing in a given situation. Most teachers' observations include their impressions along with their more objective observations.

Observations made by almost two hundred teachers and personnel workers in junior high schools, senior high schools, and colleges in different parts of the country show convincingly the manifold variations of adolescent behavior in different situations. Observed behavior varies with each combination of factors: the home background, ability, and interests of the student; the morale and philosophy of the school; the personality and instructional methods of the teacher. Consequently, we see one class showing initiative, cooperation, high scholastic achievement, consideration for the teacher and for one another. Another class, though pleasant enough, is absorbed in nonacademic interests and is lacking in ambition to do more than "get by" scholastically. Still another class will show antagonism toward teachers, a competitive attitude toward one another, and defiance of the rules of the school. There may be many variations within these few patterns.

The self-reports of children and adolescents are often at odds with appraisals by the teacher or by their classmates. Only validation by other methods can determine which is the truer picture. Perhaps both are true pictures: the self-report mirrors the inner world of the adolescent; observations by others show the way in which he manages to handle life situations.

Interviews

Counseling and psychotherapeutic interviews often yield an understanding of adolescents' inner worlds and of the ways they perceive their environment and themselves, an understanding which is essential to successful counseling. In an atmosphere in which the counselee feels understood and accepted, he is most likely to reveal and deal with his inner feelings. From the many recorded interviews, excerpts revealing a wealth of understand-

ing of their moods of happiness and depression, their warm feelings for others and their suspicions, their capacity for tenderness and their feelings of hostility, their troubled thoughts and fears, their friendships and their loneliness, their aspirations and their hopelessness give a glimpse of the kind of understanding that may be obtained in counseling interviews.

In response to an open-end question, "Suppose you tell me something about yourself, Charles," a seventeen-year-old boy in the tenth grade, who is not interested in school, hates women teachers, and is doing very poor work, spoke freely:

Oh well, I like sports. I like outdoors. I like animals. Animals are my favorite pastime. I like dogs, and horses especially. I'd like to own a horse myself. That's why I'd like to quit school now so that I can get one myself.

I love football and baseball, and boxing. If I could only think of my studies like I think about sports, I'd have A's all the time. But I can't—I can't seem to study. I go home up to my room and try to study. In about a half hour I get lazy. I wanna, I know I wanna do it. I feel guilty if I don't do it, but—then I say, I'll do it the next morning. I just like sports, open air all the time. That's all. I like girls too, but if I had a choice between getting married and having my own horse, I rather take the horse any day. . . . Sports, that's all I'm interested in. And gettin' built up. That's why I wanna get a construction job—to get built up.

He went on to speak of his relations with boys and with his father, and expressed his resentment of the discrepancy between what his father *says* and what he *does:*

He wants *me* to lay the cards on the table, but when I ask him to, he just gets sore. You see, he can get sore because he's my father . . . you have to have respect—but sometimes he gets me so mad, when you know you're right and you know he's wrong, but he won't admit it. And he's trying to teach me to be a good sport. But boy, when I find that he's not a good sport. . . . Like last night he said, "I'll show you who's the master of this house." Master! As though this was the South and I'm a slave to him. That's what gets me mad. I'm no slave. He's my father . . . sometimes I talk to him for a while and he just says, "Yeah," and he doesn't talk with me. If he talked with me I'd feel great. If I keep talkin' for a while he says,

"Can't you think of somethin' else besides that?" That's what gets me mad.

In this interview Charles made an unusually keen analysis of his feelings and the situation at home and at school.

A withdrawn seventeen-year-old girl, referred to the counselor because of repeated absences from school and a constantly unhappy expression, at first responded in monosyllables. Her most characteristic responses to suggestions were, "I wouldn't like it." "That doesn't interest me." "Well, I don't know." Later in the interview she gave a number of clues concerning her poor adjustment:

"You see, I wanted to be a secretary and then I got discouraged and I wanted to go to college but I'm too stupid to take the academic course."

When the counselor asked, "Who told you you were stupid?" the girl said, "I know myself. I can't grasp the subject. In the other school it was more simpler and slower for the girls than it is here."

The hopeless way in which she perceived herself is evident throughout the interview:

You see, as soon as I say my mother's been sick and I've had to take care of her the teachers think, "That's why she's failing in her subjects—because she has her mind on her mother's illness." No. It's me. That might have held me back a little—maybe stopped me from studying or something like that, but nothing—nothing just interests me. I just sit home . . . looking at the dog. He even thought I was nuts. Nothing just interests me at all. My mother didn't know what to do with me. She sits down and talks with me but it just doesn't do no good. I don't know what I want to be. I don't belong to no clubs. Nothing interests me any more.

In this interview an adolescent bared clues to a serious disturbance of the self-concept, deep-seated and possibly inaccessible to school counseling and even to psychiatric treatment. Some progress was made by offering opportunities to work in a friendly group and to get a part-time job which she could do competently.

From psychological and psychiatric interviews deeper recesses of adolescent personality may be reached. Even though the individual's statements bear little relation to reality, they show how he perceives himself or how he wants to present himself in a given face-to-face relationship. The discrepancy between how the individual perceives the situation and how it appears to others often yields important clues concerning his adjustment. In every interview we can gain additional understanding of adolescents' motivations and behavior.

Tests and Inventories

Standardized intelligence and achievement tests yield information as to certain kinds of mental ability and competence in different fields. In other areas of personal development wide use has been made of check lists of adolescent problems, especially the carefully constructed Mooney Problem Check List published by the Ohio State University Press and the Billett-Starr Youth Problems Inventory. However, even when thoughtfully checked by the students, these inventories reveal only the frequency and the bare bones of adolescent problems or interests in briefly stated categories. Thus they miss much of the real significance of what young people have to say and of how they say it.

Interest and personality inventories likewise give much quantitative information, but are difficult to interpret. So much depends on the student's ability to appraise himself and on his interpretation of the situation and the specific items on the inventory. Given under favorable conditions, well-constructed inventories serve as a springboard for further study of the individual.

Measures of Bodily Growth

Precise measures of height, weight, sitting height or stem length, leg length, tests of strength, photographs showing changes in body form, and X rays of bone development have been described in detail by Stolz and Stolz.[12] When obtained

---

[12] Herbert R. Stolz and Lois Meek Stolz, *Somatic Development of Adolescent Boys.* New York: The Macmillan Company, 1951.

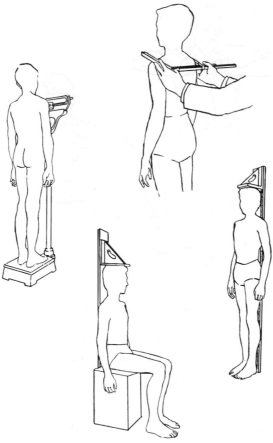

Technic of measuring weight.
Technic of measuring biacromial width.
Technic of measuring standing height.
Technic of measuring sitting height.

over a period of time, such measures show great variation among individuals in growth patterns. Rhythms in growth and relations among different aspects of physical growth and physiological maturity are also shown by these development studies (see Chapter 5). It is important to understand as much as possible about the relationships among the various aspects of the individual's total development, such as growth in height and weight,

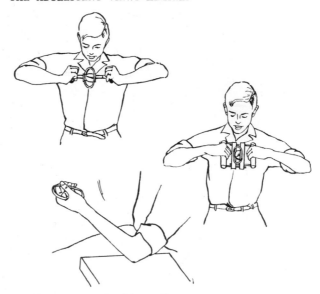

Technic of measuring shoulder pull.
Technic of measuring hand grip strength with Collin's dynamometer.

in intelligence, in achievement, in physiological maturity, and in social and emotional adjustment—all considered in the light of environmental influences.

Projective Techniques

It is generally agreed that the projective techniques add to our understanding of the unique inner world of adolescents. The Rorschach test, using specially selected ink blots to evoke responses, gives clues as to the individual's personality structure and the seriousness of his maladjustment. The Thematic Apperception Test, consisting of intentionally ambiguous and provocative pictures, throws light on the areas in which a person may be maladjusted. The incomplete sentence technique likewise may reveal areas of conflict or concern. Similarly, other projective techniques presenting unstructured material for which the person has no ready-made response, may evoke responses that reveal hidden aspects of the individual's personality.

Certain cautions should be observed in using these projective techniques. Despite the scoring systems, the interpretation of the results of projective techniques is quite subjective and sometimes seems stereotyped. Moreover, during the instability of early adolescence, a single test result may represent a mood rather than a permanent or pervasive personality trend. Since some strong motives, such as hunger, may not be revealed at all by projective methods, a combination of direct methods and projective techniques would give the most complete picture.

Case Studies

The case study is the best single method of studying the adolescent as a whole. It shows interrelationships among various personality factors and takes into account personal development over a period of time. The comprehensive case study synthesizes data from many sources, including standardized tests, inventories, and projective techniques. At its best, a case study reveals psychological changes that have been taking place within the individual as a result of his efforts to adjust to his environment.

The traditional case study began with information about the maternal and paternal grandparents and continued with more data on parents, birth conditions, early childhood and school experiences. The modern case study often begins with the present problem and explores each lead that seems significant in understanding and helping the individual.

More case studies of "normal" adolescents are needed. These would give a genetic approach to the study of adolescence. Ideally, they should begin at birth, and a psychologically discerning record of interpersonal relations be kept through the eras of infancy, childhood, juvenile socialization, and preadolescence. In this way we should gain an understanding of adolescent development that could be obtained in no other way.

INFORMATION LEADING TO UNDERSTANDING

Information is not enough. To lead to understanding, bare facts must be interpreted. "A fact is like a sack which won't stand up when it is empty. In order that it may stand up, one has to put into it the reason and sentiment which have caused it to exist." [13]

In this book we shall present as the main original sources of data (1) freely expressed, frank statements by adolescents themselves as made in written form, in group discussions, and in interviews, and (2) observations by teachers and personnel workers who have been in intimate contact with adolescents in classes, clubs, and summer camps. The interpretation of these original data will be aided by general insights into the psychology and sociology of adolescence derived by other workers from experiments and experience. The reader will note many agreements between the statements made by psychologists and the psychological insights of the adolescents themselves.

SEQUENCE OF TOPICS

In this book we shall begin in Part 1 with the world as adolescents see it, because the contemporary culture exerts such a strong influence on child and adolescent development. Next we shall see how adolescents view themselves and how they feel about growing up. At the beginning of Part 2 we shall review the continuity of development from early childhood through the preadolescent acceleration in physical growth, through puberty into the teens, and up to the age when persons legally assume adult responsibility. This brief overview will serve as an introduction to adolescents' perception of their major developmental tasks: achieving physical maturity and competency; achieving scholastic success, desirable relations with one's peers, good adjustment to the other sex; gaining reasonable independence from the family without undue antagonism; progressing toward appropriate educational and vocational goals; and achieving socially responsible behavior. In Part 3 providing favorable learning conditions and the role of guidance will be briefly considered, also from adolescents' point of view. For further reading a few selected references

[13] Luigi Pirandello, *Six Characters in Search of an Author,* in *Three Plays,* Act I, p. 22. New York: E. P. Dutton & Co., Inc., 1931.

are given: (1) comprehensive books on adolescence, (2) reports of research, and (3) popular books and articles.

Understanding adolescents is necessary for effective teaching and guidance. From their own statements we can gain insight and perspective into their frequently disturbing and inexplicable behavior. If this understanding is applied to the school program, it may suggest changes in policy, methods of instruction, and curriculum; faults to be corrected; and sound features to be reinforced. If parents understood their adolescent sons and daughters better, they could reduce family conflict and offer more sympathetic and effective guidance.

COMPREHENSION QUESTIONS

1. What are two common errors to avoid in studying adolescents? Give instances in which you have seen these errors made.

2. Describe what you consider a common pattern of adolescent behavior, and then observe an individual adolescent to see how his unique version differs from this.

3. What is meant by "interrelations within total growth"?

4. Why is it important to know how the adolescent perceives himself and his world?

5. Mention ways of gaining understanding of adolescents, and point out the relative value of each method.

6. What advantages do you see in having the organization of this book based on adolescents' perception of themselves, the world in which they live, and the goals to be achieved during adolescence?

7. What are the most important kinds of information an adult can obtain about a situation in which an adolescent is involved?

STUDY PROJECTS

1. Observe adolescents and note the ways in which they are alike and the ways in which they are different. What kind of characteristics seem to be most common among adolescents? In what respects are they most likely to be different? Try to find two or more adolescents who have the same pattern of personality and behavior. Why is it difficult to find "two of a kind"?

2. Note instances of the tendency to generalize from the specific case, as, for example, with respect to the prevalence of delinquency among adolescents.

3. Obtain descriptions of a certain person from a group of adolescents. Note how differently individuals perceive the same person.

4. Give examples of the use of each of the methods mentioned in the study of adolescence. For example, write a dated series of observations, obtain a tape recording or full notes of an interview, make a case study of an adolescent about whom you can obtain information. Use one of these methods yourself to gain an increased understanding of some individual or group of adolescents.

5. Read a report of research on adolescence. What methods were used? How significant do you think the findings were and why?

6. Read popular articles and news stories about adolescents. From what sources did the writers obtain their information?

7. Conduct or listen to a panel discussion of adults on the subject of adolescence. Then conduct or listen to a panel of young people discussing the same subject. Note differences, both in the views expressed and in frankness and originality of expression.

FOR FURTHER STUDY

FRANK, L. K., R. HARRISON, E. HELLERSBERG, K. MACHOVER, and M. STEINER, *Personality Development in Adolescent Girls.* New Orleans: Child Development Publications, 1953.

FRICK, WILLARD B., "The Adolescent Dilemma: An Interpretation," *Peabody Journal of Education,* vol. 32 (July, 1954–May, 1955), pp. 206–210.

GESELL, ARNOLD, FRANCES L. ILG, and LOUISE BATES AMES, *Youth, the Years from Ten to Sixteen,* pp. 7–12, 506–508. New York: Harper & Brothers, 1956.

JENNINGS, HELEN H., *Sociometry in Group Relations: A Work Guide for Teachers.* Washington, D.C.: American Council on Education, 1948.

KUHLEN, RAYMOND G., *The Psychology of Adolescent Development,* chap. I. New York: Harper & Brothers, 1952.

MACFARLANE, JEAN W., LUCILE ALLEN, and MARJORIE P. A. HONZIK, *Developmental Study of the Behavior Problems of Normal Children between Twenty-one Months and Fourteen Years.* University of California Publications in Child Development, vol. 2. Berkeley, Calif.: University of California Press, 1954.

MOONEY, ROSS, "Surveying High School Students' Problems by Means of a Problem Check List," *Educational Research Bulletin,* vol. 21 (March, 1942), pp. 57–69.

MURRAY, HENRY A., and OTHERS, *Explorations in Personality.* New York: Oxford University Press, 1938.

SEIDMAN, JEROME M., editor, *The Adolescent,* chap. II. New York: The Dryden Press, Inc., 1953.

SOLOMON, JOSEPH C., *A Synthesis of Human Behavior.* New York: Grune & Stratton, Inc., 1954.

TRYON, CAROLINE, *Evaluations of Adolescent Personality,* monograph of the Society for Research in Child Development, Washington, D.C., vol. 4, no. 4, 1939.

WATTENBERG, WILLIAM W., *The Adolescent Years,* chap. I. New York: Harcourt, Brace and Company, Inc., 1955.

PART ONE

How Adolescents View
Themselves and Their World

CHAPTER 2

The World in Which Adolescents Live

To most people in the United States the modern world has certain dominant characteristics. This common view of the world we call "reality." From common feelings, ideas, and purposes, the behavior of members of a given culture emerges, modified by the individual personality. Some writers such as Cantril [1] emphasize the role of the person in "the total environment-person situation," while others like Benedict [2] emphasize the role of the cultural environment—an environment which members of the society have helped to create.

THE WORLD AS WE SEE IT

Viewing it as objectively as possible, adults see the modern world as entering an atomic age, an age characterized by a pervasive fear of war, an age in which destructive competition persists despite counter-currents of cooperation, an age of shifting values influenced by the spectacular development of mass methods of communication. Adults are puzzled and uncertain. Adolescents are living in a world that has lost its security and stability.

Feelings of anxiety and fear permeate modern society. These are manifested in tension, irritability, depression, vague feelings of uneasiness and hopelessness. Some of these feelings arise

---

[1] Hadley Cantril, *The "Why" of Man's Experience.* New York: The Macmillan Company, 1950.

[2] Ruth Benedict, *Patterns of Culture,* Boston: Houghton Mifflin Company, 1934.

from people's unresolved inner conflicts, but many reflect the objective reality of a world in imminent danger of a conflict that might demolish it. Ours is a culture, according to Milton E. Kirkpatrick [3] speaking on "Mental Health in the Anglo-American Culture," which is status-minded; future-oriented, neglecting the potentialities of the present moment; and overconcerned with economic gain, placing security in possessions instead of in personality.

Yet there is "much of good and much of ill" in this world. Examples of genuine altruism are not lacking; there is an extraordinary upward social mobility, and huge sums of money are voluntarily spent for the benefit of needy persons. According to Gillespie and Allport, [4] the rugged individualist bent on financial success above everything else seems to be changing into an "outer-directed" person who wants "a full rich life," which includes sociability, pleasant suburban living with family and friends, hobbies, and travel, as well as business interests. Hidden behind the façade of materialism, there also seems to be a yearning for spiritual values. This is indicated by the popularity of books that emphasize peace of mind and positive thinking and by the reverence people feel for a man like Dr. Albert Schweitzer, who has demonstrated a way of life in marked contrast to current competitive materialism. These often conflicting patterns create many of the adolescent's problems of adjustment.

However, there is cause for hope as well as for alarm: "Youth can be the growing edge of a creative culture; . . . they can plant the seeds of disorganization, or be seduced by a Hitler and reverse the slow, slow ascent of civilization. The status of youth in an era of change is both fortunate and precarious." [5]

[3] Milton E. Kirkpatrick, "The Mental Hygiene of Adolescence in the Anglo-American Culture," *Mental Hygiene*, vol. 36 (July, 1952), pp. 394–405.

[4] James M. Gillespie and Gordon W. Allport, *Youth's Outlook on the Future: A Cross-national Study*. New York: Doubleday & Company, Inc., 1955.

[5] Howard Y. McClusky, "The Status of Youth in Our Culture," *Education*, vol. 76 (December, 1955), p. 208.

THE WORLD AS ADOLESCENTS VIEW IT

How do adolescents view this era of threatened warfare and rapid, pervasive social change, in which they have been brought up? What roles do they picture themselves assuming in this modern world? To what extent are they aware of the inter- and intragroup tensions about which adults talk so much? How keen are their anxieties? What are the sources of their unrest and frustration? We can answer these questions only by listening to what adolescents tell us in anonymous compositions, in the face-to-face relationship of the interview, or in response to the stimulus of discussion or therapy groups. In a panel discussion, after reviewing what the world was like in previous decades from 1900 on, one girl concluded, "This is the most crucial period we have ever lived through. We are faced with many problems—bombs, tension, crime. Teen-agers do consider these problems, though parents don't realize it. I'm one of a group of teen-agers who think more seriously about the future. Sometimes I just think of the worst that could happen."

In most adolescent groups we find a wide range of opinions regarding the state of the world. The following summary is based on a study of three seventh-grade classes in a small town in Connecticut, of a general and a college preparatory ninth-grade class, and of a general and a commercial tenth-grade class in Pennsylvania.

In their appraisals of the state of the world the seventh-grade youngsters covered a range from naïve enthusiasm to unmitigated pessimism: "The world in which we are living is a wonderful place," "high in social achievements, plenty of money if you work for it," "a freedom-loving world in which practically everyone has faith, hope, and believes in God," "a world that is making steady progress." (This point of view was expressed almost exclusively by girls.)

A modified optimism was expressed by both boys and girls in the same classes: "All in all, the world looks very promising but it could become better," "it has some good sides and some bad sides." These students mentioned a curious conglomeration of ills: "some of the people in the world today are cruel," "fear that the Russians will come over and take our country," "accidents caused by carelessness and drunks," "many diseases," "contrasts between luxuries and poverty." One twelve-year-old boy had this view: "The world and its people are mostly good but some people are forced to do bad things when they want to do good. I think the world has too much money. Nobody should be poor or very rich." Another boy tempered his critical comments by mentioning the possibility of making things better: ". . . progress in conquest of diseases, better education. There is race discrimination, but there are exceptions; bad living conditions for some people, but these conditions are being changed. Rome wasn't built in a day."

Others, too, emphasized the progress that is being made. One twelve-year-old girl wrote:

From my point of view this world is prospering more and more. Something new is being invented every day. Science research and health research will make this world an even healthier place to live in. Our own country will keep on prospering unless we elect a wrong leader, which I don't think will happen. Since all people in our country are freedom loving and have been used to freedom, I think we'll always keep our freedom.

These youngsters also expressed hope for the future; they believed that this was a good world growing better:

This world is in good shape and will be in better shape in years to come.

I think the world will become a better and better place to live. It may be a long, long time, but I think it will all turn out OK.

On the other hand, uncertainty about the future is indicated in quotations such as this: "The world, the way it stands today, seems to me in half decent shape, but in the future, who knows?"

A few of these twelve-year-olds merely expressed acceptance of the world as it is: "an interesting world and something to look forward to," "a world of opportunities where we the people have the Bill of Rights and the Constitution of America." The take-the-world-as-it-is view was most fully expressed in the following philosophical statement by a twelve-year-old boy: "I feel that I'll just go along with the world and whatever comes up (you can't change it) it's there, no matter how good or how bad it happens to be. I feel people should take things as they come, one by one, and figure them out, instead of just getting excited over them. You can expect a lot of fun but a lot of tragedy."

There were a few who felt that the world as a whole is very bad but that conditions are good here in the United States. One of the seventh-grade boys went on to say, "Most countries are run by dictators, or people who tell you what God to worship and who to vote for. In this country you are free to worship and to vote for whoever you want."

A generally pessimistic view of the world was held by the majority of seventh-grade boys: "The adult world which I will enter sometime in the future is not something to look forward to. It is a world of war, destruction, and desolation." They mentioned specifically "the cold war—each country trying to be one jump ahead of the other countries," "the last meeting of the Big Four was not a success," "mistrust between nations," "the atom bombs with which the world seems bent on destroying itself," "discrimination against Negroes, communists trying to overthrow the world," "countries that have one government one year and another the next year," "economic inequality—most people in the United States have a lot of luxuries but in India some people don't have necessities."

Essentially the same range of viewpoints was expressed by ninth- and tenth-grade students in a different kind of community. However, these older youngsters held a still more generally pessimistic view. A number of the boys spoke bitterly about fighting: "We are forever and ever fighting and fighting, causing war, disrupting peace." A fourteen-year-old boy in the ninth grade hoped, after school, "to get married to a woman who would like being a farmer's wife," and went on to say: "I would like to know what people get out of fighting, fighting, and fighting some more. It doesn't get them anywhere except in a graveyard."

The students' diverse attitudes toward the UN and other efforts to establish a peaceful world may reflect family or community opinions or school instruction, or they may represent independent thinking. For example, two fourteen-year-old boys in the same ninth-grade college preparatory class in world history expressed opposite points of view. One of these boys began by saying, "The world is all right except for certain things," and he mentioned the powerful weapons we have and the difficulty of controlling them. He continued:

I know we are now trying to start up an atoms for peace plan. If this would be put into action, peace would follow. All countries should be interested in it and when they see how good it works to live together peacefully the results should be very satisfactory. Take the UN. Because of the veto power many countries are being kept out. No veto power should be possible and countries allowed to join. In all the different parts of the UN all countries should be allowed to vote. In this way the majority of the countries would vote for what they think is right and no one country would be able to stop the action by vetoing it. What I think is, "Come on, fellows. Let's make this world a better place to live in. Let's get these high taxes down and divided more evenly." Why not let peace and friendship be a major factor in the world?

The other boy took a dim view of the world and of efforts to promote peace.

I think that the world is going to pot, because of wars. I do not think that sitting down at a so called Press Table is any good at all. In 1938 the Prime Minister of Britain had a peace talk with Hitler. One year later there was World War II where some 30,000,000 people all over the world were killed. I think that most of the deligates of all countries in the world that meet at peace tables really want war. I believe that we want war as much as Russia. Back in 1870 France and Germany both wanted a war, but no side could find an excuse. After a while they did find one which I don't remember because it was a very little one. I think both sides want an excuse for a war just as in 1870. I don't think the people are going to trust so much in Peace Talks any more. I don't think wars can be prevented and I don't think there is any such thing as a free country.

Other students expressed equally one-sided opinions, with little consideration for the facts. Many adolescents become disillusioned as they see the inconsistencies and discrepancies in the adult world.

About one in ten made some reference to tolerance of other races and nationalities, and to poverty. Some merely described discriminatory practices; others expressed a desire to have all people treated justly. This desire for universal tolerance and fair play, professed by adults and exemplified in the play of small children, often causes conflict during adolescence, when young people contemplate more intimate relations, such as marriage, which demand a certain degree of compatibility in backgrounds and beliefs.

In the Pennsylvania sampling of ninth- and tenth-grade students, religious influence was evident. About a fifth of the students made some reference to God. "If more people had more faith in God the world would be better," was a typical response. Others said, "With a little more religional devotion we might be able to save ourselves," and "If this world keeps going on like it is, God will be very displeased with the world." The most extreme religious point of view was expressed by a fifteen-year-old tenth-grade boy in the general course: "The UN is not helping matters. Not that it doesn't mean well, but it is standing in the way of Christ."

It is encouraging that a few of these young people recognized their responsibility for a better world and were eager to have a part in making it better: "If the younger generation could have more to do with this world . . . it would be better." "I think we should be active in the world and do all we can for it." These students suggested certain improvements:

. . . if there wouldn't be so much confusion between different countries . . .

. . . if prices of all things should go down . . .

. . . if more people would have more faith in God . . .

. . . if there was a Bible in every home (being read) or if people attended church and paid attention . . .

Each of these *if's* was followed by the clause "it would be a better world." One fourteen-year-old girl said, "The world's OK, but the people that live in it are the fault."

It would be interesting to obtain adolescents' viewpoints on each of the specific topics which they mentioned in their compositions on the general state of the world. One teacher in this country did this. He asked a senior high school economics class in a suburban community to write how they honestly felt about the hydrogen bomb. They had previously discussed it in class. Their replies indicated feelings ranging from extreme insecurity to resignation and suppression of thoughts about it. This range of attitude is indicated by the following excerpts:

I feel as if there is a great deal of hatred in this world and that some day these boms shall be dropped and the earth will disappear.

I am in the younger years of my life and do not even want or allow myself to think of what might happen.

It doesn't bother me in any way only when we have air raid drills I get awfully disturbed and get a funny feeling inside of me.

If a foreign country boms the U.S., the U.S. is ready. The U.S. air force has bases all over the world.

It's silly to worry. Every citizen should be prepared; everyone who can should take first aid. If God wills that we should be killed by a bomb, we will be. I can't speak for my friends because we never have discussed the problem.

Many others of my age do not believe as I do. They look at the whole thing in 2 ways: (1) the whole thing is just a big joke to them, and (2) the whole thing is just too dreadful to talk or think about.

What is the significance of this conglomeration of ideas expressed by teen-age youngsters? It is evident that some of them are oblivious of, or uninterested in, world conditions. Others, perhaps because they come from sheltered environments, have an unrealistic view of the world. The majority see many things that are wrong, especially with respect to war and social conditions. Most take an either-or position; only a few see both the good and the ill and the ways in which improvement is actually taking place.

Many students thought primarily of "the world" as their own

local community and seemed most concerned about school problems and teen-age crimes. They wrote more frequently about their immediate concerns than about international problems. The counselor should recognize this tendency. He cannot expect to get far in promoting international understanding with a student whose whole attention at the moment is focused on getting a date for the Saturday night dance. There has to be a readiness for the kind of counseling which involves international understanding.[6] The statements made by the students in these few communities cannot be considered typical of the views of adolescents in general, though they do represent a wide range of possible viewpoints.

Another approach, using an attitude scale, presents a picture of greater maturity. Horton and Remmers [7] found the high school seniors whom they studied evenly divided on these questions: whether there is hope for a peaceful world some day; whether democracy is endangered by foreign ideas within the country; and whether we should give up some of our national sovereignty in the best interests of a better world. With respect to race relations, these seniors were positive (about 3 to 1) in their beliefs that people of any race or national origin can become good Americans, should attend school together, should be allowed to eat in the same public eating places, and sit where they wish in theaters. They were not so positive that people of different races should dance together, use the same swimming pools, or marry one another. They were sympathetic toward criminals, recognizing that some criminal acts result from mental disorders, but considered that "obedience and proper respect for authority should be the first requirements of a good citizen." Almost nine-tenths approved of the statement that we should feel "great love, gratitude, and respect for our flag." At the same time they were definitely world-minded; their attitude toward people from foreign countries was generally favorable.

[6] Ruth Strang, "How Can the Guidance Worker Promote International Understanding?" *Bulletin of the National Association of Secondary-school Principals,* vol. 40 (December, 1956), pp. 216–227.

[7] R. E. Horton and H. H. Remmers, *Some Ethical Values of Youth, Compared over the Years,* Report No. 38, Purdue Opinion Panel, 1954.

The question of world-mindedness was brought up in a discussion by high school students who had recently visited the United Nations. The question arose, What does "world-mindedness" mean?

JOANNE: Well, I think it means thinking in terms of the whole world.

TEACHER: Yes, and what else and why?

TOM: It's more than thinking of the world; it's thinking of all the different kinds of people in the world. I think it means understanding these people.

TEACHER: Good, but why?

JOANNE: There's no sense to a United Nations if we don't think of the whole world as part of it, is there? And we must try to understand people of all nationalities to make the UN work as best it can.

TEACHER: What exactly do you mean, Joanne, when you say we must understand people of all nationalities to make the UN work?

JOANNE: Well, we should be able to understand their customs and habits, so we can understand why they live the way they do. I think if we understood the way they live, we wouldn't make fun of them like so many people do. Making fun of people doesn't help to understand them.

Discussions based on knowledge and led by a skillful teacher encourage serious thinking about world conditions. People who have attended youth forums are invariably impressed with the older adolescents' interest and information on major problems relating to government and international relations.

Adolescents' views of the world in which they live vary with their method of study as well as with their intelligence, personality, and previous experience, with the opinions expressed in their homes and churches, and with the quality of the instruction they receive in school. In general, boys seem to be more concerned with world conditions than do girls. Doubtless many young adolescents are too preoccupied with their personal problems to think much about world affairs.

The university women studied by Gillespie and Allport [8] were more "family-oriented" than the men, but students in the ten

8 Gillespie and Allport, op. cit., p. 30.

different cultures were looking forward to families of their own, and desired to have three or four children, who they thought should be given affection and brought up in a permissive atmosphere. One-third of these university students believed that the world will escape another great war. Only 15 per cent anticipated a world government, though 25 per cent thought a federal union of most noncommunist countries was possible.

Regardless of the source of the opinions which adolescents express, it is important for teachers to know the present content of their students' minds. Without this understanding, teachers cannot help pupils to make connections between what they now know and the new knowledge which they are about to receive. With this understanding, teachers can also avoid unnecessary conflicts and antagonisms between the home and the school; if they know how the students are thinking, they can modify and build constructively on what is best in students' present points of view.

INFLUENCE OF THE ENVIRONMENT ON ADOLESCENT PERSONALITY

Many personal-environmental conditions exert varying degrees of influence on the way the adolescent views himself, his world, and the future. Variations in the social setting may make adolescence a more or less difficult period for individuals and groups.

Geographical location may have some influence on people's way of life and dominant characteristics. For example, the alleged thriftiness of the Scots may have developed in response to the need to wrest a livelihood from a fairly unproductive land. Rural boys and girls tend to have somewhat different standards and values from urban youth, for rural life inculcates a sense of responsibility for tasks that must be done and equips the adolescent boy with a variety of manual skills. Fewer rural children graduate from high school; fewer rural high school students obtain scholarships for college. These differences, however, are decreasing with the increase in suburban population, with the diffusion of mass communication, with increased ease of transpor-

tation to and from the city, and with the rise of central high schools where rural and town youngsters mingle.

World conditions and general economic conditions influence the length of time elapsing between attaining adult appearance and assuming adult responsibility. The age at which young people are expected to assume adult responsibility shifts with the times. In periods of depression, adolescents are held back in their efforts to gain financial independence: there are not enough jobs to go around. In times of war and rumors of war, young boys are precipitated into experiences for which they are emotionally and morally unprepared.

The form of government and the methods used to implement it have produced characteristic youth patterns. Certainly, Nazi and Soviet youth have perceived themselves, their world, and their destiny differently from young people growing up in a democratic society. In the latter, however, young people may experience more conflict between their ideals and their practices.

The attitude of adults toward adolescents often makes the achieving of adult status difficult. For various reasons, except in times of war, adults tend to hinder youngsters from growing up. They expect them to assume adult responsibilities but deny them adult privileges.

In our culture the immaturity of adolescents is over-emphasized. Being so concerned with their faults and lapses into childish behavior, we forget that a large number of teen-agers are more intelligent, more capable in making and carrying out plans, and more emotionally mature than some of their parents and their teachers.

"I think one of our chief difficulties," a seventeen-year-old boy said, "is having people realize that you are no longer a little kid. The teachers try to do the thinking for you as if you could not think for yourself."

Many young people have to deal with "problem parents and grandparents" and "problem teachers." And they do it fairly well. In society as a whole, youngsters today are "striving against the massed immaturity of adults." [9]

The child-rearing practices common to a culture and other culturally influenced patterns of parent behavior have their effect on adolescent development. This influence has been shown most dramatically by anthropological studies. For example, the Alorese customs do not provide satisfaction of the child's basic needs for security. Infants are nursed at odd times, disciplined haphazardly, sometimes picked up and comforted when they cry, sometimes given no attention or care. Such early experiences tend to produce adults who are anxious and insecure, suspicious and unambitious.

However, merely changing certain child-care practices is not enough; the newer methods must be in accord with the whole cultural pattern. It is also true that experiences during later childhood, adolescence, and adulthood may modify the favorable or unfavorable influences of early childhood. Kluckhohn [10] noted that the Navaho Indians are permissive and indulgent to their children during the first two years of life. But this early childhood experience of acceptance and gratification is not sufficient to counteract the difficulties and hardships of their later life. Consequently, "as a people they are realistically worried and suspicious." [11] Two other tribes, both economically insecure,

[9] Ruth Strang, "Manifestations of Immaturity in Adolescents," *Mental Hygiene,* vol. 33 (October, 1949), p. 563.

[10] Clyde Kluckhohn, *Mirror for Man.* New York: McGraw-Hill Book Company, Inc., 1949.

[11] *Ibid.,* p. 201.

avoid marked anxiety, apparently by refusing to face reality.

Anthropologists have also shown that cultural expectations and pressures during preadolescence and adolescence affect the individual's adjustment. For example, according to Margaret Mead's *Studies of Adolescence in Primitive Society,* out of the Arapesh culture an ideal adolescent development emerges. Psychological conflict about sex seems to be absent among Arapesh adolescents. The basis of relations between boys and girls, men and women, is affection. Intercourse after marriage becomes a natural, acceptable, more complete expression of the husband's and wife's affection for each other. The cultural expectation is that adolescent groups will not experiment with sex. When they are ready to enter the adult world, young people are accepted warmly in a noncompetitive culture.

The Samoan adolescents likewise experience little psychological conflict about sex. Prior to adolescence they consider physiological sex urges natural and pleasurable. In their sex relations there is general premarital promiscuity and lack of emotional involvement. But their relatively unstressful adolescence, as Ausubel so well pointed out, cannot be attributed solely to uninhibited sex expression. They also enjoy an easy-going way of life and have comparatively little struggle for status.

Quite different is the adjustment of the Mundugumor adolescents, where severe restrictions are placed on premarital sex relations. The result is considerable conflict about sex and clandestine sex relations. Yet, here, too, the stress and strain of adolescence cannot be attributed solely to the way in which the sex impulse is handled. In this tribe the adolescent has to fight for status in an aggressive, competitive culture.

Similarly in the Manus culture, strict taboos regarding sex are enforced. For boys there is a dual standard of sex morality; for girls, sex desires seem nonexistent, but shame and repugnance are associated with sex. After a carefree childhood, adolescents are suddenly thrust into a ruthless, competitive adult society. These and other conditions give rise to adolescent stresses.

Since development is gradual and each era depends on what has gone before, continuing cultural conditions during childhood and adolescence would seem to be more important than the adolescent initiation rites which, in some tribes, dramatically mark the transition from childhood to adulthood. However, the rites are a direct way of attaining adult status through traditional ordeals and rituals. Accompanying the changes in social and economic status conferred through these ceremonies are changes in adolescents' attitudes toward their place and privileges in adult society. Without these rites the adolescent is less certain of his role in society and whether or not he has accomplished certain developmental tasks.

Within the United States there are many sub-cultures or patterns of culture. Child care practices vary; parent-child relations cover a range from total rejection to a high degree of understanding and genuinue affection. Teen-agers, while resenting domination by parents, are equally aware of parental neglect and indifference. Instead of writing about his view of the world, one fourteen-year-old boy wrote:

Instead of worrying about Russia and their atomic weapons, people should pay more attention to raising their family. The children are left on their own too much. They get into gangs and have races with their cars, steal, and even kill sometimes. If less attention would be payed to other things and more to children we wouldn't be reading in the paper about kid gangs, robberys, and teen-agers getting killed in follish stunts.

Some of the present conflict between adolescents and their parents can be attributed to the rapidly changing American culture. Modern teen-age behavior seems inappropriate to parents, and this makes understanding difficult. This is especially noticeable with regard to the sex roles. Here differences in supervision, standards of conduct, and differential treatment of the sexes are very great in different communities, and even among families in the same community. Some adolescents have every opportunity to develop their intellectual and interpersonal potentialities, while others must either overcome or succumb to deprivation or demoralizing conditions. The amount of leisure time available and how it is spent, the quality of radio and television programs, opportunities or lack of opportunities for part-time

work are other conditions that influence adolescents in inde-
finable ways.

The effect of social class on adolescent development has been
frequently described. Hollingshead,[12] in his sociological study
of an American community, gives much anecdotal material on
the social behavior of adolescents of high school age. He reports
that their behavior is related to the position their families occupy
in the community's social structure. He concludes that "the home
an adolescent comes from conditions in a very definite manner
the way he behaves in his relations with the school, the church,
the job, recreation, his peers and his family." [13] Nevertheless, the
fact that adolescents within the same socio-economic group be-

have differently in their day-to-day activities indicates influences
other than social class at work. In interpreting studies of this
kind, one easily falls into the errors of imputing a causal relation between adolescent behavior and social class, of failing to
recognize that factors such as mental ability and personal traits
may underlie both social position and adolescent behavior.

[12] August B. Hollingshead, *Elmtown's Youth: The Impact of Social Classes
on Adolescents,* chaps. IV and XVII. New York: John Wiley & Sons, Inc.,
1949.
[13] *Ibid.,* p. 441.

Other studies have shown little consciousness of family background among children and preadolescents; their cliques cut across social-class lines. High school students, however, become more aware of socio-economic status. They tend to choose their best friends from higher socio-economic levels than their own. McGuire[14] reported that considerable social mobility was achieved during high school years by girls from lower social classes. They were socially popular in school, made friends with upper- or middle-class girls, and often went to college. At college they came in contact with young men whom they married, and thus maintained an upper-middle-class position. Boys of lower social class whose scholarship enabled them to obtain a college education were more likely to move upward in social standing than boys who were only temporarily popular and accepted because of their success in athletics.

Fluidity of American society, according to Florence R. Kluckhohn,[15] is related to the amount of freedom which the family allows to individual members, and to the occupational success of the father. To quote:

The marked fluidity of American society and its relative lack of a rigid class system depend more than anything else upon a weakness in family bonds. . . . Another fact to be noted is how much more a particular family's class or social position is a result of the father's occupation than is the father's occupation a result of his having been born in a particular family. The main rewards, social and otherwise, go to the successful producers.[16]

In high schools in which a pervasive attitude of respect for every individual has been built through example and discussion, social distance is minimized. In many American high schools we find students of different backgrounds, races, nationalities, and socio-economic levels holding equal positions of leadership in student activities.

[14] John Carson McGuire, "Adolescent Society and Social Mobility," unpublished doctoral thesis, University of Chicago, Chicago, 1949.

[15] Florence Rockwood Kluckhohn, "The American Family and the Feminine Role," *Human Relations* (Hugh Cabot and Joseph A. Kahl, eds.), pp. 240–281. Cambridge, Mass.: Harvard University Press, 1954.

[16] *Ibid.*, p. 250.

All the difficulties of adolescent growth toward maturity cannot be attributed to cultural factors. Even in Samoa, where the general level of aspiration is low and the attitude toward sex permissive, there is not complete absence of adolescent conflict.[17] In various social settings the length of the adolescent transition period and the intensity of problems will vary, but there will also be some psychobiological uniformities and individual variations within a culture, due to differences in personality.[18]

THE ADOLESCENT'S HANDLING OF HIS ENVIRONMENT

The way an adolescent "perceives a situation may be determined objectively by the dominant quality of the situation itself, by the individual's subjective attitudes and values, and by the impact of social traditions, customs, and values." [19] He is faced with the problem of maintaining a balance "between cultural requirements and individual needs."

One of the dominant conditions in our culture that makes growing up most difficult is the long period between the individual's recognition of his adult status and its realization. The factors frequently mentioned—adult attitudes, lack of employment for young people, the many years required in preparing for a profession, delayed marriage—are difficult for the adolescent to handle. He can at least be made aware of the conflicting demands and of the courses of action acceptable to society. To know the specific behavior patterns needed will at least spare him the emotional turmoil of constant uncertainty and indecision.

Much of his successful adjustment depends on the way he perceives these conflicts and demands. If he believes that man

---

[17] Muzafer Sherif and Hadley Cantril, *The Psychology of Ego-involvements.* New York: John Wiley & Sons, Inc., 1946.

[18] David P. Ausubel, *Ego Development and the Personality Disorders,* pp. 84–86. New York: Grune & Stratton, Inc., 1952.

[19] Ruth Strang, "Many-sided Aspects of Mental Health," Forty-fourth Yearbook of the National Society for the Study of Education, part II, p. 44. Chicago: University of Chicago Press, 1955.

is not entirely a creature of his environment, he will be more active in changing it. In a panel discussion of the influence of environment on behavior, one adolescent said, in opposition to the prevalent viewpoint that delinquency is caused by poor home and neighborhood conditions, "But don't we ourselves have some responsibility for behavior? Isn't it largely up to us?" The child may influence the parent's behavior and the man may play a part in changing the social order. If adolescents perceive the social world as man-made and capable of being changed, they will have less fear of the future.[20] They will not view their environment as completely black and threatening, but will discern rifts in the clouds, revealing glimpses of a brighter day toward which they may make some small contribution.

In a number of communities young people have contributed to community betterment. They have made surveys of tuberculosis and hookworm and cooperated with local doctors and public health agencies in reducing the incidence of these diseases. They have planted fruit trees on barren hillsides, landscaped homes and school grounds, built recreation centers. In these and many other ways, young people have made their community a better place to live in. To them, changing the environment has not been a mere possibility; they have made it a reality through their own efforts.

This positive attitude is more hopeful and gives a nobler picture of man than one which views him merely as the passive product of his environment. To consider man as predestined to become merely "what his environment makes him" puts a low evaluation on the human being.

As we have said repeatedly, the influence of the environment depends a great deal on how the individual perceives it. For this reason it is important to know how adolescents view their home, their neighborhood, members of their family, their teachers and companions, whether or not their descriptions correspond with our impressions of "reality." An "objective" description of

[20] Margaret Mead, "Technological Change and Child Development," *Understanding the Child*, vol. 21 (October, 1952), pp. 109–112.

the environment does not tell how individuals will respond to it. Each person will respond somewhat differently to conditions that appear to be identical.

The direct study of the culture is a third factor in determining how an adolescent perceives and responds to a situation. Apart from the indirect influence which the culture exerts on the child through the "culturally patterned behavior of his parents and the attitudes and expectations of other people toward him," the adolescent may learn directly from his own observation, or from instruction, what is the best thing to do in his culture.

ADOLESCENTS IN DIVERSE COMMUNITIES

The concept of "the typical adolescent" is shown to be inadequate by glimpses of young people in different situations. A certain kind of school within a given community will make a difference in the attitudes and behavior of its students. In different classes within the same school, one teacher will describe adolescents as cooperative, creative, responsible. Another will say they are noisy, competitive, defiant. They may behave well in one class with a teacher whom they like and respect, but go wild in another teacher's room. Diverse kinds of behavior can be evoked from almost any adolescent group. Descriptions of adolescents as observed by teachers or counselors in diverse types of communities will illustrate some of the infinitely varied patterns of behavior in adolescent groups.

Young Adolescents in a Rural Environment

Young adolescents tend to stay in the country during their high school years, but after the age of seventeen they migrate to cities in increasing numbers. According to several reports, about one-half of the young people between the ages of fourteen and seventeen and two-thirds of those between the ages of eighteen and twenty live in cities. These figures do not include the children of migratory laborers who follow agricultural employment from place to place and present special problems. Even those rural adolescents who have a permanent residence get less schooling, in general, than urban youth. The following is a description of a class of seventh-grade boys and girls who, with a few exceptions, lived on farms in a rural community in the South. It was written by their teacher, who lived with them for a year:

In general, their appearance was good. They were clean, almost to the point of shining. The boys wore tight-fitting blue jeans and gay sports shirts—the shirts hanging loosely about their pole-like bodies.

The girls seemed more concerned with their appearance than the boys. Their hair seemed always freshly washed and well kept. They wore it in pigtails or bangs. They wore gaily-colored blouses and gathered skirts, usually accentuated by a wide leather belt of contrasting color. Sandals were the fad, and the more forward, faster-maturing girls were experimenting with lipstick. All of these youngsters appeared to be equally well-dressed. It took close observation to differentiate those who represented a lower economic status.

These youngsters were eager, happy, curious, lovable, and energetic. At no time did they present serious behavior problems. Their limits of behavior were defined, and within those limits they were given freedom of movement and expression. As in any class, however, there were some who displayed aggressive tendencies, as in the case of Herby whose father was a drunkard. To these, the teacher gave ample opportunity to channel or work off their aggression through meaningful activities—new desks to be put together, Christmas tree bases to be built, and other real jobs.

All of them were self-conscious. The girls were sensitive to their physiological changes. They were also becoming boy-conscious and practiced their emerging powers of womanly charm on the somewhat slower-developing boys of the class. Since the boys had not quite reached puberty, they were not as yet interested in girls. Sometimes one of them would proclaim vehemently, "Girls! You can have 'em! Come on, Joe, let's go play catch."

The girls, only slightly dismayed by this rejection, set their sights upon the "older men" in the eighth and ninth grades, casting sly glances, passing notes, or just plain telling them that they were their chosen love!

Though the girls seemed to be mainly interested in boys, they did try to give some appearance of studiousness. Some of them would concentrate so hard on a textbook that the teacher was sure there must be a picture of that handsome boy in the ninth grade pasted in over the page on the gladiators of ancient Rome!

The interests of many of these boys and girls lay in 4-H Club projects. "How many bushels of corn do you expect to make on that acre project of yours, Bill?" "Do you think my lamp will win in the 4-H lamp-making contest?"—their conversation often touched upon questions like these.

There were some whose interests seemed excessively intellectual. They were the ones who were naturally gifted in verbal ability, who feared parental repercussions from low marks, or who were perfectionists. They desired praise, prestige, and power; they also needed challenge.

And then there were those who just didn't seem to care about school achievement. They were not encouraged at home; they could not compete at school; and so they simply dragged along, hoping somehow they'd pass. They never sought achievement for its own sake. These were the ones whose ambitions had not become crystallized. Their apparent indifference represented broken homes, working parents, dominating mothers, or low mental ability.

The majority of the class, however, liked school more or less—anyway they knew they must attend. "So why not get the most out of it?" remarked one whose efforts were devoted to the baseball team to the detriment of his subjects.

With respect to sports, when seasonal ball games rolled around, there were invariably a few who were not allowed to play because of their low scholastic status. The ways in which they coped with this problem were phenomenal. All the rationalizations they uttered would fill a book: "Oh, well, I didn't want to play anyway." Or, "Gee, I forgot I've got to baby-sit this afternoon. It's a good thing I can't play 'cause I wouldn't be able to if I could."

Sportsmanship was sometimes lacking. If they won the softball games between the grades, they would boast loudly, "We really did 'em up good today, boy!" But if they lost, they resented "those little old squirts in the sixth grade" who had beaten them by one point.

This adolescent group enjoyed play activities, the freedom of unassigned periods, and discussions of TV shows and other matters closely related to their lives. Especially did they like to divert the teacher from the subject matter. These informal class discussions on topics of special interest to them were very helpful to the teacher in affording insight into their personalities.

Their dislikes were pronounced. They especially disliked one of their other teachers. A well-liked teacher often found herself unintentionally hearing their discussions of the disliked teacher's merits, or rather lack of merits: "Why can't Mrs. T be more like you?" "She thinks all there is to know is her subject!" "Do you know she gave us *four* pages of problems to do for tomorrow!" Her subject became a chore, despised because of her authoritarian manner and presentation. The teacher who taught the class that had just come from her room would often have to allow a few moments of freedom to relax the tensions which her rigid discipline had created.

Perhaps there were more deep-seated emotional problems in this group which were not obvious to this discerning teacher. On the surface these students seemed to accept themselves, their classmates, the inevitability of school, and the business of growing up. In physiological maturity they were distributed over the wide range characteristic of the age group. Their varied responses to schoolwork seemed to be the result of differences in ability, home background, goals and purposes, and adults' expectations of them.

Slow Learners in a Prosperous Community

The behavior of the young adolescents in a slow-learning seventh grade, who were also below average in socio-economic status, was quite different from that of the rural group just described. The IQs of this class ranged from 75 to 90; their reading ability was at the third- or fourth-grade level. They were especially poor in spelling, penmanship, and mathematics. Only a few of the brighter ones were good in athletics. In intramural competition in softball, touch tackle, and basketball, they invariably lost.

They had a tolerant but rather passive attitude toward school, not really enjoying it, but accepting it.

The majority of the students seemed to have a happy home life, although the school clinic and guidance department noted the fact that four of the boys suffered occasional beatings.

The majority of the pupils rode to school on bikes, but some used the school bus or other means of transportation. They wore moderately expensive clothing but looked unkempt and disheveled. Usually their fingernails were dirty and their clothing had food stains on it. Although they received an average allowance of approximately two dollars a week, they felt this was insufficient and wanted to supplement it by money earned in part-time jobs. Many of the boys delivered newspapers.

Although the majority of these seventh-graders were not yet interested in boy-girl relations, they had already obtained sex information or misinformation from outside sources. Two of the girls openly encouraged boys to engage in petting and showed tendencies toward sex delinquency.

There were many discipline problems in this class, including frequent fist fights, even among the girls. The major type of misconduct took the form of antisocial destructiveness. Students were reported for willfully tearing up textbooks, throwing food in the cafeteria, marring desks and school walls, and even attempting to damage the cars of faculty members. They were sometimes guilty of such misdemeanors as smoking, truancy, and stealing from the lockers; in such cases it invariably developed that they had been influenced by an older student of the school.

Every member of the class went to the movies at least once a week and looked at television at least a half hour per night. Of the fourteen girls in the class, only one did not habitually buy movie magazines. The only other recreation of appreciable importance was roller skating. Practically everyone in the class went to "the rink" on Saturday afternoon. Nothing aroused their enthusiasm except a forthcoming class softball game, a party, a movie, or the rink.

They were not interested in educational or vocational plans; questionnaires on this subject they invariably left blank.

Group work resulted in many arguments. The students often accused one another of shirking their responsibilities in the various projects. However, they enjoyed giving radio plays and other dramatic productions in class.

Their attention span was short. They were rarely interested in anything that would take more than a few days to finish. They did not comprehend easily, and would frequently repeat questions that had already been asked. They did their best work in spelling, simple language-usage drills, and other concrete assignments. They had difficulty in writing up information without copying it from a book. They enjoyed pasting pictures in their reports, and a few of them would draw illustrations in conjunction with their art workshop. Vocabulary lists based on these reports proved an excellent means of helping them assimilate new words.

Their textbooks were usually far beyond their reading level. Their parents, though practically all skilled workers—electricians, toolmakers, etc.—were not in the habit of doing much reading. Consequently their homes were usually devoid of good reading material. When the group went to the school library, there would be an immediate dash for the magazine rack. Some of the students complained that their books did not contain pictures. They evidently profited a great deal from visual aids; they remembered what they saw in a movie much better than what they read in a book.

The social behavior of this group of adolescents, under this combination of home and school conditions, left much to be desired. This may have been due in part to a deep-rooted feeling of inferiority stemming from their below-average mental ability and intensified by too difficult school tasks and lack of praise and recognition. Moreover, they were observing undesirable patterns of social behavior as set by older boys and girls, by characters in movies and on television, and, probably, by many adults in their community.

This group of young teen-age pupils, below average in mental ability and socio-economic status, were not aware of their potentialities as to personal appearance, school achievement, and social relationships. They accepted a self-concept which showed them as inferior people, and they did nothing to improve. Being below average socially and economically in a prosperous community probably contributed to their sense of inferiority. Underneath their apparent indifference, unconsciously perhaps, they had a sense of failure. Latent resentment against conditions that prevented them from achieving self-realization seemed to take the form of wanton destructiveness.

Under a varied program in which they might deal concretely with realistic problems, take part in discussions that would have meaning and use for them, set for themselves specific goals, and be given enough time to understand clearly stated, concrete explanations, they would probably show quite different "adolescent behavior."

An Eighth Grade in a Semislum

These junior high school students come from a neighborhood to which Puerto Rican and Negro families have migrated. As a group they are handicapped socially, economically, and mentally. They come from homes where a foreign language is spoken. They lack not only proper food and clothing, but also a minimum amount of parental care and affection. Many of the parents seem more concerned about the effect of the child's behavior on them than about the child himself. They say, "I have enough trouble with my other seven kids without having him bother me."

Although one occasionally finds in their compositions a statement about a warm, happy family life, most of their comments reveal disordered, broken homes: "I have one sister and a brother but my brother don't live with us. I have no father."

"I come from Puerto Rico with my mother. My mother tell me if I like to go staid in Puerto Rico and I said no because I like better in here. I have four sister and one brother. My father died. I have only one mother."

Animal pets mean much to them; they long for some personal possession to cherish. "I have a dog, her name is Queeny. She looks like Lassey. I think she is the most boutiful dog in the world."

They express their concept of themselves in these ways:

I'm not bad and not good but I well be good for the rest of the term.

I am rufe and I am younger than most of the boys in this class. I am too short for my age.

The slow learners reveal feelings of inferiority; they contrast the skills they have acquired with those they feel they should have acquired. They have always been in classes where progress was slow, where there was very little individualized attention, and where classroom procedures were constantly disrupted by violent behavioral disturbances. They say, as one did:

I didn't learn anything from the orther teachers, but I think I'll learn something from you. I would like you to give us a test every friday and Wendsday, so the boys in this class won't come and disturb me; and if you wan't this class to be good you have to watch the sneeky ones.
I like to work in Eng. I usest to foule around in Eng. but now maybe I can learn something.

Many of these young adolescents seem to sense that they have potential learning ability. Perhaps their academic hopefulness stems from their parents' expectations of a land of promise, which motivated their migration to this country. The children desperately need help in learning to speak and to read the English words which are basic to school learning. They need help in becoming acquainted with their new environment—in acquiring firsthand experiences which are necessary to the understanding of new concepts. They need to be taught step by step with sympathy and understanding. Otherwise their disillusionment and frustration will be too intense for them to cope with.

A Senior Class in a Mill Town

The behavior of groups of adolescents reflects community organization as well as family disorganization. In a mill town where the industry was autocratically but benevolently administered, there was marked conformity in adolescent conduct. The standard dress for boys was jeans, for girls, sweater and skirt. In the senior class of the high school discipline was not a problem. Peer pressure was all on the side of obedience to authority. No sooner did the teacher enter the classroom than a series of "Sh's!" brought the class to respectful attention.

The group reflected the pride that the community felt in its impressive and functional community house, equipped with a swimming pool and offering a well-balanced recreational program directed by trained persons. The leisure activities of all the children and young people revolved around the community house. All but one of the senior class participated in some community-house activity and were thoroughly at home in the sports program.

Most of the class members were from the homes of mill workers, although about 15 per cent came from the surrounding agricultural community. On a group intelligence test the average intelligence quotient was 92.

In general, the seniors' goals and purposes were limited. They admitted that all they wanted was simply to meet the minimum academic requirements. Few went beyond the letter of the assignment. Financially, most of them could not expect further education without scholarship aid, and their interests and abilities limited their vocational choices.

These young people were seriously concerned about values and much impressed by the religious teachings of the churches they attended. Many were questioning literal interpretations of the Bible. In discussing dancing they said, "I can't see anything wrong with dancing, but how are you going to get around the fact that the Bible says it is wrong?" They were torn between following the social practices of their peers and abiding by the strict injunctions of their churches against dancing and card playing.

The class was marked by a singular cohesiveness; no subgroup offered conflicting points of view. For suggestions, the majority looked to the two class members whose parents were executives in the mill, and considered it as their role to carry out these suggestions. The students were kind and helpful to one another. One member of the class was a deaf-mute. Although she had a student assigned to help her, there were times when the helper was busy in another group. Almost always some member of the class would assist her before the teacher could get to it. If no student was able to supply the help she needed, someone was sure to say to the teacher, "You mustn't forget Mary." This same kindness extended to younger children as well as to the handicapped. When elementary teachers were called out of their rooms, they usually asked a member of this senior class to take charge.

Like most other adolescents, these seniors had a strong desire for approval and recognition. Often, in connection with student activities, they wanted to know if they were as good as last year's class or better.

In this environment characterized by uniformity of socio-economic status and of housing facilities, by dependence on the mill owners for education and recreation as well as for livelihood, and by a strong religious influence, the adolescent personality was overtly quite different from that of the "flaming youth" of delinquent city areas, and from that of the ambitious and socially sophisticated groups often found in wealthy residential communities. They accepted the way of life laid down for them— a way of life that emphasized obedience, religious sanctions, kindness, and contentment with one's lot. Since choice was limited and cultural conflicts were few, adolescence for this group seemed to have little of the storm and stress characteristic of this stage of development in more turbulent communities, whose members have higher socio-economic aspirations.

Tenth-graders from the Upper Middle Class

Although younger chronologically, a sophomore high school honors English class was far more mature and creative than the senior group just described. The boys wore jeans and sport shirts to class and the girls wore plain but expensive clothes. They were all above average in intelligence and all of them planned to go to college. They had allowances of about five dollars a week and were given more when the occasion arose. The parents had all finished high school, and most of them were college graduates. Although none of the students in this group owned automobiles, many of those over sixteen were permitted to use the family car.

Many were leaders in the school. All belonged to at least

one club and held at least one office. They were all well liked by the rest of the student body and could be relied upon to help any student or faculty member when the occasion presented itself. As an example: Their English teacher was asked by the president of the PTA to prepare a program for a meeting to be held a week later. At the time he was busy with the senior play and had no free time. He presented the problem to this English class and told them if they were interested to see him after class. Five of the group stayed after class. They were very much interested and chose to form a panel to discuss civil defense, since that was a problem of current interest in the community. The teacher forgot about the program until the day of the meeting; he then found that this group had done as much research as possible and was ready to present a discussion before the PTA. The program was highly successful.

Although they enjoyed working with one another and spent a great deal of time together, this group by no means constituted an exclusive clique. They constantly brought other students into their various activities. They even pitched in to save the junior-senior reception when the president of the junior class got very little cooperation from the members of his class who were called on to serve on various committees. This sophomore English class worked for a week in their free time making decorations, planning entertainment, and assisting the juniors with their preparations. They did this entirely in a spirit of helpfulness.

Their attitude toward the faculty was exemplary. None of them ever had a run-in with any faculty member. It is interesting to note how they handled a problem, involving the faculty, which arose as to exemptions from final tests. It had previously been the custom that if a student had one B and all the rest A's he would be exempt from final examinations. But in the preceding year this policy had been changed without explanation. Two of the students in this group interviewed the principal and various faculty members to find out why they had changed the ruling. They learned that the faculty and principal believed that a student should take the examination in any subject in which his mark was lower than A, because this would help him in his college entrance examination. The group was satisfied with this explanation and accepted the ruling.

A member of the group was editor of the school paper. Finding herself short of funds for the last two issues, she immediately enlisted the aid of several students, who made and sold candy after lunch and thus raised the necessary money to publish the paper.

The English teacher made this general comment: "I think that this was the finest class I have ever worked with. They were all intelligent and understanding; you did not have to tell them twice what you wanted done and how. They seemed to have a sixth sense and always had a solution to any problem."

This was indeed a superior group of adolescents who had learned to work together, and were given opportunities to use their initiative and to take responsibility. It would be interesting to know "how they got that way"—what lucky combination of heredity, harmonious home conditions, adult example, and school instruction had resulted in producing adolescents who were creative, considerate of and helpful to others, fair-minded, and apparently well on the way to developing their potentialities.

We might describe many more groups of adolescents, equally diverse. Their infinite variety arises out of varied patterns of native ability, early childhood experience, family and community attitudes, community structure, and school pressures, opportunities, and satisfactions. Within almost any group we find a wide range of individual differences. Adolescent development, while having common features arising from characteristic biological changes and psychological principles, will vary somewhat from culture to culture, as the maturing person tries to incorporate into his own ego development the values, standards, and expectations of his particular environment. It is amazing how well many young people cope with their changing adolescent status and also with a changing society.

COMPREHENSION QUESTIONS

1. What are the characteristics of the modern world as adults view it?

2. What factors other than social class may account for differences in adolescents' behavior and attitudes?

3. In what ways may the culture affect adolescent development and personality?

4. What is the most constructive and hopeful attitude for adolescents to take toward a changing world?

5. Compare the descriptions of adolescents in diverse communities with your own observation. Why do you find marked differences in adolescent behavior in various social settings, e.g., rural, mill town

large city, and also within the same community, school, or classroom?

6. Is adolescence inevitably a difficult time for many teen-agers? Why or why not?

7. How are problems of adolescent group conduct related to the organization, pressures, and conflicting standards of the community?

STUDY PROJECTS

1. Listen to young people as they talk informally among themselves. What do they discuss? How much concern do they show for the state of the world?

2. Discuss the statement: "The American high school is an important factor in social mobility." How do young people from lower socio-economic levels become friends with students from higher levels? Give examples from your own experience and observation.

3. Make a scholarly, critical review of research on the relation between the family's socio-economic status and the adolescent's social status in his peer group.

4. Study a class to find evidence of family, school, and community influences on the behavior of individual adolescents.

FOR FURTHER STUDY

Ausubel, David P., *Theory and Problems of Adolescent Development*, chap. II. New York: Grune & Stratton, Inc., 1954.

Blair, Arthur Witt, and William H. Burton, *Growth and Development of the Preadolescent*, chap. III. New York: Appleton-Century-Crofts, Inc., 1951.

Bossard, James H. S., *The Sociology of Child Development*, 2d ed. New York: Harper & Brothers, 1954.

Hollingshead, August B., *Elmtown's Youth*, chaps. IV, XVII. New York: John Wiley & Sons, Inc., 1949.

Horrocks, John E., *The Psychology of Adolescence*, chap. XII. Boston: Houghton Mifflin Company, 1951.

Josselyn, Irene M., *The Adolescent and His World*, chap. III. New York: Family Service Association of America, 1952.

Kluckhohn, Clyde, and Dorothea Leighton, *Children of the People: The Navaho Individual and His Development*. Cambridge, Mass.: Harvard University Press, 1947.

Kuhlen, Raymond G., *The Psychology of Adolescent Development*, chap. IV. New York: Harper & Brothers, 1952.

LINTON, RALPH, *The Cultural Background of Personality.* New York: Appleton-Century-Crofts, Inc., 1945.

MARQUARDT, JOHN L., "English Language Instruction in the American High School as Viewed within the Framework of the Adolescent-needs Concept," doctoral project, Teachers College, Columbia University, New York, 1955.

MEAD, MARGARET, *Coming of Age in Samoa.* New York: William Morrow & Company, Inc., 1928.

————, *From the South Seas: Studies of Adolescence in Primitive Society.* New York: William Morrow & Company, Inc., 1939.

OLSON, CLARA M., "The Adolescent: His Society," *Review of Educational Research,* vol. 24 (February, 1954), pp. 5–10.

PARTRIDGE, ERNEST DEALTON, *Social Psychology of Adolescence.* Englewood Cliffs, N.J.: Prentice-Hall, Inc., 1938.

SEIDMAN, JEROME M. (ed.), *The Adolescent,* chaps. I, IV. New York: The Dryden Press, Inc., 1953.

STRANG, RUTH, "How Children and Adolescents View Their World," *Mental Hygiene,* vol. 38 (January, 1954), pp. 28–33.

WATTENBERG, WILLIAM W., *The Adolescent Years,* chaps. II, XIII, XXVII. New York: Harcourt, Brace and Company, Inc., 1955.

Fiction

* CHILDS, MARQUIS W., *The Cabin.* New York: Harper & Brothers, 1944.

* DAVIS, CLYDE B., *The Newcomer.* Philadelphia: J. B. Lippincott Company, 1954.

* FRANK, ANNE, *The Diary of a Young Girl.* New York: Doubleday & Company, Inc., 1952.

* McCAULEY, ROSE, *The World My Wilderness.* Boston: Little, Brown & Company, 1950.

* WOUK, HERMAN, *City Boy.* New York: Simon and Schuster, Inc., 1948.

* ————, *Marjorie Morningstar.* New York: Doubleday & Company, Inc., 1955.

Audio-visual Aids

The Devil Is a Sissy. 16 minutes. Sound. Teaching Film Custodians.
Near Home. 25 minutes. Sound. International Film Bureau.
Passion for Life. 85 minutes. Sound. Black and white. Brandon Films.
Youth in Crisis. 18 minutes. Sound. March of Time.

* Fiction.

CHAPTER 3

Developing an Adequate Self-concept
and Philosophy of Life

When I was sixteen or seventeen . . . I had not yet found my-self. I was still in search, less of abstract truth, than of a very private and personal destiny. Youth is without finality, and, like all young and ardent creatures, I craved change, adventure, delight. I felt a thrilling sense that mystery surrounded me, that life stretched ahead, like a forest of luminous vistas. . . .[1]

Achieving identity, as Ellen Glasgow implied, is a process extending into and beyond the adolescent years. The adolescent must learn to reorganize his self-concept in accordance with his changing bodily structure and functions, as well as with his new relationships with his peers and with adults. Achieving identity involves answering questions such as these:

Who am I?
What are my goals in life?
What kind of person will I be ten or fifteen years from now?

Havighurst [2] asked a group of college graduates, "At what age did you become aware of yourself as a full-fledged adult?" About three-fourths of the men and half of the women felt that they

[1] Ellen Glasgow, *The Woman Within,* pp. 82–83. New York: Harcourt, Brace and Company, Inc., 1954.
[2] Robert Havighurst, "Poised at the Crossroads of Life: Suggestions to Parents and Teachers of Young Adolescents," *School Review,* vol. 61 (September, 1953), pp. 329–336.

had achieved this degree of maturity before twenty-five years of age. The events with which the men associated this feeling of having become adults were: supporting themselves in college, graduating and getting their first job, marrying, setting up their own home, or having their first child. Changes in social attitudes and social behavior usually accompany changes in self-concept as part of a total pattern of growing toward maturity.[3]

Those aspects or characteristics of the individual which are "peculiarly his," which give a sense of unity to his personality, have been variously designated as the *self* by William James, the *ego* by Freud, the *self-system* by Sullivan, the *proprium* by Allport. Although these concepts vary greatly in comprehensiveness, they have certain characteristics in common. The self has a biological base; from birth it develops through interpersonal relations; it has continuity, maintaining its identity from day to day; it seeks to reduce interpersonal anxiety and to make itself as "good," secure, and complete as possible.

FOUR DIMENSIONS OF THE SELF

The Basic Self-concept

The self as the person perceives it has at least four dimensions. First, there is the self-concept proper which has been defined as the individual's perception of his abilities and his status and roles in the outer world. This is his concept of the kind of person he thinks he is. It is influenced by his physical self, his personal appearance, dress, and grooming; by his abilities and disposition, his values, beliefs, and aspirations. The following statement by a fourteen-year-old girl we shall call Ellen, in the eighth grade, is quite typical of many bright young adolescents:

Who am I? I'm just an average, healthy American girl. . . . I am a person of many interests. I consider myself very active. I enjoy almost every kind of sport. Being an only child I am spoiled because I like to have my way about things. I think I'm fairly smart, but I

[3] John W. Gustad, "Factors Associated with Social Behavior and Adjustment: A Review of the Literature," *Educational and Psychological Measurement*, vol. 12 (Spring, 1952), pp. 3–19.

could do better in my school work if I studied a little harder. I love animals and have two of my own dogs. I don't think I'm too moody or temperamental, as some people are.

More unusual and deeply introspective is the statement of Joan, another girl of similar age and ability: "In a personal self-analysis of myself I prove to be very selfish. I don't mean outwardly selfish, but an inward selfishness that possesses me. I wish to tell you that I do everything for the good of or to the satisfaction of myself."

The rapid changes that take place during adolescence in height, weight, body build, facial appearance, and voice necessitate a change in the adolescent's body image. "The changing body becomes a symbol, not only of being different from last month or last year, but of a new attitude toward self, toward others, toward life." [4]

Closely related to the physical characteristics is the influence of dress, grooming, and material possessions. Not having clothes like the other youngsters, being disheveled in personal appearance, not having a home where one can entertain friends without feeling embarrassed decreases a person's conception of his own importance, his feeling of social competence, his ability to appraise his true ability and worth. Lack of attention to personal appearance may be an outward manifestation of inner self-depreciation.

Having the mental ability to meet the demands of the environment also enhances the self-concept. On the other hand, the slow-learning adolescent who has not learned to read not only feels inadequate as a reader but also as a person. We find the influence of negative self-concepts operating in many learning situations. For example, many youngsters come to a reading clinic or special reading class with a fixed idea of themselves as persons who cannot learn to read. Until they obtain a more hopeful concept of themselves they will make little progress.

[4] H. R. Stolz and L. M. Stolz, "Adolescent Problems Related to Somatic Variations," *Adolescence,* Forty-third Yearbook, National Society for the Study of Education, part I, p. 83. Chicago: University of Chicago Press, 1944.

A long-time goal or purpose may become a central core or radix of self-motivating behavior. When an adolescent sees a task as a means of self-expression, he puts forth his maximum effort to accomplish it. According to Snygg and Combs,[5] the individual has a strong drive to maintain and enhance his phenomenal self. The self-image may be "compulsive, compensatory, and unrealistic" or it may be "an insightful cognitive map closely geared to reality and defining a wholesome ambition."[6] It involves time past, time present, and time future.

The Transitory Perception of Self

Second, there is the self-perception which an individual holds at the present time. This view may be lacking in perspective and may be influenced by the mood of the moment or by some recent experience. It is a transitory attitude. Many adolescents do not recognize its transitory nature; they act as though this temporary elation or depression, optimism or pessimism with reference to the self, would last forever. This dimension often includes a negative view—a picture of the kind of self the person fears he is.

Something of this transitory view of self was expressed by Anne, a thirteen-year-old girl in a class of gifted eighth-grade pupils:

I am, at least I think I am, the kind of person I would want to be except for a few minor details which sometimes seem awfully big. I guess some people think I'm awfully careless and carefree, and sometimes I wonder whether I'm too much so. My mother thinks I'm too slow even when I'm going as fast as I possibly can. She also thinks I'm much too forgetful and irresponsible. I guess she'd like to trade me in for somebody like my cousin who is so helpful. I have many friends but too many are girls and must think that I don't care about anything but fun. But I do think about my marks but thinking about them doesn't make them any better. Every marking period I vow not to say a word to neighbors in class and study

[5] Donald Snygg and Arthur W. Combs, *Individual Behavior*. New York: Harper & Brothers, 1949.

[6] Gordon W. Allport, *Becoming: Basic Considerations for a Psychology of Personality*, p. 47. New Haven, Conn.: Yale University Press, 1955.

and get good marks but every marking period the same thing happens.

The Social Self

The third dimension is the social self. This is the self as the person thinks others see it. This concept may not correspond with other people's perceptions of him; nevertheless it has an important effect on his behavior. If an adolescent has the impression that others think he is "dumb," retarded in reading, socially unacceptable, he tends to see himself in these negative ways. His feeling of insecurity about himself, his sense of unworthiness, colors his impression of the way others feel about him: "How could anyone really like *me!*" If, on the other hand, his parents, teachers, and friends have realistically accentuated the positive in his personality, he will take a more hopeful attitude toward himself.

In their compositions, many youngsters think that people have mixed feelings about them or that other people's impressions of them are diffcrent from their own. Ellen said, "I consider myself generally liked although there's nothing outstanding about me when it comes to making friends." Joan thought, "Other people think I am responsible, but I am either too stubborn or too dominating. I am not saying that they don't like me, but I think I could improve myself. When I am with a crowd everyone enjoys themselves because I don't think anyone should be left out." Less able learners write more briefly and more negatively about other persons' opinions of them, as in the following quotations from the compositions of eighth-grade boys and girls:

Other people think I'm a stupid jerk.
Other people don't think too good of me, but some do.
Some think I'm bright and some think I'm dull. (Boy)
Other people think I'm fairly quiet and a little shy. (Girl)
Well, I think people think that I'm a nice boy, a handsome boy, but one girl thinks I'm out of this world.

Some say, "I don't know what kind of person others think I am."

The Ideal Self

The fourth dimension is the ideal self or the self-ideal—the kind of person the individual hopes to be or would like to be. This may be realistic, too low, or too high, depending upon the individual's level of aspiration in relation to his ability and opportunities for self-realization. If the ideal self is set too low, it may be destructive of self-esteem as the individual compares himself with others who have had higher aspirations and have achieved much more. If the ideal self is set at an unrealistically high level, he may experience continuous frustration and be more subject to feelings of depression than if there were less discrepancy between the self-perception and the ideal self.[7] One's level of aspiration tends to go up with success and down with failure. Youngsters who have a fairly accurate, objective self-concept set realistic, attainable goals which present just enough challenge.

In writing about the kind of person she would like to be, Ellen emphasized character and her ideal of service rather than material things:

I would like to be fair and just in my judgment of others. I want to always remember that we are all imperfect and can make mistakes. I want to be kind and helpful to all persons. I'd like to have other people think I am like this. I would like to become a person who could bring joy and happiness to others. I don't particularly want to become a famous person. My goal in life is to become a missionary.

Joan, who was more introspective than most young adolescents, described her ideal self as follows:

I would like to be a person well liked through the years. I would also like to be a person that can look back through the years and feel satisfied with everything I have done. The kind of person I would like to become is rather common. In the sense of my future career I would like to be successful. In my personal career I would like to become just average. My goal in life is either to become a

[7] Robert E. Bills, "Self Concepts and Rorschach Signs of Depression," *Journal of Consulting Psychology*, vol. 18 (April, 1954), pp. 135–137.

lawyer or a secondary school teacher. In either of these careers I would like to be successful.

A boy in the same class as Ellen and Joan wrote as follows about his ideal self:

I would like to be just a normal person. Doing my job and having a wife to come home to. I'd like to mind my own business, never getting into trouble and going to jail.

When I grow up I would like to go into the medical field or become a pilot. I guess I could never really pick out which one I want to be. But who knows, I might become a flying doctor, going from state to state performing delicate operations.

My goals and purposes in life are to become a somebody. I don't want to walk down the street and have people say, "There goes Mr. Nobody."

The slow-learning pupils of the same age want to be "smart," to finish school, to make money, to be like a big brother or big sister. Some of their vocational choices are realistic, others clearly fantasy.

The ideal self is derived in many ways. According to Havighurst and MacDonald,[8] the development of the ideal self goes through an early stage of identification with a parent or parent substitute; an intermediate, somewhat unrealistic and glamorous stage, omitted by some children; and a stage of identification with an attractive young adult or an imaginary character who has a combination of many admirable qualities. Since, in early adolescence, the individual often models his ideal self after someone in his environment who is not a great deal older than he, adolescents need attractive young adults as models. One thirteen-year-old boy found his ideals in the college boys who served as his counselors in a summer camp. These young men had a marked influence on this youngster, who was at the crossroads. Before going to camp he had set foot on the road toward juvenile delinquency. After his summer at camp he started off in a

[8] Robert J. Havighurst and Donald V. MacDonald, "Development of the Ideal Self in New Zealand and American Children," *Journal of Educational Research,* vol. 49 (December, 1955), pp. 263–273.

far better direction and made such excellent progress in school the next year that he was put in the rapid advance class; in the previous year he had been failing in his subjects. Some parents do not set good examples. Even if they do, they may not be accepted as models by adolescents who are striving to achieve psychological independence from the family.

Reading may aid in the development of the ideal self. Characters in books may serve as useful objects for identification and imitation.[9] Although fewer adolescents than might be expected report conscious identification with specific characters in fiction, it is possible that many youngsters draw upon various fictional sources for qualities which they may incorporate into their ideal selves. For example, they may get clues for solving their own problems of adjustment from characters who know how to get along with others (e.g., Antonia in Cather's *My Antonia*), or those who have a good set of values (e.g., Kristin in Undset's *Kristin Lavransdatter*), or those who can transcend major tragedies in their lives (e.g., Jane Eyre in Brontë's *Jane Eyre*).

Acceptance of Self

Adolescents often refuse to accept themselves as they are. One bright ninth-grade girl recognized her feeling of self-acceptance

[9] Samuel Weingarten, "Reading as a Source of the Ideal Self," *Reading Teacher*, vol. 8 (February, 1955), pp. 159–164.

as unique: "I belong to a very small minority group which likes Carol Allen [her name]. This point alone makes some of my schoolmates think I am real wierd." Another girl, sixteen, expressed an apparently hopeless self-rejection: "Why am I ugly? Everybody hates me for I am unbearable to look at. My teachers can't stand the sight of me and they fail me. My name is Gertrude so you can see that my face goes well with my name. I have a puss only my mother could love—(and even she doesn't)."

Matteson's study [10] of the self-estimates of college freshmen showed a strong tendency in both men and women toward unrealistic objectives and aspirations; they came to college with grandiose expectations. There is a disparity between what they are and what they would like to be.

Successful therapy tends to narrow the gap between the "real self" and the "ideal self." Self-acceptance also seems to be increased by therapeutic counseling, in the course of which the client tends to acquire understanding, to become more secure, more self-accepting, less apologetic and self-condemnatory, more realistic in his self-appraisal, and more self-reliant. He may become able to change patterns in himself that he recognizes as undesirable. The self-image "helps us bring our view of the present into line with our view of the future." [11]

All these dimensions of the self are of great significance because they guide and, in many instances, determine an individual's behavior.

THE DYNAMIC NATURE OF THE SELF-CONCEPT

The very origin of the self-concept is dynamic. It arises out of the complex of the person's interpersonal relations and, according to Sullivan,[12] is determined by the way he organizes his experience to avoid or diminish anxiety. It is molded by approval

[10] Ross W. Matteson, "Self-estimates of College Freshmen," *Personnel and Guidance Journal*, vol. 34 (January, 1956), pp. 280–284.

[11] Allport, *op. cit.*, p. 47.

[12] Harry S. Sullivan, *The Interpersonal Theory of Psychiatry*, pp. 164–168. New York: W. W. Norton & Company, Inc., 1953.

and disapproval, praise and blame, reward and punishment, the giving or withholding of love, especially by the persons most significant in the individual's life. If parents and teachers hold a critical, disparaging attitude toward a person, he may take a similar attitude toward himself and others.

The self-concept is dynamic in its efforts to maintain its individuality. Despite the influence of family, close friends, and peer groups, adolescents, to different degrees, resist the demands for conformity made upon them. "All his life long this being will be attempting to reconcile these two modes of becoming—the tribal and the personal: the one makes him into a mirror, the other lights the lamp of individuality within." [13]

The question may be raised as to whether "the lamp of individuality" is burning low in young people today. A survey of college seniors conducted by *Time* magazine indicated that the ideal of many college students was conformity and competence. They do not aspire to originality and individuality. They have few dreams. One college senior said, "I think contentment is the main thing." Even in the junior high school age, this tendency toward contentment is evident.

The self-concept is persistent. Lecky [14] went so far as to say

[13] Allport, *op. cit.*, p. 35.
[14] Prescott Lecky, *Self Consistency, a Theory of Personality*, New York: Island Press Co-operative, Inc., 1945.

that "preserving one's perception of one's self intact is the prime motive in all behavior." A person will twist and turn new experiences so that they will conform to his preconceived idea of himself, and thus will introduce no inconsistencies. Even if a person conceives of himself as weak or despicable or stupid, he may hold to this "me" concept, whatever it is. This he does to maintain self-consistency—in order not to lose his self.

Excessive activity is sometimes a manifestation of "loss of self." If an adolescent accepts his parents' values and goals completely, he may feel an emptiness, an absence of identity, which he tries to fill with incessant work or recreational activities.

The dynamic aspect of the self-concept is also evidenced in adolescents' desire to understand themselves and to realize their most acceptable selves. Some build self-assurance by demonstrating their competency. Others, who are overanxious to gain recognition or affection, may strive for perfection; they may overwork or resort to attention-getting devices. Still others withdraw or otherwise escape from the situation. Some resort to self-blame and self-depreciation. When their feelings are hurt, some try to destroy things or hurt people. However, many cope with varying evaluations of themselves by learning "modes of self-realization that are acceptable and constructive." [15]

Harmony is achieved in various ways. According to Allport, the ego "synthesizes inner needs and outer reality." [16] The individual may succeed in fitting his experiences into his total self-concept. Or he may ignore the implication of any experiences that disturb or do not reinforce his preconceived ideas. Or he may misinterpret an experience—change his perception of it so that it will no longer cause conflict.

In successful therapy research workers [17] have demonstrated the possibility of change (1) from a negative to a positive attitude toward the self, (2) from frustration or depression to

[15] Caroline B. Zachry and Margaret Lighty, *Emotion and Conduct in Adolescence*, pp. 175–218. New York: Appleton-Century-Crofts, Inc., 1940.

[16] Allport, *op. cit.*, p. 37.

[17] Carl R. Rogers and Rosalind F. Diamond (eds.), *Psychotherapy and Personality Change*. Chicago: University of Chicago Press, 1954.

higher feelings of worth and social acceptance, and (3) from rebellion or withdrawal to some corresponding improvement in attitude toward others.

A positive attitude toward the self in all aspects of life is a most important determinant of successful life adjustment. The individual's concept of himself is at the core of his thinking, motivation, and behavior. It largely determines how an adolescent perceives his friends, his family, his potential vocation, and other aspects of his life. A "currently popular hypothesis [is] that human behavior in any particular context is largely determined by one's perception of himself," [18] and of his situation. Faulty growth results from faulty perception of oneself and one's situation. "As a man thinketh in his heart, so he is." If the person understands why he needs to behave as he does and how his behavior is affecting others, he will be in a better position to change his behavior. An adolescent's behavior is most fully understood in the light of his concept of himself.

DEVELOPMENT OF THE SELF-CONCEPT

To understand the self-concept of adolescents it is necessary to review the personal history of individuals and to note sequences of development. Changes in the individual's self-concept may occur at any time during his life, but especially at the beginning of each developmental phase. According to one theory,[19] an important step in the development of the self-concept occurs when the child strives to break away from the complete dependency of infancy. This is a tremendous first step toward achieving identity, toward asserting a recognizable self-concept. The child is still dependent on his parents and usually, after a period of attempting to demonstrate his omnipotence, he finds security through alliance with the parent, whom he now recognizes as all-powerful and not obligated to minister to his helplessness.

18 Emory Cowen, "The 'Negative Self-concept' as a Personality Measure," *Journal of Consulting Psychology,* vol. 18 (April, 1954), pp. 138–142.

19 David P. Ausubel, *Ego Development and the Personality Disorders.* New York: Grune & Stratton, Inc., 1952.

By thus identifying with his parents, the little child gains security and, indirectly, a sense of status. This is what Ausubel has called the process of *satellizing*. It is a process that goes on intermittently throughout life as the child fluctuates between self-assertiveness arising from a feeling of confidence in his own growing powers and the need for a certain amount of dependence upon someone more powerful than himself.

Beginning school contributes to the process of desatellization by introducing the child to a wider world and by lessening his attachment to his parents. At first the little child may transfer some of his dependency feelings to the teacher, but soon his peer relations become more important, and he begins to depend more on their approval than on the approval of his parents.

During preadolescence the school and the peer group satisfy his newer needs for status—needs that his parents cannot satisfy.[20] He is strongly influenced by the pressure of his peer group. He changes his behavior in accordance with the way his age-

[20] *Ibid.*, p. 168.

mates respond to him. He sees himself through others' eyes; their approval or criticism affect his attitude toward himself. At first the pressure of the peer group may be an asset. It gives the adolescent an opportunity to play various roles in his peer culture. Later on this pressure may interfere with his freedom and prevent him from being himself. A healthy peer culture aids the adolescent in achieving identity; a bad peer culture may cause him to identify himself with the underworld.

Parents have been replaced by other models; there has been "a reallocation of loyalties"; conformity to group standards has taken first place. Yet, despite "the tyranny of the group," the preadolescent and adolescent show a certain amount of resistance to complete conformity to the group, to being like everyone else; each, to some extent, desires to be himself, a unique individual. This desire, as previously stated, leads to the development of individuality.

During preadolescence the capacity for intimacy develops—

Preadolescents achieve intimacy with a best friend of the same sex; this is the beginning of a real affection for and sensitivity to the happiness and welfare of another person. (*Courtesy of H. Armstrong Roberts and of the National Committee of Boys and Girls Club Work, 4-H Clubs.*)

Close chums move into expanding relationships in groups of three or more, like these girl scouts at camp. (*Courtesy of the Girl Scouts of the U.S.A.*)

Square dancing meets many adolescent needs; it takes lots of energy; young people enjoy the colorful calls and the opportunity for spontaneity. (*Courtesy of* Sets In Order *magazine.*)

intimacy with a close friend or chum of the same sex. According to Harry Stack Sullivan, this relationship is exceedingly important. It may correct certain unreal ideas about the individual and others; it may lead to desirable changes in personality as he tries to make himself more acceptable to his friend and to contribute to his chum's prestige and sense of worth.[21]

During early adolescence acceptance of bodily changes contributes greatly to the self-concept. The physically mature adolescent tends to accept roles associated with the adult image of himself. Changes in his attitude toward himself are interwoven with changes in his expectancies of others and their expectancies of him. Toward adults, the change is from childish dependency to reciprocity based on respect for himself and for others. Maturity develops out of (1) demonstrated competence to deal with his experience, (2) community attitudes toward the development of adolescent independence, and (3) the adolescent's previous progress in setting goals, making decisions, and taking on responsibility. One way of building an adolescent's self-esteem and self-confidence is by placing him in situations in which he can succeed. Enabling him to see for himself that he can do the task required or relate himself happily to others is more effective than giving him a pep talk or reassurance. Every experience contributes to the adolescent's evolving picture of himself which, in turn, becomes a guide to future action. Previous persistent, unanalyzed failure does not give immunity to future failure; on the contrary, it usually produces a greater susceptibility to failure.

During later adolescence many young people find that, despite their adult stature and competency, they have no standing in the adult world. They are in a no man's land where they have lost the privileges and security of childhood but have not yet gained acceptance as adults. This is a difficult period. They may retreat into a dependent relation, or become hostile and aggressive, or find status and orientation in the peer culture.

These problems of adjusting to change of status continue

---

[21] Sullivan, *op. cit.*, pp. 245–262.

PERSONNEL

throughout life. Many young married people have the problem of revising their self-concept in accordance with the needs of the marriage partner and the children. The mother whose adolescent children no longer need her constant care often suffers a loss of status. Equally severe may be the loss of prestige and companionship associated with retirement from an absorbing career.

Achieving identity is a long and arduous process. Sometimes the individual in desperation reverts to a behavior pattern that used to be successful. The development of selfhood accelerates with increased capacity to think, to feel, to decide for oneself. It thrives on interaction with other people. However, the course of self-understanding and self-realization is not smooth. Some stumbling and fumbling are inevitable. The impulse to self-assertion competes with the instinct to resist change; the individual sets up defenses to preserve his present idea of himself. He rationalizes. He resists the impact of thoughts that would make it necessary for him to reexamine his self-concept. Growth in self-understanding implies a search, a struggle, a continual endeavor. It is a process, rather than an end result. The search for self requires courage, humility, a willingness to feel, and a desire to grow.[22]

METHODS OF STUDYING THE SELF-CONCEPT

The discrepancy between the individual's perception of himself and a more objective evaluation of him by others is often great. Some aspects of the self-concept may be hidden from the person himself. His evaluation of himself may be unreliable because it is based on distorted values or because he is holding the lid on certain aspects of his self that he does not want to recognize.

For several reasons it is often difficult to obtain an accurate picture of an individual's self-concept. Some adolescents depreciate themselves because they are afraid of appearing conceited. Others may lack the verbal ability to express their feelings about themselves. The very process of self-assessment may cause some changes as they see themselves in a somewhat different light. A number of college students in the author's study recognized the difficulties in writing about oneself:

Most people, even to themselves, don't like to admit their faults, but I shall try to be as open-minded as possible.

We often overrate or underrate ourselves. Many people are not really honest with themselves despite the famous saying, "Know thyself."

To answer these questions . . . requires self-exploration and complete frankness. I shall try honestly to evaluate myself as I know myself.

And one added: "Since we live with ourselves twenty-four hours a day, we should have a fairly good idea as to what we are."

[22] Arthur T. Jersild, *In Search of Self, an Exploration of the Role of the School in Promoting Self-understanding.* New York: Bureau of Publications, Teachers College, Columbia University, 1952.

Having recognized the possibility of self-deception, these young people are more likely to resist this tendency and to describe their actual, their "social," and their ideal selves as they really perceive them.

Despite the difficulty of introspection, it is important to examine an adolescent's concept of himself and his perception of his environment. We have too often observed only his outward behavior: his boisterousness, quick changes in mood, rebellion against adults, and other manifestations of what we call immaturity or "problem behavior." We usually focus on "what's wrong with adolescents," instead of "what's right with them." We should give them an opportunity to present themselves in their own way. Over a period of time we may be able to see how a new self is emerging out of the instability of this stage of growth. Adolescents will reveal themselves. They speak and write freely and frankly when they know that whatever they reveal of themselves will be accepted. They often welcome the invitation to think about themselves. Their effort to discover, release, and develop their potentialities is part of a creative process.

Considerable success has been achieved in objectifying the individual's perception of himself. Six main techniques have been used to reveal the self-concept:

1. The individual's own description of himself, in the form of
   a. Diaries and letters
   b. Autobiography
   c. Conversations—informal, casual, and unstructured, or more formal interviews
2. Relatively unstructured compositions, such as those described in this book, which give us a glimpse into how he perceives himself or, at least, into how he wants to present himself. An individual may also reveal himself in what he says or writes about others.
3. Free responses to questions such as
   a. "What I like about myself and what I dislike"
   b. "Who are you?"
   c. "The kind of person I think I am; the kind of person others think I am; the kind of person I would like to become"

4. Tests or questionnaires
   a. The Kuder Preference Record [23]
   b. The Minnesota Multiphasic [24] and the California Test of Personality,[25] which have certain items relating to the self-concept
   c. Bills' Index of Adjustment and Values,[26] which was developed from Allport's study of traits. Attitudes toward forty-nine traits, such as *acceptable, accurate, cruel, dependable,* are elicited by various ratings of these statements:
      "I am a [an] _____ person."
      "I would like to be a [an] _____ person."
      The subjects indicate on a 5-point scale their degree of liking for each trait, and rate themselves with respect to each trait.
   d. Stephenson's "Q-sort" technique [27]—presenting the individual with statements of a large number of possible self-concepts, which he may sort in various ways to show which apply to him.
5. Projective techniques; [28] among these, in addition to the Rorschach, which has been mentioned in Chapter 1, are:
   a. The Thematic Apperception Test,[29] in which the individual feels free to express himself through projection in story form

[23] *Kuder Preference Record,* Science Research Associates, Inc., Chicago, 1948.

[24] *Minnesota Multiphasic Personality Inventory,* by Starke R. Hathaway and J. Charnley McKinley, The Psychological Corporation, New York, 1951.

[25] *California Test of Personality,* by Louis P. Thorp, Willis W. Clark, and Ernest W. Tiegs, The California Test Bureau, Los Angeles, 1953.

[26] Robert E. Bills, Edgar L. Vance, and Orison S. McLean, "An Index of Adjustment and Values," *Journal of Consulting Psychology,* vol. 15 (June, 1951), pp. 257–261.

[27] William Stephenson, "A Statistical Approach to Typology: The Study of Trait Universes," *Journal of Clinical Psychology,* vol. 6 (January, 1950), pp. 26–38.

[28] Lawrence K. Frank, R. Harrison, E. Hellersberg, K. Machover, and M. Steiner, *Personality Development in Adolescent Girls.* New Orleans: Child Development Publications, 1953.

[29] Henry A. Murray, *The Thematic Apperception Test.* Cambridge: Harvard University Press, 1943.

b. The incomplete sentence technique, which includes items such as these:

I like to . . . .
I brag about . . . .
I feel hurt when . . . .
My hero is . . . .
I want to get even with . . . .
I make believe that . . . .
I get disgusted when . . . .
I want . . . .
I am afraid . . . .
I hate . . . .
I am happy about . . . .
I worry about . . . .
I pity . . . .
I love . . . .
I feel ashamed when . . . .
I feel proud when . . . .
My most important three wishes are . . . .

c. The "Draw a Person" test [30]

d. Play diagnosis, and the use of art forms such as puppets

6. Observation of individuals in a natural or controlled situation. After careful observation, one may be able to infer something of the individual's concept of himself.

ADOLESCENTS' CONCEPTS OF THEMSELVES

Since the older adolescent tends to be more introspective and more willing to think and write or talk about his inner world than the preadolescent, we can obtain our most significant data on the self-concept from the older group. Very small children usually identify themselves simply by their first name. Older children usually associate themselves with sports and other ac-

[30] Karen Machover, *Personality Projection in the Drawing of the Human Figure*. Springfield, Ill.: Charles C Thomas, Publisher, 1948. See also Karen Machover, *Draw-a-Person Test*. Springfield, Ill.: Charles C Thomas, Publisher, 1949.

tivities; young adolescents, with social relations; and older adolescents, to a greater extent, with their own inner thoughts and feelings.

A sixth-grade class of boys and girls eleven and twelve years old, in a well-to-do residential suburb, expressed rather conventional concepts of themselves as they are and as they would like to be. Their views parallel quite closely those of twelfth-grade high school students in the same community. However, in general, the high school students were more introspective, showed greater individual differences in response, and seemed more concerned with scholastic success than the younger students. The first of the following compositions represents the realistic views of a bright boy, 140 IQ; the second is quite typical of the "girl social" in this community, and the third was written by a relatively slow learner in a class in which more than half had IQs of 125 or higher:

1. A boy, eleven years old:

"I am a boy, 11 years old, I enjoy reading and I think I am fairly smart. I have several hobbies and favorite sports, all dealing with the water, fishing, swimming, sailing, and fly-tying. I love animals and have several pets. I have a hot temper and blow my top often.

"Other people think I am a queer and always tease me about my temper, so I blow my top; they tease me some more and my lid goes higher, and so it goes. I have a few freinds who don't taunt me, thank goodness.

"I would like to be more aimiable and not lose my temper so often. I want to become an architect or an author and own a big yawl to sail in the Annual Race and to do a lot of fishing. I want to be smart and be able to help others."

2. A girl, aged twelve:

"I am the kind of person that likes to be with people. I enjoy such sports as swimming, ice skating, tennis, etc. I like to be up to date, and know what's going on in the world. I have a hot temper, but it's learning to keep cool.

"I *hope* that other people enjoy being with me, as I enjoy being with them. I can think of some people who think that I am sometimes conceited, and I must admit that sometimes I think so too, and some people that think I am fun to be with.

"I'd like to be the kind of person that just about everyone enjoys playing, or being with. I most certainly would not like to be the most popular girl in school, but I would like to be rather popular. I'd like to become a person that is always helping people. I'd like to become a child's private nurse, or be a nurse in the children's ward of the hospital. My ambitions in life are just like most any girl's. I would like to go to Europe, and when I finish high school, I would like to be accepted by William and Mary College. At about the age of twenty-one I'd like to be married, and live a happy, healthy life."

3. A boy, eleven years old:

"I am a boy and my age is 11. I am a slow worker and the things I do are mostly always right. I get pretty good grades in my report card. In school I try to do my best but sometimes I have trouble.

"I think that some people like me and others don't.

"When I go to collage I want to study to be a pilot. When I grow up I want to be a good worker. I want to accomplish my arithmetic and spelling."

The dominant tone of the self-appraisals of these sixth-grade, mostly upper-class children is one of self-acceptance and satisfaction. A fault they do not seem to mind admitting is a hot temper. Both boys and girls emphasize marriage, a family, and a comfortable home, thus anticipating the trend toward less intense striving for success that Allport noted in his study of university students. Many speak of wanting to be of service. It would be interesting to make a developmental study of these youngsters and also to compare their self-appraisals with those of children of different socio-economic backgrounds.

Dependence on Their Peers for Self-concept

The following compositions were written by seventh-grade girls who described themselves with reference to a group, usually their peer group:

I am the kind of person who enjoys sports, and schoolwork. I am not too popular with the "gang" because they think I'm too serious. This really doesn't get me down, because I consider what I do is my own business. I like most everyone, especially those boys and girls who are "sports minded."

My family and I are very close, and we enjoy doing things together, such as picnicking, sailing, and skiing. We never seem to have spats as some of the girls and their families have.

Another girl in the same grade also viewed herself in relation to friends, and to her growing interest in boys:

I believe that I am an honest girl, and I try to be loyal to my classmates and friends at all times, because I consider this important. Making and keeping friends is not very hard for me. I try to join clubs and to "keep up with things," if you know what I mean.

Boys are beginning to notice me, but I don't date, as my folks say I'm too young. I enjoy being with boys, provided they are "nice."

Young Adolescents' Concepts of Themselves

Compositions from two eighth-grade classes in the same school give insight into the way slow learners and able learners view themselves. In one class of twenty-four the IQs on a group intelligence test covered a range from about 55 to 90. In the other class of twenty-eight, the range was from 117 to 144 IQ. They both responded to the same request, which was worded as follows:

Directions for students:

Just put the class (English, for example), your age, grade, and whether you are a boy or girl at the top of the paper.

Once in a while, it is interesting to write about oneself. You will have about half an hour to write about three views of yourself:

1. Who am I? What kind of a person do I think I am?
2. What kind of person do other people think I am?
3. What kind of person would I like to be? What kind of person do I want to become? What are my goals or purposes in life?

If you do not write your name on your paper, you can write more freely and frankly on these questions. Just write whatever comes to mind; there is no right answer; it's just what *you* think.

To teachers:

Try to create an atmosphere of interest and cooperation (largely through your own attitude), and make some connection between the class work and the subject. For example, in English—"You've been writing a lot of compositions about all sorts of things. Here's a chance to write about something you know very well—yourself." Or in social studies—"You've been reading about many kinds of people, alike in some ways, different in other ways. You can understand people better if you understand yourself. What kind of a person are you? Let's take a half hour . . . etc."

Only one failed to respond. He said, "I don't know what kind of person I am. I don't know what kind of person other people think I am. I don't know what my goals are yet! I don't know what purposes I have in life."

Taken as a whole, both groups mentioned all the factors that enter into the self-system: physical characteristics, clothes, attitude of persons toward them, interests, and future vocation. They often expressed an ambivalent feeling toward themselves: "I'm not perfect but I'm not very, very bad either." They have a need to find something good in themselves: "I am not a very good person, sometimes I get in trouble, but sometimes I do good. I smoke but not steady." Another said, "Sometimes I am a very selfish person; other times very grumpy. But I can be very pleasant and kind also." They also often feel that they impress other persons in different ways: "Some people don't think too good of me, but others do."

Low-achievement Group. There is a wide discrepancy between the kind of person they think they are and their ideal self; also between the kind of future they want and the more realistic, realizable future which they would be able to attain. The low-achievement group wanted to be "smart," successful, popular; have lots of friends; be a doctor, "a very good teacher," an engineer, an airplane pilot. One girl wanted to join "the Wax." Others set their sights on money and prestige; they wanted to be "a millionaire," "a big shot," a rich man with a nice wife. Some of the more realistic goals mentioned were policeman, farmer, electrician, mechanic, secretary.

The self-concepts of even this one group covered a restricted range from that of the very good docile boy or girl to that of a "not very good boy." The common pattern was to mention both

their faults and their good points. They seemed to have Hous-
man's attitude that there was "much of good and much of ill" in
all of us. In this group of slow learners there was less disparage-
ment of themselves than might be expected. Perhaps these youngsters had a greater need to bolster up their self-esteem, a greater
need to avoid the anxiety caused by a recognition of the discrepancy between their real and their ideal self.

Several compositions quoted in detail will give an idea of the
unique patterns of these eighth-grade low-achievement youngsters.

The *"satellizer"*—a girl, fourteen years old, who reduces anxiety by attaching herself to people and doing just what they
want her to do:

I like all my teachers very much. I think I get a long with people, I try very much to.

I think that other people like me, and I try to keep them my
friends and then I try to become there best friend. I think I'm neat,
I keep my hair combed an have my self clean at all times. But some
times I get mad to quick thats one thing I shouldent do.

I'd like to become a populary person, I'd like to become a good
getar player. I would not like to become such a quick tempered person.

I'd like to become a nurse because I like to help other people and
try to make them feel beter.

An unrealistic pattern of common adolescent interests, apparently growing out of affectionate family relations and meager information about the world of work:

I'm on the plump side, putting it mildly, I have brown eyes, and
brown hair.

I like lots of friends, and like to be active and popular. I also like
boys. I think I would not be noral if I wasn't a Rock 'n Roll fan. I
take a big interest in my school work, and also I am clothes crazy!
I don't think I'm spoiled because I have two parents who make sure
of that. But I love them both so much, and of coure I love my little
brother too.

I hope all my friends like me. And I want to be liked for what

I am. I am also choosie about the kids I go around with. I think most grownups I meet think I'm a respectable girl too. My Mom and Dad can take a lot of credit fo that.

I'd like to be friendly, smart, easy to get along with. Well, I guess I just would like to be like my father. But also to have a nicer figure too.

I'd like to become a person that people like to be with and when I leave them, they would say, "Gee, what a nice girl she is."

Well, I want to get married and raise a big family, but I don't want to have to work. I want a smart husband that I know will support his family. My parents want me to become a teacher, secretary (although I know I can't spell), or a nurse. But maybe I will have a job like that or maybe I'll be a wife and mother, who knows?

Another girl of the same age expressed her fantasy about the future in this way: "I will like to be a secretary in a business office, and maybe marry the boss. I would like to be a person that has a great personality, intelligent, and very loyal. My purposes in life are to help other human being by understanding them."

A *dominant interest* may prevent a young adolescent from feeling completely discouraged about other areas of his life. For example, one boy's interest was in hunting:

I like to hunt. I've shot sixteen rabbit, thurty two woodchuck, twenty-four chipmonks, sex squrrows, eight patrige, five Fezent, and one deer.

Many people think I am stupid and silly. When I grow up and out of the air force I would like to be a farner or a macinal enjoneer.

I have one goald and that is to get out of high school with a daploma.

Even with the lack of academic achievement represented in this letter, this boy seems hopeful about his future. Is his view due to ignorance, or is he whistling in the dark, or do his thoughts turn resolutely to some corner of his life in which he is successful?

Similarly another boy, also fourteen years old in the same

class, turned his thoughts away from his failure in school to his work in a garage where he felt successful:

I am a kind of person that dont no like school and do not like to go but I have to. Sume people like me and sume do not like very well. I would like to be a person that likes cars and motorcles and I do like them. I what to become a person that like mimit raceing car and I would like to diver one sume day. And my goals are to be a machine in a coupel of years. I have had three year of exsperient I helps out at a garage for three years. I did not get paided but the exsperient was paid in it self.

The compositions quoted represent the most verbal members of this low-scholarship class. The majority follow this kind of pattern: "I am _____ [gives name]. I think I am a pretty good boy. Most people I am around think I am a good boy but some people thing I am a bum. I would like to be a smart person. I wand to become a baseball player in the army. I want to finish school."

Several errors in the education of these youngsters are indicated. In addition to the atrocious spelling, which should have been better taught all during elementary school years, most of them could have been helped to acquire a more accurate self-concept and a more realistic self-ideal. Thus the anxiety concerning a disclosure of their inability to meet school and life situations might have been reduced.

Group of Able Learners. The eighth-grade class of able learners likewise made frequent reference to sports, friends, and being well liked by others. More seemed to think of themselves as average than as superior. One boy expressed it this way: "I am what you might call an unnormal normal boy. I think other people think of me as a shy and modest boy. I don't try to show off. I just sit down and listen to what they have to say, or else I go and look at television, so I won't get in trouble with my brother and sister."

Their level of aspiration is not as unrealistically high as that of the slow-learning group; in fact, it was sometimes below their potentialities. Four were interested in being farmers; five, teachers; two, nurses; only two mentioned other professions. There was also less discrepancy between their concept of themselves and how they thought others saw them. In general, too, their ideal self was more like their self-concept.

However, the most vivid impression obtained from reading these compositions was that of individuality of personality patterns and relations between the three aspects of the self. The only way to present this uniqueness is to quote several of the compositions.

Alternate interests are recognized by this eighth-grade boy who sees himself quite clearly, recognizing his dominant interest and having in mind another vocational choice if his choice of athletics is not realistic. He writes:

I think I am a pretty good person. I am not a juvinile delinwen. I am not a very noisy person in school, but when I get out of school at quarter of three then I become quite noisy. I like to play all kinds of sports and sometimes I like school. I like to play with almost everybody I meet. I am a very shy person when I first go where there are strange people and strange surroundings, but it doesn't take me long to get use to it.

I guess people think of me what I have already wrote. A noisy-outside-quiet-inside kind of person.

I would like to become a great atlete and be able to make a major league baseball team. I am not counting on making the big league so if I don't make a team I am going to college to become an arcitectual engineer.

I would like to be a person like Duke Snider or Pee Wee Reese, two good atletes.

My goal in life is to become a ball player, but I will probually end up being arcitect. I would like to get married and have two children.

Self-analytical tendencies are shown by this eighth-grade boy in the gifted group who is quite introspective and expressed his feeling of worry about many things:

I am a person who has a feeling for other people. Even for ani-mals I have a strong feeling. I don't think I could kill or harm an animal. I always seem to have some sort of worry on my mind. When I have no worries on me I feel terrific. I am a very shy person. I do not like to take responsibilities. When a good chance for me to do something or what I want to do comes around I back out. In short I am a hermit.

I think some other people think I am a nice person. Many people I knew and still know in school think I am nice. Sometimes I worry about what other people think of me. Many grown-ups I know think I am nice with an exception of a few of course.

I would like to become an independent person. I don't like to have to ask somebody about things. I worry often about the things I do. I would like to be a well liked person. I don't like being a hermit. I would like to get a good mathamatical brain so I have a good chance of getting a good job. In life all I care to get is a good job and a wife. I do not care to be a great, famous person in life. I just want a good job and normal life.

Striving to maintain one's individuality is a real but not always recognized problem. This eighth-grade girl with an IQ of 140 reflected the pressure to conform, which is so common in society today. She described her desire to maintain her individuality:

Sometimes I wonder about myself. I think that sometimes I am not enough of a follower. One of my teachers once said that in order to become a leader one has to become a good follower. That is one of my weak points. I do not want to be just one of the bunch. I want to stand out, not be like everybody else. Sometimes I try to accomplish that and I am sure that it must be a bother to other people. It's as if I wanted to be the center of attraction, but I just want to be different.

As I grow older I hope I can lose that habit and try to become a follower. I want people to appreciate me because I can get along well with everyone and add something to the group not just be aggressive.

My greatest ambition is too secure a Ph.D. in a field of science. Yet the strange thing is that I don't want to become famous as my attitude now seems to suggest. I also just don't want to become an ordinary, everyday housewife. I hope maybe to become a professor of science or mathematics at a college.

I hope earnestly that I can mend my bad points and try to become a person who adds something to society.

Exceedingly troubled and confused are some intellectually superior young adolescents. The following composition, written by a girl in the eighth grade with an IQ of 135, is an SOS call for help. It is an extreme example of lack of self-esteem in a group of much more happy-go-lucky youngsters:

Who am I? I am a girl. I'll give you a physical description first. I'm five feet, brown eyes, brown hair, and quite pudgy. All around, not too attractive, but it doesn't bother me too much. Mental description. I'm headstrong, terribly. I don't trust anybody. I'm terribly moody. I have an awful temper. I'm boy-crazy. Very. I'm crazy about two boys in the room. What happens they like someone else. Oh, well! That's life. I am very sensitive. Too much so, I'm afraid. I'd like to tell people my troubles, but people just don't like to listen to them. They've got too many troubles of their own to worry about.

People don't like me too much from what I can gather, because I can be hurt so easily and I show it. They think I am too sensitive, moody, temperamental, corny and quite a few other things but I can't think of them write now.

I'd like to be pretty, gay, witty and respected. Unsensitive. A person able to think out my troubles, and not bother anyone else. I daydream. I wish I could be able to pay attention without going off into another world.

I'd like to be a fashion designer or something in the fashions field. I like clothes. Although I myself do not look too good in anything right now, I like to see nice things on other people.

Self-concepts of Senior High School Students

A senior high school class, above average in intelligence and socio-economic background, were at first nonplused when asked to write on the same three questions:

However, they soon became interested in these questions, and wrote freely and frankly. Some followed certain cultural patterns with respect to their goals of "success" and marriage, but many expressed keen insight about themselves and their relations to others. A tabulation of the responses of these twenty-four students showed a preponderance of satisfaction and self-accept-ance, and much more concern about having friends than about intellectual and educational matters. A large number of person-ality characteristics were mentioned: laziness, selfishness, pride, worrying, procrastinating, inferiority feeling, shyness, passive-ness, confidence, social poise, honesty, cheerfulness, sense of hu-mor, being friendly, thoughtful, sympathetic, sincere, well-bal-anced. Typical responses under each category of *"I" as I See Myself* are listed in Table 1.

TABLE 1

	Boys	Girls	Total
Dissatisfaction:	1	0	1
"In living with other people I feel inferior"			
Satisfaction:	2	8	10
"I am a very contented person"			
"I come from a wonderful family and have had a sat-isfying life"			
"I am an average American girl"			
Acceptance of self, recognizing both positive and nega-tive sides:	4	3	7
"I am governed by the normal prejudices and fears, but I think I make an honest effort to overcome them"			
"I have my faults which I am aware of, and I have my good points"			
Inability to analyze self:	1	2	3
"This question is unreasonable"			
"I am a person who has been exposed to many facets of life, and I am therefore a combination and a mixed result of all. I cannot analyze myself at this time"			
Doubt:	1	1	2
"I am not sure what kind of person I am"			
No response			1
Total	9	14	24

As Table 2 shows, there was considerable consistency between their self-concept and *"I" as I Feel Others See Me.*

TABLE 2

	Boys	Girls	Total
Agreement: "I think that most people see me as I myself see me"	3	6	9

Disagreement:
  "Others see me differently from the way I see myself"
  "I always fear that on the next test I'll fail . . . Other people consider me intelligent and well informed"
  "I suppose others think I am a person of fairly high standards and ideals, but I myself am not sure whether the ideals I hold are the truest, or are suitable ones for others to live by"
  "Other people think I am happy-go-lucky (don't see serious thoughtful side). They think I am more capable in student affairs than I really am"
  "I don't think that other people . . . know what kind of person I really am, or at least my opinion of myself"
	2	2	4

Not sure what others think about one: "I hope they think . . ."	2	2	4
No response	3	4	7
Total	10	14	24

The expression of satisfaction with themselves is also indicated by a low proportion, as compared with other groups, who express a desire to change. Table 3 indicates the *Distance between "I" as I Am and "I" as I Would Like to Be.*

Their specific goals followed a stereotyped pattern. These were most frequently mentioned: success, general and financial; education; marriage; service to others and self-fulfillment. The personality traits they wanted to develop in their ideal self were happiness, trustworthiness, emotional maturity, friendliness, self-assertion, self-confidence, and self-sufficiency; they also wanted to be just and fair. Each of these traits was mentioned only once or twice.

TABLE 3

	Boys	Girls	Total
Desire to change (these students indicated a definite desire to change at least some part of themselves): "I would like to be a person who would stand up and defend his arguments" "I would like to get along easier and not feel so shy"	2	2	4
Desire to stay the same or to continue in the direction of growth they were experiencing: "I would like to be a person who always has good friends and one who knew her place in life and reached it" "In a sense, my goal can never be reached for I feel that if I live the best life at all times that is possible I will have carried out my desires"	4	9	16
No response		3	4
Total	9	14	24

Three of these compositions, quoted in full, will illustrate several approaches to the self—the first represents a combination of idealism and realism; the second is perhaps unduly disparaging; the third shows resistance to introspection and probably reflects a prevalent attitude in his social environment.

I'm an above average teenager, presently termed a sub-freshman. I think I am far away from being what I wish I were. However, I do attempt to be intellectually honest and morally fair. I am governed by the normal prejudices and fears, but I think I make an honest effort to overcome both.

Other people think I'm a nice enough person but perhaps a bit different from the norm. Perhaps I am considered moody and mercurial but neither of these feelings is powerful enough to incur the displeasure of others.

I'd like to be a person who could be counted on to help others in an emergency. I'd like to do things for people but in an inconspicuous manner. My present goals include making my life and the lives of others pleasant, beneficial, and meaningful.

I feel that I am a rather average individual. I feel my marks are of an average nature. I could perhaps, if I had tried harder, raised my marks. Therefore I think that I am a little bit lazy. I like to watch all the sports a natural American boy likes to watch and I try to play them, but I am a little clumsy and therefore I am not outstanding in any sport. I feel I am very honest and seldom even tell a little white lie.

I think that most people see me as I myself see me. I make friends quite easily and therefore I feel other people must like me.

I would like to be successful in everything I did in life. Because now everything I do is rather mediocre, I would like to be successful in business and some day get married. I would like to be able to help my community in many ways.

This question is unreasonable for I feel objective judgment is necessary and it is impossible for one to correctly analyze himself because he must be free of emotional sensations. I suppose that a moment of self-realization comes to all eventually, but we who are not yet set into our more or less final molds cannot realize what we are.

I suppose others think I am a person of fairly high standards and ideals, but I myself am not at all sure whether the ideals I hold are the truest ideals, or are suitable ones for others to live by. I believe in honesty, not only because it is right but because it is the surest way to do the best without hurting others through unfair competition. I do believe in competition and think that those who get ahead by fair means should be rewarded for doing so, and in proportion to the distance they are above others. I do not believe that anyone should be helped if he is an underdog *just* because he is not living well. He *must* be *willing* and able to do *more* than his share to lift himself from poverty before others help him. Otherwise those who help are wasting their time and efforts.

Naturally, I wish to be a person fairly high up on the ladder. I do not mean only in a monetary way, but a person who is able to enjoy and understand those things which make man great. I would like to be able to aid those who wish to help themselves to get the benefits of being a human being; for then I would be giving as well as receiving in life.

None of these high school seniors expressed total acceptance or total rejection of themselves, or even a very disturbing discrepancy between their presently perceived and their ideal selves.

They avoided the extremes of complete complacency and of abject rejection of themselves. Instead, they recognized their good qualities, but were also aware of personality faults that might still be modified or corrected. This seems a healthy attitude to take—an attitude leading to the realization of the individual's most acceptable self.

Unique Patterns of Older Adolescents

We should expect older adolescents to penetrate more deeply into their self-concepts than do younger adolescents. An analysis of twenty compositions written by college students eighteen to twenty-one years of age shows a wide range of unique responses to three questions which served as a stimulus to their introspection:

> What kind of person do you really think you are?
> What kind of person do other people think you are?
> What kind of person would you like to become?

These three questions helped the students to distinguish their own appraisal of themselves, other people's opinions of them, and their conception of their ideal self. That these students welcomed the opportunity to write on these questions was indicated by the thoughtfulness, directness, and length of their compositions, which ran from three to five pages.

In their self-descriptions the negative qualities which they mentioned with greatest frequency were a "hot temper," "laziness," and "moodiness." Almost all expressed a liking for people and a desire to have people like them. But apart from these fairly commonplace comments, they showed the greatest diversity. The only way to convey this diversity is to present a number of individual patterns, some abbreviated, some in their writers' exact words.

A Chameleon-like Self-concept. One pattern shows the self-concept in a period of instability. For example, one eighteen-year-old girl has clearly not yet achieved identification. She saw herself as "quite moody" and vacillating: "I secretly compare myself with a salamander who changes his color to blend with his environment." With relatives she feels considerable tension; with "outsiders" she feels at ease; with children, she gets along very well: "I adore them all."

This same trait of presenting different sides of her personality to different persons and under different circumstances is also brought out in her answer to the second question, "What kind of a person do other people think I am?" Her grandmother, she thinks, has nothing but criticism for her. Her grandfather thinks she is clever and a good conversationalist; he is proud of her. Boys say she is "different"; they can't figure her out ("I seem like a different person with each date"). Her girl friends say she is "spoiled." Her ideal self is built on some of her recognized assets: ability to "amuse the young and entertain the old." She wants to solve her own problems and control her quick temper, while still keeping her ability to forgive others. Each of her statements was supported by illustrations, and the whole composition seemed to be a keen and accurate appraisal.

Low Estimate of Self, High Level of Aspiration. It is common to find this pattern among college students, even among those of above-average ability and home background. A study of Harvard freshmen [31] showed a pattern of feelings of inferiority and considerable anxiety about success. A high school boy insists that he is "just an average boy" although intelligence tests rate him as a "superior adult." A boy of twenty-one thinks of himself as a person of average intelligence who has difficulty in carrying on a conversation. "I guess I am the type of person that most people can take or leave." He again identifies himself with average people when he says, "Like most people, I either have to be prodded or have a very special reason to do something." His marks in school are above average; this makes him hopeful of success in life. However, "Unless I plan and hope for a very successful future there will never be any." Concerning religion he says he "would have to again be rated as average." With parents he has some "generally minor, run-of-the-mill arguments."

[31] Henry A. Murray and others, *Explorations in Personality.* New York: Oxford University Press, 1938.

According to his own statement, other people consider him "likeable enough but a little quiet"; they think he gets along "fairly well with his parents."

In his picture of his ideal self, however, he discards this concept of mediocrity. He would like to be "full of personality," "perfect as far as religion is concerned," "the kind of person that gives everything he has to the people close to him." His secret ambition has always been to become a professional athlete. Realizing that this goal is unrealistic, he is "planning and hoping to some day become a successful executive," which seems to be equally unrealistic. Although this boy's idea of being only average seems to be central in his thinking about his present self, he aspires to exceptional personal qualities and achievement.

Multiple Dissatisfactions with Self. Sometimes a negative self-concept is accompanied by indifference or even a fatalistic attitude. As one sixteen-year-old poor reader said in an interview, "I'm the black sheep of the family, and I guess every family has to have one black sheep." A nineteen-year-old college boy expressed indifference rather than a fatalistic attitude toward change for the better. He considers himself a pessimist, "always looking at the worst angle that could happen." He speaks, however, of "wishful thinking, always dreaming up some crazy way I could get out of things, looking for a miracle." It is part of his pattern to put things off till the last minute, even forget to do things, and to get angry and excited about the slightest thing. "Whenever something goes wrong with me, I'd blame it on someone or something instead of blaming myself. . . . I guess I feel sorry for myself, always making excuses." He is not unique in hating "to be told to do things by my parents, teachers, or anyone else. I'd rather do things on my own." He feels that he lacks ambition and drive, rushes at the last minute to complete an assignment.

However, he mentions some satisfactions, too: self-satisfaction in doing something well; enjoyment of music—"I'd rather play music eight hours a day than do anything else"; satisfaction when someone pays him a compliment.

Alone he is quiet and shy, in a crowd he tries to act like the others and sometimes overdoes it. He likes "regular girls, not loud girls or wallflowers."

He thinks other people may think him either conceited or just naturally quiet. They tell him that he has ability and that he ought to have more ambition and plan for his future.

The kind of person I'd like to become? It doesn't matter to me if I care to change. I guess I could use some changes in my attitude towards things, people and life in general. Each person cuts their own path and keeps on following it. Life is just like a handwriting. You can change it any time you want. You can copy it like any other person's.

I guess I would like to be able to get up and go after something more.

One of the things I like about this paper is once you start writing about yourself, you can't stop.

This young man underemphasizes the difficulty of making changes in his attitude toward life and work. Perhaps he is just "whistling in the dark" here. His pessimistic attitude may have arisen from a feeling of dissatisfaction in many areas of his life —in his inability to face facts, to get assignments done, to get along better with girls, to change his attitude "toward things, people, and life in general."

Confused and Unrealistic. Central to another pattern of self-perception is an overestimate of one's ability, coupled with doubt about its accuracy. A boy of nineteen who presents data that suggest he is about average, thinks of himself as above average in intelligence and physical appearance. He says, "My personality is about the only thing below par." This below-average rating he attributes largely to shyness. He says:

What people think of me is far more important to me than what I think of myself. I find that intelligent people do not think me as able as do the more ignorant people. These less intelligent people probably think I am superior because they do not know me well and cannot see my faults as well as the intelligent person. Nobody, as yet, has told me exactly where I stand, so I have no basis for knowing.

This uncertainty as to "where he stands" seems to stem partly from a lack of objective information about himself, and from too great a dependence on the opinions of others regarding his ability. However, he might not be able to harmonize the objective evidence, if it were available, with his self-concept. Despite the fact that his ability is apparently no more than average (he quotes his IQ as 110), he wants "to become a person of fame . . . who will receive the highest respect from men, and affection from women . . . who should go down in history as a great leader who made life on earth better."

Acceptance of Self. A pattern of self-acceptance would include recognition of one's good points as well as one's faults. One boy, nineteen years old, first recognized his good points, on the theory that "we all live with ourselves twenty-four hours a day and therefore we should think much of ourselves, at least enough to give confidence to our ego to improve ourselves." He characterized himself as friendly, fair, good at sports and music. He thinks things out before making a decision, "would go far to find a true friend or companion," and has the initiative to complete difficult tasks.

As to faults, he thinks he may "go overboard in trying to create a good time for myself as well as others." Like so many other adolescents, he mentioned having difficulty controlling his temper, especially when arguing with members of his family.

He feels other persons recognize his good qualities and are also aware of some of his faults, especially selfishness.

His view of his future self is somewhat anxious, vague, and idealistic: "I feel I have gained much to date, but now have a harder climb ahead because of the setbacks which are likely to occur and which I feel I am not prepared for. As a future leader I would like to keep the good traits I have and lose the bad ones."

This boy's desire for self-control may be variously interpreted. Jersild [32] emphasized the desirability of expressing genuine emotions, of not trying to maintain a calm, courageous façade. There is something to be said on the other side, however. Outbursts of

[32] Jersild, *op. cit.*, pp. 37–44.

anger may set off reciprocal responses which, in a family or among friends, often lead to prolonged bitterness: "a soft answer turneth away wrath: but grievous words stir up anger" (Proverbs 15:1). Moreover, the James Lange theory of emotions has not been entirely disproved: if one acts calm and courageous, he may begin to feel that way; there may be some psychological justification for making a soft answer or "whistling a merry tune."

Discrepancy between Self-concept and Behavior. Another pattern that occurs, to some extent, in everyone includes an inability to carry out one's good intentions: "the good that I would I do not: but the evil which I would not, that I do" (Romans 8:19). A twenty-year-old college boy reveals many conflicts between his self-concept and his actual behavior. He feels that he is easy to get along with, softhearted and religious, very emotional when he sees a person in trouble. Yet he has a bad temper which erupts seldom with his age-mates, but very often at home. "Girls seem to like me but the ones I seem to enjoy are already taken." "Although I believe deeply in my religion, I seem to break every law of God repeatedly." He becomes depressed at times when everything seems to go wrong.

The person he would like to become is patterned on a person whom he knew: "a wonderful school teacher, who was also a Sunday school teacher, a devoted father, a successful businessman, and a man respected and admired by all." In psychoanalytical theory, reduction of the demands of the super ego, as represented by this ideal character, is frequently suggested. That, of course, is one way to reduce inner conflict. Another way is to strengthen and reinforce the ego so that it will be able to meet the demands of the super ego.

Persistently and Profoundly Pessimistic. Unique among the compositions collected is the profoundly and persistently pessimistic outlook of a Korean War veteran, twenty-one years old, who is completing his college work:

The kind of a person I think I am isn't worth writing on paper. To the best of my knowledge, I think I am selfish and ungrateful. In the social world I think I am a complete failure. I talk to all the people I know but somehow can't keep their attention. In school I jump down everybody's throat. When everyone asks me if I am going to the dance or the party, I tell them, "No," because I have to work. I tell the truth almost all the time about things I have done or would want to do.

I think I am underweight, look like a Frankenstein, and have no success with the opposite sex, although I try. When talking to someone I like to hear what they have to say. When they are finished I don't say anything. I don't know what to talk about when I meet someone for the first time. When working, I put my heart into the job. I don't talk to the opposite sex because I am scared or something. I have had only about 12 dates in my life. I never know what to do except go dancing or to a show. I go to a show by myself most of the time. I have a sense of humor which may or may not be equaled. So far all my friends think I must be nuts or something. Even my own family don't like me. I have the feeling of not belonging to social groups. I don't even feel like staying in school any more. I noticed when I play sports like baseball and basketball, if I make a good play or score a run or a basket, I feel good inside but I don't like people to pat you on the back or the crowds cheering, although if it's in the paper I like to see it there. I have the feeling that no one on earth feels like I do. I like a girl whom I probably won't see the rest of my life because she is of a higher standard than myself. I am afraid to ask people for things, like asking a girl for a date. I get butterflies and seem fearful for some reason or other, mostly because I talk myself out of such things.

The other people I know must think the same thing deep down under. In school everyone seems to think I am friendly. Some of them must really think I am unsociable because I don't go to games, dances, or parties. I think they believe I am really unworthy of anything.

This college senior's deep-seated sense of unworthiness and failure permeates every area of his life. Even when he is successful in sports, he is able to extract little satisfaction from it. He twists and turns and interprets all his experiences to make them conform to his preconceived concept of himself. Such a case would have to be handled by individual or group psychotherapy.

Identity Achieved through Purpose. A self-concept shaped by a worthy purpose represents a mature pattern. If the purpose is appropriate to the individual, realistic, and socially desirable, this is a pattern we should hope to find more frequently among college students. A definite philosophy of life molds the self-concept of a college girl of nineteen. It is a pattern shaped by purpose. She writes: "I would like to be a person who can honestly say that they have put their time to good use and have not wasted their life in some unworthy cause. I want to feel as though I have actually done some good. I want to feel the self-satisfaction that goes along with a wholesome life, and this self-satisfaction is the clue to happiness."

She wants to be open-minded and honest with herself; she admires these qualities in other people. For the most part she looks at the future realistically, but sometimes lapses into fantasy: "I find myself quite often slipping into a world of make-believe, especially when I have time on my hands."

But the course of purposeful activity does not always run smooth. She thinks of herself as moody: "If all goes well one day, I'm exceptionally happy. If all doesn't go well, I become dull and sullen and I'm sometimes rude and 'jump' at my friends for the least little thing." She feels she is "spoiled" and usually gets her own way at home.

Knowing exactly what she wants helps her to make up her mind quickly. "If I decide on something, I try my best to get it." This applies to her schoolwork also: "In the field in which I intend to make my career, I work especially hard and try to learn all that I possibly can." But she also succeeds in keeping her other marks above average.

She tries to be friendly with everyone but finds she gets along better with boys than with girls. "I have been told by many boys that they prefer a girl who can talk openly and not pretend to be stupid." She admits she appreciates compliments. Although she gets along best with persons who share her interests, she always seems to find something in common with different people.

On the whole, she feels that people like her, that she makes a good first impression through her conversation, and that those who hold an unfavorable opinion of her are in the minority.

The person she would like to be "is a combination of people I've met who have made a lasting impression on me." She would like to be cheerful and friendly to everyone and make people feel at ease when talking with her. She wants first to make good on a job, and after that "settle down and get married."

This girl has apparently achieved considerable harmony in her philosophy of life, value system, and concept of her ideal self. She does not, however, expect perfection in herself, but recognizes and apparently accepts a normal amount of daydreaming and moodiness, and occasional flashes of temper.

Uniqueness of Patterns. This one small group of college students shows a wide variety of self-concepts. They vary not only in the qualities they think they possess, but in their personality organization, attitude toward changing themselves, self-satisfaction, and concern for the opinion of others. They vary also with respect to the relation of the ideal self to the actual self as they perceive it. Some conceive the ideal self as built on present good qualities; others build the ideal self on faults corrected. One profoundly pessimistic student considers change neither desirable nor possible. There is evidence accumulating, however, that personality does change during college years, that these years can be of critical importance.

In all of these varied patterns the students made some reference to social relations—to peer relations more often than to family relations, to the opposite sex more often than to the same sex. Heterosexual adjustment often seems to have a central place as an expression of social competence. Recreation, if mentioned at all, is related to social relations; this is also the case with reference to physical development and personal appearance. The negative characteristic most frequently mentioned is "getting angry" with family or friends. It would be interesting to explore the meaning of this characteristic to the individuals who mention it. Although these young people were still in school, still coping with the problem of achieving academic success, they rarely mentioned intelligence in connection with the self-concept.

In a larger number of cases we would undoubtedly find these same patterns, plus many others, in endless variation. However, these few pictures of the way some adolescents view themselves will serve to emphasize the individuality of the self-concept.

QUALITIES RELATED TO THE SELF-CONCEPT

Closely related to the dynamic nature of the self, already discussed, are certain qualities that are interwoven with the self-concept. Among these are understanding and acceptance of others, level of aspiration, emotional adjustment, and value system.

Understanding of Others

Self-understanding appears to be related to understanding of others, and vice versa; awareness of self is attained through the

recognition of the attitude of others toward oneself. Since "the language of emotion" is common to people of various ages and backgrounds, one would expect a person who has experienced anger, hate, love, fear, or compassion, to understand these feelings in others. To gain information on how well parents and children understand each other's feelings, Tarwater [33] asked two

[33] Jesse W. Tarwater, "The Adolescent's Question: 'Who Understands Who I Am?'" *Understanding the Child*, vol. 24 (January, 1955), pp. 11–14.

questions of adolescents: "How I feel about myself" and "How I predict my parents would respond for me" [on this question]. He also asked two questions of parents: "How I think my adolescent child really feels" and "How my adolescent child will respond" [to the question of how he feels]. By comparing parents' and children's responses, he found that adolescents seemed to understand parents better than parents understood adolescents. There was least agreement between adolescents and parents in the areas of adolescent peer relations and self-concepts. The adolescents also showed more acceptance of parents than parents predicted they would.

Does the person who accepts himself also tend to be tolerant toward others? The evidence on this question is somewhat conflicting. Research by Carl Rogers and his associates [34] has shown self-acceptance and acceptance of others to be positively related. Jersild [35] suggested that the individual's attitude toward others reflects his attitude toward himself and that the individual evaluates himself through his interpretation of what others think of him.

Level of Aspiration

The self-concept is also related to one's level of aspiration. The "ideal goal" is associated with the ideal self; the "action goal," with the realistic self-concept. Although level of aspiration is an individual matter, people tend to set their levels of aspiration relatively high when they are dissatisfied with their present status, or when they are confident and successful. They tend to set their levels of aspiration relatively low when their motivation is poor, when they fear failure, when they do not face failure frankly or the situation realistically, when others think poorly of them, and when they feel insecure or have other personality problems.[36]

[34] Rogers and Diamond, *op. cit.*

[35] Jersild, *op. cit.*

[36] Kurt Lewin, Tamara Dembo, Leon Festinger, and Pauline Snedden Sears, "The Level of Aspiration Theory," in *Personality and the Behavior Disorders* (J. McV. Hunt, ed.), part I, pp. 333–378. New York: The Ronald Press Company, 1944.

Having experienced failure from trying to emulate models or accomplish tasks too difficult for them, youngsters respond in different ways. Some may give up and put forth no further effort; others may set their goals more realistically; others will doggedly continue to try to do the impossible. In the case of youngsters with high capacity who have low levels of aspiration, who think they can do anything with very little effort, the adult should try to put them in situations in which they have to work hard to accomplish a task that is difficult but seems worthwhile to them.

Emotional Adjustment

There is probably a reciprocal relation between a realistic, clearly conceived self-concept and good adjustment. The self-concept gives a consistent orientation to experience. When varied ideas of the self are somehow blended with conflicting outside pressures into a unified whole, the individual feels comfortable and free. When inner conflicts are unresolved, the individual feels insecure, anxious, restless, or otherwise disturbed. Satisfaction and happiness are closely associated with the self-concept; they are a natural consequence of the harmonious functioning of the total personality. To make progress toward realizing one's most acceptable and realistic self is a joyful experience; it is a more positive satisfaction than the mere relief which one feels at overcoming a personality fault or correcting a defect.

Anxiety arises when there is enough disparity to cause unhappiness between the adolescent's idealized self and his "real self." The greater the chasm, the greater the possible anxiety. Anxiety may also be caused by an unrealistic view of one's future. Through reading oversimplified success stories or failing to recognize his economic or cultural limitations, an adolescent may be led to adopt fantastic vocational goals. These temporarily bolster his self-esteem, but frustration is inevitable when he is finally forced to face reality. The adolescent will often find himself in situations that will reveal the inadequacy or inappropriateness of his self-concept. This evokes anxiety, which may cause withdrawal from such situations rather than any attempt to change

Membership in a constructive peer group in a small democracy, Boys' Nation, helps young people learn to share in making decisions, taking responsibility, carrying through and evaluating projects in local community, state, and national groups. (*Courtesy of the American Legion.*)

Personal involvement and parental pressure may combine to cause intense anxiety in an adolescent taking an examination such as the Merit Scholarship Test. (*Courtesy of Wide World Photos.*)

Adolescent girls today can choose a career, homemaking and a career, or a career of homemaking. (*Courtesy of the National Committee of Boys and Girls Club Work, 4-H Clubs.*)

High achievement like that of a Georgia boy, winner of a $400 scholarship at the fifteenth annual Science Talent ·Institute, brings personal satisfaction and a sense of social usefulness. What makes the difference between the gifted underachievers and a boy like John H. Venable? (*Courtesy of Westinghouse Science Talent Institute.*)

himself. He cannot analyze or learn from severe anxiety, which may have its roots in infancy or very early childhood experiences.[37]

Older adolescents are often moody; sometimes they wish they had never been born. A surprisingly large number have had thoughts of suicide. They dwell on things they want to forget, and are concerned about their bad habits. They could bear some of their frustrations more readily and exert more effort to overcome their difficulties in accomplishing their adolescent tasks if their self-concepts were clear, realistic, and positive—if they knew who they really were and where they wanted to go.

RELATION OF GOALS AND VALUES TO THE SELF-CONCEPT

Values have been described as "ideas-tied-to-feelings." For example, a dominant concept of oneself as a kind person would be associated with many ideas of how one ought to respond

[37] Sullivan, op. cit., pp. 300–302.

toward various kinds of people. These ideas, in turn, would guide one's behavior. The individual's values and philosophy are part of his concept of the ideal self.

Genesis and Development of Values

Children reflect their parents' values. Parental influence is especially strong during stages of development in which the child feels dependent upon the parent and identifies closely with him. Later, persons derive certain values from their observation of behavior.

The values of older adolescents show considerable agreement with those of their parents. College students' ideas about politics and social planning seemed to agree fairly well with those of their parents. Conflicts with parental values were more likely to be in the areas of love, courtship and marriage, sex instruction, and religion.[38]

Variation of Value with the Culture

Adolescents' values vary with the different sub-cultures in which they have grown up. Children from lower socio-economic backgrounds may have values that are quite different from those of the teacher and middle-class students. For example, in several seventh-grade classes, boys and girls of higher socio-economic status put a higher value on conformity to adult standards and conventional rules of conduct. Those of lower socio-economic status placed a higher value on self-assertion and aggression. Teachers should recognize that many differences in values exist; they should try to understand, not condemn, youngsters whose values are different from their own.

This does not mean that the teacher must condone values that are detrimental to the individual or to society. On the contrary, the public school teacher should take advantage of his contacts with "all the children of all the people," to help adolescents reorganize their value systems on a higher level. He can do this by setting an example himself and establishing a friendly rela-

[38] R. Grann Lloyd, "Parent-Youth Conflict of College Students," *Sociology and Social Research,* vol. 36 (March–April, 1952), pp. 227–230.

tion with the youngsters which they will want to maintain by behaving acceptably. The teacher will show that he understands their feelings, but be firm in distinguishing between how one feels and how one acts. He will make it clear that one can control one's behavior even when prompted by feelings to act in anti-social ways. The adolescent's goals should be acceptable not only to himself, but also to society.

Changing Ethical Values of Youth

One has the general impression that the ethical values of youth have deteriorated a great deal over the past twenty-five or fifty years. However, Horton and Remmers [39] found minor changes in both rural and urban high school students' rating

TABLE 4

1919	Rank	1954
Killing or murdering.....	1	Killing or murdering
Sexual misbehaving......	2	Using or selling narcotics
Stealing...............	3	Sexual misbehaving
Cheating..............	4	Stealing
Lying.................	5	Drinking (alcohol)
Drinking (alcohol).......	6	Cheating
Gambling.............	7	Lying
Swearing, vulgar talk....	8	Being cruel
Not being religious.......	9	Not being religious
Being selfish...........	10	Reckless driving
Gossiping.............	11	Swearing
Idleness..............	12	Being undependable
Snobbishness...........	13	Gossiping
Extravagance..........	14	Being inconsiderate
Smoking..............	15	Smoking
Dancing..............	16	Being conceited

of what they considered "worst practices." The differences in students' rankings of "worst practices" in 1919 and in 1954 are illustrated in Table 4.

[39] R. E. Horton and H. H. Remmers, *Some Ethical Values of Youth, Compared Over the Years,* Report No. 38, Purdue Opinion Panel, vol. 13, no. 2 (April, 1954), pp. 1–3.

It will be noted that some behaviors listed as "worst practices" in 1919 were not even mentioned in 1954: "Dancing," "Idleness," "Extravagance," and "Snobbishness." These social practices have been replaced with more fundamental personality traits, such as "Being cruel," "Being inconsiderate," and "Being undependable." "Using or selling narcotics" was ranked in second place in 1954, whereas it did not even appear on the 1919 list. In general, the rankings on ethical practices of boys and girls are similar except for "Sexual misbehaving," which was rated as one of the four worst by 48 per cent of the boys and 72 per cent of the girls. On the list of best practices, "Being courteous and friendly" was rated by the largest percentage of students and "Being religious," second. A comparison of results in different parts of the country, using the same opinion scale, would probably show marked differences, for example, between a "blackboard jungle" area and a rural New England community.

Modification of Values

Most parents and teachers hope to achieve this goal of socialization through criticism of the child. They point out his faults, correct his mistakes, order or forbid him to behave in certain ways. This is humiliating to the child and more so to the adolescent; it decreases his self-esteem and undermines his self-confidence. It often gives him a concept of himself as a person who does not have "what it takes" to become an acceptable adult or to achieve the kind of self to which he aspires. Instead, young people need to be told occasionally "what is good about them" and encouraged, through social and creative experiences, to develop their individuality. Children and young people tend to feel toward themselves as other people who are significant in their lives feel toward them.

Values are further modified, as the child grows older, by persons whom he admires. As children reach and pass the age of ten, parents as prestige figures are gradually replaced by persons outside the family circle. Boys become attached to historical and public figures. They seldom mention teachers, per-

haps because so many of their teachers have been women. Girls still look to their parents as models, and also to teachers to some extent. The effect which radio and television programs are having on the development of values should be carefully studied. Sports heroes and figures in public life are vividly presented; they may, in the present generation, serve as models far more frequently than did historical figures in the past. More important is the insidious influence of certain ideas which are incessantly dinned into the thoughts and feelings of children and adolescents as they listen for long hours to radio and television. For all we know this may be resulting in unconscious conditioning with respect to drinking, smoking, sex practices, crime, indiscriminate use of drugs to relieve pain, and the appraisal of possessions and material values above everything else.

As these influences change the values of adolescents and are built into codes of conduct in peer groups, their effect on the individual adolescent is intensified. He chooses his friends from among those who have similar values, and association with them reinforces his ideals, whether constructive or destructive. The urge toward conformity is strong.

Problems arise from conflicting values. Parents' values clash with peer values. Environmental pressures make it difficult for the individual to maintain his values. Conflicting practices of adults cannot be reconciled with the ethical code they have taught him.

Can values and ideals be taught? Or are they caught? While not discounting the necessity of knowing what is the right thing to do, we should recognize the discrepancy between knowing and doing, between the ideal and its practical application. Under the best conditions adolescents can be helped to develop ideals and standards. Religious conferences for young people, such as those held for many years at Northfield, Massachusetts, have probably helped impressionable adolescents to perceive that the world needs them, and to see their ideal self in terms of service. Youth-serving organizations such as the 4-H Clubs, Scouts, Hi-Y, and Campfire Girls reinforce the social values which children and young people have a readiness to accept. It is more difficult for these organizations to attract youngsters with anti-social attitudes and help them to reorganize their value systems.

Ideals and values are not superimposed from without; they develop, to some extent, in response to some need on the part of the individual. To fulfill the need to be esteemed and accepted, some individuals will conceive of themselves as kind, thoughtful, and considerate. Such behavior on their part will tend to evoke similar responses from others. There is no objection to this; the strongest personality belongs to one who has been able to integrate what is good for himself with what is good for others. Less wholesome is the acceptable behavior which is assumed merely to cover up or hide inclinations about which one feels guilty.

The roots of adolescent goals and values spread wide and deep into the individual's past, and into his family, school, and peer relations. Being aware of the manifold situations in which values develop and are modified helps adults to provide conditions conductive to the growth of a socially acceptable and psychologically sound value system.

Moral and Spiritual Values

Concern with moral and spiritual values represents a high point in the development of the self-concept. In general, older adolescents are more concerned about the destiny of man and the meaning of life than are younger boys and girls. Religion emphasizes love, faith, and hope. In a sense, moral and spiritual values are basic to self-esteem, for without hope for the future, it does not matter much what one becomes. Some system of beliefs which gives meaning to life is characteristic of the mature personality. The ultimate in self-realization involves love for something outside and beyond the self.

When asked to write anonymously on "What life means to me," a surprisingly large number of adolescents expressed views in marked contrast to the cynical, hedonistic attitudes that adults often associate with modern adolescents. One of the most exceptional statements was written by a fifteen-year-old girl in the tenth grade:

Life? You ask what it means to me: Life as I've seen it is a few moments of joys, sadness, or happiness. How can I be a judge of life when I've lived but a fraction of years? But my life means to me something that is a gift. For the greatest gift in this world is to be alive. To me life is happiness, love—having someone love you and loving someone (mother, father, etc.). It means sadness, learning, meeting people, but mainly it means living from day to day, whether it brings new thoughts, new experiences, or new learning.

A boy of the same age and grade wrote:

What is the meaning of life? Life is an existence which should have a purpose. Every person should do good on this earth. I think there should be humor in life but I believe that life should be mainly serious.

I am here for a reason. God has a reason for everyone being here. We are all part of a plan. I am here to do good and lead a good life. . . .

I feel responsible for what I do because I feel I can make my own decisions. . . .

Usually what helps one to do the right thing is just knowing that it is right and the thing to do. . . .

I finally believe that life should be enjoyed doing right things.

To this boy religion seemed to mean self-fulfillment.

During the late teens, some young people seem particularly sensitive to religious influences. They are thrilled to attend a religious conference; they sometimes seriously consider a religious vocation. They picture themselves idealistically serving or saving the world.

Doubt and Dissatisfaction

Some high school students are greatly disturbed because their fundamentalist beliefs are being challenged by their reading and their associates. They no longer feel secure or certain about anything that has to do with religion; doubt and bewilderment fill their minds. Yet it is important that they progress from reliance on parents to self-reliance. A high school girl with keen insight described this dichotomy of feelings as follows:

During adolescence, one's whole outlook on life changes. He sees things with his own eyes and not through the eyes of his parents. He must judge people and the world by his own standards. At this point he has two philosophies of life, we might say: that of his parents, and his own. These two philosophies are in constant conflict until the youth can get them straightened out in his mind. This has been one of my main problems. I find my own ideas in conflict with those of my parents and this results in a disturbing situation.

Some youngsters also have periods of doubt and antagonism toward established religious programs. Honest doubt often leads to faith. A person who does not have the courage to doubt may not acquire the wisdom to believe. Part of the antagonism which often occurs at this stage may arise from resentment at having to attend church services in which one no longer finds interest and value.

Antagonism may also stem from inability to reconcile certain scientific facts with childhood beliefs. This conflict is intensified by adults who represent science as inimical to religion. Actually some of the most able scientists are deeply religious and humble. They feel that science has not invalidated the simple Biblical statement, "In the beginning, God. . . ."

Adolescents express increasing dissatisfaction with church services as they grow older. At the same time they are concerned about not going to church often enough. In one study of eighteen-year-olds, 60 per cent said that they "dislike church service." [40] This decreased interest in church services is a challenge to religious workers.

Rejection of established religious services is sometimes caused by the chasm between what is preached and what is practiced. For many persons, religion is not continuous with life; it is set apart from the workaday world. It does not furnish young people with a faith to live by or help them to learn techniques of living.

Antagonistic responses to religion may also stem from a basic hostility toward parents, which has been projected into the area of religion. It may have little to do with any real cynicism concerning religion. Although adolescents may reject the God of their parents, they may be trying to find Him in their own rebellious way. Harry Emerson Fosdick told of a young man who came to him and said defiantly, "I don't believe in God." Dr. Fosdick replied, "Suppose you tell me about the God you don't believe in." The boy then proceeded to describe a God of wrath and vengeance. "I don't believe in that God, either," Dr. Fosdick told him, and then described the God that he believed in—a God who is sympathetically working with mankind for a better world.

[40] Raymond G. Kuhlen and Martha Arnold, "Age Differences in Religious Beliefs and Problems during Adolescence," *Pedagogical Seminary and Journal of Genetic Psychology,* vol. 65 (December, 1944), p. 296.

Religious perplexity may also be all mixed up with a disturbed relationship with one's boy or girl friend. Quite frequently a counselor finds that an adolescent's request to talk about her religious doubts is a cover for an underlying problem involving a quarrel with her boy friend. In fact, religious faith is part of the individual's total development and experience.

Adolescents respond differently to religious doubts and antagonisms. Some will keep up appearances and continue their church-going and other religious observances in order to avoid criticism or to reassure themselves. Others will become cynical and openly critical. Both of these responses indicate unresolved conflict. Still others will resolve or temporarily bypass their doubts by means of an increasingly mature faith, which integrates the personality.

One might expect improvement in insight during the college years. In a midwestern university [41] the attitudes of college students toward God and toward the church were increasingly favorable during a twelve-year period which included World War II. Women students, in general, have a more favorable attitude toward the church than men, and those who belong to and attend church have a more favorable attitude toward church than those who do not.

Positive Attitudes toward Religion

Many adolescents have a fine attitude toward religion. They recognize its positive personal values. Such a point of view was expressed by a girl, sixteen years old, in the eleventh grade, who was concerned about "the growing absence of religion in the home." She raised many questions about her religion and concluded by saying:

I'll probably never find out anyway. But I would like to say that I think a lot of this current wave of juvenile delinquency would not have occured had religion been brought into the home. For religion ties one closer to those he loves through a common understanding of

[41] Adam R. Gilliland, "Changes in Religious Beliefs of College Students," *Journal of Social Psychology*, vol. 37 (February, 1953), pp. 113–116.

God and the life He meant us to live. It can all be illustrated in the following diagram:

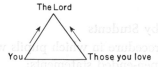

The closer you get to the Lord the closer you become to your family.

Well, I've finally gotten it out of my system, as I have never written about it before, but I don't want you to think I'm a fanatic or something like that. I'm a pretty normal kid. I get average grades in school and I want to be a nurse when I get out of school.

Self-realization in the psychological realm is connected with religious faith. An adolescent who believes in God as a "very present help" not only in time of trouble but also as a daily source of guidance for his best development, has a certain resource of strength and courage. He is not alone. His concept of himself extends into infinity.

ADOLESCENTS' WISHES AND INTERESTS

An individual's self-concept may be partially revealed by his interests. In fact, "the hierarchy of interests" is, from adolescence onward, "the surest clue to personality." [42] In general, young adolescents' interests reflect the instability of the period. Some childish interests are being discarded, new interests being built. Some of these may be quite temporary. The dominant adolescent interests are in social activities that involve the other sex, personal appearance that attracts the other sex, and what the future holds for them. In their compositions, the older adolescents less often expressed the childish wishes for specific objects; they tended to wish for more general benefits for themselves and others, such as peace in the world. However, their wishes usually remain quite concrete and realistic, predominantly for things outside themselves, infrequently for corrections of their personal shortcomings. Their replies are undoubtedly influenced by the form

[42] Allport, *op. cit.*, p. 29.

of the request and the conditions under which the responses are obtained.

Wishes Expressed by Students

Cobb [43] used a procedure in which pupils were asked to complete twenty-four open-ended statements:

1. I wish I were . . . .
2. I wish I were not . . . .
3. I wish I could . . . .
4. I wish I did not . . . .
5. I wish I had . . . .
6. I wish my folks were . . . .
7. I wish my folks would . . . .
8. I wish my mother would . . . .
9. I wish my mother did not . . . .
10. I wish my father would . . . .
11. I wish my father did not . . . .
12. I wish my family lived . . . .
13. I wish our home were . . . .
14. I wish our home were not . . . .
15. I wish my brother(s) . . . .
16. I wish my sister(s) . . . .
17. I wish my teacher(s) were . . . .
18. I wish my teacher(s) would . . . .
19. I wish my teacher(s) did not . . . .
20. I wish . . . friends . . . .
21. I wish my girl friends . . . .
22. I wish my boy friends . . . .
23. I wish my best friend . . . .
24. I wish more than *anything* that . . . .

In obtaining responses to these incomplete sentences, teachers emphasized permissiveness and anonymity. "The vast majority of responses were seriously made." On the statement, "I wish I were . . . ," the responses of elementary children in grades

[43] Henry V. Z. Cobb, "Role-wishes and General Wishes of Children and Adolescents," *Child Development,* vol. 25 (September, 1954), pp. 161–171.

four, five, and six compared with those of pupils in junior and senior high school were as follows: The senior high school boys and girls more often wanted to be out of school and earning money than did the elementary and junior high school pupils. The girls increasingly desired social ease and popularity and a better personality. In elementary school most of the girls seemed to be interested in professional careers; in high school their choices were more realistically focused on jobs as clerks and stenographers. Boys became more concerned with social acceptance and less interested in "action-daring" careers as they grew older. Boys on all age levels expressed more wishes for personal achievement than did girls; for boys, this was the most frequently mentioned category. The smallest percentages expressed wishes for possessions, changes in living conditions, and changes in identity, as for example, to be of the opposite sex. Both boys and girls reached their peak with respect to wishes relating to school and physical appearance during junior high school years.

The senior high school pupils made surprisingly little reference to physical appearance, except in the item, "better looking," which concerned 5.8 per cent of the girls. In the junior high school group, 7.8 per cent of the boys and 3.9 per cent of the girls wished to be bigger. None of the boys of this age wished to be smaller, though 4.5 per cent of the girls did.

The responses to the item, "I wish more than *anything* that . . . ," were still more diverse. Wishes in the realm of personal-social relations were highest in frequency; they became more numerous from elementary through senior high school. Interest in love and courtship did not become prominent until senior high school. Desire for unbroken or more congenial homes, general well-being, financial security, and considerate parents and siblings was expressed almost as frequently as desire for love and marriage. Gesell, Ilg, and Ames [44] also found a decrease in the expressed wishes for material things beginning at thirteen years. In these later years—fourteen, fifteen, and sixteen—the most frequently mentioned wishes were for "peace," "to be

[44] Arnold Gesell, Frances L. Ilg, and Louise B. Ames, *Youth, the Years from Ten to Sixteen,* p. 510. New York: Harper & Brothers, 1956.

better, smarter, nicer," for "happiness (for self or others)," and for the "betterment of others."

Children's wishes are influenced by the culture and the socio-economic level of the groups studied. In some circumstances the majority of children from nine to twelve wish for material things; in others, for intangibles such as peace, a good education, and various happy experiences. In another culture children of the same age may wish for very simple things like a paint box or a pocket knife, and also to have no more war or food shortages and to be strong, healthy, and rich.

Interests in Social Behavior

A variation of the "Guess Who" technique was used to study how students thought they should and should not act in a variety of typical school situations.[45] The subjects were 225 students enrolled in the seventh to twelfth grades at the Ohio State University school. The order of frequency for the total responses was as follows:

1. Respectful, polite
2. Identification with group
3. Unobtrusive
4. Constructive
5. Creative

Girls emphasized a "respectful and polite" behavior, while boys more frequently mentioned "constructive and creative" behavior. A common pattern increasing in frequency from grades seven to twelve was unobtrusive behavior—not tearing down others, identification with the group, and "maturity." Parents gave maturity the highest rating, and were in general agreement with teachers. A common negative attitude was indicated by the fact that all tended to describe how students *should* behave by pointing out undesirable activities in which they *should not* engage.

[45] Laurence Siegel, Herbert L. Coon, Harold B. Pepinsky, and Stanley Rubin, "Expressed Standards of Behavior of High School Students, Teachers and Parents," *Personnel and Guidance Journal*, vol. 34 (January, 1956), pp. 261–266.

Friendly relations with other persons are one of the most important sources of happiness for junior and senior high school students. They are also more interested in self-improvement and more concerned with the happiness and welfare of others than younger children. Their behavior, however, does not always coincide with their expressed interests.

THE CONTRIBUTION OF LITERATURE
TO SELF-UNDERSTANDING

True-to-life literature can be used to help adolescents gain understanding of themselves and others. The special contribution of literature in developing the self-concept should be pointed out here. Fictional characters the same age or slightly older than the adolescent reader, "living" through the period of rapid adolescent growth, at first bewildered and insecure, but eventually developing a reintegrated personality, can help the reader bring his own feelings to the surface, where he will be better able to cope with them. The reader will see how these teen-age characters develop satisfying relations with their peers, handle conflicts with parents, gain independence courteously, face the consequences of their own acts, find satisfaction through co-operation, and find ways of helping to build a better, freer world. Such books should not only record true feelings and behavior, but also open up new insights or possibilities.[46]

CONCLUDING STATEMENT

Adolescence should be viewed as an opportunity for achieving a realistic, stable, socially acceptable, and personally satisfying self-concept. Adolescents need experiences that help them to "move toward others with friendliness." They need to understand their development and take pride in their growth in wisdom, stature, human relations, and specific skills. In helping children and adolescents to find themselves, adults can assist in several ways: by providing conditions in which they can discover and develop their capacities; by offering opportunities for them to be creative, socially successful, responsible, and competent within the limits of their capacity; by accentuating the positive in their behavior; by setting consistently good examples of attitude and conduct; and by helping them to recognize a power and purpose greater than themselves. Through counseling, also, the student may be helped to develop appropriate goals. He may gain insights as a result of "talking it out." He may experience relief through examining his newly recognized fears and anxieties in the security of the counselor's presence. In short, there may be a process of reeducation as the adolescent progressively formulates appropriate goals and determines ways of reaching them.

COMPREHENSION QUESTIONS

1. Explain why the self-concept is central to adolescent development.

2. In what four ways may an individual view himself?

[46] Richard Braddock, "Selecting Novels for Group Reading," unpublished doctoral project, Teachers College, Columbia University, New York, 1956.

3. What effect may a chasm between the "real self" and the "idealized self" have on an adolescent?

4. Why are our efforts to understand an adolescent so dependent on our knowing how he perceives himself?

5. Compare the passage from the complete dependency of infancy to the accepted dependency (satellization) of childhood with the emancipation from the family that occurs during adolescence. When does a person usually achieve identity as a full-fledged adult?

6. Describe the methods that have been used to study the self-concept. What is the special contribution of each?

7. Which interests and attitudes show the greatest intensification during the adolescent years—interest in the opposite sex, religious feelings, hero worship of teachers?

8. How is understanding of oneself related to understanding of others, to level of aspiration, to satisfaction and happiness, to goals and values?

STUDY PROJECTS

1. Answer for yourself the three questions asked of older adolescents (page 101).

2. If you are working with any groups of adolescents, ask them to write on these three questions after you have established a good relationship with them.

3. Read the self-descriptions given by students, and consider how you as a teacher, counselor, or parent might help individuals obtain a more adequate and realistic self-concept.

4. Consider how you might help an individual adolescent, by changing his environment, to reorganize his value system on a higher level. First try to understand the experiences that are now shaping his values—associates, books, magazines, radio programs, movies, television, amusement places, and so on. Then consider how more constructive experiences might be substituted.

5. Form an advisory committee of young people in a church to suggest ways of making the church services and young people's activities contribute more to the development of adolescents.

6. Analyze the interests of one or more adolescents.

7. Compare your judgment of an adolescent's self-concept, as derived from observation, with an estimate which he has written.

FOR FURTHER STUDY

AUSUBEL, DAVID P., *Theory and Problems of Adolescent Development*, chap. IX. New York: Grune & Stratton, Inc., 1954.

BEHRMAN, S. N., *Biography*. New York: Rinehart & Company, Inc., 1932.

CRUICKSHANK, WILLIAM M. (ed.), *Psychology of Exceptional Children and Youth*. Englewood Cliffs, N.J.: Prentice-Hall, Inc., 1955.

GESELL, ARNOLD, FRANCES L. ILG, and LOUISE BATES AMES, *Youth, the Years from Ten to Sixteen*, chaps. XIV, XVIII. New York: Harper & Brothers, 1956.

HAVIGHURST, ROBERT J., *Ways of Growth toward Christian Objectives*. Chicago: University of Chicago, Committee on Human Development, 1956.

HAVIGHURST, ROBERT J., and HILDA TABA, *Adolescent Character and Personality*. New York: John Wiley & Sons, Inc., 1949.

HURLOCK, ELIZABETH B., *Adolescent Development*, 2d ed., chaps. VII, VIII, IX. New York: McGraw-Hill Book Company, Inc., 1955.

JERSILD, ARTHUR T., *In Search of Self: an Exploration of the Role of the School in Promoting Self-understanding*. New York: Bureau of Publications, Teachers College, Columbia University, 1952.

KUHLEN, RAYMOND G., and MARTHA ARNOLD, "Age Differences in Religious Beliefs and Problems during Adolescence," *Pedagogical Seminary and Journal of Genetic Psychology*, vol. 65 (December, 1944), pp. 291–300.

LECKY, PRESCOTT, *Self Consistency, a Theory of Personality*. New York: Island Press Co-operative, Inc., 1945.

MATTESON, ROSS W., "Self-estimates of College Freshmen," *Personnel and Guidance Journal*, vol. 34 (January, 1956), pp. 280–284.

MENNINGER, WILLIAM C., *Self Understanding*. Chicago: Science Research Associates, 1951.

SHERIF, M., and H. CANTRIL, *The Psychology of Ego-involvements*. New York: John Wiley & Sons, Inc., 1947.

SNYGG, DONALD, and ARTHUR W. COMBS, *Individual Behavior*. New York: Harper & Brothers, 1949.

SULLIVAN, HARRY S., *The Interpersonal Theory of Psychiatry*. New York: W. W. Norton & Company, Inc., 1953.

TORRANCE, E. PAUL, "Some Practical Uses of a Knowledge of Self Concepts in Counseling and Guidance," *Educational and Psychological Measurement*, vol. 14 (Spring, 1954), pp. 120–127.

WATTENBERG, WILLIAM W., *The Adolescent Years*, chaps. II, XVI, XVII. New York: Harcourt, Brace and Company, Inc., 1955.

Fiction and Popular Articles

* FRY, CHRISTOPHER, *The Dark Is Light Enough*. New York: Oxford University Press, 1954.

LAMBORN, ROBERT L., "Must They Be 'Crazy, Mixed-up Kids'?" *New York Times Magazine* (June 26, 1955), pp. 20, 46.

* SANDBURG, CARL, *Always the Young Strangers*. New York: Harcourt, Brace and Company, Inc., 1953.

Audio-visual Aids

Facing Reality. 12 minutes. Sound. McGraw-Hill.
Toward Emotional Maturity. 11 minutes. Sound. McGraw-Hill.

* Fiction.

CHAPTER 4

How It Feels to be Growing Up

Adults have had many different viewpoints about what growing up means to adolescents. From observation of their occasional moodiness, their rebellion, their restlessness, their inconsistencies and erratic ups and downs, adults have inferred that growing up in our culture is a turbulent transition period. Young people's obvious difficulties in getting jobs during periods of unemployment, in being permitted to assume responsibilities, in reconciling discrepancies between what adults say and teach and what they do, and in finding some place to go and something worthwhile to do reinforce the impression that adolescence is a frustrating experience. But is it, in general, a peculiarly dramatic or disturbing stage of human development?

For many adolescents in our society the teen years are indeed a period of difficult adjustment. Bettelheim has made an excellent brief summary of the emotional problems of adolescents:

It is not his physiological development alone which reduces the adolescent to a state of insecurity. He also lives in a continuous, anxiety-evoking dilemma—biologically, emotionally, and culturally. His biological dilemma originates in the conflict between the re-awakening of his sex drives and his inability to gratify them because of inhibitions and societal pressure. His emotional dilemma centers in the fact that, though he is no longer a child, he is not yet grown up; that, though he desires to free himself from his ties to his parents, he cannot afford to give them up. His cultural dilemma is highlighted by the many new grown-up duties and responsibilities

132

which he is expected to fulfil although he does not yet enjoy adult rights.[1]

The demands made upon adolescents in our culture are, indeed, extreme. If the adjustments adolescents make seem extreme, we should consider their behavior in relation to the conditions that evoke it. Most of the so-called problems of adolescents are attempts to achieve their normal developmental tasks.

It has been estimated that approximately nine-tenths of adolescents pass through this period without permanent emotional disturbances. In fact, at the beginning of the early and the late adolescent phases, they may correct some personality "fault lines" and make desirable changes in their self-concept. Research reported during the last twenty-five years has tended to dispel the belief that adolescents inevitably pass through a period of "storm and stress." Whether they do or not depends on the nature and intensity of their earlier experiences, their level of aspiration, their resources for coping with the problems and conflicting goals, their ability to appraise themselves, and their frustration tolerance. Their adjustment also depends on whether the home, the school, and the wider environment facilitate or complicate the normal process of coping with new sensations, desires, and experiences.

How do adolescents themselves feel about the changes they are experiencing during this period? Do they feel that the changes are sudden and unexpected, or is it only adults who are unprepared for these changes? Do they think of adolescence as a calamity or as an opportunity? Do they view the years ahead with optimism or pessimism? How do they perceive themselves as maturing persons?

SOURCES OF INFORMATION

The most direct way of obtaining answers to these questions is to ask the adolescents themselves. In response to the invitation

[1] Bruno Bettelheim, "The Social-studies Teacher and the Emotional Needs of Adolescents," *The School Review,* vol. 56 (December, 1948), p. 586.

to write on "How it feels to be growing up," teen-age students give us views such as the following—the first two by sixteen-year-old boys and the third by a girl of the same age in the same English class:

Many years ago I thought I would never get out of the "cry baby" stage. Every time I was corrected or scolded I would tune up and cry. It seemed that all the boys at school were always picking on me or taking my hat and many other things which always sent me home crying. It seemed that I would never get out of that stage. I stayed in it until I started playing junior varsity football in the seventh grade. Then I guess I got the cry baby knocked out of me. Playing varsity football for the past three years has helped me to grow up, too.

When I was a little younger, my dad always was jumping down my back or tanning my hide. I had always spent too much money or had lost it. I used to ask him for money all the time. As I grew older I was ashamed to ask for money so I started playing in a dance band and doing other kinds of odd jobs to get my spending money. My dad says it really helps a lot and it makes me feel that I have a responsibility.

Now most of the teen-agers feel that they don't need any more financial help from their parents except on special occasions. Most teen-agers like to date and when they start dating it makes them feel as if they are growing up.

This first composition shows the possibility of change in personality during preadolescence and early adolescence through the influence of interpersonal relations and certain environmental conditions such as sports, part-time employment, and dating. Thus the young person growing up is able to accomplish successfully his adolescent tasks.

The second composition likewise reflects the self-assurance characteristic of some teen-agers:

In the eighth grade I began to notice how fast I was maturing. Soon I discovered how differently people began to treat me. As I grew older, I began to find myself being respected, a feeling that I had never had before.

I began to leave my childish ways behind and mix with my friends.

Almost every day someone would stop me on the street to remark how fast I was growing.

In my sophomore year I realized that I had but two more years to be with my friends. Just thinking about leaving them would upset me.

When I got my driver's license I thought I was one of the big people of the town, but it didn't take me long to find out differently. Somehow before I got the license I thought being able to drive a car would turn me into a different person, and that I would be grown up. I thought it would do for me what other teen-agers thought whiskey and smoking would do for them.

I wish that I could find a vocation that I like to go into. I have about six picked out. They are all in the scientific field. I believe I would like to go in either electronics or astronomy. Boy, is it tough trying to find a future in the wide blue yonder!

But I feel that sometime, somehow, and somewhere in the future I will find what I am looking for. I believe that I have a good future in front of me and I am waiting for it.

This composition also illustrates the influence of people's attitudes toward the young person, the importance of friends, the search for some symbol of maturity, the complexity of vocational choice, and the way the future grows out of the past.

A sixteen-year-old girl described her mixed feelings about growing up in this way:

For the last three years I have been more conscious than ever of the fact that I am growing up. No one can ever completely describe this feeling.

At times I want to cry but I feel ashamed because I am a big girl now. Other times I want to read big books but I am laughed at for this. "Why, I'm only a little girl!" they say. I am just an in-between age—too big for dolls and too little for big books.

A lot of times I feel self-conscious while in a crowd or when company comes and I am wearing dungarees and a faded shirt.

Every adult has to go through this stage of life but to me it seems they can't understand the way I feel. I have problems that an adult could never understand even if they tried—which so few do. If I try to talk to one, I either get laughed at or am told that as a teen-ager I think I know everything, or for me to go away and leave them alone.

It seems that my parents expect the impossible of me. I am to have the brains of an adult and act the same but still I'm too young to know any of the family affairs.

In this composition the influence of adults' attitudes toward adolescents and their expectations of them is highlighted, as is also their need for an understanding personal relation.

Many compositions, to some extent, express the optimism and integration which seems to be characteristic of a certain stage of growing up. They also emphasize one of the most generally recognized adolescent problems—having adult capabilities and being expected to act like an adult, but still being treated in many ways like a child and denied adult status.

As a basis for the detailed analysis in this chapter on adolescents' feelings about growing up, three separate samples of unstructured compositions were obtained and analyzed. This free-response approach yielded information on what was uppermost in their thoughts; it avoided suggesting adult ideas to them; it afforded much insight into how they perceived the process of growing up. Sample 1 consisted of 277 anonymous compositions by junior and senior high school students from various environments: urban, suburban, semi-rural; lower, middle, and upper socio-economic levels; public, private, and parochial schools.[2] Sample 2 consisted of 231 anonymous compositions from a similarly diverse population in grades nine to twelve; it also included forty-one compositions from fifth- and sixth-grade children. Between these two samples there was a rank order correlation of .85 for twenty-five response categories. Sample 3 consisted of 1,124 slightly more structured, signed compositions from grades seven to twelve, about half from urban and half from rural areas in the same county. Although a wide range of socio-economic levels was represented, the middle and lower socio-economic groups predominated. Since these compositions in sample 3 were signed, it was possible to relate the students' responses to their IQs as obtained on group intelligence tests.

[2] For detail on this sampling see Ruth Strang, "Adolescents' Views on One Aspect of Their Development," *Journal of Educational Psychology,* vol. 46 (November, 1955), pp. 423–432.

Each composition was read; common points of view were tabulated under main categories. Typical responses and unusual psychological insights expressed by individual adolescents were also noted; some of these will be quoted in this chapter. Most of the boys and girls described their present feelings; a few projected themselves into the future and viewed the present from that vantage point. Their comments are convincing because they are based on their immediate firsthand experience. This chapter presents a detailed original analysis of adolescent feelings about growing up.

DOMINANT FEELINGS ABOUT GROWING UP

The dominant feelings about growing up expressed in the total number of compositions, exclusive of those from children in grades five to six, are summarized in Table 5. Differences as to age, IQ, and sex, which are small in most of the items, will be discussed later. Here we shall see which feelings seem to be uppermost. Are adolescents most concerned with negative factors, such as conflict with parents and feelings of stress and strain, or with positive concerns about making the most of their increasing independence? Do they welcome new opportunities for self-direction? Are they looking forward to the future with a certain degree of anticipation, with realistic concern, or with dread?

In the compositions collected, the positive point of view was dominant. The second highest ranking item for the entire sample was "Feeling of increasing independence and self-direction." Many of the less frequently mentioned items were likewise positive in tone, reflecting the students' concern about developing into mature persons. The same positive emphasis was indicated by their interest in major adolescent tasks—boy-girl relations, marriage and raising a family, and religion and morality. Even the statements expressing concern about vocation or the future more often showed indecision and uncertainty rather than fear or anxious dread. From reading the compositions, one gained the impression that the majority of those who mentioned the vocational problem felt that, with guidance and information, they could solve it themselves. Only a few (4 per cent) mentioned reluctance to relinquish the security of childhood, whereas about twice as many expressed a feeling of frustration at adults' failure to recognize their ability to be "on their own."

They welcomed responsibility. Many items in Table 5 represent

TABLE 5

Rank	Category	Per Cent *
1	Concern with boy-girl relationships	33.4
2	Feeling of increasing independence and self-direction	27.6
3	Concern about vocation or the future	26.4
4	Concern with social relationships	25.6
5	Concern with marriage and raising a family	23.1
6	Awareness of increased responsibilities	19.9
7	Feelings about religion or morality	17.6
8	Concern about school success or grades	17.5
9	Problems of sibling relationships	14.9
10	Dissatisfaction with school experiences	12.9
11	Interest in sports	12.3
12	Concern with larger social problems (national, international)	10.5
13	Concern with clothes or appearance	10.3
14	Feels "good," it is "fun," it is a "nice" time of life	9.4
15	Feeling of frustration that independence is not recognized	8.4
16	Viewpoint that adults do not "understand" adolescents	6.1
17	Problems about money	6.1
18	Suggestion of reluctance to lose dependence	4.4
19	Awareness of increasing acceptance in the adult world	4.1
20	Concern with military service	3.6

* Figures are relative percentage frequencies—the number of times a given category occurred divided by the number of compositions.

a combination of the desire to be independent and a willingness to assume responsibility. Certainly adolescents' own statements do not bear out the popular impression of adolescent irresponsibility.

Another indication of their positive attitude toward growing

up was their rather frequent characterization of adolescence as
"good," "fun," "a nice time of life." Approximately one-tenth of
the total sample made statements of this kind. About 4 per cent
expressed satisfaction at their increasing acceptance in the adult
world. Responses of this kind varied with the situation. In sample
1, 23 per cent of the senior high school and 12 per cent of the
junior high school students spoke of growing up as "fun" or a
good time of life, whereas in sample 3, from a single county,
only 1 per cent of those in the senior high school and 6 per cent
in the junior high school definitely expressed this feeling of satisfaction.

From their spontaneous written statements we get the impression that, by and large, adolescents have a positive approach
to life. Many see growing up as an adventure, despite its difficulties and uncertainties. They "accentuate the positive," while
not ignoring reality or glossing over the negative aspects of growing up. We get the feeling from reading the compositions as a
whole that the students who wrote them are realistic and ex-
pectant.

Possibly the general impression that adolescence is a time
of problems—problems in a negative sense—has been gained
largely from interviews and case studies of maladjusted adolescents. Teachers, counselors, psychologists, and psychiatrists commonly work with the adolescents who are having difficulties in
adjustment and need their help most; they seldom systematically
interview a random sampling of young people.

Commonality of response is presented in Table 5; individuality
of response will now be represented by direct quotations. Of
course, there are wide individual differences among adolescents.
The tone of the compositions ranges from delight to despair.
These variations in response will be brought out in the detailed
analysis which follows.

INDIVIDUAL FEELINGS AND VIEWPOINTS

Although the frequency of different types of response varies
with the situation, in a sample as large as this a wide range of

feelings will be represented. Awareness of this diversity of view-points is most helpful in working with individual adolescents, any one of whom may show a unique, rather than a common, attitude.

Feeling of Increasing Independence

Satisfaction with increasing independence is a relatively common feeling, expressed in various ways by junior and senior high school students.

1. To them, independence means more freedom to go places and do things by themselves. In their own words:

"As I grow older, I can do more things without my parents having to worry about me."

"I can do more traveling by myself."

"I now choose my own styles in clothes and wear what I like to school."

"The things you couldn't do when you were younger you can do now."

2. Independence means making up your own mind:

"When you get older, you form your own opinions and many are adverse to your parents'."

"As I grew older, the problem of making practical decisions confronted me and the idea that I was old enough to think for myself."

3. Independence means solving your own problems:

"I feel less dependent upon my parents. When something goes wrong, I do not always run to them—instead I try to solve my problems for myself."

"When a problem, big or small, arises, you can work it out without getting yourself and everyone around you confused and nervous."

"I am beginning to understand the responsibilities of my position, and most amazing of all, to tackle them. I derive a great satisfaction from their solution and even anticipate the advent of new ones with a curious mixture of anxiety and exhilaration."

4. Independence means more emotional maturity:

"As you grow up you are not so much of a burden to your parents and they do not worry about you but pass on the worries to you, and you carry your worries yourself."

5. Independence means increased self-esteem and self-reliance:

"Growing up makes me feel as if I were somebody important."

"It is making me feel more dignified and more self-reliant."

These responses suggest and illustrate certain developmental phases in the meaning which independence has for adolescents. The younger adolescents seemed a little more eager for "freedom," as they viewed it, than did the senior high school students (31.5 per cent, as compared with 23.8 per cent in senior high school, in the total sample); they more often emphasized "being on their own," having freedom to go places by themselves, to do things they want to do, to choose their own clothes, to make their own decisions. The more thoughtful senior high school students spoke oftener of thinking for themselves, forming their own opinions, solving their own problems. Doing this successfully increases their self-esteem—their sense of being competent persons.

Variation in emphasis in different localities is indicated by a comparison of two samples. In sample 1 (277 compositions from different types of schools and communities) the frequency with which pupils on various grade levels expressed their desire for and satisfaction in independence is shown in Table 6.

TABLE 6

Grade Level	Number of Compositions	Number Expressing Satisfaction in Independence	Per Cent
7-8-9	185	68	37
10–11–12	92	40	44
7–12	277	108	39

In view of the fact that these were free responses—no particular item was suggested—it is significant that between one-third and one-half of the students mentioned the feeling of increasing independence and self-direction. For samples 1 and 2 combined—these samples were similar in the diversity of the situations from which the compositions were obtained—the frequency for this category was 41 per cent. Apparently the satisfaction of feeling independent was uppermost in these students' minds.

In sample 3 (1,124 high school students, all from one county, generally of low socio-economic status though representing a variety of family backgrounds) the results were quite different,

TABLE 7

Grade Level and IQ	Number of Compositions	Number Expressing Satisfaction in Independence	Per Cent
7–8–9; Average IQ: 95.2	247	58	23
7–8–9; IQ: 120–129	121	25	21 ⎱ 19
7–8–9; IQ: 130 and over	135	5	14 ⎰
10–11–12; Average IQ: 94.9	636	133	21
10–11–12; IQ: 120–129	65	10	15 ⎱ 14
10–11–12; IQ: 130 and over	20	2	10 ⎰
7–12	1,124	233	21

as shown in Table 7. In this sample about one-fifth welcomed increasing independence—a much smaller proportion than in samples 1 and 2.

The students of average and below-average intelligence in sample 3 expressed satisfaction in their increasing independence slightly more frequently than did those with IQs of 120 or over. Several possible explanations of this difference may be suggested. Probably those with lower IQs have always felt pushed and prodded and restricted more than have those of higher intelligence; consequently, they may have welcomed the time when they would have less close supervision. Then, too, they may not have seen so clearly as the gifted the difficulties and responsibilities lying ahead. It is also possible that adolescents with low IQs associated with low economic status actually have been more on their own and liked it. Even though somewhat fewer youngsters of high ability welcomed increasing independence, the proportion who did is still substantial. This may be explained as reflecting their confidence in their competence to handle the new situations that confront them.

In these samplings boys seemed to show as much eagerness for independence as did girls, though each sex was irked by different kinds of restrictions. The girls looked forward to more freedom in choosing their clothes, having dates, being allowed to stay out later. The boys especially resented domination by their fathers and "being tied to their mothers' apron strings." The feelings of the two sexes would show variations influenced by different cultural attitudes toward proper behavior for boys and girls, and also by home relationships. Gaining independence, however, has long been regarded as a major goal of adolescence, and teen-agers of both sexes are keenly aware of this aspect of growing up.

Frustration when Independence Is Not Recognized

Accompanying the desire for independence are feelings of frustration that this desire is not recognized by adults, especially by parents. While some students expressed happiness at the prospect of having more freedom, a considerable number (8 per cent in the total sample, 13 per cent in sample 1) expressed present resentments.

1. They resented being treated like children:

"Nothing angers me more than to have someone say, 'Oh, you are still young, with no problems yet.'"

"A lot of parents . . . like to keep their children as babies as long as they can."

"Parents worry too much about our welfare. But that is simply because they are under a false impression. We are grown up long before they have a chance to realize it."

2. They objected to too close supervision:

"I don't think my mother should remind me all the time of certain things I shouldn't do. I think I am old enough to know better and not be told all the time."

"I will be glad when I won't have to take orders and be bossed around by so many people."

3. They were irked by inconsistencies in adults' attitudes toward them:

"I'm expected to have manners like an adult, yet have to go to bed early like a little child."

"Parents say, 'You're old enough to help out with this' and 'You can't do that, you're much too young.'"

It is well for adults to be aware that teen-agers resent being considered more immature than they really are, being treated as less capable than they really are, and being treated inconsistently.

Appreciation of Acceptance by Adults

On the other hand, some groups showed an awareness of being increasingly accepted in the adult world. They expressed this feeling in such statements as these:

When people see you, they talk to you as a grown-up. I feel that I am one of the family now.

At home, they will listen to your ideas about things. Before this year I never took part in family discussions.

When deciding upon things in the family I have more to say than I used to.

My parents talk to me as if I were an equal; they confide in me more.

Adults begin to ask our opinion on various subjects.

Parents, friends, and relatives begin to gain confidence in you and begin to depend on you.

In both sample 2 and sample 3, more responses of this kind came from the junior than from the senior high school students. In sample 1, however, 8 per cent of the junior high, as compared with 15 per cent of the senior high students, mentioned adults' increasing respect for them. Perhaps the younger age group is more aware of this changed adult attitude because it is a new experience. On the other hand, as adolescents become more mature, we should expect adults to listen to them, confide in them, and respect their opinions. Too often, however, older adolescents meet an unexpected rejection of their maturity by adults. Both cultural differences and family relations have a great influence on the extent to which parents and teachers accept teen-agers on a man-to-man basis. For example, in a well-to-do residential community almost half of the senior high school students mentioned adult acceptance of their increasing maturity.

Awareness of Increasing Responsibilities

According to Table 5, awareness of increasing responsibilities was sixth among the various categories in frequency of mention. It would seem that the feeling of increasing independence and self-direction, mentioned still more often, might be related to this awareness of increased responsibility. Adolescents' expressions of this awareness give insight into the meanings which responsibility has for them, and the feeling tones which accompany their sense of responsibility.

1. Some feel that new responsibilities have been added gradually: "Each year I am given a little more responsibility."

"My parents are willing to let me grow up and assume as much responsibility as I feel I am capable of handling."

2. Responsibility means helping parents in various ways. Some youngsters like this; others see disadvantages, too:

"Growing up means a lot to me. I can help parents more—help with younger sisters and things around the house."

"Since I've been growing up my parents have given me more responsibility for doing things. I don't like this very much because it takes away some of my fun."

"Because I have these extra responsibilities and privileges I like being a teen-ager."

Both junior and senior high school students accept responsibility as part of growing up, and most of them seem to do so willingly. In sample 1, the number who mentioned increased responsibilities was almost as large as the number who spoke of more freedom and privileges. In the total sample, 20 per cent mentioned awareness of increased responsibility as contrasted with 28 per cent who referred to increasing independence and self-direction. The very fact that one-fifth of these adolescents mentioned, of their own accord, the responsibilities associated with growing up indicates considerable awareness of the serious side of freedom.

We would expect the senior high school students to be more aware of the increasing responsibilities of growing up than the junior high school pupils. This was true in the two samplings from a variety of communities. In sample 1 the percentage mentioning this increased awareness was, for junior high school, 28 per cent; for senior high school, 46 per cent. In the composite total sample, junior and senior high school students mentioned increased responsibility with almost equal frequency. Among the students in sample 3, only a very small number, all with IQs of 120 or over, spoke specifically of the responsibilities of growing up.

Various factors would influence adolescents' awareness of the increased responsibilities of growing up: intelligence; opportunities to take responsibility, which would be greater in rural than in urban localities; family background and attitudes. Adolescents in homes where the children have to assume responsibilities early would naturally become aware of the serious side of growing up sooner than those in more sheltered environments. Any of these conditions might account for the differences, in the various samples, between junior and senior high school students' awareness of their increasing responsibilities.

Mixed Feelings about Growing Up

In view of G. Stanley Hall's early emphasis on adolescence as an inevitable time of "storm and stress," it is surprising that so many youngsters (9 per cent of the total sample) felt that growing up was "fun," "exciting," "wonderful," "enjoyable." An examination of the separate samples, however, shows what was so dramatically demonstrated by Margaret Mead in her *Coming of Age in Samoa:* that whether adolescence is turbulent or placid depends a great deal on the culture, and, we should add more specifically, on family attitude and relations. Some parents and teachers seem to be highly successful in taking the joy out of adolescence. In sample 1, 16 per cent made some reference to the pleasures of growing up; in sample 2 it was 42 per cent, and in sample 3, only 2 per cent. These differences raise many questions: Is growing up in a rural community, a small town, or a suburb more or less difficult than growing up in a city? Do some school systems provide more enjoyable school activities than do others? Do rural youngsters engage in more enjoyable church and community activities and have more real jobs to do than city children and young people? What personal and family conditions contribute to the marked differences in young people's enthusiasm for growing up? Apparently adolescence is a difficult time of life and a period of strain and stress for some but not for others. The following quotations were characteristic of seventh-, eighth-, and ninth-grade pupils:

All and all, it feels great to be growing up.

Growing up is to me exciting.

Being a teenager is lots of fun, too. I don't remember when I enjoyed life as much as I do now.

I know I'll enjoy life later on if it keeps up this way.

The comments of senior high school students were similar, though somewhat more perceptive:

Far from feeling odd or awkward as is supposedly the fashion, I have had a wonderful time preparing to be an adult.

I love growing up. The last two years especially have been a great joy to me.

One ninth-grade student compared the process of growing up to seeing "the curtain rising on a new and fabulous play."

In contrast with these buoyant feelings, there were some negative responses such as these:

On the whole growing up is the biggest ordeal anyone goes through. I believe I have had more troubles now than I ever had—disappointments and let-downs. One thing I learned to do is never build up my hopes.

Some days I wish I wasn't born, because everything went wrong.

One is impressed with the wholehearted enjoyment of life that is indicated in some of these comments, and with the extreme unhappiness of others. These mixed feelings may reflect the fluctuations in mood that are often observed in adolescents, as well as differences in personality, age, and home and school experiences.

Some of those who have reservations about the desirability of growing up mention their reluctance to lose the dependency of childhood. These are some typical responses of this kind:

You wonder what it will be like when there aren't any mother and father to guide you and it scares you.

You now [at 17] wish that you were young again—you had no worries.

Growing up is a hard thing to face because childhood is so dear to our hearts.

I sometimes dread the thought of growing up because of the many responsibilities. Adults are held responsible for all their mistakes and are rarely excused like youngsters are. I wish I could stay about sixteen years old for the rest of my life.

The feeling that comes with growing up sometimes frightens you —the thought that now you are responsible for all your actions. People can't say, "She is only a child and you can't blame her for her bad actions."

There is a feeling of being afraid—afraid to face the world and all its problems alone.

A few adolescents, on the other hand, are impatient to arrive at adulthood. This impatience generally stems from dissatisfaction with school, the feeling that work experience is more satisfactory than school experience, or a desire to have more spending money.

Feelings of Indecision and Confusion

Psychologists and sociologists have frequently called attention to the fact that adolescents are affected by a changing culture and conflicting standards within a given community. They have described discrepancies and discontinuities between home and school, between social peer pressures and adult demands, between biological urges and lack of opportunities to satisfy them. These discrepancies and discontinuities do not seem to be clearly recognized by the younger adolescents in our samples. Relatively few junior high school youngsters wrote about their feelings of indecision and confusion. Many of these youngsters may have been in a stage in which they felt relatively adequate as persons; later they may have more difficulty in coping with the multiplicity of decisions and problems pressing upon them. Increased confusion is mentioned by 12 per cent of the senior high school students in sample 1, but is not specifically mentioned at all by the senior high school students in the other two samples. Concern about the complex and conflicting attitudes within one's own mind and in one's environment is illustrated by the following quotations from the compositions of two seventeen-year-old girls:

Growing up is a complex process having many changes in attitude on just one subject—perhaps two unlike feelings in one day—depending on surrounding attitudes or opinions.

Though I understand right from wrong, it is really difficult to act as I know I should. My mind tells me to do one thing but my hurt feelings or angry emotions disregard all direction. . . . Growing up is not easy. I have to act like a lady when I feel like just going wild.

The following statement, also written by a senior high school girl, is unique in the insight it expresses:

Growing up is a time of confusion and uncertainty. You begin to question principles that you had always considered concrete fact. Ideas, all conflicting, pour in from all directions—parents, teachers, adults, and teen-age friends, movies, radio, TV, books. You decide you are for one thing, then someone talks you into the opposite side. Adults are confused, also, but they have had time to form their opinions and standards, whereas we teen-agers are floundering in a sea of indecision.

Many other adolescents may feel considerable confusion and anxiety without being able to verbalize it. On the other hand, younger boys and girls and those less keen to see relationships may not recognize the conflicting standards and values in their environment.

Moodiness

Moodiness, generally considered one of the most common characteristics of adolescents, is seldom mentioned in these compositions. In fact, it was not specifically described by the junior high school youngsters in sample 1, and was mentioned by only about 5 per cent of those in senior high school. The latter seemed to be more aware of unpredictable and inexplicable variations in mood than were the younger pupils.

There are a number of possible explanations for this apparent omission. Perhaps these adolescents experience and recognize fluctuations in mood but do not want to tell about them. Or perhaps they actually experience shifts in mood but do not identify or recognize them. Some may not have the words to express their feelings. It may be, also, that changes in mood are such ordinary daily occurrences that they do not seem worth writing about. Or, finally, the large majority of adolescents may be more emotionally stable than adults have given them credit for being.

Whatever the reasons why change of mood is infrequently mentioned, some of those who do speak of it describe their feelings vividly, as in the following quotations from the compositions of senior high school girls:

One of the first difficulties that teen-agers discuss is their moods. Sometimes they get up in the morning feeling wonderful. Instead of walking, they feel like running; instead of talking, they feel like singing. Other days they feel wretched and depressed. They can hardly drag themselves around. Every time someone speaks to them they feel like slapping him. . . . These moods come and go in a mysterious way, for just no reason at all.

The most frequent feeling . . . is a blithe feeling. I am happy, gay, and glad to be alive. I may start the day with such a feeling but by night . . . I would feel depressed, discontented, annoyed and mad at everyone including myself. Often I have the feeling of wanting to cry bitterly at nothing.

Fluctuations in physical energy, as described by one girl, are probably related to fluctuations in mood: "There are some times that I could scrub all the floors in the house, wash windows . . . go out dancing at night until one or two o'clock, and come home still ready and raring (but not permitted) to go. Yet there are times when I don't do anything, and I'm exhausted."

Although it may not be specifically mentioned in many compositions, moodiness is often implied in descriptions of conflicting feelings, of ups and downs. An individual adolescent will often express two diverse viewpoints; this may indicate lack of consistency in mood.

BROADENING KNOWLEDGE AND CHANGING INTERESTS

Although an expanding adolescent world would naturally imply expanding knowledge and interests, other factors enter in to affect the number and maturity of adolescents' interests. The very fact of sexual maturation expands interests related to the opposite sex. For boys, interest in more complex and highly organized sports increases during early adolescence. On the other hand, many childhood games are abandoned. Lack of time due to increase in work experiences, study, and travel limits the development of broad recreational interests. Instead of being ends in themselves, as in childhood, teen-age interests become means by which youngsters gain social prestige, opportunity to get acquainted with the other sex, and, sometimes, preparation for a vocation.

The intellectual stimulation offered by the home and the school has a great deal to do with whether a broadening of certain interests occurs. About 5 per cent of the adolescents in sample 1 and 12 per cent in sample 2 mentioned the possibility of developing new interests. This response was not discovered at all as a possible category in sample 3. Unless adolescents receive some guidance, they may merely repeat familiar activities rather than discover new ones. Those who were aware of expanding interests made such remarks as, "Every day I learn something new and look forward to the next day." "School work is going to get harder now," wrote an eighth-grade boy, "but we don't mind it, because when you are growing up you like to learn new and important things."

Voluntary reading may be considered as one means of broadening one's knowledge. In the large sampling from one county (sample 3), the students of lower and higher intelligence showed a marked difference in the degree to which they expressed enjoyment of voluntary reading. Of the pupils in seventh, eighth, and ninth grades, only 13 per cent of those with an average IQ of 95 mentioned the pleasure of voluntary reading, as contrasted with 40 to 50 per cent of those with IQs of 120 or over. Among the smaller number of senior high school students, the difference in voluntary reading between IQ levels was less. In general, the brighter students referred more frequently to their enjoyment of reading than did those with a lower average intelligence. But in senior high school, especially among the boys, required reading and other activities tended to decrease the amount of voluntary reading. The poor readers, low in intelligence, cannot get much pleasure from voluntary reading, because it is too difficult for them.

For the investigation of possible IQ and sex differences for the various categories of a particular grade level, 461 eleventh-grade compositions were extracted from sample 3, and the responses were tabulated according to the sex of the writer and according to whether the IQ was over or under 100. The following percentages mentioned the category of "enjoyment of voluntary reading":

123 eleventh-grade boys, IQ under 100 . . . . 17%
 82 eleventh-grade boys, IQ 100 or over 16%
159 eleventh-grade girls, IQ under 100 . . . . 26%
 97 eleventh-grade girls, IQ 100 or over 41%

The fact that only about 16 per cent of the 205 eleventh-grade boys, in contrast with 31 per cent of the 256 girls, expressed enjoyment in voluntary reading indicates a sex difference at this grade level for this sample of 461 adolescents. This difference may be attributable to an essential difference between boys and girls in this respect, or to more particular factors which influence girls but not boys, or vice versa, and thus operate to differentiate the voluntary reading interests of boys from those of girls. Whether this difference would hold in a sample from another community or in the entire population of eleventh-grade boys and girls is a question that would require further study.

Among adolescents of all ages there is undoubtedly a potential, at present unrealized, for growth in knowledge and worthwhile interests. During early adolescence especially, boys and girls have more energy, time, and eagerness to develop permanent interests than they will have in later years. Home, school, and community should provide the opportunities for them to do so.

Adolescent interests may expand to include larger social problems and national and international issues. In this set of compositions references to national and world conditions occurred with the following frequency:

Sample 1	4%
Sample 2	7%
Sample 3	14%
Composite sample	10%

The data for this category may be a little distorted by the fact that some of the writers were expressing concern about international affairs primarily because they were personally involved through relatives and close friends who were on active duty abroad. Results of any investigation of this aspect of adolescent interests could be expected to vary with the times. Other studies have reported various degrees of interest in these wider relationships. The degree of interest expressed would vary according to the form in which the question was put, as well as with the times and with the students' home and community backgrounds and school instruction. For many adolescents, their immediate personal problems may be so pressing as to crowd out consideration of more remote matters. However, their expression of various points of view and their earnestness in discussing world conditions evidences potential sensitivity to social problems beyond their immediate environment (see Chapter 2).

OTHER CONCERNS AND PROBLEMS OF GROWING UP

In writing about "How it feels to be growing up," junior and senior high school students mentioned practically all the major adolescent goals and problems already cited. These will be briefly summarized here and treated in more detail in succeeding chapters.

Physical Changes and Concerns

In view of the degree to which books on adolescence emphasize physical changes, we might expect more reference to these
changes in teen-age compositions on growing up. In samples 1
and 2, there were not enough responses dealing with bodily
changes to warrant tabulating them as a category. This particular concern seems to have a very low relative frequency of mention in freely written compositions on "How it feels to be growing up." Even other students who wrote on "When I have felt
disturbed or at a loss," and even those in sample 3, whose in-
structions included a phrase or two that might have suggested
physical changes, referred to physical changes relatively seldom.

When statements concerning problems of height, weight, and
changes in bodily form are integrated with references to social
and emotional factors, we find that 18 per cent of both the junior
and senior high school students in sample 3 with an average IQ
of 95 expressed satisfaction with body growth, change, or status;
slightly more of the same group expressed dissatisfaction. Among
the students with IQs over 120 in the same schools, the percentages of those who expressed satisfaction and dissatisfaction were
both somewhat larger. This suggests that the brighter students
have a greater awareness of the role of physical change in adolescent development. Adolescents are most concerned with the
results of health and good physical development—facility in
sports and attractive personal appearance.

Interest in sports was specifically mentioned by 12 per cent
of the composite sample. In writing about growing up, junior
high school students referred to sports slightly more frequently
than did those in senior high. In the junior high schools in sample 3, this interest was mentioned more frequently by students
of 120 IQ or higher (25 per cent) than by those with an average IQ of 95 (11 per cent). The reverse was true in senior high
schools: 8 per cent among the higher IQs mentioned interest in
sports, as contrasted with 13 per cent of those with an average
IQ of 95. Possibly the older gifted students recognized that in
order to reach their goals they needed to devote more time to

study. Or perhaps the multiplicity of activities accessible to certain high school students—part-time remunerative work, departmental clubs, school publications, and so on—has crowded sports out of their schedule. Actual participation in sports, especially by boys, would be much higher than indicated by frequency of mention in these compositions.

It was also true that the responses relating to sports occurred mainly in compositions written by boys. An analysis of 461 eleventh-grade compositions—a subsample of sample 3—showed that the sports category contained forty-seven items mentioned by boys and only fifteen mentioned by girls. For the entire sample, the proportion of girls who referred to sports was probably still smaller.

Concern with clothes and personal appearance was mentioned in 10 per cent of the compositions in the composite sample. Practically all of the contributions to this category were by girls. These data reinforce the general impression that boys are much more interested in sports and much less interested in personal appearance than are girls. Concern with clothes seems to be closely related to the desire not to be different from one's agemates and, especially with girls, the desire to be attractive to the opposite sex.

Concept of Oneself

In the compositions about growing up, expressions or indications of self-acceptance were much more frequent than indications of lack of self-acceptance or expressions of desire to change one's personality. Adolescents with lower IQs gave about as much evidence of self-acceptance as did those with IQs above 120. However, those with IQs above 130, especially in the junior high school, more often expressed desire to change their personalities. Perhaps these students recognized early adolescence as an appropriate time for sorting out childish traits and reorganizing the personality on a more mature level. Identification with fictional and movie characters was mentioned by only one student in junior high school and by three senior high school students among 277. This is surprising in view of the common tendency to attribute adolescent characteristics to the influence of magazines and movies. However, such influence may be insidious; it may be accomplished by such a gradual process of conditioning that the individual is unaware that he is being influenced. Another explanation of the few references to mass media of communication in this set of compositions is that the youngsters did not associate these influences with the process of growing up.

Concern about School

When adolescents are given check lists of problems, they usually mark those relating to schoolwork more frequently than any others. In writing freely about problems of growing up, the junior and senior high school students in our samplings were apparently more concerned about other aspects of growing up. In Table 5, it will be noted that concern about school success or grades was mentioned in 17.5 per cent of the compositions; thus it was outranked by seven of the twenty categories common to the entire sample. In samples 1 and 2 combined, the position of this item was still less prominent: it was outranked by sixteen of the twenty-five categories. About one-tenth of those in sample 3 and only 3 per cent in the other two samples expressed dissatisfaction with school experiences and impatience to be through with school. In Chapters 6 and 12 more detail is given about the feelings which students have toward marks and report cards, and about factors that make studying hard or easy for them.

Concern with Social Behavior

One of the concerns which these adolescents mentioned most frequently was social relations in general, mentioned by about one-fourth of the students in the composite sample; another was boy-girl relations, the highest-ranking item, mentioned by one-third. In this sample of 1,591 compositions, students in senior high school mentioned both these items slightly more frequently than did those in junior high school.

In sample 3 as a whole, the students expressed much satisfaction with peer relations, as shown by the following percentages:

Satisfaction with peer relations 34%
Desire for greater acceptance by peers 7%

The percentages for sample 3 students with IQs of 120 or more were:

Satisfaction with peer relations 43%
Desire for greater acceptance by peers 11%

These data reinforce the well-established fact that superior mental ability tends to be associated with better-than-average social adjustment. However, some of the brighter students expressed desire for greater acceptance by their peers. This is a common problem among the more able students in high school; they frequently say, "The other kids don't like me."

Relations in the Family

In writing about growing up the students frequently referred to family relations in connection with other problems, such as freedom and responsibility. Brothers and sisters seemed to be more frequent causes of conflict with both junior and senior high school students than did parents; the percentages for the composite summary are as follows:

Problems of sibling relations, junior high 14%
    "   "   "   "   senior high 16%
Feelings of frustration that independence is not
   recognized 8%
Viewpoint that adults do not understand adolescents.. 6%

Sample 3 yielded these percentages on the following categories:

Expression of satisfaction with parent relations 45%
Problems related to broken homes 8%
Concern for welfare of family or parents 11%
Parental interference with vocational plans 1%
Parental interference in dating or in choice of friends.. 3%

From these freely written compositions we do not get the impression that most adolescents are antagonistic toward their parents. On the contrary, about half of those in sample 3 spontaneously expressed either satisfaction in their relations with parents or concern for their welfare. More direct reference to family relations is reported in Chapter 10. Perhaps these young people were reluctant to write about family troubles; perhaps they did not associate problems of growing up specifically with family relations; or perhaps the majority of adolescents in average homes are really fond of their parents and get along fairly well with them. It may be, too, that child-study and parent-education projects are having some effect on the relations of adolescents with their families.

Money Problems

One gets the general impression that money problems loom large for many adolescents, and many do check money items on a problem check list. However, in these compositions focused on feelings about growing up, only 6 per cent of the total sample mentioned money problems; this item ranked fourth from the bottom among the twenty categories. There was only a slight difference between the frequencies with which this item was mentioned by junior and senior high school students. Perhaps this is owing to the fact that, although the older adolescent's need for money is usually greater than the younger one's, his ability to earn money is correspondingly greater. As one ninth-grade boy said, "Your conception of money also changes as you grow up. At the age of eight or nine, fifty cents might be a pile of money to you, but now you think in terms of five or ten dollars." And a girl of sixteen in senior high school expressed a point of view common to both boys and girls: "Some of the pleasures in growing up is that you don't have to depend on your parents so much. You can get a job and earn money to buy your own clothes."

One of the major reasons why teen-age boys want money is so that they can sport, and support, a car. In sample 3, about 15 per cent of those with an average IQ of 95 wrote of their

desire to own or operate a car. One of them put it this way:
"If I had three wishes the first would be to be 16 and drive a
cattlelike." Another was willing to settle for "a Buick convertible." Perhaps driving a car gives, or would give, these youngsters the prestige they cannot obtain from academic work. Only
7 per cent of those with IQs of 120 or more in sample 3 specifically associated a desire to have a car with the problems of
growing up.

Educational and Vocational Plans

Concern about a vocation and about the future in general was
voiced frequently in these compositions as well as on the check
lists reported in other investigations. In sample 3, about one-
third expressed a desire for a particular vocation, while between
one-fifth and one-fourth indicated that vocational choice was an
area of conflict and indecision. For some young people vocational choice is complicated by differences of opinion in the
family. A fourteen-year-old boy described his situation in this

way: "When I was a very small boy I wondered what I would be. A doctor, as my mother wants me to be, or a lawyer, as my father wants me to be, or what I wanted to be—soldier, baseball player, cowboy. Well, as I grew older, that was taken out of my mind by my mother when she said, 'Son, you are going to be a doctor.'"

For students in college preparatory courses, decisions about future education seem to be of more immediate concern than vocational choice. In sample 3 of this study, about 13 per cent of the boys with IQs of 120 or more were thinking seriously about military service, whereas this concern was mentioned by only 6 per cent of those with average IQs of 95. Perhaps this is because military service represents an interruption of one's schooling, and is therefore more of a threat to the brighter boys than to the less able boys.

Morality and Religion

Much has been written about the religious perplexities of adolescence. According to our data these problems increase markedly from junior to senior high school, as shown in the percentages in Table 8.

TABLE 8

	Junior High	Senior High
Combined samples 1 and 2....	6%	34%
Sample 3.................	12%	24%
Composite summary.........	9%	25%

In sample 1, which contained a larger proportion of compositions from Roman Catholic schools, references to questions of right and wrong and to religious beliefs, practices, and perplexities were more frequent than in the other two samples. One gifted sixteen-year-old girl wrote: "Growing up has made me feel different about religion. When I try to understand and ask questions, I either get a confusing answer or my question cannot be answered." In general, the brighter youngsters become concerned with religious and moral questions earlier than the slow learners. In all cases, however, moral and religious aspects of growing up can only be built on the total personality as it exists. Many adolescents are troubled; they are frightened, lonely, aloof, and do not expect people to accept them. Religion offers them a relationship with Someone who is always present and will never leave or forsake them. A few compositions expressed this deep religious feeling.

Concluding Statement

The concerns briefly mentioned in the foregoing pages are commonly recognized by adolescents, especially by those of average socio-economic backgrounds. More detailed knowledge is needed about how young people of different abilities and backgrounds perceive these problems of growing up, how they are coping with them at present, how they might handle various situations more competently, and what help adults can give.

HOPES FOR THE FUTURE

Adolescent behavior is influenced by the past and the future. Thoughts of things to come impinge upon the present, sometimes withdrawing energy from immediate tasks, sometimes motivating the individual to greater achievement. Adolescents in the junior and senior high schools surveyed in this study expressed three main hopes for the future. The first in frequency of mention was desire for marriage and children (23 per cent of the total sample). The percentage making this response was twice as large in the senior high school (30 per cent) as in the junior high school (15 per cent). Of the senior high school students in sample 3, more of the below average (34 per cent) than of the gifted (25 per cent) expressed this desire. Said one eighth-grade boy with an IQ of 95: "I would like to have a good job, a nice home in the country and a good wife." What more could one desire!

The second desire was for world peace. This wish was mentioned slightly more frequently in senior high school than in junior high school and by twice as many mentally superior as average students. In sample 3, the figures were as follows:

Senior high school 14%
Junior high school 11%
Those with IQs 120 or more 22%
Those with average IQ of 95 .... 11%

It was an eighteen-year-old boy with an IQ of 120 who wrote: "I wish the world would be unified into one cooperating body, not by war because regardless who is the victor, both sides lose. One little word PEACE to the world and all humanity."

Looking realistically at the present, one seventeen-year-old girl wrote: "Growing up in the world today means an uncertain future. It means bringing our own children into a troubled world."

Unusual in its clarity and in its literary quality is the comment of a gifted senior boy: "Whenever someone mentions growing up, I always have a feeling of doubt. This doubt is caused chiefly by the critical international situation. What wars will the U.S. be involved in? How may the problem of co-existence be worked out peaceably? These situations will undoubtedly spin their web around my adult life."

The third desire was for future financial security. Here, too, the frequency increased with age—7 per cent at the junior high school level and 16 per cent at the senior high school level in sample 3. There was only a slight difference in this respect between intelligence levels.

Some students also mentioned the desire for a happy future, and wrote about dreams of travel and adventure. A high school senior wanted to "travel around the world and see how people in other countries live." These same three desires—for a happy family life, for peace, for travel—were also uppermost in the minds of university students in ten different cultures who wrote compositions for Gillespie and Allport.[3] Dreams and hopes for

[3] James M. Gillespie and Gordon W. Allport, *Youth's Outlook on the Future: A Cross-national Study.* New York: Doubleday & Company, Inc., 1955.

the future, as well as fears and anxieties, are woven into adolescents' feelings about growing up. The way in which they perceive themselves with reference to their future probably has an important influence on their present behavior.

A PLEA FOR UNDERSTANDING

Lack of adult understanding is implied in many of the compositions on growing up. This feeling is specifically expressed by 6 per cent of the composite sample; the percentage is higher among senior high school students. In the combined sample 1 and 2:

in junior high school 1%
in senior high school 13%

In the composite sample:

in junior high school 4%
in senior high school 8%

As one student put it, "Though parents were young once, they do not fully understand teen-agers."

Adolescents often seem to understand adults better than adults understand adolescents. They make perceptive comments like the following:

They [parents] judge their own teen-agers from what other kids have done.

They don't realize that we live in a different world than they did when they were growing up.

Grownups say they remember what it was like to be growing up; that they understand our problems. I disagree, as they forget the unpleasant memories. Only someone who is going through the process knows what it is like to be growing up.

The writers of the first two comments expressed the general semantic principle that "adolescent A is not the same as adolescent 'A.'" They recognized that adults have a faulty tendency to generalize, although generalization is not warranted because of differences in persons and times. In the third quotation a seventeen-year-old boy expressed the tendency which one psychologist called "the obliviscence of the disagreeable," and pointed out the authenticity of firsthand experience as contrasted with delayed memory.

A still more serious indictment was made by a senior high school girl in a small textile town: "My friends and I have, at one time or another, felt that our parents did not understand us, *nor care to*." And by a boy from a middle-class family: "I have problems which an adult could never understand, even if they tried—which so few do."

This plea for understanding has been echoed by large numbers of adolescents. It has also been expressed by adults writing about adolescents:

All who wish to help the young rebel adjust to his physical and social environment must first understand him. It helps to know that (a) the difficulties are not new, not a development of the younger generation, (b) behavior is not all bad but a curious mixture of good and bad, and (c) that even the seeming bad behaviors hold great significance for future growth along approved lines.[4]

In this paragraph Burton has admirably summed up the essentials of an understanding which many youngsters think is still lacking in the adults they know.

AGE DIFFERENCES IN VIEWS OF GROWING UP

Although there are wide individual differences within each age and local group, and though the views expressed by the various age groups overlap a good deal, some age trends are discernible.

Children's Views

Children in the intermediate grades of elementary school tend to live in the present; their ideas of the future, though somewhat fanciful from an adult point of view, are, within the limits of their experience, fairly reasonable and sensible. They view

[4] William H. Burton, "The Preadolescent: Rebel in our Society," *Education*, vol. 76 (December, 1955), p. 223.

the future, as they do the present, in a matter-of-fact, confident way.

There are marked differences in the responses of boys and girls. Even before the prepubescent growth spurt, girls are thinking of getting married. The following points of view are fairly typical:

I am nine years old. I haven't thought much about growing up. When I get big I am getting married and I will have 3 kids because I like babies. I have a boy friend. His name is Albert, he goes to my church.

I am nine years old. I don't want to grow up very much, but I know I have to so I might as well plan. When I grow up I want to get married at about twenty-one. I want a pretty baby girl. I would name her Sheila. I want to be able to make dresses for my girl. If I can't be a dressmaker I want to be a beautician.

Some are thinking of college, too. This ten-year-old girl mapped out her future as follows: "In seven more years I will be seventeen. I am very anxious to go to college. I haven't decided whether I want to get married, but if I do I want to have a church wedding. And after the wedding I would like to go to Hawaii on my honeymoon. After I come back I would take up my career again."

Boys of these ages, as was indicated in Chapter 2, are intensely active and are quite uninterested in girls. They sometimes let their present antagonisms toward girls color their plans for the future: "I am nine years old and I don't like girls. I am going to be a bachelor and I'd like to be a mechanical engner. I like every kind of sports. I am going to be a dective in the White House, too, when I grow up."

These quotations are probably quite typical of nine- and ten-year-old children. Many of their replies to the question about growing up sound quaint to us, but are probably realistic to them. According to Gesell in *Youth, the Years from Ten to Sixteen*,[5] at the developmental phase represented by ten-year-olds,

[5] Arnold Gesell, Frances L. Ilg, and Louise B. Ames, *Youth, the Years from Ten to Sixteen.* New York: Harper & Brothers, 1956.

children are especially good about caring for children under five. Despite their keen interest in present activities, girls sometimes daydream about marrying.

Views of Preadolescents

When the boys, especially, are experiencing a spurt in growth, the accent is on the increased freedom and privileges which accompany growing up. The following views were common among groups of boys eleven to thirteen years old living, for the most part, in urban or suburban neighborhoods:

You can go more places by yourself—like riding a bike or going to stores or buildings. When you were younger you couldn't ride on the road or do anything dangerous.

You can do things you couldn't do when you were younger, like building things or using different tools, playing basketball or football.

You can stay up late, go out with girls and talk with adults.

You're trusted more.

You think you can do everything. You learn to take care of yourself. It feels good to be growing up.

A few have begun to look forward to leaving school: "Soon I'll be over with school. Then I'll be working and I like working."

These youngsters sometimes recall some of the advantages they had as children—getting more attention, having more things done for them, paying half price at the movies. A very small number express reluctance to relinquish childish things: "I'll have to stop playing and start working, and I hate that."

While looking toward the future, some seem quite content with the present. One eleven-year-old boy put it in these words: "My age is about the best because you have a lot of freedom and privileges and sometimes even more privileges and freedom than older people. Of course, I have my duties to perform but I don't find it difficult." Another boy of the same age summarized the advantages of growing up as follows: "I think it's good because I know more and I can do more. I have more priviliges. I have more fun. I go to more places. I get more allowance. I

have more frends and I know more people. I go to a new school."
He listed no disadvantages.

Although many girls of this age mention the advantages of
growing up, they have more reservations about it than do boys
of the same age. Their responses cover a range of feelings from
anticipation to skepticism. Many are ambivalent; some express
disappointment: "Growing up isn't as much fun as I expected
it to be. Of course, there are its priviledges like dates and an
allowance, but still there are its drawbacks."

For one reason or another, preadolescents are fairly optimistic
about growing up. This optimism may stem partly from their
general confidence in their ability to deal with reality and partly
from their lack of knowledge of the problems that will later
confront them. They like the feeling of independence and self-
direction and describe growing up as fun more frequently than
the senior high school groups. Since they are still socially immature, they express considerable concern about social behavior
in their peer culture and about ways of making friends. "Best
friends" are of great importance to them. Despite frequent references in the literature to family conflicts, especially around
eleven years of age, many of the youngsters in these samples
wrote of satisfaction in parental and even in sibling relations,
and expressed concern about the solution of their family's problems. It would be interesting to study these compositions according to chronological age, and to compare them with Gesell's
more objective data. However, as Gesell pointed out, one youngster may reach a certain stage earlier or later than another of
the same chronological age. The 746 compositions obtained from
this age group displayed a great diversity of views about what
it means to grow up, owing to individual differences and differences in home, school, and neighborhood environments.

Views of Junior High School Students

Early adolescents, even in the same class, show a great diversity in points of view—a diversity which may be related to
variations in their stages of physiological maturity. Most of them
are still fairly optimistic about growing up: "I think that grow-

ing up is wonderful. I think it's wonderful to be a teen-ager—
not to have any responsibilities; to have the privedge to go on
dates, to have fun. I think the best part of your life is when
you're a teen-ager." Some take growing up philosophically: "The
way I feel now is that I'm not going to rush into things, but
take each year as it is and be satisfied." A good philosophy of
life and sound psychology, too! Some take growing up noncha-
lantly: "To me growing up isn't anything different; you just look
older every year that passes. When I was nine years, I used to
say I wished I was fifteen, and now that I am past fifteen, I
don't even notice it." So imperceptible is the process of growing old!

Some of these youngsters also mention mixed feelings, rebel-
liousness, and various problems, but not so frequently as one
might expect. The accent on problems is illustrated by one, who
writes: "All the problems you never had before flock together
all at once and you're left in a quandary as to which problem
you should try to solve first. Schoolwork gets harder and you
get more homework in one night than you ever got before in
a week. There are more problems at home than you can face
at once." This is indeed true. The young adolescent must face
the problems of loss of childhood status, disenchantment with
respect to his unrealistic expectations of growing up, establishing himself in his peer group, and making the transition to heterosexual relations.

A pessimistic view toward growing up was expressed by a
youngster who wrote: "There are times when you feel like you
wanted to grow up as fast as you can, to get it over with."

One highly gifted young adolescent, only fourteen years old,
wrote a most perceptive account of the process of growing up.
The way she thought through the problem will be helpful to
others who are still floundering around in their teen-age perplexities. The following excerpt highlights the importance of parents who understand:

I think that most children are very anxious to be "old" and "sophisticated," and to be treated as such. This is only a natural attitude. You begin to think about people, and the future. You try to

reason out in your own mind, for your personal satisfaction, just what you think about *life, religion,* and *your* pursuit of happiness. In other words, you are beginning to mold your philosophy of life, which you will probably follow through all the future years.

Of course, it is impossible to go from a child right to an adult without going through this in-between stage. You *worry* and you *worry* and you *worry*. However, you simply detest the idea of being adolescent . . . so you decide that you'll just skip it all and be an adult. It all seems *so* simple.

But . . . it is obviously impossible to understand how to even *act* at being an adult unless you've been through a bit of adolescence and thought a few things out. So—it seems to me that the adolescent who goes off on wild binges, drinking and smoking and becoming what is popularly called a juvenile delinquent, is merely "copying" what he thinks a sophisticated man of the world would be doing.

I know this is true, because I went through it myself. I thought I was being sophisticated and old as the *devil,* while actually I was being twice as young and foolish as I was before it all started.

I was lucky—and I can thank my parents for it. Being able to confide in my parents meant that I could get their advice on the whole business without flinching a minute in telling them about it. . . . It's up to the parents *always,* from the very beginning, to make the child feel that, no matter how horrible, they are always there to help. After all, that's what parents are for. . . . There is nothing more comforting to a worried and confused adolescent than parents whom they feel they can go to freely and get aid on a problem good or bad—aid from parents who will understand.

Truly, the children I feel genuine pity for . . . are those who don't feel that they can confide in their parents.[6]

Views of Senior High School Students

Older adolescents are usually more introspective than those in the younger age groups. But the same kind of comments occur with surprising frequency in both junior and senior high school compositions. Both groups show a wide range of attitudes toward growing up—all the way from optimism to pes-

[6] Ruth Strang, *Investing in Yourself,* pp. 79–81, Consumer Education Study. Washington, D.C.: National Association of Secondary-school Principals, 1945.

simism. They mention many of the same problems. They describe similar relations with adults. In the tenth grade some students are optimistic about the future; others recognize that the future holds the possibility of both happiness and unhappiness. Seniors show serious concern about the draft and about finding a vocation.

However, there do seem to be certain trends among older adolescents, although these would have to be verified by developmental studies of the same individuals:

1. An acceptance of increasing freedom plus responsibilities
2. More feelings of indecision and confusion
3. A keener, more realistic recognition of the serious concerns of growing up, such as marriage and military service
4. Increasing concern with problems of morality and religion.

Conflicts with parents still occur, along with the feeling that parents do not understand one. A few older adolescents still seem reluctant to lose the advantages of dependence. These are probably the "satellizers," who from early childhood have chosen dependency rather than independence.

However, we must not expect young people to achieve full emotional and social maturity even by the end of adolescence; one moves toward such maturity all through life. Only a small proportion of the groups studied were aware of all the main manifestations of maturity. They emphasized the capacity for self-direction and for vocational competency. They mentioned less frequently increased sensitivity to and feeling with people, and the ability to relate themselves warmly, constructively, and creatively to others. Very few mentioned ability to set long-range goals and to persist in a worthwhile line of endeavor, to tolerate delayed satisfaction and solitude, and to maintain their integrity as unique persons.

CONCLUDING STATEMENT

Although adults have inferred from observation and recollection how adolescents feel about growing up, it is refreshing to have young people tell us about this in their own words. For some, growing up seems to be an uneventful, gradual process. "Really," wrote a sixteen-year-old, "we don't feel any different, though changes are taking place all the time." For others, growing up means having more privileges and freedom, along with more responsibility. It means making decisions and sometimes learning the hard way. For some, the high point of growing up is acquiring a driver's license and driving a car. To many girls, growing up means dating, marriage, and a family. A large number of boys throughout the high school years are also thinking about a home and a family of their own. Growing up also means receiving more respect and acceptance by adults.

Many face life quite realistically but hopefully. Said one sixteen-year-old, "I've found that most problems can be solved if you put forth a little effort. There's always someone willing to help for the asking."

There are some adolescents, however, to whom growing up is a source of anxiety. They dread relinquishing childhood dependency and assuming responsibility for their own actions. Sometimes they feel completely overwhelmed with problems. In these cases, previous blighting experiences have made them hostile or excessively submissive. Some move against people; some move away from people into their own world of fantasy.

All we can say is that adolescents' feelings about growing up cover a wide range, that most have mixed feelings about it, and that many have feelings of positive expectancy.

Deeper Interpretation

In their own words, adolescents have expressed several basic psychological and psychoanalytical points of view. They have expressed "the impulse toward growth"—social and emotional. The young adolescents have implied increasing "ego strength except in those cases in which the child is struggling with conflicts of such intensity that his ego is powerless to deal with them." [7]

As parents learn to become more understanding and reason-

[7] Irene M. Josselyn, *The Adolescent and His World,* p. 16. New York: Family Service Association of America, 1952.

ably permissive, conflicts in values between parent and child are minimized. Perhaps such changes in parental attitudes may account for the fact that a relatively small number of adolescents mentioned serious conflict with their parents. If we knew the time of puberty for each individual case included in this study, we might find the bulk of negative comments occurring shortly before and after its onset: puberty has been described as a period of increased sensitivity, resentment, and irritability. According to Josselyn, "practically every child is somewhat overwhelmed for a short period by the effects of the physiological maturing process. His defenses are inadequate to deal with the strain to which he is exposed." [8]

In the adolescents' compositions we do not get an appreciation of the influence of the past on their present adjustment. They do not show how the groundwork for their present struggle toward emancipation and toward resolving their more serious conflicts is laid in their previous experiences of growing up.

Nor do many of them emphasize the loss of stability and security which is involved in a change from a period of relative equilibrium to a new status. It is surprising that so few refer to uncertainties and pain, to "resistance to change and ambivalent feelings," to feelings of anxiety and insecurity,[9] and that so many emphasize the positive aspects of growing up. It may be that in some cases the feelings of anxiety are too intense and deep-seated to be analyzed. Still it is significant that in the written statements of these groups of adolescents "the impulse toward growth" is expressed more frequently than the resistance to change.

COMPREHENSION QUESTIONS

1. What was Stanley Hall's view of the way adolescents feel about growing up? What is the modern view? What do adolescents themselves say about it?

[8] *Ibid.*, p. 24.
[9] David P. Ausubel, *Ego Development and the Personality Disorders*, p. 105. New York: Grune & Stratton, Inc., 1952.

2. What range of attitudes toward growing up do you find in any group?

3. What are some of the factors that might influence adolescents to take a positive or a negative view of growing up?

4. Which feelings about growing up are mentioned most frequently by adolescents?

5. What common causes of frustration do young people mention?

6. How does the recognition by adolescents of the responsibilities of growing up compare with the general feeling among adults that adolescents are irresponsible? How do you account for this discrepancy?

7. As you read the chapter as a whole, what is your impression of the relative degrees of optimism and pessimism with which adolescents view growing up?

STUDY PROJECTS

1. If you are working with adolescents, get their views about "How it feels to be growing up." Use the interview, discussion, or composition technique.

2. Interview some adolescents who have written compositions on this subject to see if they can tell how they arrived at their present attitude toward growing up. Relate their attitudes to their stage of physiological maturity.

3. Try to find out why there are such wide individual differences in adolescents' expressed attitudes about growing up.

4. Try to help an insecure adolescent view the process of growing up more hopefully; help him to perceive more clearly its possible advantages; consider with him ways in which he may cope with his environment more successfully.

FOR FURTHER STUDY

BARUCH, DOROTHY W., *How to Live with Your Teen-ager.* New York: McGraw-Hill Book Company, Inc., 1953.

BELL, HOWARD M., *Youth Tell Their Story.* Washington, D.C.: American Council on Education, 1938.

BLOS, PETER, *The Adolescent Personality.* New York: Appleton-Century-Crofts, Inc., 1941.

FRANK, LAWRENCE K., *Individual Development.* New York: Double-day & Company, Inc., 1955.

GESELL, ARNOLD, FRANCES L. ILG, and LOUISE BATES AMES, *Youth, the Years from Ten to Sixteen,* chap. XIV. New York: Harper & Brothers, 1956.

LANDIS, PAUL H., *Understanding Teen-agers.* New York: Appleton-Century-Crofts, Inc., 1955.

MALM, MARGUERITE, and OLIS G. JAMISON, *Adolescence.* New York: McGraw-Hill Book Company, Inc., 1952.

OJEMANN, RALPH H., *What Research Says to the Teacher: Personality Adjustment of Individual Children.* Washington, D.C.: National Education Association, American Educational Research Association, Department of Classroom Teachers, 1954.

REDL, FRITZ, and DAVID WINEMAN, *Controls from Within.* Glencoe, Ill.: Free Press, 1952.

REDL, FRITZ, and WILLIAM W. WATTENBERG, *Mental Hygiene in Teaching.* New York: Harcourt, Brace and Company, Inc., 1951.

ROTHNEY, JOHN W. M., *The High School Student: A Book of Cases.* New York: The Dryden Press, Inc., 1953.

STRANG, RUTH, "Inner World of Gifted Adolescents," *Journal of Exceptional Children,* vol. 16 (January, 1950), pp. 97–101.

———, *Introduction to Child Study.* New York: The Macmillan Company, 1951.

———, "Manifestations of Maturity in Adolescents," *Mental Hygiene,* vol. 33 (October, 1949), pp. 563–569.

Fiction and Popular Articles

BENET, STEPHEN VINCENT, "Freedom's a Hard-bought Thing," *Selected Works,* vol. II. New York: Rinehart & Company, Inc., 1942.

* CATHER, WILLA, "Paul's Case," in Bennett Cerf (ed.), *Great Modern Short Stories.* New York: Modern Library, Inc., 1942.

EVANS, ELIZABETH, "In Defense of My Generation," *NEA Journal,* vol. 64 (March, 1955), pp. 139–140.

LANDIS, PAUL H., *Coming of Age: Problems of Teen-agers,* Public Affairs Pamphlet No. 234. New York: Public Affairs Press, 1956.

* McCULLERS, CARSON, *The Member of the Wedding.* New York: New Directions, 1951.

REDL, FRITZ, *Preadolescents, What Makes Them Tick.* Chicago: Association for Family Living, 1944.

SHAW, CLIFFORD, *The Jack-roller.* Chicago: University of Chicago Press, 1930.

* TARKINGTON, BOOTH, *Alice Adams.* New York: Grosset & Dunlap, Inc., 1921.

* Fiction.

Audio-visual Aids

He Acts His Age. 15 minutes. Sound. McGraw-Hill.

Meeting the Needs of Adolescence. 19 minutes. Sound. McGraw-Hill.

Personal Problems of Adolescent Youth. 43 frames. Ohio State University.

The Wedding of Palo. 70 minutes. Sound, black and white. Brandon Films, Inc.

PART TWO

Adolescents' Perception and Attainment of Their Developmental Tasks

THE ADOLESCENT VIEWS HIMSELF

CHAPTER 5

Continuity of Growth toward Maturity

Adolescence is both a unique period and a continuous part of an individual's total life span. Viewed in the context of what has gone before, the stages of preadolescence and adolescence are psychologically explainable. Adolescents pass through phases, just as the baby does in learning to walk or talk, and, like the baby, they may reach these stages at different rates. Each period of physical, social, and emotional growth has its special tasks and challenges, the response to which is shadowed by the individual's past and guided by his expectations of what is still to come. The best preparation for the future is to live fully in the present.

A certain psychological predestination has begun to operate before the age of ten. Basic personality patterns have been established; intellectual development can be predicted, under nor-

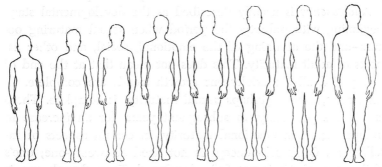

The same individual at different stages of growth. Note changes in size and body build.

179

mal environmental conditions, with considerable accuracy. Even characteristics observed during the first year of life seem to persist—for example, the tendency to laugh or to cry readily. Predictions made on the basis of careful observation of preschool children's behavior are remarkably accurate. The kind of problems an adolescent faces and the kind of adjustment he makes to them depend a great deal on the kind of child he was prior to adolescence.

Much that appears to be inexplicable in teen-age behavior could be understood if more were known about the individual's early relationships and experiences. The child who feels secure in his parents' love, confident of his own abilities, and successful in making and keeping friends is likely to achieve adolescent independence without much emotional "storm and stress"; he is likely to be able to accept and appreciate others as he himself has been accepted and appreciated. On the other hand, extreme anxiety, aggression, or withdrawal may arise from deprivation of affection or lack of tenderness, frequent experience of failure, domination by an adult or older brother or sister, or innumerable other early experiences. However, this does not mean that maladjusted children always become maladjusted adolescents. Some are able, through satisfying interpersonal relations, to perceive themselves in a new light, to modify their behavior, to sort out childhood habits and build on the positive factors in their personality. Others find the additional strains and pressures of adolescence more than they can cope with.

Adolescence is usually described as the developmental stage beginning with puberty—the period when sexual maturing occurs—and the attaining of the emotional, social, and other aspects of adult maturity. This does not mean that at the end of this period all the adolescent growth trends are complete. In fact, none, except perhaps sexual maturity, is complete. There is still the possibility, in subsequent years, for an increase in independence, in emotional maturity, in certain aspects of intelligence. One's self-concept is not fixed at twenty-one; one's philosophy of life is not fully developed. Even though one is hemmed in by a rigid pattern of life, there is a possibility of progress as long as one retains the capacity to learn. Adolescence simply marks a peak in human growth and change; it does not complete growth nor preclude further change. After adolescence, however, change is usually less marked and more difficult to achieve.

The word "adolescence" is derived from the Latin verb *adolescere*, meaning *to grow, to grow to maturity*. In *A Winter's Tale* Shakespeare sets about the same age limits to adolescence as do modern psychologists, but speaks disparagingly of it: "I would there were no age between ten and three and twenty, or that youth would sleep out the rest." Quite the opposite view of adolescence was recently expressed by a seventeen-year-old boy in an interview: "Teen-age years are the best. You're coming out of childhood and going into manhood. You don't have to bother with military service or voting yet. You're not responsible for a family, or other things that tie you down." It is true, however, that adolescence involves a series of changes that make individuals especially vulnerable during this period.

The Gesell Institute report [1] describes growth patterns from ten to sixteen similar to the developmental sequences of infancy and childhood. While appropriate, perhaps, for children below the age of six, this method of describing characteristics of adolescents according to specific ages is invalid because of the varying rates of physical maturing and the diversity of environmental conditions during these years. However, in the development of any child growing up, there are probably periods of relative equilibrium, "seasons of calm weather," times when he withdraws from his parents into his own thoughts and times when he is more outgoing, enthusiastic, and energetic. There comes a time, too, when he is more ready to examine his own feelings and to weave the loose strands of personality together into a more mature pattern. The course of adolescent behavior cannot be definitely charted year by year because "every child has an individual pattern of growth unique to him. . . ." [2]

[1] Arnold Gesell, Frances L. Ilg, and Louise B. Ames, *Youth, the Years from Ten to Sixteen.* New York: Harper & Brothers, 1956.

[2] *Ibid.,* p. 15.

Adults are faced with the practical problem of helping teenagers during this period of their life. Parents especially may find this a stormy period for them. Some may be unable to relinquish the emotional satisfaction of having their children dependent on them, or to tolerate intellectual superiority or greater emotional maturity in an adolescent son or daughter.

The goal of growth is maturity, evolving over many years. Although maturity is manifested in many ways and in different degrees in various individuals, a few characteristics of the emotionally mature person may be mentioned:

1. Ability to feel with others, see things from their point of view, and be creative and happy rather than antagonistic or indifferent in one's relation with others

2. Objectivity toward oneself and acceptance of one's emotions as natural; ability to examine one's behavior critically and modify it accordingly

3. Ability to select realistic, worthwhile goals, both immediate and long term; to organize one's thinking and acting around these goals, and sustain the tension needed to achieve them

4. Ability to make adjustments to situations, to remain flexible in one's roles, and to modify one's concepts in line with reality

5. Ability to accept unexpected stresses, frustrations, and disappointments as inevitable parts of life, without experiencing intense emotional reactions and without abandoning well-considered, appropriate goals

6. Ability to give as well as to receive affection

7. Ability to form opinions based on facts and sound reasoning and to hold to them when compromises would violate fundamental convictions [3]

During the adolescent years, progress toward emotional as well as physical maturity can be expected.

PREPARATORY YEARS

Every adolescent has a past. He is born with certain capacities and resources. Among the most pervasive and determining

[3] Ruth Strang, "Manifestations of Maturity in Adolescents," *Mental Hygiene,* vol. 33 (October, 1949), pp. 563–564.

is the ability to see relationships and to organize the experiences provided by persons and objects in his environment. The fulfillment of his intellectual potential depends not only on whether he has opportunities to organize and relate all sorts of things and symbols in his environment, but also on whether the people who surround him have realistic and positive expectations of him, and on whether he gets satisfaction from his efforts. The fulfillment of his emotional potential depends a great deal on

whether the parent or parent-substitute provides conditions in which the infant can build a sense of trust and in which the older child can achieve independence without hostility and socially acceptable behavior without intense, unanalyzable anxiety.

Important studies have demonstrated the continuity of development. Every aspect of adolescent development has its roots in the preceding years. For example, differences between early- and late-maturing boys and girls have been traced back to early childhood; unequal increases in the amount of the sex hormone affect the rate at which the individual evolves appropriate masculine or feminine behavior. Early experiences greatly influence particular phases of his ego development, such as the degree to which an adolescent clings to childhood dependence. Adolescence tests the quality of personality structure built during preceding years. Adolescent personality problems can be traced back to early roots, although adolescents themselves may not be aware of their origins.

During early adolescence, environmental conditions, such as overprotective or possessive parents, too exacting social pressures, conflicting attitudes among adults, and discontinuity of values between childhood and adulthood may increase the number and severity of problems, which may persist into subsequent adolescent and adult years. But adolescence per se does not create basic personality problems; it may precipitate long-existent or long-dormant difficulties by putting the individual under special stress.

Many adolescents may not be so successful in coping with their problems as this sixteen-year-old girl apparently was:

When I moved from a town into this larger city, it was the middle of the year. It was in kindergarten. The children whom the teachers thought might have trouble in learning to read were given special attention, so that when they reached the first grade, they would be able to work along at the same speed as the others. But I entered after this special help in reading had been started. Consequently, when I got to the first grade I wasn't up to par, and ever since then I have had some difficulty in my reading.

In different classes, when I have been called on to read aloud, I would sometimes pronounce a word wrong. This seemed to sound funny to the class and they would laugh at me. This was always embarrassing to me. Some of my teachers would say to the class, "Everyone sometimes makes mistakes." I tried my best not to mind, and I practiced reading at home to improve. Since the teachers didn't help me to overcome my problem, I tried myself. In my later years if I made a slight slip in reading I would just laugh with the class. I have cured myself from getting all upset.

However, when it comes my turn to read aloud in class, I still get a little nervous for I always am wondering whether the class will laugh at me if I make a mistake.

This girl apparently built up an inner world of perceptions and convictions that determined whether she would be upset by ridicule or criticism, or accept it. She worked harder, practiced more, and obtained help on her reading rather than saying,

"I can't learn to read; I'm hopeless." By changing her perception of this situation she was able to exert some control over it. She tried to change her attitude toward conditions that could not be corrected in the present. Such learned ways of meeting life situations are very important in adolescent adjustment.

If conditions have been and continue to be favorable, the transition from childhood into adult life can be fairly smooth sailing. It need not be characterized by severe emotional upheavals. Studies of people in other cultures, as well as of adolescents in our own, have shown this to be possible.

THREE STAGES OF GROWTH

Three phases or periods of adolescence may be recognized, each merging imperceptibly into the next, each dependent upon earlier growth trends and experiences. First is the prepubescent period, in which the growth spurt occurs. It begins at about the age of ten or eleven and extends to fourteen or fifteen, or whenever puberty occurs. Second is the early adolescent period, starting with physiological maturity. It extends from puberty to the sixteenth or seventeenth year. Most youngsters in this stage are in high school, though some are in the last years of elementary school and a few are in college. By the end of this period major physical changes are generally complete. Third is later adolescence. A few of the young people in this stage are in the last years of high school; most are of college age. They are either in a college or other educational institution, or married, or working, or trying to find work.

The Prepubescent Period

This is the period of the growth spurt preceding puberty. During this period children tend to be self-sufficient and unabashed. Most of them have learned ways of dealing with the demands made upon them and have their own standards of fair play and justice. This gives them self-confidence. They look forward to growing up. Most of them are looking forward to

entering high school and to gaining more personal-social freedom. A chum of the same sex means much to them. Each of the two friends feels genuine affection for the other; they want to do what is best for their chum and to meet his or her expectations of them. As a result of this friendship they may correct certain undesirable personality trends. In general, they are most concerned with the immediate future: what teacher they are going to have next, how a projected trip is going to turn out.

Nine- and ten-year-olds may speak very positively about growing up. The girls are concerned with marriage. "When I get about nineteen," one nine-year-old girl said, "I wish to be married. I hope to go to college and be a doctor and then have about seven children. I will not marry a farmer. I think I've had enough of farms." Another girl of the same age was worried about getting "a good husband that will work and behave." Some have their future all worked out in detail, as did this girl:

I am ten years old. I wish I will grow older soon. Because I want to be married, because I want to get a baby girl. I want to be twenty-one when I get married. I am glad I am a girl because girls have prettier clothes then boys do. My baby's name is going to be

Bridget Ann. I want to go to Texas on my honeymoon. I am going to buy a house in Texas.

Girls of this age commonly take a favorable attitude toward future marriage. But their interest at this stage seems to be rather like playing house, imaginatively, with little emotional involvement and concern for reality as adults perceive it.

Most boys of the same age, though equally positive about their future, have little use for womenfolk. The following comment by a ten-year-old boy is quite typical: "I have thought a lot about growing up. I want to take over science. I don't like girls. I want to be a bachelor and be a mechanical enginer. I like to go hunting. I want to drive a plane."

Even though changes in body-size and the appearance of secondary sex characteristics may give maturing girls a sense of unfamiliarity with their bodies, these changes are not so disturbing as the later attainment of full physiological maturity. When they are playing games they have learned or sports they have practiced, their coordination is usually good.

They are trying to break away from childhood, sorting over their childish ways of behaving, discarding some and retaining and modifying others. Finding a close friend and a place in a peer group is one of the major developmental tasks of this period.

Within the limitations of their experience, children moving rapidly toward puberty are fairly comfortable in a world of reality which they are learning to master. If they cannot master it, they are more likely to avoid its unpleasant aspects than to resort to neurotic defenses. Their protests to parents more often represent a clash in standards and values than any deep inner conflicts. Even in major tragedies, they keep their balance by turning to the real world of people and interests. One older girl wrote in an autobiography of the loss of an only brother and a much-loved grandmother during this earlier period; yet she was apparently able to carry on her school and other activities without any serious breakdown.

Parents and teachers expect prepubescent children to take on more responsibility and to be fairly reliable. They should recognize their self-assertion as a path toward achieving individuality and self-direction. They should welcome their interest in the group as an opportunity to learn to get along with other persons and as another step toward emancipation from close family ties. If the preadolescent's behavior annoys them, they should try to see its significance in the child's development.[4] Adults are often pleased with the way these youngsters assert their growing independence while retaining a reasonable conformity to accepted standards. Teachers should treat these children with respect, enrich the curriculum with new experiences and practical applications of science and social studies, and with art, music, and literature, and provide opportunities for group activity.

Early Adolescence

Preadolescence merges into early adolescence with different degrees of abruptness. The transition is usually marked by increasing instability. Even six months before puberty, manifested in girls by the onset of menstruation, and less easily identified in boys by the increased prominence of secondary sex characteristics and seminal emissions, there seems to be an increasing instability. The early adolescent period, which coincides most nearly with the junior high school grades, is usually considered the most difficult time for youngsters and for their elders. Their emotions are often intense; their changes in mood are often rapid and violent. They seek excitement. Being treated like children almost always arouses their anger. Yet underneath their rebellion, their sloppy clothes or simulated sophistication, and their valiant efforts to grow up is a pervasive feeling of insecurity and bewilderment. They worry about their appearance and about being normal. Believe it or not, many worry about their schoolwork. On check lists of problems, they mention concern about study methods, failure in a subject, and other academic considerations more frequently than any other kind of problem. Though they may not mention problems of social relations as often, they worry a great deal about being liked and being ac-

[4] William H. Burton, "The Preadolescent: Rebel in Our Society," *Education*, vol. 76 (December, 1955), pp. 222–225.

cepted in groups of their own age. Some of them have religious doubts and feel guilty about things they have done in secret.

There is likely to be a considerable change in young adolescents from the seventh to the eighth grade. One teacher noted the following changes:

There is a tremendous change in their personal appearance. By their own efforts, the eighth-graders are the neatest and cleanest pupils in our school. Some of the girls begin to use lipstick, but may wipe it off before returning home.

The boys still do not want the girls to participate in their games very often, nor to work with them on class projects. They do, however, like square dancing and often ask for more time than I had at first scheduled for it. The girls also prefer most often to participate in activities by themselves. They tend to break into smaller groups, which are sometimes critical of one another. "Did you see that picture Sue and Anne are making?" they will say. "They copied it from ours."

Very few of my eighth-grade boys have any clear idea of their life work. And fewer still could give any sound reason for the vocation they have happened to choose. The girls know more about the careers they have tentatively chosen—mostly teaching, nursing, secretarial work, airplane stewardess.

In relationships with their peers the boys are superior to the girls. They have arguments, of course, and sometimes a fist fight, but become reconciled within a few days. When girls run into difficulty with each other, they usually do not "make up" so quickly.

Even the eighth-graders whose behavior is least desirable in my room have good relations with the younger children in our school. For example, in choosing two first-grade children to be marshals at graduation, they tried to prevent the children who were not chosen from being too disappointed. Some will sing songs and play games with groups of first-grade children on the playground, and set a good example to the younger children in the school.

My greatest difficulty in working with eighth-grade pupils has been during the last few weeks of the school year. When they are almost finished with elementary school education and anticipating high school with its forms, parties, and other activities, they seem to become sophisticated too quickly.

They listen intently and have great respect for what the high school

students tell them. I have asked some of these high school youngsters to come back to give their advice to the eighth grade. What they say makes a definite impression on my class.

One of their greatest concerns is about their report cards. They have learned that in high school they will be put into ability groups, determined in part by the marks they earn in my eighth grade. Consequently their anxiety is evident for a few days before report cards are handed out. Some pupils put forth greater effort after the marking period; with others I have noticed no such effort.

I consider working with eighth-grade youngsters a challenge and an opportunity.

This seems to be a fairly representative general description of youngsters of this age in a small middle-class town or suburban community. In a delinquency area of a large city, or in a wealthy residential section or a private school, the pupils' behavior would deviate markedly, as suggested in Chapter 2.

The unique characteristic of this early adolescent period, extending from the rather abrupt appearance of the sex drive to the establishment of an individual pattern of sexual behavior, is the tensions associated with sex expression. According to Sullivan,[5] three interacting and sometimes contradictory needs must be handled in early adolescence: "the need for personal security," or reduction of anxiety; "the need for intimacy" as expressed in friendship with the same sex during preadolescence; and the need for satisfaction of the sex drive. Young adolescents are faced with the problem of extending the intimacy they had enjoyed with their chum to a member of the other sex. Even much of their group activity may be concerned with establishing hetero-sexual relations.

Young adolescents are at the crossroads. Circumstances in their environment, interacting with the instability of this stage of growth, often cause marked changes in their behavior, un-favorable or favorable. A teacher noticed great changes in the behavior of a girl called Susie, whom she had observed over a period of five years.

After the death of her parents when she was eleven years old, Susie went to live with her grandmother. Until she reached the eighth grade her attendance and conduct had been commendable. Soon after the beginning of that school year the eighth-grade pupils were practicing a play. Susie volunteered to help with the singing. She was not in the play because the girls in the cast were to wear white dresses, and she said that she felt she should not ask her grandmother to buy her a white dress. At that time Susie seemed to get along amiably with the other mem-bers of her class. She had a best friend with whom she sometimes traded part of her lunch. They palled around at school and saw each other on the week ends. During the latter part of the eighth-grade year, she began to do poorer work and to be absent a great deal. She said her absences were due to the fact that her grandmother could not provide the proper clothes for her. Her clothes had become shabby, and she no longer had spending

[5] Harry S. Sullivan, *The Interpersonal Theory of Psychiatry*, pp. 263–296. New York: W. W. Norton & Company, Inc., 1953.

money for lunch times or for school purposes. At this time Susie's behavior began to change. Instead of being timid, she was getting "uppity" and boisterous. She was becoming very much interested in boys and no longer seemed interested in school.

The change in Susie's behavior may have resulted from any of a number of conditions: a changed relationship with her grandmother, to whom Susie was becoming a heavy burden; the awakening of sex interests as her reproductive system matured; a shift from playing with friends at home to playing away from home; repressed hostility arising from early deprivation of affection. These or other conditions might account for Susie's restlessness, moodiness, rebellion, and changed attitude toward adults.

The following picture of a gifted boy (IQ 130) in the last year of junior high school also illustrates concretely some of the characteristics of the early adolescent period:

Terry was of medium build and not yet physiologically mature. He was interested in all sports, particularly basketball. He wore overalls to school and a white shirt and tie to church. He readily worked in small groups of his own age. Although he did not particularly appreciate having girls in the groups, he would manage to cooperate with them. At parties he would mingle with boys and leave the girls to themselves. He had one definite goal: to go to college. His vocational ambitions were varied, and changed from day to day. He had several home duties, such as mowing the yard, washing dishes, etc., which he attended to faithfully. He took responsibility for taking several younger neighborhood children to and from school. He enjoyed associating with older boys during the noon hour but did not usually like to work with them in club projects or school activities. He had apparently learned that the most comfortable way to get along with his teachers, parents, and other adults was to cooperate with them rather than to rebel against demands that were fairly reasonable. In solving his everyday problems he would first arrive at a solution himself and, if in doubt, discuss his solution with an adult.

Terry had passed through the stage of being antagonistic toward adults, and was beginning to meet them on a more mature level. Through a period of increasing self-awareness he had succeeded in reconciling the conflicting desires for independent responsibilities and home and group loyalties.

Early adolescence is characterized (1) by a variety of changes in physical development, (2) by increased emotional stress arising from the difficulties encountered in adapting to a changing self as well as from the revival of old problems unsolved in early childhood, and finally, (3) by the tension created by altered social status and by confusion in re-orienting to both the peer group and the adult world.[6]

The role of the parent changes, but is nonetheless important. Owing to increasing age and changing circumstances, the parents of adolescents may be so preoccupied with their own problems that they may not be as patient or as understanding as they once were. They may neglect their teen-age children or make excessive demands on them. A combination of unfavorable conditions may prove overwhelming to a child who enters adolescence with emotional difficulties. Such a bewildered adolescent may be helped to handle at least one problem area successfully. During this transition period the adolescent often appears to be confused and inconsistent. "The support which he receives must not only include acceptance and stimulation but must also furnish controls when his own are not functioning adequately."[7]

Later Adolescence

The later adolescent period, following the period just described, generally begins with the junior and senior years of high school and extends to the legal age of entering adulthood. These older adolescents constitute a sizeable group. In 1954 there were more than 13 million young people aged eighteen to twenty-one. This number is increasing. It has been estimated

---

[6] Irwin M. Marcus, M.D., "The Problem of Evaluation," *The Adolescent Exceptional Child*, Proceedings of the 1954 Spring Conference of The Woods Schools, p. 11. Langhorne, Pa.: The Woods Schools, 1954. Reprinted by permission of the author and The Woods Schools.

[7] *Ibid.*, p. 12.

that the eighteen-to-twenty-one age group will increase by 70 per cent from 1954 to 1970.[8]

During this period adolescents tend to complete their physical growth, attain mature attitudes toward achieving identity, and move toward emotional maturity. They continue to develop intellectually, with sub-abilities showing somewhat different growth patterns and increasing divergence from one another. The older adolescents' capacity for independence increases with their advance in self-direction. Faced with the immediate prospect of going to work, they think of themselves in relation to vocational plans. In the process of coming to terms with themselves, many struggle to achieve a philosophy of life and to understand life's purpose, values, and meaning.

One of their most important developmental goals is to learn about themselves and find themselves (see Chapter 13). They need to know their strengths and weaknesses—to assess what they can do and what they probably cannot do successfully. Their self-concept includes, as a very important element, their feelings about themselves, which range from self-contempt to complacency. This self-concept has been developing ever since they experienced their earliest awareness of themselves. Experiences of being loved and cherished as a baby, of achieving autonomy during the middle preschool years, of succeeding in beginning reading and other school subjects, of being liked by one's peers, of contributing to and being accepted by a group— all contribute to the adolescent's concept of himself. Since many of these factors are exterior to the personality, depending upon environmental conditions, one would not expect the curve of self-discovery to be closely related to other growth curves.

Another important achievement is what Erikson has called "achieving intimacy." This involves establishing a warm, mature relation, usually with a person of the opposite sex, but sometimes with a friend or relative. Everyone needs someone with whom, as Stevenson put it, he can talk "out of his heart freely." Early

---

[8] Joseph G. Smith and Dael L. Wolfle, "Some General Problems of Educating Post-high-school Youth," *Review of Educational Research*, vol. 24 (October, 1954), pp. 269–276.

relations with parents, brothers and sisters, and friends often persist into later life. Some persons even achieve the intimacy of marriage before the end of adolescence. An increasing number of boys and girls marry before or soon after graduating from high school. There are so many married students now attending college that many institutions provide special housing facilities for them and conduct special programs for students' wives.

During this period antagonism toward adults decreases. Having established their status with their age group, older adolescents may reestablish their relations with adults on a man-to-man basis. Realizing that adults are influential in helping them to achieve their educational and vocational goals, older adolescents tend to control their behavior with adults better than their behavior with peers. They are still worried about relations with the opposite sex; dating problems loom large. Increasingly concerned with preparation for a career, they may be expected to develop more serious and sustained interests. Wasting time and flitting from one thing to another are indications that an older adolescent is not "acting his age." Through introspection they can understand themselves better and can gain insight into their own strengths and weaknesses and those of others. They should achieve a certain stability and coordination of personality and grow in spiritual qualities through being of service. Helping them to succeed in these adolescent tasks is the responsibility of adults. While recognizing the common tendencies we have just mentioned, adults must be very flexible to allow for individual differences, which widen with age.

This is a time when binding decisions are made—choosing whether to quit school or to seek further education, choosing a life partner, choosing a vocation.

They are expected to develop desirable attitudes and function as good citizens. This goal can best be accomplished by taking advantage of opportunities to perform responsible tasks in the community.[9]

One may obtain glimpses of the inner world of older adolescents by reading the following personal accounts by freshman college girls: [10]

When I want to study or do my homework, I just can't do it. I want to study yet I can't seem to make myself sit down and actually do it.

I've always been timid about participating in class discussions.

There has been animosity between my father and me for the past few years. I sincerely would like to have a better understanding with him, but I do not know how to go about it.

My mother died six months ago. As a result of this I was left alone with only my father. He sits in a dark house, brooding over my mother's death all the time. . . . He is extremely jealous of anyone who likes me. He is extremely afraid someone will take me away from him. It looks like he expects me to take care of him the rest of his life.

My girl friend is one who wants and thinks that one friend is enough. I like her but I can't spend all my time with her.

---

[9] Karl C. Garrison, "Developmental Tasks and Problems of the Late Adolescent Period," *Education,* vol. 76 (December, 1955), pp. 232–235.

[10] Kay Genet Otto, "Certain Group Procedures Applied in Health Education," unpublished doctoral project, Teachers College, Columbia University, New York. 1955.

My boy friend and I have gone in for heavy petting, because we feel it is a way of showing our love, and also because we enjoy it. But I have a guilty feeling that I'm doing something wrong. There is no one I can really talk over this problem with.

Concern with school and with future success, problems of family relations, efforts to work out satisfactory relations with age-mates, and especially with the opposite sex—these themes recur frequently when adolescents write about themselves.

How do such adolescent trends project into the future? Do interests established during adolescence persist into adult life? Can the rejected child and adolescent become a self-accepting person?

Some persons are perennial adolescents. They represent the tragedy of arrested adolescent development. This failure to accomplish the developmental tasks of childhood and adolescence is seen in the immaturity of the alcoholic, the petulance of the demanding wife, the apathy of the old person who has no interests or hobbies to occupy his time.

If, on the other hand, the individual has lived fully in each stage of his development, he is ready for the tasks ahead. Then the middle years of life have a desirable continuity with the past and become a rewarding experience.

ADULT EMOTIONAL EXPANSIVENESS

Emotional expansion in middle life partly depends on what interests and hobbies the individual has cultivated earlier. Gardening, handwork, art and music, friendships with a variety of people—these are some of the interests in which people in middle life invest their emotions. Activities and relationships like these are especially important for middle-aged mothers whose children no longer need their attentive care.

With parents who married late, the adolescence of their children often coincides with the menopause, which generally occurs between the ages of forty and fifty-five. This means that both parents and children may experience special problems of adjustment at the same time.

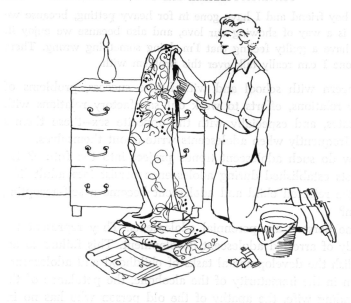

INTEGRITY IN THE LATER YEARS OF LIFE

Maintaining integrity in middle or old age means accepting one's life cycle as something that had to be. It means achieving harmony between the past and the future. Somerset Maugham described it in this way:

I have shaped my life in accordance with a certain design, with a beginning, a middle and an end. . . . We are the product of our natures and our environment. I have not made the pattern I thought best, or even the pattern I should have liked to make, but merely that which seemed feasible. There are better patterns than mine. . . . The best pattern of all is the husbandman's, who ploughs his land and reaps his crop, who enjoys his toil and enjoys his leisure, loves, marries, begets children and dies.[11]

It is difficult to accept a decrease in status as part of one's life. Most people do not want to relinquish their former activities;

[11] W. Somerset Maugham, *The Summing Up*, pp. 293–294. Copyright 1938 by W. Somerset Maugham. Reprinted by permission of Doubleday & Company, Inc.

some are temperamentally unable to accept a petering-out process.

Fortunately, aging is so gradual a process that we are scarcely aware of it most of the time. Fortunately, too, abilities decline at different rates. For example, language ability lapses least with age. Loss of ability is most apparent with respect to learning new skills and acquiring knowledge in new fields. Those who are intellectually superior resist old age better and show it less than those who are less keen. Although most people always feel "a need to be needed," this becomes more acute with age.

ADOLESCENT GOALS

The goals of adolescents are reflected in the tasks they face and the problems they are trying to solve. These tasks, often appearing in the form of problems, relate to aspects of development which must be accomplished before the individual can reach a higher stage of maturity. The adolescent may be working on a number of these tasks simultaneously. Success in one facilitates progress in another; failure in one may interfere with his accomplishment in other areas of his life.

There have been many statements of "adolescent tasks." Havighurst [12] most fully defined and described ten developmental tasks of adolescence. Erik Erikson [13] mentioned eight psycho-social tasks covering the whole life span. Corey [14] evolved a list of five hurdles for teen-agers, which corresponds closely to the perceptive formulation of adolescent problems made by Leta S. Hollingworth [15] in 1928.

[12] Robert J. Havighurst, *Developmental Tasks and Education*, pp. 33–63. New York: Longmans, Green & Co., Inc., 1952.

[13] Erik Erikson, *Childhood and Society*. New York: W. W. Norton & Company, Inc., 1950.

[14] Stephen M. Corey, "The Developmental Tasks of Youth," *The American High School: Its Responsibility and Opportunity*, Eighth Yearbook of the John Dewey Society (H. L. Caswell, ed.). New York: Harper & Brothers, 1946.

[15] Leta S. Hollingworth, *The Psychology of the Adolescent*. New York: Appleton-Century-Crofts, Inc., 1928.

These developmental tasks are accomplished over a long stretch of years. The adolescent is always working on them in one way or another. By accomplishing them he is able to bridge the gap between what he was as a child and what he is to become as an adult. These tasks constitute a unit: if a person has done well with them up to a certain age, he is likely to complete them successfully.

Many studies have been made of "adolescent problems." Most of them involve the use of some kind of inventory or check list. For example, Morris [16] gave the 1950 revision of the Mooney Problem Check List to 500 students in five central schools, grades eight to twelve, in a rural county of New York State. Nardone [17] administered the same check list to students in grades seven, eight, and nine in a rural-suburban high school. In another part of the country, Elias [18] obtained information on adolescent problems from a check list given to 5,500 high school seniors. Withey [19] interviewed over one thousand boys, ages fourteen, fifteen, and sixteen, and summarized the problems they mentioned. Little and Chapman [20] made a survey of about five thousand high school students to identify their worries. They were simply asked to write about their worries as they saw them. From their unstructured free responses the investigators obtained information about the problems that seemed of most concern to students. In making surveys of guidance work in several large cities, the present author obtained compositions on "When I felt disturbed or at a loss" from representative samplings of high school students.

[16] Glyn Morris, "A Search for Pupil Viewpoints: How Five Schools Made Plans Based on Pupil Needs," *Clearing House,* vol. 29 (November, 1954), pp. 131–134.

[17] Michael Nardone, "Guiding Oyster Bay High School Students," unpublished doctoral project, Teachers College, Columbia University, New York, 1955.

[18] L. J. Elias, *High School Youth Look at Their Problems.* Pullman, Wash.: State College of Washington, January, 1949.

[19] Stephen B. Withey, "What Boys See as Their Problem," *Education,* vol. 76 (December, 1955), pp. 210–213.

[20] Wilson Little and A. L. Chapman, *Developmental Guidance in Secondary Schools,* pp. 1–16. New York: McGraw-Hill Book Company, Inc., 1953.

There are individual and group differences in the numbers and kinds of problems which adolescents report. Groups of low socio-economic status reported a higher percentage of problems, and many more problems relating to what to do after high school, than did students in the higher socio-economic level.[21] The lower group was much more concerned about financing a college education, selecting a vocation that does not require a college degree, finding jobs open to high school graduates, and finding a part-time job to earn spending money. They also expressed more concern about acquiring social skills such as speaking before a group, carrying on a conversation, learning to dance, and gaining access to places for wholesome recreation. They complained more often than the higher socio-economic group that they had no quiet place to study and could not get along with brothers and sisters. They wished they had a room of their own. More of them reported needing attention to their teeth. More expressed the feeling that they were not so smart as others. The higher socio-economic group was not free from these worries, but fewer mentioned them in the study.

These and similar sources of information reveal major problem areas. There is a high degree of agreement among these studies. In some communities, especially rural and rural-suburban, study problems and failure in academic work are mentioned most frequently. In other schools problems of family relations and social relations among peers head the list. Next in order, usually, are concerns about the future: further education, vocation, military service; personality and character development; part-time jobs and other ways of earning money; and health. If stated positively, these "adolescent problems" become "developmental tasks." Or, looking at it in another way, we can say that adolescents encounter certain problems in attaining their developmental goals. Let us now look at adolescent growth in the latter way.

1. The goal of physical competency—accepting and making the most of one's physical capacities. Following are some of the

21 R. E. Horton and H. H. Remmers, *Some Ethical Values of Youth, Compared over the Years,* Report No. 38. Purdue Opinion Panel, vol. 13, no. 2, April, 1954.

problems most frequently mentioned in connection with this goal:

Being overweight or underweight

Not getting enough sleep

Having trouble with teeth or eyes

Having a poor complexion or skin trouble

Smoking and drinking

Being nervous

"Trying to stop a bad habit"

2. The goal of achieving scholastic success. This includes choice of course, relationships with teachers, and development of communication skills—speaking, reading, writing, listening. Problems often mentioned in relation to this goal include:

"Can't keep my mind on my studies"

Fear of failing in school work

Fear of making mistakes

Fear of speaking up in class

Worry about examinations and grades

Not spending enough time in studying

Not knowing how to read and study effectively, to outline and take notes, to give oral reports

Not budgeting time wisely

Lack of interest in some subjects

3. The goal of getting along with age-mates of both sexes, making friends, learning to work with others for a common purpose. This goal implies having a constructive attitude toward persons of different interests, abilities, and backgrounds. To accomplish this goal, adolescents feel the need of social skills—knowing how to dance, how to keep a conversation going, how to meet people, how to dress, how to entertain, how to acquire social ease. They want to be able to get along well with both boys and girls and to feel that they are socially acceptable. They worry about how they are impressing people.

4. The goal of being prepared for marriage and family life. Following are some of the problems mentioned in connection with efforts to attain this goal:

How to get dates; how often to have dates; how to get a
date with the right person

Whether to "go steady"

How to behave on a date and avoid "going too far"

"Wondering if I'll ever get married"

What makes a good marriage

How to get information and make decisions about love
and marriage

How to make marriage successful

5. The goal of getting along with one's family, of gaining emotional independence from parents and other adults without
hurting their feelings too much. These are some of the problems mentioned in this connection:

Being treated like a child

Not getting along with a brother or sister

Lack of parental understanding; refusal to take parental
advice

Incompatibility of parents, broken homes, neglect, lack
of parental supervision

Disagreements with parents; handling family disputes

Too little time with parents

Inability to get along with relatives

6. The goal of achieving identity—of discovering and developing one's most acceptable self. Problems connected with
this goal are:

Accepting one's masculine or feminine role

Accepting oneself as he can become

Breaking away from childish dependence on parents

Resisting pressures toward conformity with the age group

7. The goal of being economically independent. This includes
not only the ability eventually to make a living, but also
the ability to earn enough money, while going to school,
to satisfy one's needs and desires. Adolescents frequently
mention these problems connected with getting enough money
to do the things they want to do:

"How to earn some money of my own"

Needing a part-time or vacation job

How to earn money while going to school
How to spend money wisely
How to save money

8. The goal of making sound educational plans and choosing, preparing for, and entering a vocation for which one has the necessary ability and interest. Achieving this goal involves discovering one's abilities and developing them as fully as possible, beginning in the early years. It also implies remaining flexible enough about vocational choices to modify them in the light of changes in economic conditions or in one's own interests and abilities. Military service concerns the older adolescents.

9. The goal of developing a workable set of values, moral standards, and religious beliefs—of evolving a functional philosophy of life which takes account of one's place in the world. Following are some of the problems that may be associated with attaining this goal:

Accepting oneself—recognizing limitations but focusing one's attention on assets
Developing tolerance, tact, broadmindedness
Overcoming bad temper, moodiness, daydreaming, selfishness, and jealousy
Developing character and poise
Being forced to go to church, or refusing to go
Having feelings of guilt and feelings of inferiority
Having doubts and questions about religious beliefs
Conflicts between science and religion
Not knowing what to believe or how to believe

10. The goal of socially responsible behavior. Problems connected with this goal are:

Learning to consider the welfare of others as well as one's own desires, acquiring self-control and self-discipline
Finding socially useful things to do; helping make the world a better place in which to live
Resisting pressures of delinquent groups
Restlessness in class
Losing one's temper

Lack of self-confidence
Being bored
Truancy
Staying out late at night
Lack of knowledge of law, government, social institutions
    in the modern world

The central goal of adolescence seems to be to move from the dependence of childhood to the new relations and responsibilities of adulthood. To help adolescents achieve this goal, adults must see things through their eyes and understand their difficulties in trying to break away from their "parent-centered life." Many adults fail to establish in the early years the kind of relationship that will give the child a feeling of confidence and a willingness to discuss his problems. Consequently, many problem areas are never discussed at all, or, if they are brought out into the open, are merely quarreled over. It is important, therefore, for adults to see the whole picture, which includes knowledge of adolescent goals and the difficulties in achieving them, knowledge of the kind of relationships which they can and should have with the adolescents in their charge, and understanding of their roles as parents and teachers. If they expect young people to assume adult responsibilities, they should not withhold adult status.

Adolescence should be viewed as an opportunity, not a calamity. The very instability of early adolescence makes it easier to sort out childish ways of thinking, feeling, and acting and to reorganize them on a more mature basis. In their concern to conform in dress, activities, and interests, adolescents must not be allowed to fence themselves in—to fail to develop individuality and to take advantage of their youth and make the most of these years.

COMPREHENSION QUESTIONS

1. How does continuity of development affect adolescent adjustment?

2. What characteristics would you look for in the emotionally mature person? Do some adolescents possess these characteristics to a greater extent than some adults you know?

3. What are the main phases in the life span? Which three are treated in this book?

4. How is the physical-growth spurt in the prepubescent period related to social and emotional development?

5. How are the physiological changes of early adolescence related to behavior?

6. Why do adolescents vary so widely in their progress toward maturity, and in the stresses and strains which they experience during this period?

7. What are the main goals to be achieved during adolescence? Which of these seem to be recognized most clearly by adolescents themselves? How are these goals or tasks related to adolescent problems?

STUDY PROJECTS

1. Study differences in height and body form in a seventh- and eighth-grade class. Identify the stages in maturity represented in these groups.

2. Compare the ages of parents you know with the ages of their adolescent children. In how many instances do the social-biological adjustments of middle life coincide with the adjustments of adolescence?

3. As you read the direct quotations from the younger and from the older age groups, what differences in tone do you notice?

4. Ask classes in junior and senior high school to write about their goals. How do their own statements compare with the goals listed in this chapter?

FOR FURTHER STUDY

AUSUBEL, DAVID P., *Theory and Problems of Adolescent Development*, chap. VII. New York: Grune & Stratton, Inc., 1954.

BLAIR, ARTHUR WITT, and WILLIAM H. BURTON, *Growth and Development of the Preadolescent*. New York: Appleton-Century-Crofts, Inc., 1951.

COLE, LUELLA, *Psychology of Adolescence,* 4th ed. New York: Rinehart & Company, Inc., 1954.

CROW, LESTER D., and ALICE CROW, *Adolescent Development and Adjustment.* New York: McGraw-Hill Book Company, Inc., 1956.

DIMOCK, HEDLEY S., *Rediscovering the Adolescent.* New York: Association Press, 1937.

ERIKSON, ERIK H., *Childhood and Society.* New York: W. W. Norton & Company, Inc., 1950.

HAVIGHURST, ROBERT J., *Developmental Tasks and Education.* New York: Longmans, Green & Co., Inc., 1952.

———, "Research on the Developmental-task Concept," *School Review,* vol. 64 (May, 1956), pp. 215–223.

HOLLINGWORTH, LETA S., *The Psychology of the Adolescent.* New York: Appleton-Century-Crofts, Inc., 1928.

LANDIS, PAUL H., *Understanding Teen-agers.* New York: Appleton-Century-Crofts, Inc., 1955.

MOSER, CLARENCE G., *Understanding Boys.* New York: Association Press, 1953.

NATIONAL SOCIETY FOR THE STUDY OF EDUCATION, *Adolescence,* Forty-third Yearbook, part I. Chicago: University of Chicago Press, 1944.

REED, BRYAN H., *Eighty Thousand Adolescents,* chaps. I–X. London: George Allen & Unwin, Ltd., 1950.

SANFORD, NEVITT, "Personality Development during College Years," *The Personnel and Guidance Journal,* vol. 35 (October, 1956), pp. 74–80.

STRANG, RUTH, "The Psychology of Gifted Children and Youth," chap. X, *Psychology of Exceptional Children and Youth* (William Cruickshank, ed.), Englewood Cliffs, N.J.: Prentice-Hall, Inc., 1955.

WATTENBERG, WILLIAM W., *The Adolescent Years,* chaps. III–VI. New York: Harcourt, Brace and Company, Inc., 1955.

ZACHRY, CAROLINE B., and MARGARET LIGHTY, *Emotion and Conduct in Adolescence.* New York: Appleton-Century-Crofts, Inc., 1940.

ZUBEK, JOHN P., and PATRICIA A. SOLBERG, *Human Development.* New York: McGraw-Hill Book Company, Inc., 1954.

Fiction and Popular Articles

* BARKER, A. L., *Innocents.* New York: Charles Scribner's Sons, 1947.

* BURT, NATHANIEL, *Scotland's Burning.* Boston: Little, Brown & Company, 1954.

* Fiction.

* CRONIN, A. J., *The Green Years*. Boston: Little, Brown & Company, 1944.
* MANN, THOMAS, *Stories of Three Decades*. New York: Alfred A. Knopf, Inc., 1938.
* MAUGHAM, SOMERSET, *Of Human Bondage*. New York: Doubleday & Company, Inc., 1915.
WITTENBERG, RUDOLPH M., *On Call for Youth: How to Understand and Help Young People*. New York: Association Press, 1955.

Audio-visual Aids

Age of Turmoil. 16 minutes. Sound. McGraw-Hill.
The Meaning of Adolescence. 16 minutes. Sound. McGraw-Hill.

* Fiction.

CHAPTER 6

Achieving Physical and Sexual Maturity

Facts about the physical growth preceding and following puberty are important for a number of reasons. Bodily changes, especially if sudden, change the adolescent's body image and self-concept; he may now see himself as an adult with adult privileges and responsibilities. Biological changes give rise to physical sensations; these are translated into emotional states, which, in turn, may be expressed in social behavior. Slow or rapid growth, unevenness of growth, or abnormalities of growth may affect an adolescent's total development. During the years in the life continuum when individuals are achieving physical maturity and competency, a complex of changes evolves—physical, social, emotional—all interrelated. The process begins with the physical-growth spurt and continues until the other aspects of maturation are relatively complete.

PHYSICAL DEVELOPMENT—ANATOMICAL AGE

Growth during adolescence is a phase of the individual's total development. In general, the growth curves of individual boys resemble the average growth curve for boys of the same physiological age; this is also true for girls. For individuals of the same chronological age, however, the growth curves vary greatly.

The growth of children and adolescents has its ups and downs. During the life span there are two marked spurts in growth, followed by periods in which growth proceeds at a slower rate.

The first of these is in early infancy; the second begins one or two years preceding puberty and continues for six months to a year after puberty. Then growth continues at a slower rate for about five or six years. Although each individual's pattern of growth is unique, a certain rhythm in growth rate is evident in many physical measurements prior to and during adolescence.

The sequences of development common to most adolescents, but occurring at different chronological ages, are:

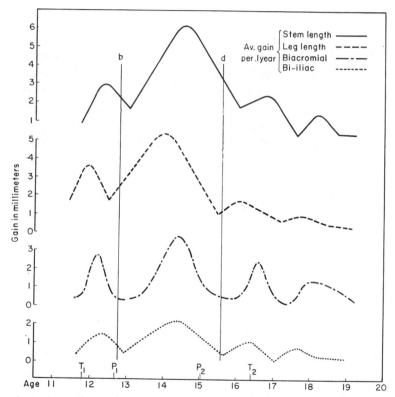

These are schematic phase-pattern profiles for the stem length, leg length, biacromial width, and bi-iliac width. The timing relations to the puberal period for height are indicated by the letters *b* and *d*. The timing relations to puberal growth in testes and to puberal growth in glans penis are indicated by T_1 and T_2, P_1 and P_2. (*From H. R. Stolz and L. M. Stolz, Somatic Development of Adolescent Boys, copyright 1951, p. 417. Used with permission of The Macmillan Company.*)

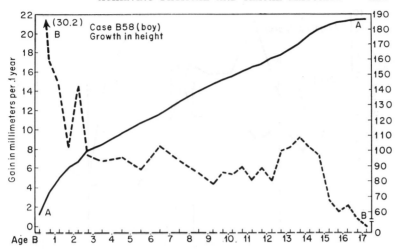

These profiles illustrate two ways in which the same growth data may be arranged and presented. Profile A shows how tall a boy was at successive chronological ages and what was the general trend of his growth. Profile B shows the changes in the same boy's growth rate during successive periods. Changes from acceleration to deceleration, or the reverse, and changes of gradients from one period to the next constitute the outstanding features of Profile B, but are scarcely noticeable in Profile A. (*From H. R. Stolz and L. M. Stolz,* Somatic Development of Adolescent Boys, *copyright 1951, p. 6. Used with permission of The Macmillan Company.*)

1. Accelerated growth in height one or two years before puberty, followed by a rapid decrease in the growth rate. The growth spurt begins with the long bones of arms and legs. The peak in rapid growth is one of the easiest ways of estimating maturity. There also seem to be rhythmic ups and downs in the growth rates of different parts of the body during adolescence.

2. Increase in weight begins a little later than accelerated growth in height. During the three years before and after puberty girls make their greatest gains—an average of 34 pounds. Boys make their greatest gains a year or two later than girls. In the early stages at least half of the boys are somewhat fat and feminine in appearance.

3. Changes in body proportions of trunk, legs, arms, head, and face are likewise associated with the patterns for growth in height and weight.

The preadolescent growth spurt is thought to be initiated by one of the secretions of the pituitary gland. This secretion

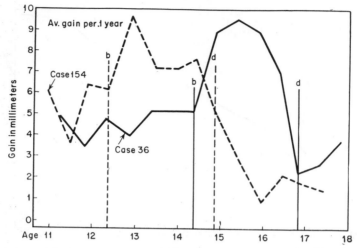

Height-growth curves showing same amount of gain during the puberal growth period, but with different timing and configuration. (*From H. R. Stolz and L. M. Stolz,* Somatic Development of Adolescent Boys, *copyright 1951, p. 101. Used with permission of The Macmillan Company.*)

stimulates the growth of bones, muscles, and tissues; secretion from the sex glands checks growth. If sexual development is premature, the boy or girl completes the pubertal growth period early. If the production of sex hormones is delayed, growth continues longer than the average.

Accompanying the accelerated growth just before puberty, there is, in many cases, a corresponding rise in basal metabolism. Owing to this increase in basal metabolism and in height, weight, and physical activity, a higher intake of food is needed. No wonder the appetite of adolescent boys is phenomenal!

Individual Variation in Growth and Size

The onset of the pubertal growth period shows great individual variations. In the majority of girls the acceleration in growth rate begins between the ages of ten and fifteen; in the majority of boys, between the ages of eleven and sixteen. This means that one boy may be entering adolescence in the fifth grade when he is only ten years old, while a classmate of the same chronological age may not begin to change from his childhood pattern until he

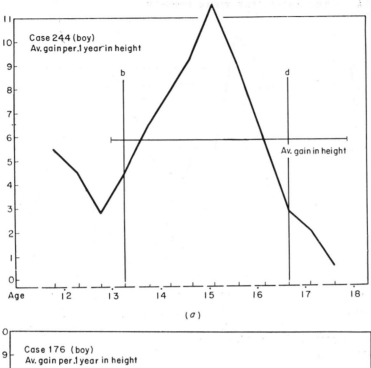

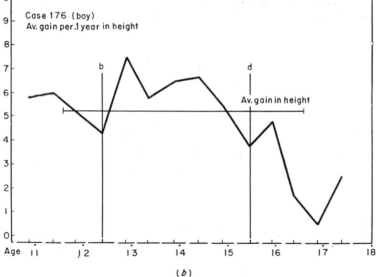

Height-growth curves of two boys representing contrasts in configuration. (*From H. R. Stolz and L. M. Stolz,* Somatic Development of Adolescent Boys, *copyright 1951, p. 111. Used with permission of The Macmillan Company.*)

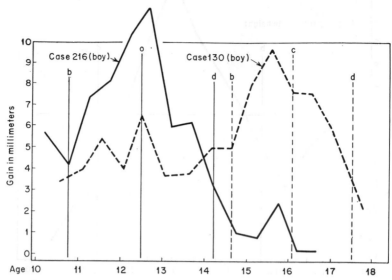

Height-growth curves for two boys illustrating early and late development. (*From H. R. Stolz and L. M. Stolz*, Somatic Development of Adolescent Boys, *copyright 1951, p. 61. Used with permission of The Macmillan Company.*)

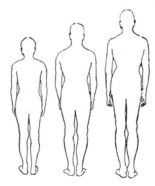

Three early developers at a corresponding point in the postpuberal period. The first became a short man; the second, medium in height; and the third, tall.

is fifteen or sixteen and in the middle years of high school. In general, the early maturers, even as children, are taller and heavier than late maturers.

Boys who begin the pubertal growth period early tend to complete this phase earlier. But if a boy is short at the beginning of the growth spurt, he will tend to be relatively short at the end; similarly, an initially tall boy will tend to maintain his relative height during the period of rapid growth. If the duration of the growth spurt is long, a corresponding gain in height may be expected. However, the individual variations are so great that "the chronological age of a boy at the onset of the pubertal period could not be used as a basis for predicting his mature height with any degree of certainty." [1] Physical growth is difficult to predict.

The duration of this period of rapid growth in height also varies. For boys it may extend from 2 to 4 years. Girls show less variation and are more likely to require about 3 to 3½ years for the process.

Early adolescents come in all shapes and sizes. In any group there will be some who are quite short and want to grow taller. There are others who have begun to grow rapidly; some of the girls are very tall. For example, in an eighth-grade class there were two girls who were 5 feet, 7 inches tall. In a ninth-grade class sizes ranged from Jim, 5 feet, 10 inches, 200 pounds, to Steve, 5 feet, 2 inches, 100 pounds.

Sex Differences

Sex differences in physical development are most marked during the period of rapid growth. Because their growth spurt has started one to two years earlier than boys, girls around thirteen years of age tend to be bigger than the boys in their classes. In fact, between the ages of eleven and fourteen is the only time in the human life span when girls tend to be relatively taller than boys of the same chronological age. For girls, the greatest increase in height usually occurs from six months to a

[1] Herbert R. Stolz and Lois M. Stolz, *Somatic Development of Adolescent Boys,* p. 115. New York: The Macmillan Company, 1951.

year before the menarche; their greatest increases in weight come just before and just after puberty. Boys may be expected to attain their maximal growth rate about a year after the initial signs of sexual maturation. Their greatest increase in weight comes a year or two later than for girls.

Observation at a class picnic or informal party will give one a vivid sense of these physical differences. For example, at an eighth-grade picnic, out of the entire class of thirty, only two boys danced with girls, although there were fifteen or more girls dancing. These boys were several inches shorter than their partners. The rest of the boys and girls were playing softball or other active games in which partners were not necessary. In a combined junior-senior high school, girls tend to prefer boys a year or two older than themselves.

Rapid changes in physical growth have social and emotional consequences. Differences in size between boys and girls may make girls in the junior high school feel awkward and out of place with boys of their own chronological age. Tall girls may become over-quiet, studious, and stoop-shouldered, or loud and boisterous.

Boys of the same age, many of whom have just started their growth spurt, often wonder whether they will always be short, or skinny, or fat. Some small boys try to conceal their feeling of inferiority about their size by becoming loud, "showing off," or seeking to excel in some sport. They usually avoid girls. They are often interested in exercises to develop strength and physical fitness. Both boys and girls need to be reassured that most irregularities of growth will eventually be ironed out, and that their present feelings of inferiority will not be permanent.

Special Causes for Concern

In addition to the individual variations and the differences between boys and girls in rate of development, there are special causes for concern. Most disturbing to boys is the "fat period," which occurs near the beginning of the growth spurt. If this tendency is pronounced, boys will have conspicuous accumulations of fat around the nipples and over the abdomen and hips.

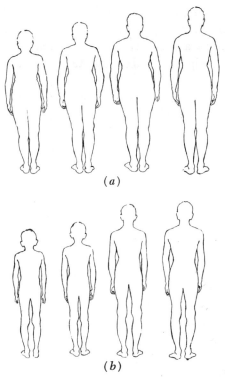

(*a*) Changes in size and body form of a fat boy during the prepuberal, at the beginning and end of the puberal period, and during the postpuberal period. (*b*) Changes in size and body form of a lightweight boy during the same periods.

This gives them a feminine appearance. Although this "fat period" may last for only two years, the unfavorable effect on the boy's concept of himself and his achievement of masculine identification may persist for many years. Girls, too, may be concerned about this period when fat tends to accumulate over the abdomen and hips. They try to curb their normal appetite and sometimes go to extremes in dieting.

Although, in general, other aspects of development are closely related to patterns for growth in height and weight, uneven growth of some parts of the body sometimes causes concern. Although a serious discrepancy between various aspects of an individual's growth, as for example, more rapid growth of nose or chin, will be disturbing to the adolescent, variability of growth has some positive aspects. It may, for example, emphasize individuality and help to combat the tendency toward over-conformity.

It is encouraging to note how well some teen-agers adjust to physical liabilities and make the most of their assets. Lois was the largest girl in the senior class. She was not only tall but also heavily built, and, in general, physically unattractive. However, she was always well-groomed, and had learned to carry herself with poise. She was highly intelligent and a natural leader. In class she would often bring up a thought-provoking question or lead a discussion; in any group, she could be depended upon for ideas. She also had a fine sense of humor and was always ready for a good time.

Adolescents perceive changes in size and body form in dif-

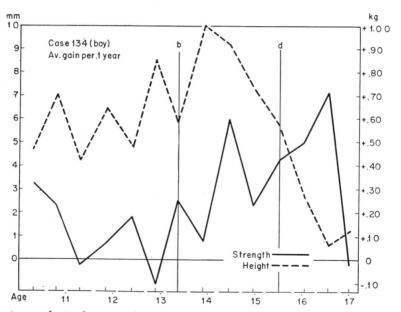

Apex velocity for strength growth following end of puberal growth period for height. (*From H. R. Stolz and L. M. Stolz,* Somatic Development of Adolescent Boys, *copyright 1951, p. 311. Used with permission of The Macmillan Company.*)

ferent ways. Some are proud of their increase in size and the other manifestations of physical maturity. Others are anxious about certain aspects of their growth. Still others are concerned about looking different from their age-mates. Some feel ashamed of their atypical growth patterns. They need to become used to their new body image as perceived by themselves and by others.

When teen-agers begin to look like adults, they try to act and think like adults. As we have already noted, they become conscious of their expanding world and their increasing responsibilities. Parents and teachers should sympathize with young people's efforts to "gear in" to adult life. They should not laugh at their efforts or block their first attempts to be "on their own." Instead they should learn when to allow the adolescent to take it easy, to speed up, or to put on the brakes.

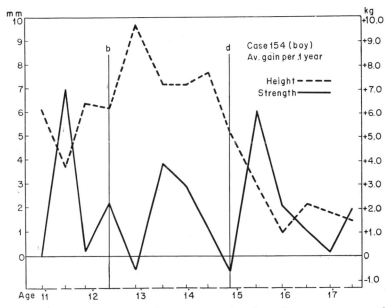

This was the only instance from one sample where the maximum growth velocity for strength occurred before the onset of the puberal period for height. (*From H. R. Stolz and L. M. Stolz,* Somatic Development of Adolescent Boys, *copyright 1951, p. 311. Used with permission of The Macmillan Company.*)

Since muscular strength lags behind growth in height and weight, there is the danger of causing overstrain by expecting too much of a big, growing boy. Even though he looks like a man, he may not have the corresponding strength. An individual's strength will also vary with his general physiological condition, which is affected by fatigue, lack of sleep, and infections. During this period of rapid growth, it is easy to overestimate a youngster's physical capacity and plunge him into too strenuous activities.

Increase in physical activity, often accompanying increase in size, may also be caused by secretions of the thyroid gland. This internal secretion contributes to the restlessness, the "nervousness," the desire to be "on the go" until all hours, which is so characteristic of teen-agers, at the very time they need more sleep than usual. Within a few years nature usually achieves the normal balance of glandular functioning without need for medication.

Appraisal of Adolescent Growth

The appraisement of adolescent growth should be based on a not-too-complicated record kept throughout the elementary school years and continued into high school. Meredith's *Physical Growth Record* [2] for reporting and interpreting height and weight with respect to age would seem to be the most practical device for widespread use in the schools at the present time. For schools able to obtain X-rays of the bones of the wrist, this measure of skeletal age is much more indicative of an individual's growth status than is chronological age.

The very individuality of adolescents makes it difficult to appraise their growth. As Stolz and Stolz have pointed out, interpretation of growth figures for an individual should be made by comparison, not with average figures at a given chronological age, but with the sequence of development common to most adolescents. One must recognize the wide variation among adolescents

[2] Howard V. Meredith, "A 'Physical Growth Record' for Use in Elementary and High Schools," *American Journal of Public Health*, vol. 39 (July, 1949), pp. 878–885.

in height, weight, bone development, and sexual maturity, and also take into consideration individual differences in body structure, total development, and family heritage. Patterns of growth cannot be predicted without a knowledge of the individual's physiological age. "In the final analysis, appraisal of growth is largely subjective." [3]

SEXUAL DEVELOPMENT—PHYSIOLOGICAL AGE

Sexual maturation covers a period of time; it is not a point in time. No single event marks the specific time when the reproductive organs begin to function. Puberty is best considered as a gradual change in all aspects of development, rather than as a sudden, specific change occurring at a certain date. However, it arrives more abruptly for girls than for boys. There is evidence from primitive societies and case studies that reproduction may not be possible immediately after the first menstruation. It is also true that sex feelings and sex behavior often occur in childhood, before pubescence.

Signs of Sexual Maturing

It is biological changes that set the adolescent period apart for special consideration. Of the various changes that take place during adolescence, sexual maturation seems to be of central importance. This change is initiated by hormones, or internal secretions. The pituitary gland, which stimulates physical growth, emits another secretion which stimulates the development of the sex glands. Their secretions, in turn, promote development of the secondary sex characteristics—pubic and axillary hair in both sexes; facial hair and growth of testes and penis in boys. Change of voice in boys occurs relatively late, usually following the other bodily changes just mentioned.

In girls, these changes include the rounding out of hips and breasts. These signs, together with the peak in the growth spurt, the first menstruation in girls, and the first emission in boys,

---

[3] Wesley M. Staton, "The Adolescent; His Physical Growth and Health," *Review of Educational Research,* vol. 24 (February, 1954), p. 20.

mark the beginning of sexual maturation. Teachers and parents may anticipate the menarche when they see that the growth curve is reaching its peak. They can then check the attainment of sexual maturity by the other signs just mentioned.

Most girls reach sexual maturity near the thirteenth birthday. Recent investigators have reported a slightly earlier mean age— 12.8 years. In a New York study, the mean time of occurrence of the menarche was 13.5 years; in a Cleveland study of girls in better economic circumstances, it was 12.5 years. Both boys and girls are likely to reach sexual maturity during the junior high school years. Girls of the present generation begin to menstruate earlier than did their mothers, and American girls tend to have their first menstruation earlier than do girls in other countries. Individual variation, however, is still wide; normal range covers the ages from ten to sixteen or even seventeen. Girls mature one to three years earlier than boys.

More specifically, at 9½ years of age neither boys nor girls have reached puberty. At 13½, half of the girls but only 3 or 4 per cent of the boys have passed through puberty. It is around 15½ years, or in the ninth grade, that teachers find the greatest diversity: the large majority of the girls will have attained biological maturity; a smaller proportion of the boys will have reached maturity; about a third of the boys will be passing through puberty; and a few will still be children. At 17½ practically all of the girls and all but about 10 per cent of the boys will have passed through puberty. Considering various developmental and social factors, pubertal changes may occur at an especially appropriate time for one individual and at a most inopportune time for another.

Attitudes toward Physiological Changes

Achievement of sexual maturity is of great importance to the adolescent. It may be either a welcomed event or a cause of embarrassment and uneasiness. Girls may respond to menstruation in various ways:

Dreading these physiological changes and being frightened by them
Resenting the limitations imposed by menstruation

Being embarrassed when they cannot go swimming or play vigorous games with the boys

Being merely secretive about it

Being proud of this sign of maturity as a woman

Often these youngsters have no one to whom they can turn for help. Their peers often give them misinformation; their parents are often embarrassed or evasive.

When boys begin to show signs of sexual maturity, they are likely to perceive them favorably. They welcome the growth of hair on chin and chest, the deepening voice, and other evidences of maturation as heralds of masculinity rather than as causes for embarrassment.

"Early" and "Late" Maturers

Between the extremes of early and late maturing stretches a continuum from the youngest to the oldest age of sexual maturation. To avoid perpetuating the dichotomy of "early" and "late" maturers, Nicolson and Hanley [4] recommended using standard scores in appraising maturation. Nevertheless, the concept of "earlier" and "later" maturers has practical value in helping us to describe adolescent development. Some of the problems of growing up stem from extreme differences in age or rate of maturing. They are intensified by previous unfortunate experiences and by ineffective sex education or lack of it when it is needed. Both earlier-maturing and later-maturing boys and girls should be identified and helped to cope with their special problems. [5]

The earlier-maturing boy is perhaps the most fortunate. He usually has fun, feels superior because he is in demand with other boys for sports, and with the mature girls in his class for social events. He may feel fairly adequate in his emerging adult

[4] Arline B. Nicolson and Charles Hanley, "Indices of Physiological Maturity; Derivation and Interrelationships," *Child Development,* vol. 24 (March, 1953), pp. 3–38.

[5] Elizabeth Lee Vincent, "Physical and Psychological Aspects of Puberty and Adolescence," *Journal of the National Association of Deans of Women,* vol. 19 (October, 1955), pp. 3–10.

role, though unable to meet some adults' unrealistic expectations of him. If too much is expected of him intellectually and emotionally, he can at least turn to some activities in which he is successful. A senior high school boy described this happy state of affairs as follows:

When I was younger I couldn't wait till I grew up. Every time I wanted to play baseball or football they would say I was too small. Now I'm about six feet tall. Every time a game is played now I get into it. In baseball I'm a fast runner, a good catcher and a strong hitter. In football my weight, now 165 pounds, is not too heavy but I carry it well. I play quarterback. In basketball I use my six feet height to get rebounds which helps you get a game. I feel good always getting a game; I feel grown up. I feel like a man, which I am. At night if I want to go to a movie I go, no cashier stops me to ask my age like they use to. All I can say is, it feels good to grow up.

Other fast-growing boys experience social awkwardness as a result of their rapid growth. A very tall sixteen-year-old senior described this aspect of growing up:

When you are growing up it is a very awkward stage of life. You suddenly find yourself with big, long, gawky legs. Your voice gets hoarse as it gets lower. After several months of this you suddenly realize that you have a deep voice just like most men. You have gotten taller and taller and wonder if you will stop. First you get taller than your mother, then your father. And finally you find yourself the tallest in the family. Because of your awkwardness you have social problems. It seems hard at first to talk with the other sex. And because they are also at the awkward stage it is doubly hard. The biggest problem is to get socially adjusted because of your awkwardness. Also you get yelled at a lot for kicking things and being just plain clumsy. You trip over those big feet and your extra long legs don't help any.

The earlier-maturing girl is at a decided disadvantage. She feels conspicuous among her smaller classmates, finds boys of her own age immature and uninteresting. As in the case of the earlier-maturing boy, too much may be expected of her intellectually and emotionally because of her more mature appearance. If she joins an older group, she may get into serious trouble. If she loses interest in her less mature childhood friends and is not accepted by the older boys and girls, she may be lonely and unhappy. One girl wrote: "I had difficulties the first year I went to high school, because I was so tall. All the other girls were short and they got the fellows. No one would dance with me." However, the earlier-maturing girls may show greater ability to respond appropriately to social situations, being less influenced by their moods and more independent and rational in their judgments.

It is the later-maturing boy, however, who usually has the most serious problems of adjustment. He often worries about his small size, cannot get on teams, is not dated by girls. He may feel socially rejected, inadequate, and dissatisfied with himself; he may sense that his parents are disappointed in him. These feelings may lead him to withdraw from normal social contacts. He needs to be assured that he will eventually grow up, and that he can become skillful in certain sports even though he does not have sufficient height and weight to engage in others.

Later maturing is not so serious a problem for girls as for boys. The girl has the advantage of associating with the many later-maturing boys in her class. Her parents are often glad not to lose "their little girl." However, as time goes on, she may become more aware of her difference from the other girls and may either try to keep up with them socially or withdraw into solitary activities.

In various ways glandular changes and the resulting physical development that occurs during this period affect adolescents' self-concepts and their social relations. As a result of attaining sexual maturity, adolescents begin to feel impulses which they do not know how to handle. Many youngsters are bewildered by their conflicting impulses. If parents understood that there is some physiological reason for much exasperating adolescent behavior, they would be more sympathetic and understanding toward their children's struggle to grow up.

PHYSICAL EFFICIENCY

In this, as in other areas, research has produced conflicting results, and there is much undocumented opinion. Although pre-adolescents, as a group, tend to be healthy, active, physically efficient, there is potential for improvement. According to some studies, strength and physical efficiency increase during the early years of adolescence. From thirteen to seventeen years of age boys show a rapid increase in strength. Girls increase less rapidly.[6] This tendency for adolescent boys to increase in strength much faster than girls may be explained by differences in physique due to the male sex hormones and to cultural conditioning. The hormones affect the boys' muscular development and also height, weight, breadth of shoulders, and length of bone. These and other skeletal and physiological conditions generally give boys an advantage over girls in strength. Boys also usually have more opportunity for exercise than girls. Most girls begin to curtail their physical activity around the time of puberty, through lack of interest, motivation, or opportunities. They abandon their childish outdoor games but do not immediately develop skill in adult sports. One fourteen-year-old girl presented the problem in these words:

> There comes a time when you are baffled as to whether or not to play with boys—playing such things as football and other rough sports. If you don't, you don't get very much exercise, as an all-girl unorganized game is awful. Most of us decide to play with the boys but to take it easy.

Boys, on the other hand, tend to move without a break from childhood games into adult sports; consequently they may be expected to improve in physical efficiency during the teens. Although the normal heart is not damaged by ordinary vigorous activity, a cardiologic examination should certainly be required

[6] F. K. Shuttleworth, *The Adolescent Period: A Graphic Atlas,* monograph of the Society for Research in Child Development, vol. 14, no. 1. Evanston, Ill.: Child Development Publications, 1951.

before an adolescent is allowed to participate in competitive sports.

Under favorable conditions we can assume that physical efficiency will increase during adolescence. Good nutrition as well as exercise underlies muscular strength. Motor coordination tends to improve as muscular strength develops. Boys tend to increase steadily in motor coordination until about the age of seventeen; girls, until about fourteen. But both boys and girls can develop specific motor coordination in certain sports and dances. There is little evidence to show that lack of motor coordination is a cause of awkwardness; this seems to be more social than physical in origin.

Some motor abilities reach their peak in the teens; others continue to develop into the twenties or later. With boys, engaging in sports is an essential part of the growing-up process. In compositions on "IIow it feels to be growing up" interest in sports was specifically mentioned by the percentages of boys and girls in Table 9.

TABLE 9

Grade Level and IQ	Number of Compositions	Number Mentioning Interest in Sports	Per Cent
7–8–9; Average IQ: 95.2	247	27	11
7–8–9; IQ: 120–129	121	28	23
7–8–9; IQ: 130 and over	35	11	31
10–11–12; Average IQ: 94.9	636	80	13
10–11–12; IQ: 120–129	65	6	9.2
10–11–12; IQ: 130 and over	20	1	5

For the most part, these students merely mentioned the kinds of games they liked or would like to play—football, baseball, basketball, and others. Some stated that they were good in certain sports. Others voiced aspirations. One eighth-grade boy wrote: "I wish I was bigger so I could get picked to play ball more often."

When athletics hold a prominent place in school and community life, as they do in many situations, the boy who cannot participate often feels "left out" and inferior. It was especially difficult for Bill: after a year of outstanding success on the football team, he gave up sports because of his low marks in school subjects. His grades improved, but he had such a feeling of frustration and loneliness that he felt he must find some way to participate in sports again. This he did by budgeting his time better and acquiring more effective reading and study methods.

Junior high school girls are interested in sports, but their interest lags behind that of boys as they grow older. Many older adolescent girls are more interested in the boys who play on the teams and in being cheer leaders, twirlers, or drum majorettes than they are in actual participation in the sports.

In planning the athletic program for teen-age boys and girls, it is necessary to consider a number of factors other than the contribution a particular activity may make to physical efficiency. Among these factors are the students' readiness in motor learning, the emotional concomitants of athletic contests, and the educational worth and social contribution of different games and sports. For example, success in some sports depends more on brain than brawn. This knowledge is encouraging to the alert boy of slight body build. Adolescents should be helped to recognize that physical competency of an appropriate kind is an important part of their total development.

HEALTH DURING ADOLESCENCE

Adolescence is a relatively healthy period of life. Adolescent youngsters have a lower rate of absence from school due to illness than any other age group. The lowest rates of illness, death, and disability are reported for the fifteen-to-twenty-four age group. Recent progress in disease prevention and medical care has reduced the mortality rates among adolescents.

Still there is considerable illness among adolescents, and many suffer from physical handicaps. The number one cause of death is accidents. Next in order of frequency are cancer and leukemia, heart disease and rheumatic fever, tuberculosis, pneumonia and

influenza, kidney disease, poliomyelitis, congenital malforma-
tions, suicide, and homicide.[7] Illness may be at the root of some
behavior problems such as restlessness and "laziness." A main
objective of health education is to help adolescents perceive their
health problems differently and to put health in its proper place
as basic to whatever they want to do or become.

Health problems per se do not seem to be uppermost in adolescents' minds. In their freely written compositions, they mention a minimum of health problems. Likewise on the Mooney
Problem Check List, urban, suburban, and rural students tend
to show less recognition of health problems than of other kinds
of worries or difficulties. However, according to one study,[8] involving almost two hundred adolescents, 31 per cent of the boys
and 41 per cent of the girls said they were at some time during the study disturbed about physical factors. On the Billett-
Starr Youth Problems Inventory, concern about physical health,
fitness, and safety ranked third in frequency of mention by a
suburban high school group. When adolescents are asked directly about their health problems or when a recording is made
of their comments during a physical examination, they will express more concern about physical factors than they usually do
in compositions or check lists.

The health problems with which younger adolescents seem
most concerned are headaches, trouble with teeth, being overweight or underweight, and being "not good looking." Senior
high school students also mentioned "tiring easily," lack of sleep,
poor complexion or skin troubles, being too short, allergies, and
smoking. In their freely written responses they mentioned concern for the illness of their parents as well as their own health
problems.

The importance of the problems which these adolescents mentioned is confirmed by health surveys. The American Dental As-

[7] Metropolitan Life Insurance Company, "Health of Teen-agers," *Statistical Bulletin*, vol. 34 (August, 1953), pp. 1–4.

[8] Herbert R. Stolz and Lois Meek Stolz, "Adolescent Problems Related
to Somatic Variation," *Adolescence*, Forty-third Yearbook of the National
Society for the Study of Education, part I, pp. 81–99. Chicago: University
of Chicago Press, 1944.

sociation reported that less than 4 per cent of high school students were free from dental defects. Poor nutrition, which is a factor in most of the problems mentioned, is widespread. In general, the eating habits of high school students are the poorest of any age group. Their diets are deficient in milk, green and yellow vegetables, and citrus fruits, suggesting vitamin and mineral deficiency.

Nutritional deficiency may be related to mental health as well as to physical growth and health.[9] There is still much to be learned about the effect of the chemistry of the body on emotional health. An inadequate diet may also be indirectly related to poor school achievement.

Often the solution to the problem is not so simple as merely providing a well-balanced diet. Psychological factors enter in, such as the youngster's attitude toward food. Although some young people have genuine allergies to certain foods, their refusals to eat are usually, as one boy said, "just notions." The eating customs of "the crowd" often condition adolescents' eating habits.

Breakfast is the most common bone of contention. Many teenagers go to school without a decent breakfast. Parents cannot solve this problem by merely putting on pressure. In fact, if going without breakfast is part of an adolescent's resistance to a morning routine, or one way of asserting independence, parental insistence may cause emotional disturbances in family relations more serious than the nutritional consequences of not eating a bowl of cereal and milk. If the parent can discover the reasons why his son or daughter has lost interest in breakfast, he may create more favorable conditions. Sometimes the child just wants a change. An egg beaten up in a glass of orange juice and one or two pieces of buttered toast are nutritious, quick to eat, and "different." Bananas can be substituted for cereal. Toasted cheese sandwiches, suggested by one adolescent who was permitted to plan the breakfast menu, are about as nutritious as the more

[9] Tom D. Spies and others, "Detection and Treatment of Nutritive Failure in Children," *Journal of the American Medical Association,* vol. 148 (April 19, 1952), pp. 1376–1382.

conventional menu of cereal and milk. If parents would take the trouble to see the breakfast problem as their teen-agers view it, they would be well on the road to its solution.

It is bad enough to be fat and forty, but to be fat and four-teen is still harder to bear. The inevitable nicknames are dis-tressing: "Fatty," "Lard," "Tubby," "Five-by-five," "Square Baby." Youngsters often take these characterizations good-naturedly, but underneath they may be quite embarrassed by their excessive weight. One boy played truant from school on those days when he had to take a special gym class with a cold shower afterward. When he did attend, he was sitting on the sidelines most of the time for being out of breath or out of step. Certain facts about obesity and weight control are useful in counseling adolescents.[10]

When slimness is the vogue, teen-age girls who imagine that they are overweight or are afraid they will become fat subject themselves to diets that may be injurious. One girl in her daily schedule reported eating for breakfast each day nothing but "4 prunes and juice." Some teen-age girls who are very fond of sweets will abstain from desserts for days if they think they are getting fat, or if sweets seem to cause acne.

Pimples, or acne, are one of their most disturbing health prob-lems. Inappropriate diet, uncleanliness of the skin, increased ac-tivity of certain glands of internal secretion, and emotional dis-turbance all may contribute to this teen-age affliction. Skin spe-cialists recommend avoidance of chocolate, rich cakes, and fatty foods, and thorough cleansing of the skin—massaging in a pure mild soap lather and rinsing with warm water followed by cold. Medical research has shown that an outburst of rage or hate is often followed by an outbreak of pimples. The understanding of a sympathetic doctor who can relieve the young person's fears about the causation of acne may be of more help than the med-ication he gives.

Just as physical defects may cause emotional disturbances, in-ner psychological conflicts may become manifest in bodily diffi-

[10] Jean Mayer and Frederick J. Stare, "Exercise and Control: Frequent Misconceptions," *Journal of the American Dietetic Association*, vol. 29 (April, 1953), pp. 340–343.

culties. Acne, obesity, and dysmenorrhea (painful menstruation) are common psychosomatic ailments of adolescence. Any emotional unrest can work through the autonomic nervous system and affect the physiology of the individual. In any psychosomatic ailment a thorough examination should be made to detect any organic conditions or constitutional defects. Improvement in general health and regular prescribed exercise are also basic.

In the case of dysmenorrhea, when no physical or glandular causes have been found, attention should be turned to psychological factors. Among these may be (1) lack of preparation for the onset of menstruation (if it occurs unexpectedly, it comes as a shock); (2) association of blood with sickness and injury; (3) greater than average sensitivity to pain; (4) false beliefs and superstitions, such as persistent primitive taboos; (5) resentment, especially on the part of the "tomboy," against unreasonable restriction of her swimming, horseback riding, and other activities in which she normally engaged (many taboos and superstitions still cling to the menstrual period, although authorities emphasize the desirability of continuing one's normal habits of bathing and engaging in all but the most strenuous exercises); (6) fear of having a baby now that the girl is capable of sexual reproduction; and (7) tendency to use painful menstruation as an excuse for getting out of school and home duties, or social gatherings in which one would feel insecure. Any of these psychological conditions may affect the autonomic nervous system and produce contraction of the cervical muscles of the uterus, which causes pain. This periodic pain makes the girl's days miserable and prevents her from realizing her full potentialities. Since the causation is often partly psychological, it helps to emphasize not her disabilities but her potentialities for the realization of her desires for marriage and/or a career.

THE PHYSICALLY HANDICAPPED ADOLESCENT

Although relatively few high school students mention physical handicaps in their compositions or on check lists, it has been estimated that 7 per cent of the population fourteen to seventeen years old are physically disabled to some extent. These young people are faced with the special limitations imposed by their handicaps as well as by the problems common to other adolescents. Despite this, handicapped children often make a good adjustment to their environment and learn to live with their physical impairment. However, recent research [11] has shown that physically incapacitated children's responses to feelings of fear may take the form of withdrawal, and that they have a greater need than the average for acceptance.

Parents, teachers, and fellow students can best help the physically incapacitated child in three ways:

1. By treating him as a normal child except where necessary adjustments must be made to his impairment.

2. By providing suitable activities in which he can engage successfully. For example, one physical education teacher in a large city high school expected the physically handicapped girls who would benefit by mild and moderate activities to engage in ring toss, shuffleboard, Chinese checkers, dominoes, checkers, and similar games, which could take the form of tournaments.

3. By accepting their best efforts and providing opportunities for them to get recognition through genuine service to the group. For example, one shy girl, with many fears about her physical disability, is happily assisting the school doctor and nurse in keeping the teacher's medical records up to date. The correction of a physical defect may make a vast difference in an adolescent's competency and self-confidence.

PERSONAL APPEARANCE

Improved personal appearance for girls and increased strength for boys are among the strongest motivations for healthful living. Teen-age girls show concern about improving their personal appearance earlier than boys. Junior high school boys, especially in the seventh and eighth grades, from homes of all economic levels, commonly have a "don't care" attitude about grooming.

[11] Howard J. Norris and William M. Cruickshank, "Adjustment of Physically Handicapped Adolescent Youth," *Journal of the International Council for Exceptional Children*, vol. 21 (May, 1955), pp. 282–288.

By the time they reach the twelfth grade, their attitude has usually changed. They are concerned about doing and wearing the right thing, as, for example, at the junior-senior banquet. There are exceptions, of course, depending on home training, current teen-age styles, and individual personality. Among 6,000 high school seniors in the state of Washington, more than one in every six reported being worried about personal appearance. An equal number were concerned about being underweight or overweight, and more than one-eighth were worried about poor complexion.[12]

Personal appearance may be related to conformity to the group, to behavior, and to the self-concept. Adolescents' uniformity in dress reflects their desire to "belong" and their fear of being "different." On a cold, snowy day, when one mother remonstrated with her daughter about not wearing a hat, the daughter exclaimed, "If I wear a hat, I'll look different from

[12] L. J. Elias, *High School Youth Look at Their Problems*. Pullman, Wash.: State College of Washington, January, 1949.

all the others. They'll think me crazy. It's bad enough that I have to wear galoshes!" On rainy days similar conflict arises regarding umbrellas and rubbers.

Excessive attention to make-up and clothes may indicate a certain lack of self-acceptance. Extreme neglect of personal appearance may indicate self-rejection. Posture, too, may reflect the self-concept.

Although this interest in clothes and personal appearance has been stimulated, in some instances, by teen-age magazines such as *Seventeen* and *Glamour,* the local mode prevails. In one city senior high school, for example, teen-age girls were wearing these main types of footwear: loafers, saddle shoes, ballerinas, and "heels." They wore heels only on more formal occasions, such as graduation and evening dances, and then only after consultation with their best friends.

Adolescent styles may change overnight. These youngsters are quick to take up new fads such as wearing dog collars on their ankles or bells on their shoelaces. Girls will spend money that they really need for other purposes, just to conform. And when no money is available, they make pitiful attempts to construct a suitable facsimile from something they have on hand. Adolescent girls want to be individual and to outshine one another to some extent, and yet, at the same time, to conform to the group.

Nail biting, which arises from stresses of various kinds, is often related to personal appearance. One ninth-grade boy said he stopped biting his nails only after he got a girl friend and a job where his appearance was important. Youngsters try various ways of stopping this habit: they chew gum, put nail polish or iodine on their nails, stop drinking coffee, use "will power." They need help in reducing the sources of tension that are causing the habit.

ADOLESCENTS' PERCEPTION OF THEIR PHYSICAL DEVELOPMENT

How do young people view the physical development that occurs between childhood and adult maturity? What influence does the change in body image have on an adolescent's concept of himself and on the way he is viewed by others? How does he feel about himself? How does an adolescent feel about being different from others of his chronological age in height, weight, body form, rate of growth, or biological maturity? Does he think, "Am I normal?" Or does he realize that there is no "normal boy" or "normal girl," but only individuals with an infinite variety of growth patterns? The answers to these questions depend a great deal on the individual's past, and exert a strong influence on his future behavior.

Of the 1,124 compositions obtained from junior and senior high school students in the single-county sample previously mentioned, 238, or 21 per cent, expressed satisfaction with body growth, change, or status; 260, or 23 per cent, expressed dissatisfaction. As might be expected, the more intelligent (IQs 120–129), whose physical development is usually superior, were more satisfied with their growth than were those of average or low IQ. The figures in Table 10 show the number and percentage of different grade and IQ levels who expressed satisfaction or dissatisfaction with their own body growth:

TABLE 10

Grade Level and IQ	Number of Compositions	Those Expressing Satisfaction with Own Body Growth		Those Expressing Dissatisfaction with Own Body Growth	
		No.	Per Cent	No.	Per Cent
7–8–9; Average IQ: 95.2	247	45	18	54	22
7–8–9; IQ: 120–129	121	39	32	29	24
7–8–9; IQ: 130 and over	35	10	29	13	37
10–11–12; Average IQ: 94.9	636	113	18	144	23
10–11–12; IQ: 120–129	65	25	38	15	23
10–11–12; IQ: 130 and over	20	6	30	5	25

These percentages suggest that we should recognize not only the dissatisfactions but also the satisfactions which young people feel in the physical aspects of growing up and in their changing growth status.

The many disadvantages of late maturing are mentioned more frequently by boys than by girls. One fourteen-year-old boy referred to the way people reacted to his small size: "Being small is no help in growing up. A small boy is always recognized as an eighth grader instead of a ninth. Whenever I'm introduced to somebody bigger than me they always seem surprised to learn I'm a ninth grader." Being small for his age made it difficult for him to achieve status in his group.

Another boy of the same age and grade went into more detail on the difficulty a small boy has in participating in sports and making a good social adjustment:

Size means a lot in the ninth grade, especially when you are small, you get pushed around by all the biger boys. To be in sports you have to be big and brawny. On the football field you always get the bad positions. When you play basketball they never pass to you. If you get the ball, they expect you to pass it immediately to them, and if you don't you're a stupid dope. You never get a chance to show how good you are. If you miss a shot they tell you that you ought to learn to shoot, but they don't let you learn to shoot because they are always hogging the ball. When you are small they never invite you to a party.

According to another ninth-grade youngster, it is even worse if one is both short and thin:

My problem is being short and kind of skinny. So I'm not good in baseball and can't go out for football and can't play basketball. The rest of the sports I don't like. . . . And girls don't like boys shorter than them. I've tried a few things: exercise to build up the body, eating more than usual, eating the right kind of food to put on weight, drinking more milk, and trying to get more sleep—they say you grow more in your sleep.

This boy added as objective evidence of the success of his multiple efforts: "In the past couple of months I've outgrown all my clothes!"

A senior boy who had unusual understanding of normal fluctuations in rate of growth rejoiced at having at last "come up to a half-way decent height" and concluded, "All in all, I'm thankful I have come this far and fervently hope I keep on growing."

Unfortunately, the feelings of inferiority which originate during a period of delayed growth may persist even after the growth spurt begins. One ninth-grade boy explained how being short and fat in his earlier years had made him self-conscious. Even after he began to get taller and "started to stretch" and his weight did not show so much, it took a long time for him to get over his self-consciousness and to mingle with the crowd. He concluded, "It seems like a small problem to me now, but when I was younger, it was the biggest problem I had to face."

Girls, too, have their problems related to physical growth. Most serious is that of being much taller than one's classmates, especially the boys. As one gifted girl said, "If you're taller than boys, it's bad enough, but if you're brighter, it's fatal." An eighth-grade girl with an IQ of 76 wrote, "I wish I was built cute."

Abruptness of physical and physiological change may be even more important than deviations in height and weight. We are quite sure that the changes are more abrupt for girls than for boys and that they are more sudden for some individuals than for others. Mental, social, and emotional as well as physical changes come quickly for the girl who matures early. When bodily changes are gradual, the individual adjusts to them unconsciously. Possibly this is why more adolescents did not mention problems of physical growth in their compositions. Instead, they frequently expressed a positive attitude toward attaining physical maturity.

RELATION OF PHYSICAL TO EMOTIONAL
AND SOCIAL DEVELOPMENT

Physical and physiological changes may have pervasive emotional overtones. Young adolescents who have a well-balanced physical development and accept their changing bodies move into the responsibilities of later adolescence quite smoothly, other things being equal. Adequate physical development helps to give them self-confidence. According to Irene M. Josselyn:

The shifts in the interaction between physical growth and emotional growth, when both follow the average pattern, can almost be charted. . . . In the early period of rapid physical growth, the characteristic psychological pattern is one of increased ego capacity to deal with reality. When the reproductive organs begin to function, the psychological mechanisms of adjustment are overwhelmed by the impact of the new impulses and the intensification of the older ones. As a result, earlier established ego defenses become inadequate. With the attainment of physical stability at a relatively mature level, the individual again develops capacity for psychological integration. It is usually in this latter period that the individual reveals the underlying nature of his adolescent conflicts, his attempts at solving them, and the goals toward which he is striving.[13]

It would seem advantageous for the individual to accept his changing biological self during puberty. But when the change is abrupt, it is often accompanied, especially among girls, by a restriction or suppression of feelings.

Physical, Social, and Emotional Interrelations

Important insights concerning the relation of physical to emotional and social development have been obtained from intensive studies such as the developmental study by More.[14] Among the significant insights and hypotheses gained from such research are the following:

The physical, social, and emotional aspects of development are interrelated and coordinated especially among girls.[15]

Physical status affects social status of adolescents in varying degrees. Observation has shown that the boy or girl who differs markedly in height, weight, and strength from other individuals

[13] Irene M. Josselyn, *The Adolescent and His World*, p. 7. New York: Family Service Association of America, 1952.

[14] Douglas M. More, *Developmental Concordance and Discordance during Puberty and Early Adolescence*, monograph of the Society for Research in Child Development, ser. 56, vol. 18, no. 1, 1953. Champaign, Ill.: University of Illinois, Child Development Publications, 1955.

[15] *Ibid.*, p. 39.

of the same age often feels socially inadequate. In More's study,[16] the earlier-maturing girl seemed to be more sociable, more emotionally stable and well integrated, more active and forceful than the later-maturing girl. However, with young adolescent girls, More found no significant relation between physical maturity and social interaction(For a particular girl, physical maturity might be quite important socially, while for another girl, physical maturity might have a relatively unimportant effect upon her social life. At the later age of sixteen there was a higher relation between physical maturity and warmth of feeling toward others and participation in group activities. And whatever socio-physical relationship exists seems to be much less marked for boys than for girls.

Physical status seems to be more closely related to emotional than to social development; emotional status seems to be intermediate between physical and social status. In fact, emotional development is critical in that it permits social behavior and adjustment. However, the influence of the individual's emotional pattern which persists from childhood into adolescence may outweigh the effect of two or three years' difference in the time of physical maturation.

Emotional maturity does not inevitably accompany physiological maturity, although delayed physical maturity may make it difficult for a boy or girl to feel emotionally mature and thus to make a normal social adjustment. If the earlier-maturer is not reassured that his feeling of inferiority owing to marked physical difference from his age-mates will not last forever, he is likely to become increasingly anxious about it.

Physical and emotional maturity are not always related to social maturity. Boys and girls may have the physical maturity and emotional readiness for mature living but lack the necessary social techniques to make a satisfactory adjustment with their age-mates. A few may be immature physically and emotionally, but already possessed of a social sensitivity and social skills that enable them to respond to people appropriately. However, it is possible that persons who are very late in maturing physically

16 *Ibid.*

may be lacking in the emotional perceptions which would make it possible for them to achieve good social interaction and normal social relations with their peers. Skillful guidance in social relations might help these later-maturers to make a better social adjustment.

A significant relation between physical maturation and ratings on the achievement of developmental tasks was obtained for girls but not for boys.[17] This relation was especially evident in the achievement of emotional independence. A possible explanation is that the earlier-maturing girl who has been successful in her initial attempts to be independent and make her own decisions tends to persist in this direction, whereas the later-maturing girl who made unsuccessful attempts at the same chronological age becomes discouraged from engaging in further independent thought and action.

There will always be individuals who are not in accord with any general trend or who do not follow a common pattern of development. In fact, each individual follows a unique pattern of physical-emotional-social development, and, as More so wisely concluded, "It is clear from these data that an attempt to apply such broad generalizations without modification, for the understanding of any particular adolescent girl, or small sample of such girls, could be in considerable error." [18]

Relation of Physical Fitness to Emotional and Social Behavior

A physical defect or bodily conformation that prevents the adolescent boy from participating successfully in athletics may seriously affect his emotional and social development. In a study [19] of the personal and social adjustment of 461 sophomore and junior high school boys, those ranking high in athletic achievement showed better personal and social adjustment than those whose athletic achievement was low. Physique, motor skill,

[17] *Ibid.*, p. 37.
[18] *Ibid.*, p. 31.
[19] Lowell G. Biddulph, "Athletic Achievement and the Personal and Social Adjustment of High School Boys," *Research Quarterly of the American Association for Health and Physical Education*, vol. 25 (March, 1954), pp. 1–7.

and popularity are closely associated. Especially in situations where athletics play a prominent part in school and community life and winning teams are lionized, the boy who cannot take part in athletics is likely to be considered a "sissy." Worse still, his masculine concept of himself is weakened. This anxiety about whether he is a capable, manly person may find expression in many kinds of behavior that are inexplicable to the boy himself and to his parents and teachers. He may also attribute many of his other troubles to the physical defect or deviation. Jones and Bayley [20] reported the following relationships between physical maturity and social and emotional traits in boys: the physically accelerated boys were usually accepted by their peers without having to strive for status, treated as more mature by both adults and children, and given positions of leadership in senior high school. The physically retarded boys were more likely to show immature behavior, perhaps because their classmates and elders treated them as immature, and were more likely to strive for attention or, in some cases, to withdraw.

Since the desire to be popular among one's peers is keen during the preadolescent and adolescent years, we should expect a close relation between physical fitness, physique, motor skills, and popularity among adolescent boys. This expectation has been verified by research. Hanley [21] reported a significant relation between body type and reputation among adolescent boys. McCraw and Tolbert [22] found a significant relation between sociometric status and athletic ability in boys in grades seven, eight, and nine. Supplementing an admirable statistical study, Harold E. Jones [23] presented case material confirming the quantitative

[20] Mary C. Jones and Nancy Bayley, "Physical Maturing among Boys as Related to Behavior," *Journal of Educational Psychology,* vol. 41 (March, 1950), pp. 129–148.

[21] Charles Hanley, "Physique and Reputation of Junior High School Boys," *Child Development,* vol. 22 (December, 1951), pp. 247–260.

[22] L. W. McCraw and J. W. Tolbert, "Sociometric Status and Athletic Ability of Junior High School Boys," *Research Quarterly,* vol. 24 (March, 1953), pp. 72–80.

[23] Harold E. Jones, "Physical Ability as a Factor in Social Adjustment in Adolescence," *Journal of Educational Research,* vol. 40 (December, 1946), pp. 287–301.

evidence that among boys "competitive athletic skills are among the chief sources of social esteem in the period preceding maturity."

For the awkward boy who withdraws into intellectual pursuits, or the athletic girl "attractive only by day," Lawrence S. Kubie [24] recommended a physical-evaluation program to plan sports assignments, and individual guidance and instruction to assure these students success in riding, swimming, or other socially popular activities. Lack of physical facilities for recreation and shortage of time to engage in group activities may defeat individual guidance such as Kubie mentioned. The guidance of adolescents with limited physical abilities involves a twofold approach: to help them understand and accept themselves, and to help them make the most of their assets.

HOW ADULTS CAN HELP ADOLESCENTS ACHIEVE PHYSICAL COMPETENCY

Adults should be sensitive to the wide variations in rate and to deviations in physical development as children enter the period of puberty. They should recognize that an adolescent's attitude and behavior may be attributable to such factors as social demands on him and people's expectations and treatment of him as well as to the physical and biological changes. When the youngster becomes physiologically mature, he is aware that adults expect him to behave differently. This awareness may help him to express his feelings in socially acceptable ways. But if adult standards are low and if they expect adolescents to be "crazy, mixed-up kids," the effect on teen-age behavior is serious. Adults can help adolescents understand and accept, with a certain amount of pride, their changes in size and body form and functioning and to view physical competency as a means to some worthwhile goal, not as an end in itself.

Recognizing the possible interweaving of physical, emotional, and social factors, adults will be alert to emotional concomi-

[24] Lawrence S. Kubie, "Competitive Sports and the Awkward Child," Child Study, vol. 31 (Spring, 1954), pp. 10–15.

tants that may be disturbing an individual adolescent and interfering with his social adjustment. Among the sources of emotional disturbance are the child's changing relation to his parents, the suddenness of the onset of puberty and what it means to him, the lack of opportunity to express the body image of himself as an adult, the lack of socially acceptable and creative outlets for his impulses.

Recognizing individual differences in growth patterns, the adult will help the individual to develop in his own best way, and will try to see any difficult situation through the young person's eyes; otherwise the adult may view the adolescent's inner feelings and outward behavior quite differently than it is viewed by the teen-ager himself and by his peers.

Another important adult responsibility, shared with the young persons, is to create an environment that promotes physical competency. Such an environment includes play space, time for physical activities, and instruction in skills that are appropriate and socially useful to the individual. Many values accrue when adults and adolescents work together to use natural recreational resources and make the community a better place for children and adolescents to grow toward maturity.

For adolescents who are physically incapacitated, the environment should provide activities in which they can be successful, and which will increase their self-esteem, enrich their social relations, and give them some opportunity to be of service. In fact, these are desirable characteristics for the environment of all adolescents.

COMPREHENSION QUESTIONS

1. How may the adolescent's physical development be related to his concept of himself?

2. What are some of the satisfactions adolescents may feel in growing up? What are some of their common dissatisfactions?

3. What biological factors stimulate and control physical growth and development?

4. How do boys compare with girls in their physical development? What effect may this difference have on boy-girl relations?

5. What range of feelings may girls have toward menstruation?

6. How may earlier or later maturing affect girls and boys? In what ways may early maturity be an advantage to boys and a disadvantage to girls?

7. Describe the possible interaction between physical, social, and emotional development.

8. What are the most serious and common health problems of adolescents?

STUDY PROJECTS

1. Begin a study of the growth of several preadolescents whom you know well, weighing and measuring each of them carefully each month and relating their growth curves to other signs of biological maturity.

2. Describe a school and community recreational program that would contribute to the physical and social development of both boys and girls.

3. If you are a physical education teacher, identify the early-maturing girls and refer them for counseling if they seem to be having difficulty in their social or emotional development. Similarly, identify boys who cannot excel in athletics and help them to gain prestige in other ways, such as by being sports reporters or team managers.

4. Help a youngster who is rejected by his classmates because of lack of skill in sports or unattractive appearance to acquire some athletic, musical, dramatic, or other skill, or to make the most of his physical assets through good grooming and more attractive clothing.

5. Study the breakfast problem or some other health problem by first trying to understand how adolescents perceive the situation and what their motivations are.

6. Obtain compositions on some health topic such as "The best thing I ever did for my health," "Why I sometimes don't do the healthful things I know I ought to do," or "My most serious growth and health problems and what I have done about them."

7. Interest a group of teen-agers in making a survey of local facilities for outdoor recreation and in doing something to improve them.

FOR FURTHER STUDY

AUSUBEL, DAVID P., *Theory and Problems of Adolescent Development,* chaps. IV, V, VI. New York: Grune & Stratton, Inc., 1954.

GESELL, ARNOLD, FRANCES L. ILG, and LOUISE BATES AMES, *Youth, the Years from Ten to Sixteen,* chaps. XI, XII. New York: Harper & Brothers, 1956.

HURLOCK, ELIZABETH B., *Adolescent Development,* chaps. II, III. New York: McGraw-Hill Book Company, Inc., 1955.

JONES, HAROLD E., *Development in Adolescence.* New York: Appleton-Century-Crofts, Inc., 1943.

———, "Physical Ability as a Factor in Social Adjustment in Adolescence," *Journal of Educational Research,* vol. 40 (December, 1946), pp. 287–301.

JONES, MARY C., and NANCY BAYLEY, "Physical Maturing among Boys as Related to Behavior," *Journal of Educational Psychology,* vol. 41 (March, 1950), pp. 129–148.

JOSSELYN, IRENE M., *The Adolescent and His World,* chaps. I, II. New York: Family Service Association of America, 1952.

KUHLEN, RAYMOND G., *The Psychology of Adolescent Development,* chap. II. New York: Harper & Brothers, 1952.

MORE, DOUGLAS M., *Developmental Concordance and Discordance during Puberty and Early Adolescence,* monograph of the Society for Research in Child Development, ser. 56, vol. 18, no. 1, 1953. Champaign, Ill.: University of Illinois, Child Development Publications, 1955.

SCHONFELD, W. A., "Primary and Secondary Sexual Characteristics: Study of Their Development in Males from Birth through Maturity," *American Journal of Diseases of Children,* vol. 65 (April, 1943), pp. 535–549.

SHUTTLEWORTH, F. K., *The Adolescent Period: a Graphic Atlas.* Evanston, Ill.: Child Development Publications, 1951.

STATON, WESLEY M., "The Adolescent: His Physical Growth and Health," *Review of Educational Research,* vol. 24 (February, 1954), pp. 19–29.

STOLZ, HERBERT R., and LOIS MEEK STOLZ, *Somatic Development of Adolescent Boys.* New York: The Macmillan Company, 1951.

VINCENT, ELIZABETH LEE, "Physical and Psychological Aspects of Puberty and Adolescence," *National Association of Deans of Women Journal,* vol. 19 (October, 1955), pp. 3–10.

WATTENBERG, WILLIAM W., *The Adolescent Years,* chap. VII. New York: Harcourt, Brace and Company, Inc., 1955.

Audio-visual Aids

Physical Aspects of Puberty. 19 minutes. Sound. McGraw-Hill.

Your Body during Adolescence (Health and Safety Series) 10 minutes. Sound. McGraw-Hill.

CHAPTER 7

Achieving Scholastic Success

In our culture achieving scholastic success is a generally recognized adolescent task. It is recognized as important by parents, by teachers, of course, and by the students themselves. Students in many localities and in all grades of junior and senior high school cite problems related to schoolwork as one of their major areas of concern.

PREVALENCE AND KINDS OF ACADEMIC PROBLEMS

Previous studies show that from one-third to one-half of the school population mention anxiety about school in essays and on check lists. They express fear of tests, of "speaking up in class," and of failing in schoolwork. They are worried about getting low grades or being a grade behind their age-mates. They speak of having trouble with various subjects—arithmetic, spelling, grammar, writing—and with giving oral reports. In many instances difficulties in reading underlie failure in other subjects.

Some of these difficulties they attribute to lack of interest in certain subjects—being required to take subjects they do not like —dull classes and books, poor teaching, too little freedom or too much disorder in class, and insufficient class discussion. They also recognize pupil-teacher relationships as a factor in a student's school achievement.

Some students blame themselves rather than the school or the teachers. They realize that they are not spending enough time in study, do not know how to study effectively, or cannot keep their minds on their studies. Many mention, as their biggest problem, being bored with school, being unable to get interested in their subjects.

Academic problems vary in quantity and in kind with intelligence and sex. Students in the lower quarter of intelligence check certain problems more frequently than those who are intellectually superior; these problems include anxiety about failing and not being able to finish high school, about being held a grade behind others of their age, about having difficulty in understanding words and in becoming interested in their required reading. It is possible that anxiety about schoolwork may be part of a more pervasive, general anxiety. Girls generally get along better in school than boys. They skip grades more often; they less often repeat grades; they get higher grades in all subjects except social studies and science, in which boys show a slight superiority. Yet, on intelligence test scores, boys and girls are about equal.

Success in school may have a pervasive effect on the student's personality. As a young person improves his achievement, he develops his powers, and his self-confidence increases. Whether a student has a favorable experience and attitude toward school depends a great deal on whether he has good relations with teachers and a satisfying social life with his age-mates. School offers students opportunities to make friends. Even some who have been isolates may build up friendships by working together on a class or club committee, or even by being assigned to certain tables in the school cafeteria.

MEANING OF SCHOOL SUCCESS

Adolescents want to experience success. But "success" has many different meanings, to young people and to adults. To a few it means having the highest marks in the class. To others it means reaching an individual goal or standard; anything below one's level of aspiration is failure. To many, success means passing in every subject. To some of these, barely "getting by" is enough. In a school where the morale is low, some able learners deliberately court failure, "just to be fellowed," as Sidney Lanier expressed it. They would rather fail in a subject than be branded as a "brain," a "square," or "Einstein." There are also a few who fail a subject or flunk out of school or college in order to express their hostility to parents who seem to care more for their child's achievement than for the child himself. To very mature adolescents, success means working up to their optimum capacity, realizing their intellectual potentialities.

Teachers also view scholastic success in different ways. Some define success as meeting grade standards. Others consider successful any adolescent who is achieving up to his capacity; they take into account his family background and his previous educational opportunities as well as his intelligence as observed and as indicated on intelligence tests. Teachers would profit by seeing more clearly what is the effect of interest on adolescents' learning, how students feel about school marks, and what makes study easy or hard for them.

THE ROLE OF INTEREST IN LEARNING

In writing on the topic, "How does your interest in a book or in an assignment affect what you read, how you read, and what you learn," junior and senior high school students considered interest of as great importance as John Dewey did. The tenor of their thinking was as follows: When they are not interested in a book or an assignment, they "don't care what it says," skim over it, read as little of it as possible, do not notice the important points or get much out of it, do not remember what they read, and get poor marks in the subject. On the other hand, when they are interested they enjoy it, read eagerly and quickly but carefully, note important ideas and "take in more facts," comprehend with little effort in one reading, remember what they read, go into the subject more deeply, and read more on the same subject.

One twelve-year-old boy in the seventh grade summed up his point of view in two terse sentences: "The more interest, the more reading; the more reading, the more knowledge. If you are interested in an assignment it is easier and faster to do."

Another boy, one year older and in the eighth grade, explained more introspectively how he felt about a dull book or assignment:

When I am interested in something I read faster and understand what I read with a feeling I am getting something out of it. I feel like keeping on with the same subject. And when they ask me a question I have the right answer.

When I am not interested I can't hardly read or understand what I'm studying about. I feel like the period is never going to finish. I feel like I ain't getting nothing out of what I am studying. And I feel lazying, sleepy without energy; can't wait till the period is finished so I can go to the other.

A girl in the same grade went into more detail:

If I am interested in a subject that we are discussing in class, I am much more suseptible to knowledge. I will read the subject much better and easier. I think my work would be much better if I am interested in a subject and I will like it much better.

On the other hand, if I am not interested in the subject we are working on and it is to borring, I may have some sort of a mental block. This is very foolish and I am trying to correct it. We sometimes have to work on things we don't like.

An older girl, sixteen years old, made a still more detailed analysis:

When I get a chapter in History for an assignment I usually think, "Oh this ought to be interesting" or else, "don't want to read this, it will probably be very boring. I'll just look it over if I have some spare time in Study Hall."

I think that the subject of a reading assignment greatly affects how thoroughly you read it. If I get a chapter in History that I'm interested in, I will read it and consentrate on it so that I will know what I read. But if I don't like what I have to read, I will probably just skim over it and end up not knowing anymore than I did before I started. If I'm not interested in what I'm reading, I usually have the radio on, and pay more attention to that, or else I sit and watch television while I'm reading.

If I am really interested in what I'm reading, I will understand it and I will learn a lot. I won't just read it because I feel I have to in case we have a test on it, but I will read it because I want to.

If I'm not interested in what I have to read I won't even care if I learn anything from it or not.

It also depends on the mood I'm in when I read it, how much I learn. If I feel ambitious, I will learn a lot but if I'm tired or don't feel like doing anything I won't learn anything from it.

Some of the youngsters gave a few clues as to what makes school books and assignments dull. They say that subjects may be boring because, as they are taught, they are too easy or too difficult. One sixteen-year-old boy took citizenship education as an illustration:

I look on most assignments as very dull reading. I hold the point that reading to learn is not at all as interesting as reading for your pleasure is. In a Cit. Ed. book the author makes his idea known and then goes on to the next one leaving you just getting interested in the first one. Like, he starts to tell about a war, he tells all the reasons the war started, he tells all the countries that were in it and then says something like, "The war lasted two years" and stops.

I find reading Cit. Ed. very dull but, very easy. The author gives you all the facts where I can't miss them and for this reason I can read with the radio on and still get it. If the assignment is a long one I read till I have covered six or seven pages and then I do something else for a while, while the part I have read sinks in.

I think the reading is too easy to read and that's why it's so dull. The author uses sub-titles for most of important parts and they stand out like a house on fire.

To put what I think of Cit. Ed. reading in one sentence—it is very dull but very easy.

Quite different from the compositions just quoted and atypical of the responses in general was the composition written by a seventeen-year-old boy whose severe reading disability precluded any interest in reading:

The subject that I read makes no difference to me. Because I think reading is strictly for the birds. In short, I hate anything that has to do with reading, such as books, teachers that make me read, and so on.

I can read a chapter in anything and not know a thing about it. When I read, which is very seldom, unless it's homework. . . . And if you want to know what I learn, that is a laugh. In short, nothing except how to get board.

As a follow-up of these compositions, and because so many youngsters took the attitude that "if you're not interested, that settles it—you don't learn," several classes were asked to write on the topic, "How I became interested in something I was not interested in at first." The following composition by a boy in the eighth grade is one of the most comprehensive on this topic and includes most of the items mentioned in other papers:

In going about getting interested in something that you don't particuly care for you may do a number of things.

First you could read a lot on the subject and find out weather it is interesting to you. (Sometimes you aren't interested in somcthing for the simple reason you don't know anything about it.)

You could find out about a subject from a friend who is interested in that certin subject.

You may *have* to read a book, article, story, etc., about a certin subject and then find out that you like that subject.

You may have to do some research on a subject for a certain class and find out that that subject appeals to you.

You could just pick up a book or magizine on a subject and read about it and find out that that subject is turiably interesting.

One additional suggestion made by a youngster in the same class was to "Try to find out the things about a subject that you are interested in and concentrate mostly on these. There will, of course, be some things that you won't like but try to forget these and, as I said, concentrate on the things that interest you about the subject."

Teachers will be better able to help students achieve scholastic success if they know how they feel about their subjects and under what conditions they are most interested. To do this is not to pamper or "spoon feed" students. Interest evokes effort and concentration; it aids comprehension and retention of ideas; it facilitates learning. Therefore, by knowing how students perceive their reading and study assignments, teachers can create conditions that are more conducive to effective learning.

In general, students do not learn without doing or practicing what is to be learned. That is, a child does not learn simply by being told what he is to learn; he learns what he *does;* the task must serve some purpose which the individual has originated or accepted as his own. We will get further by treating students as persons who are seeking something, rather than as persons who are avoiding something. There is always some stimulus to learning—an internal or external condition that creates a need. This problem or need arouses feeling or emotion, which leads one to think about ways of meeting the need or solving the problem. A certain amount of tension is necessary for learning. However, intense, undifferentiated anxiety will interfere with learning; the individual cannot analyze or learn from it. In such cases reduction of anxiety facilitates learning.[1] Principles of learning, emphasizing (1) interest, purpose, and need, (2) immediate application of what is learned, and (3) emotional factors, apply to all kinds of learning.

HOW ADOLESCENTS FEEL ABOUT TESTS, MARKS, AND REPORT CARDS

In the composite sample of compositions on "How it feels to be growing up" (see Chapter 4), almost one-fifth spontaneously mentioned concern with school success or grades. The percentages were about the same in junior and in senior high school, and only slightly smaller for the superior than for the less able learners. In compositions on "When I have felt disturbed or at a loss," problems of school achievement were mentioned relatively more frequently.

Adolescents are worried about marks and examinations for various reasons—because of the attitudes of their parents, because failure may affect their self-esteem and their future educational

[1] O. Hobart Mowrer, *Learning Theory and Personality Dynamics.* New York: The Ronald Press Company, 1950.

and vocational plans. Many believe in the importance of schooling as a means toward "getting along in the world."

Quotations from compositions will give a vivid impression of
the way some sensitive youngsters feel about marks and examinations.

The first composition, written by an extremely conscientious
seventeen-year-old senior girl, expresses a common anxiety created by tests and examinations:

I'm usually in good humor but every once and a while things
seem to pile up and I get discouraged. This happened only yesterday and, I think, for a good reason.

During the term, I find, I have been studying more than most of
my friends but to no avail. I come home from school, study for one
hour, eat supper and do homework for the next three hours. Now
that the finals are "just around the corner" I feel as if I still don't
know a thing, not even enough to pass a simple exam. Yesterday I
was trying to figure it out but arrived at no conclusion. I don't think
I'll be able to remember all the material we have had. If I cram I
think I'll be able to pass most of the tests. I only hope I have enough
time to learn everything or at least to review it.

In the second composition, another seventeen-year-old senior
girl describes the effect of an examination question she could
not answer, and gives her opinion of the kind of questions the
examination contained:

The day I remember the best as giving me the greatest letdown
in my high school years, happened one Monday morning last June
when I took the geometry examination.

I can laugh now but I will tell you one thing, I did not laugh
when I left that examination room or for a good week afterwards.
I was completely at a loss when I began the third part of that paper. I could not and did not do one of the proposed problems. I remember finishing the first two parts of the paper without too much
trouble but once I came face to face with that third part I can really
say I lost my wits, nerve, and all my knowledge of geometry.

I did pass the examination after all my despair at the lack of
knowledge that I had gained during the year that I had studied ge-

ometry. I can give the advice of experience to all those who in the future plan to attack this subject. Study all the little unimportant things and then you are sure to be able to work out the third part of the paper. My downfall was due to the fact that I skipped over the little ones and studied the things that I considered important.

Examinations which determine some important outcome, such as entrance to a particular high school or college, produce still more intense emotional disturbance. The effect, as seen by a 12½-year-old boy, of not passing the entrance examination to a high school of music and art, on which he had set his heart, was pervasive and persistent. He described the experience in a composition when he was 15½ years old:

I was 12½ years old, and very determined to become a concert pianist. I was to take my examination for the high school of music and art. I felt that my whole future, everything that I had ever worked for, depended on the results of that examination. I just couldn't fail.

Finally after strenuous hours of practicing, the time for the test came. To say that I was merely nervous is just putting it mildly. For it wasn't only me taking the exam, but I knew how my parents felt about it. Everything, it seemed was at stake.

The night before the exam, I had hardly slept. I couldn't eat any breakfast and showed up two hours early. Finally, the moment arrived. The time just hurried by, and before I knew it, it was over. The test itself I had found rather easy, too easy. I went home feeling confident of being accepted. But that feeling didn't last very long. We weren't to find out the results until two weeks later. Then the usual after exam jitters began to take hold of me. I kept on finding more and more mistakes that I had made. Now I was less and less confident. In fact, I was sure that I had failed miserably.

At long last, my official teacher read the names of those accepted and those refused.

I always had been an optimist, and at that moment I had a feeling that I would be accepted. The names were read—I was not on the accepted list. I had not expected it, but yet something inside of me told me that maybe, some mirical—but no. The blow had struck. I had failed my parents and myself. I can't very well explain the feeling that I had. I became very moody and sometimes melancholy. I was obsessed with a feeling of failure and inferiority.

Everything that I had ever dreamed of just crumbled before me. The worst result was that I refused to continue playing the piano. I proved to be a coward. But something happened to change that, something that to this day is unexplainable to me. One night I had a dream that my hands were crushed by the piano keyboard and woke up screaming violently, that if I could only have my hands back I would play again, and keep on playing.

That seemed to be the cure. I continued my piano lessons, but I never seemed to regain my old spark about life on the whole. Many times, I think back, and instead of taking it lightly, I again become moody and obsessed with the same feeling. I become frightened and wonder if life is worth living, because it is always full of disappointments. I don't know whether that has anything to do with my failing the music test or it is just the adolescent stage I am going through.

I feel that I can't do anything about it, and hope that as I grow older and mature, I will come to look at life in a brighter light.

This was a boy who arrived at adolescence with many emotional problems of childhood unsolved. In looking back, he attributed his subsequent depression and fear to the one experience of failing the examination, an experience that a more robust personality could have faced without such profound emotional consequences.

After reading these compositions some teachers may say, "These are very exceptional cases. The majority of teen-agers don't take school seriously enough." Perhaps. But compositions somewhat like these occurred quite frequently; all of them were written with apparent sincerity. It may be that the "indifference" and "laziness" often observed by teachers represent an attempt to camouflage deeper feelings of anxiety and discouragement.

Similar feelings of anxiety were expressed in compositions specifically dealing with the subject of report cards. Although real advances have been made in methods of reporting pupil progress, many schools continue to use some variation of the traditional type of report card, which many students and parents still regard as a picture of the student's success in school. To improve our methods of reporting to parents, we should ask three questions:

1. What is the purpose of the report?
2. How do the students feel about it?
3. What do the parents do about it?

We would all agree that the purpose of report cards or other forms of reporting is primarily to help students make the best progress possible for them. To accomplish this purpose the report should (1) include items on all the important areas of adolescent development to which the school can and should contribute, (2) represent an accurate appraisal, (3) be analytic enough so that the student and parent can see strong and weak points, (4) appraise the student's progress with reference to his ability, and (5) suggest practical ways in which he can do better. Obviously all this information cannot be included on the traditional type of report card. For this reason, in many school systems the written report is being supplemented or even supplanted by parent-teacher conferences. The trends toward holding parent-teacher conferences to promote mutual understanding of the child and of the report and toward placing more responsibility on the child for appraising his own achievement are two promising developments in reporting pupil progress.[2]

The need for improvement in methods of reporting pupil progress is shown by the way students and parents respond to them. Students express their common feeling of tension over report cards by such words as "excited," "dread," "scared," "embarrassed," "disappointed," "thrilled," "weak in the knees," "anxious." Students' responses in 567 compositions from a wide variety of school situations on the topics, "How I feel when I get my report card" and "How I feel when I get my report card, what I do about it, and what my parents say and do about it," were tabulated. Table 11 gives a quantitative picture of their feelings and viewpoints.

[2] Ruth Strang, *How to Report Pupil Progress.* Chicago: Science Research Associates, Inc., 1955.

TABLE 11

Students' Responses	Students Making a Given Response in					
	Grades 4–5–6 (No., 112)		Grades 7–8–9 (No., 281)		Grades 10–11–12 (No., 174)	
	No.	Per Cent	No.	Per Cent	No.	Per Cent
Fear of physical punishment........	28	25.0	7	2.5	1	0.6
Fear of parent disapproval or loss of privileges.....................	38	34.0	139	50.0	103	59.0
General feeling of anxiety, fear, or extreme uneasiness at the time of receiving the report.............	16	14.0	26	9.3	11	6.3
Dissatisfaction with parents' indifference......................	0	0	21	7.5	8	4.6
Alleged feeling of indifference or lack of anxiety.....................	0	0	13	4.6	17	9.8
Expectation of parental support, understanding, or assistance........	0	0	25	8.9	15	8.6
Feeling of pleasant surprise.........	8	7.1	2	0.7	8	4.6
Blame teacher...................	1	0.9	22	7.8	17	9.8
Blame system of marking or of reporting......................	0	0	19	6.8	7	4.0
Blame self for bad report.........	0	0	21	7.5	8	4.6
Determination to improve.........	15	13.0	32	11.0	23	13.0

From Table 11 and from the reading of many other compositions, several generalizations may be made:

1. Their dominant feelings were fear and anxiety; almost two-thirds of them specifically mentioned these feelings about report cards. Apparently many youngsters of all ages tend to "expect the worst" and to feel surprised and pleased when their reports are good.
2. These feelings of fear and anxiety arise primarily from dread of incurring parental disapproval and loss of privileges.
3. Relatively few youngsters:

    a. Said they were indifferent or not anxious about report cards
    b. Expected parental support or assistance
    c. Blamed the teacher
4. Still fewer:
    a. Felt surprised and pleased with their reports
    b. Blamed the marking system
    c. Blamed themselves
    d. Complained that their parents were indifferent about their
        reports

In view of the assumed purpose of reports to parents, it is significant that only about one-eighth, or 12 per cent, of the total group expressed determination to improve. In this respect there was little change from the fourth to the twelfth grades, though there were differences among schools having different methods of marking and reporting and different psychological atmospheres. Determination to improve may be short-lived, because the usual report does not suggest specific ways to improve. Students may resolve to try to do better the next time, but this feeling usually vanishes in a week or two. One youngster expressed it in this way:

On those occasions on which we get the scholastic report on our marks, if I have done my best, I feel good. But if I have not as has sometimes happened I feel a bit depressed. But I do feel temporarily ambitious saying to myself that I am going to try my hardest the next term. This urge has usually died out before the next week has passed.

This sample of compositions showed a few age differences as to the students' reactions to reports. Fear of physical punishment decreased and fear of parental disapproval or loss of privileges increased as children passed into the adolescent period. The elementary school children were less analytical about the report card situation: they did not blame the teacher, or the reporting or marking system, or themselves. They never expressed unconcern about reports. Apparently they did not expect their parents to be either indifferent or helpful or understanding, as did some of the junior and senior high school stu dents. From the elementary to the junior high school grades an increasing number of students blamed themselves when a report was "bad." This may indicate an increasingly objective attitude, in accord with the tendency to face reality at this age.

Many youngsters have mixed feelings regarding their reports, depending upon the quality of the report and their parents' response to it. An exceptionally analytical treatment of the subject was made by a seventeen-year-old boy who attached great importance to report cards:

One month my parents will congratulate me and tell me that I could do even better. But the next month my marks will drop and so will my confidence but it is here that my mother and father build it right up again. It is this little push which enables me to try harder. Instead, coming home with a bad report card, my parents scolding me or punishing will not help at all.

Something the parents and teachers don't understand is that the pupil feels bad too. Sometimes very strange things such as refusing to work any more or disobedience in class can come from the wrong attitude between teacher, parents and pupils.

HOW MARKS MAY AFFECT PUPIL-TEACHER RELATIONS

Many youngsters are more concerned with what their parents will say than with what the marks show about their growth in knowledge. Marks, like punishment, may evoke the student's hostility toward the teacher instead of directing his attention to ways of improving his record. In the eighth grade of a city school located in a delinquent area, the topic of report cards evoked a particularly violent expression of hatred for teachers. The two following compositions are typical of the twenty handed in by this class of serious behavior problems:

When I get and find out my marks I feel like giving the teachers a piece of mind. I don't mean just, "I don't deserve the mark I got." I'll tell him he is mentally unbalanced and they should be shot for being dopy freaks. I tell my mother that he hates civilization and that he talks a lot about the Trojans and never teachs us anything.

First off my first idea is to get a gun and shot a few teachers, then I know the stinking rotten teachers aint worth it. For two reasons first off a .38 bullet cost three cents and a prison term *if* you are caught. Well *if* my report card is good they say keep up the good work, if it is bad well my father don't talk much if you know what I mean.

One can only speculate as to the combination of heredity and environment that produced such attitudes in young adolescent boys. This subject will be discussed in more detail in Chapter 12.

In contrast to these expressions of violent hostility toward the teacher, other compositions present the teacher as fair-minded and helpful. For example, one eleven-year-old girl in the seventh grade in another school wrote: "Last year, in sixth grade, we had a teacher who would discuss our report cards with us. If we felt we were being marked unfairly we would tell him and he would go over it. If he was wrong he would change the mark."

WHAT PARENTS DO ABOUT REPORT CARDS

Many students anticipate their parents' reaction and try to have excuses ready and otherwise prepare them for a poor report. One youngster used the device of not giving his mother his report until he was ready to leave for school the next morning. Then he would hurriedly thrust it into her hand and say, "Hurry up and sign it, Mom, so I won't be late." A junior high school boy coped with the situation in this way:

When I bring home a bad report card my parents make all sorts of threts and I half to counteract them. On the other hand if by some chance I should bring home a good report card my parents would just look at it and say nothing to me.

Before it is time to bring home the report card I half to get them ready for the shock. I usually tell them that I saw my report card and it was very bad. The subjects that I think I failed I make up excuses why I failed them and why they are not important to me.

What do the parents do that cause so much fear, anxiety, and ingenuity on the part of youngsters?

Some ways in which youngsters perceive parental attitudes and behavior with respect to report cards are vividly brought out in these compositions. A few parents administer physical punishment, such as was described by a sixth-grade boy with

a foreign home background: "When I bring home a bad report I get 4 beatings. First my mother, then my father and my two brothers." "My father," wrote a ninth-grade boy, "is filled with rage and I am filled with fright." Two slow learners in a low socio-economic group in Harlem, New York City, spoke of being whipped or "branded with an ironing cord" if they got a D on their report cards. And an eleventh-grade student wrote, "I am fearful of the things to come. . . . My father will use harsh methods to help me remember to concentrate on my studies and nothing else. After which he does some talking."

In general, parental disapproval and deprivation of privileges are much more common than physical punishment. According to the students' accounts, parents respond to report cards in any of these ways: they give rewards for high grades; when grades are low, they scold, take away privileges, or merely tell the child "to do better"; they often overlook evidences of progress and dwell on bad points in the report, compare the child's marks with those of a brighter brother or sister, tell him to talk it over with the teacher, or try to help him themselves. The last two responses were infrequently reported, perhaps owing to deficiencies in the report card and lack of parent education. We should resist the common tendency to blame the parent. Most parents mean well; they want to help their child progress in school.

Sometimes, however, the parents' concern stems from their own personal ambition. "My father," wrote a ninth-grade boy, "always says, 'You can do better,' for you see he was in the high 90's during his high school and college years. He expects me to follow in his footsteps! ! ! !" This attitude Dr. James Plant described as "whatness" rather than "whoness"—concern for what the child achieves rather than for him as a person. Children and adolescents may sense this parental attitude as a form of rejection.

One of the commonest complaints is that their parents are never satisfied with their marks. As one parent-pressured boy wrote:

My marks all varie from 80 to 95 and I'm not surprised at my marks because I know the capacity of my ability. The way my parents see it, they always expect more than what I receive, and I am very disheartened because I know I've tried tremendously hard and like some accomodation from my parents, which I never get. They always tell me, "is that all you get in that subject? Why don't you get higher?" My feelings are of course hurt, but I always try better the next time.

A ninth-grade girl described a somewhat similar home situation: "My mother says I could be smart like my brother if I really tried hard. Then I show it to my father and he says he wants to see an improvement or he'll figure out some way of punishment, so next marking period I try harder because I think of what might happen."

Inconsistency in parents' response to their school progress is also frequently recognized by the youngsters. Sometimes it is the mother, sometimes the father who is the more lenient. "If the report is bad," one junior high school boy wrote, "I sort of sneak

it home until I get up courage to show it to my parents. I know my mother won't be bad but my father will make me come home every day after school and study until my marks improve."

As seen through children's eyes, there are some parents who are very understanding and helpful. These happy home situations were described in some compositions. The first illustrates a type of family relationship where the child is accepted and the parents' only concern is to help him do better:

When I arrive home my mother first looks at my marks. She does not usually remark on the grades but on whether or not I have improved or degenerated in my subjects. She says that if I do my best she will be satisfied. Sometimes I try to make excuses for decreased marks. But she knows my possibilities. My father does not, in my opinion, understand as well as my mother although he has never said anything unfavorable about my report. (Natch! !)

Another understanding parent-child relation and philosophy was described by an eighth-grade girl:

When my parents see the report card they usually say they are very pleased with my work. My mother said she will not promise me money because she feels that I should work for my own satisfaction and not for promises of money. My mother said that if I kept on getting high marks she will be very pleased with my work, but if my marks should slip she would not get mad but she would try to get me to work harder. As it is now I don't think she'll have to bother.

To obtain the most vivid picture of the way children and adolescents feel when they get their report cards, one should read many of these original compositions, which space does not permit us to include here. At reporting time, youngsters run the whole gamut of human emotions: panic, shame, fear, trepidation, anxiety, tension, nervousness, numbness, curiosity, satisfaction, pleasure, exhilaration.

Knowing how students feel about reports and what parents do about them is very enlightening to teachers. In the light of this knowledge we must seek answers to such questions as these: How can we protect the student who is doing his best from undeserved punishment and unrealistic parental expectations? How can we encourage self-appraisal by the student? How can we give students and parents more specific help than the general admonition to "try harder," which is all many parents can give at present?

WHAT MAKES STUDYING EASY OR DIFFICULT FOR ADOLESCENTS?

To help students make a better scholastic record, we need to know more about their study difficulties. What conditions do they consider favorable or unfavorable for study? How do these conditions change as the child grows older? Which conditions do they perceive as particularly potent? Let us first consult the adolescents themselves on these questions.

To obtain their views we have analyzed 536 compositions written on the topic, "What makes studying easy or difficult for me." The writers of these compositions represent scholastic levels from the fifth grade to the sophomore year of college, and cover a very wide range of intellectual ability and socio-economic background.

The complexity of the study problem is well brought out by the diverse and often conflicting responses in these compositions. For example, one student may write that studying with others is an effective practice for him, though there may be times when studying alone is advantageous. Another may mention the difficulty caused by not having all the necessary materials immediately at hand but also recognize that more decisive factors may still make his studying difficult. A complex of factors, varying in importance from time to time, affects the individual's studying. More detail on study conditions and individual differences among pupils in this respect will be given in Chapter 13.

Table 12 shows the relative frequency with which twenty-nine factors were mentioned. For example, the first figure represents the number of students who asserted either the positive value of privacy or the negative value of lack of privacy, plus the number of those who made both kinds of statements about privacy. Thus the per cent represents the proportion of the total number of compositions, 536, which mentioned *privacy* as a factor in study.

A few students mentioned other conditions which they thought helpful to effective study. Since frequency of mention is not always an indication of the importance of an item, these less frequently mentioned items will be listed:

Desire for good grades, promotion, or success in an imminent test
Studying in the early morning

TABLE 12

Factors Students Think Facilitate Study	Effective Frequency of Mention	Per Cent of 536 Compositions
Physical conditions:		
Privacy; no distraction by others............	297	55.5
Quiet environment (excluding reference to TV and radio).............................	254	47.4
Not trying to watch TV while studying, not putting off study to watch a TV program, or not being disturbed by someone else in the home having TV on.....................	165	30.8
Having the radio off......................	78	14.5
Having immediately at hand all materials necessary for study and no objects which distract attention.........................	64	11.9
Having the radio on......................	54	10.1
Good lighting............................	45	8.4
Physical environment that contributes to bodily comfort............................	44	8.2
Having TV on...........................	15	2.8
Study with, or assistance by, others:		
Assistance by others in the home while studying....................................	50	9.3
Studying with others.....................	30	5.6
Parental encouragement, support, or cooperation...................................	13	2.4
Personal factors:		
Freedom from other concerns and worries, and from competing personal interests........	197	36.8
Feeling well and rested...................	68	12.7
Feeling in the right "mood" to study........	39	7.3
Conditions of time and place:		
Studying in school rather than at home......	32	6.0
Having sufficient time to be thorough and careful...............................	29	5.4
Doing homework early—immediately on returning from school.....................	28	5.2

TABLE 12 (*Continued*)

Factors Students Think Facilitate Study	Effective Frequency of Mention	Per Cent of 536 Compositions
Having a definite plan for allotting time to each subject, or for studying them in a certain order...............................	18	3.4
Regularity—some studying each night, not delaying till just before a test or the due date of a report............................	15	2.8
Having a definite hour each day to study.....	10	1.9
Conditions relating to the assignment and the content of subjects:		
Particular interest in the material being studied	201	37.5
An assignment that is not too long...........	82	15.3
An assignment that comprises material that is either already "understood," or is comprehensible...............................	71	13.2
An assignment that is not of the "reading" type...................................	32	6.0
Voluntary rather than enforced study........	16	3.0
Satisfactory textbooks....................	10	1.9
An assignment that is mainly a "reading" assignment...........................	8	1.5
Teaching conditions:		
Effective teaching—this cluster of factors includes clear and complete explanations, a teacher with attractive personality and keen interest in the subject, definite assignments, satisfactory pupil-teacher relations, and other similar components directly related to teaching. (The per cent in this category was based on 505 compositions.)..........	152	30.1
Having been attentive in class; having taken good notes............................	42	7.8

Thinking about the subject in leisure moments

Short breaks during the study period

A few students said that the following things made studying difficult for them:

Being interrupted to perform household duties or run errands (10.1 per cent mentioned this.)

Putting off homework until morning and trying to get it done before going to school

Having someone else try to help

Unwelcome parental interference or advice

Absence from class

Inadequate background from earlier grades

Assignments consisting merely of material to be memorized or exercises to be done

Discouragement over low grades, or fear of failure

Though these students seldom specifically mentioned motivation, their responses show considerable awareness of the importance of this basic psychological factor.

The seven conditions most frequently mentioned by students of all grade levels as having a favorable effect on their study are listed below in order of frequency of mention:

1. Privacy

2. Quiet environment

3. Interest in the assignment

4. Freedom from other concerns and worries and from competing personal interests

5. Absence of distractions caused by television

6. Effective teaching and favorable student-teacher relations

7. Suitable assignments—not too long, challenging, and comprehensible

While these students mentioned certain environmental conditions such as privacy, quiet, and freedom from distractions, included in the usual list of recommended study hints, they put a great deal more emphasis on personal factors such as interest and peace of mind, and on the teacher's responsibility for fostering effective study. This suggests that we might often do well to attack study problems indirectly. Instead of always urging the student to get down to work promptly, to study a given subject at the same time each day, and to concentrate on the assignment, we might consider his vocational outlook, the nature of his relations with other members of his family and with his age-mates, and other factors which may be taking his mind off his school subjects. We might also critically examine our assignments, the books we require, and our methods of teaching and making assignments. Many students say that their studying is made difficult by books which are dull and unrelated to their lives, and by inability to understand what to do and how to do it.

Items less frequently mentioned correspond more closely to the usual lists of study hints, especially those concerned with physical conditions such as good lighting, a comfortable room, and having at hand the materials needed for study. Some of the items least frequently mentioned were more mature in tone than those commonly given by adolescents: studying in the early morning, thinking about the subject in casual moments, and taking short breaks between periods of study.

To make his learning more efficient a student should understand the conditions under which he learns best and the conditions that deter him from learning. We tend to generalize too much about *best* reading and study methods, ignoring individual differences. One student may reject a recommended study procedure in favor of a short cut that he himself has developed; another may need to have definite steps outlined for him. One student may work best alone; another, with a classmate; some seem to have become conditioned to listening to the radio or television while studying.

AGE DIFFERENCES IN RESPONSES

Since the compositions on this subject represented three grade levels—5–6, 7–9, and 10–12 and a few college sophomores—some comparisons may be made of the responses of students in these different age groups. The children in the fifth and sixth grades commended privacy and freedom from distractions, assistance by others in the home, and attentiveness in class more frequently than did the older students. Those in the seventh, eighth, and ninth grades emphasized the importance of feeling an interest in the subject, having all necessary materials on hand to begin with, and having clear and definite assignments. They more often criticized the teacher. Concern with over-long assignments and with distracting worries and competing personal interests increased from the elementary to the high school level. The senior high school students also seemed to be more aware of the importance of effective teaching and satisfactory student-teacher relations. All appreciated encouragement and support from parents and teachers. As one senior high school student expressed it: "Among other things, a person's home life has an effect on his schoolwork and almost everything else he may undertake. If parents take a solid interest in their children, they will be greatly encouraged to do better. Sometimes it's the problems of home that cause a student to lose interest in school and marks."

Teachers can make studying difficult or easy for their students. Effective teaching sets the stage for home study. It is enlightening for the teacher to view home study through the students' eyes. The most direct way to learn about factors that are facilitating or hindering home study is to ask students to write freely and frankly on what makes studying easy or difficult for them.

THE ROLE OF INTELLIGENCE

Students rarely mention lack of mental ability as a cause of failure in academic work. They blame their failure in school on factors other than intelligence. Perhaps they have never discussed the meaning of their intelligence test scores. Or they may think of intelligence as a sort of magic key to success, and resist the idea that they may not possess it. However, they occasionally say that "the teacher goes too fast," or admit that they cannot grasp certain subjects. The following quotation is one of the few instances in which a youngster definitely recognized his lack of mental ability: "Mothers don't realize how hard it is to do good

in school when you haven't what it takes. My mother expects me
to be a genius, which I'm not."

Students are quite right in thinking that intelligence per se
should not be considered a cause of school failure. Schoolwork
should be adjusted to the capacity of the individual; his school
tasks should be ones in which he *can* succeed, with reasonable
effort. To adjust school requirements to individual capacities,
teachers need to know certain general facts about the mental
ability of adolescents, as well as the test scores of individual
students.

Distribution of Intelligence

Intelligence is often defined as "the ability to learn," and influences all aspects of the individual's achievement at each stage
of his development. Given a certain quality of mind to begin with,
intelligence grows with experience. Mental age, obtained from
intelligence test scores, is a widely used way of measuring
brightness.

In any large group of adolescents one finds a wide distribu-
tion of mental ages. Among the general population of fourteen-
year-olds, for example, almost 25 per cent are likely to have a
mental age of 14; 20 per cent, a mental age of 13; 15 per cent,
a mental age of 15. About 2 per cent would have a mental age
of 10, and almost 4 per cent, a mental age of 18; the others would
be distributed between these two extremes. These percentages,
of course, would vary with the particular school or situation.
For example, in one district in New York State, the percentages
of children whose IQs were 125 or higher on standardized group
intelligence tests varied from 4 per cent in one high school to
25 per cent in another. We should expect differences in intelligence to increase during adolescent years as environmental differences become wider.

Individual differences within any group—boys or girls, whites
or Negroes, students with Italian or Polish backgrounds, high
or low socio-economic level—are much greater than differences
between groups. We cannot definitely predict an individual's in-

telligence from group averages. There is no substitute for study of the individual adolescent.

The Use of Intelligence-test Scores

Some differences in intelligence among adolescents are quite constant and may be attributed to "prolonged emotional or environmental influences and inherent tendencies to develop at given rates." [3] Other differences can be attributed to the temporary instability of the IQ. Although the median fluctuation from one testing to another is about 7 IQ points, 17 per cent of the population on a single retest may rise or fall 15 or more points, and nearly 1 per cent may vary as much as 30 points in either direction. The amount of fluctuation increases with the length of time between tests, with the degree of difference in the content and the method of standardization of the tests, and with the amount of coaching which the child receives before the test. Bright children show more variability in their test results than average or below-average children. Scores are most unstable before the age of five. Fluctuations in scores are still greater for group intelligence tests. Facts of this kind highlight the need for caution in the interpretation of the intelligence test scores of individual adolescents.

In using the results of intelligence tests we should also take into consideration the possibility that intellectual development has been inhibited by emotional problems. There have been instances of marked rises in IQ after successful treatment. We would expect the more intelligent adolescent to have a keener insight into his own adjustment and into social situations; in fact, Terman found his gifted group generally superior to the average in these respects. However, persons of very high intelligence may have special problems of social and personal adjustment because their intellectual world is so different from that of their fellows. [4]

[3] Nancy Bayley, "On the Growth of Intelligence," *American Psychologist,* vol. 10 (December, 1955), pp. 805–818.

[4] Leta S. Hollingworth, *Children above 180 IQ, Stanford-Binet.* Yonkers, N.Y.: World Book Company, 1942.

Growth in Intelligence

Growth in mental age and increase in intelligence-test scores are rapid during the second decade. Jones and Conrad[5] emphasized the important cumulative mental growth that takes place after the age of eleven. During the early and middle teens the development is gradual. There does not seem to be a spurt in mental growth corresponding to the physical growth spurt. But any increased power to think, to relate ideas, or to deal with abstractions facilitates achievement, and thus helps to increase self-esteem and to exert a pervasive influence on the adolescent's total development.

At one time it was thought that young people stopped growing mentally at about sixteen years of age. Later the curve was extended upward to eighteen, and then to twenty-three. Now there is evidence that individuals grow in certain aspects of intelligence even beyond these years.[6] It is encouraging to know that adolescents may keep growing intellectually during their high school and college years.

Individual growth curves show periods of fast and slow progress in intelligence, spurts and plateaus, and even regressions in relation to the individual's past performance.

Some kinds of mental ability increase more than others during the adolescent years. For example, both boys and girls may be expected to increase in vocabulary; boys generally show a greater increase in arithmetic scores than do girls; and both sexes show little or no increase in scores on items which primarily involve memory. Over a longer span of years—from the ages of ten to sixty[7]—wide differences occur in rates of growth on subtests of the Army Alpha test. By the age of twenty the rate of growth on oral directions, dissected sentences, and arithmetic problems reaches a peak and does not decline until later. On common-sense

[5] Harold E. Jones and Herbert S. Conrad, "Mental Development in Adolescence," *Adolescence*, Forty-third Yearbook of the National Society for the Study of Education, part I, chap. VIII, pp. 146–163. Chicago: University of Chicago Press, 1944.

[6] Bayley, *op. cit.*

[7] Jones and Conrad, *op. cit.*

items, analogies, and numerical completions, the peak of performance is reached before twenty, while growth in vocabulary and general information continues to a slight degree well into adult years.

Growth in mental abilities as measured by intelligence tests is influenced by the kind and amount of schooling the individual has received and the nature of his work and other experiences. Those who leave school often lose the intellectual stimulation necessary for the full development of their mental ability, while those who continue their education in high school and college may realize latent abilities. P. E. Vernon [8] found that:

1. The general intelligence factor, or g, showed a very slight increase between the ages of fourteen and seventeen in boys who had left school, but a greater increase in those who received further schooling.

2. After seventeen, general intelligence decreased among men in "lower-grade" occupations, but not among those in more "intellectual" occupations.

3. Mechanical and spatial ability, the k factor, increased even without any technical education.

He concluded that the growth of these abilities appears to depend largely on the extent to which they are used, and that educational attainments may influence that aspect of intelligence which is "largely acquired in the course of everyday living." [9]

In general, the pathways of mental growth for normal, superior, and retarded children diverge more widely as they grow older. However, we could expect that a school program which was more meaningful and challenging to the slow-learning student would tend to decrease these differences. According to Freeman and Flory,[10] at sixteen and seventeen years of age the low-scor-

[8] P. E. Vernon, "Changes in Abilities from Fourteen to Twenty Years," *Advancement of Science*, vol. 5 (April, 1948), p. 138.

[9] P. E. Vernon, "The Psychology of Intelligence and G," *Quarterly Bulletin British Psychological Society*, vol. 26 (May, 1955), p. 11.

[10] Frank N. Freeman and Charles D. Flory, *Growth in Intellectual Ability as Measured by Repeated Tests*, monograph of the Society for Research in Child Development, vol. 2, no. 2. Washington, D.C.: Society for Research in Child Development, National Research Council, 1937.

ing group was continuing to improve at a faster rate than the high-scoring group. In another more recent study, the brighter adolescents showed greater acceleration in mental growth than did the less able. These differences in research findings might be partly explained by differences in intellectual stimulation in the various samples and by variations in rate of growth. For example, some twelve-year-olds who are growing slowly may have more mental potential than others of the same age who have developed more rapidly; consequently at twelve they may make more progress than was expected. The intellectual ability and interests of the truly gifted will shine through if opportunities and encouragement are provided in the environment. This does not mean, however, that parents and teachers should expect the gifted to function constantly on a high intellectual level, any more than they would expect a physically competent adolescent always to be engaged in physical activities.

It seems clear that growth in intelligence is part of the total development of the child, and that accelerations in various aspects of growth tend to be related.

MOTIVATION

Scholastic success requires motivation or drive as well as capacity and opportunities to learn. Some students seem to have no desire to succeed in school. There are many reasons for underachievement. Some students have failed so often that they are afraid to try again; their tenseness and anxiety interfere with learning. Some seem to persist in a dependency which prevents their taking initiative and putting forth effort. A few may be using their failure in school as an expression of hostility toward their parents. Specialization of interests and experiences may provide motivation in some areas but cause neglect of others.

Extrinsic reward—prizes, honor lists, and other forms of competition—is not the answer to the problem of motivation. In the beginning, competition may stimulate those who feel that they have some chance to win. But many fall by the wayside as the competition continues and their chances of success become slim.

Then they put forth no more effort than do others of equal ability who have not been stimulated by competition. In a competition, only those who clearly see the possibility of getting the praise or the prize are motivated to put forth their best effort. Intense competition for short periods does stimulate some teenagers, but the less able quickly give up trying to achieve the impossible and feel more hopeless than ever about themselves. The efficacy of extrinsic rewards varies with the individual and with the situation. Marks have more appeal for students whose parents think schooling is important than for those from homes where "school learning" is not held in high esteem.

When schoolwork has no meaning, use, or purpose for students, it becomes drudgery. Then they have to be motivated mainly by threats of failure, marks, and prizes.

Apparently it is difficult for adolescents to explain their deeper motivations. Even gifted students in a ninth-grade English class had difficulty in explaining in unstructured, unsigned compositions, "What makes me tick." A number of their compositions began somewhat like this: "I really don't know what makes me tick for I never really thought about it before." On the other hand, one youngster who apparently had been delving into psychology wrote:

All people have reasons for what they do. Some motives may be trivial or not make much sense, but nevertheless all actions have reasons in back of them. I suppose I am no different than anyone else in this respect, but most of the time it is hard to psychoanalyze one's self.

Sometimes a person has a goal in mind and tries for it in a direct manner. Other times the person himself is not quite sure about anything and wanders aimlessly like in a fog. Luckily most people aren't like this. But, there are few if any who are in perfect mental health. Almost everyone has repressed desires, misplaced emotions or neurotic tendencies. Even the most successfull and intelligent men, when analized have a desire to do something contrary to society.

This boy went to extremes in looking below the surface of behavior. He may have been seriously disturbed emotionally or merely intellectually interested in this kind of analysis because of his reading of psychology or literature or the conversations heard in his family circle. Whatever his motivation, he was sound in emphasizing the importance of goal-directed behavior and the possibilities of hidden motives.

"School, home life, social life, all contribute to 'what makes me tick,'" wrote another boy in his opening sentence, recognizing the fact that motives originate in external conditions as well as within the individual. Some find a motivation in school life despite its routine. Many boys mentioned their enjoyment of sports as a positive factor in school life. One girl declared, "My whole life revolves around school. . . . If it weren't for school there would be nothing for me to do. The work isn't hard and the people are nice. They try to make you feel at home. I see more of some of the people at school than I see of my parents. I wouldn't want to miss one monotonous minute of this monotonous life." Certainly the social life of the school and the friendships formed there can be strong motivating factors; they keep many youngsters from dropping out of school. "Friends are a backbone to a person's personality," one of the ninth-grade girls wrote. "If your friends are with you nothing seems too terrible." She went on to make a special comment on boy friends: "I believe a boy has a good deal to do with a girl's morale. He gives you something to look forward to." A boy of the same age wrote in a similar vein, "'What makes me tick?' I have an idea it is girls."

Success in life looms large as a motive to those youngsters who are ambitious and have a high level of aspiration. One boy wrote, "My attitude on life is to make something of myself before I die. I don't wish to be a nobody all my life. Our class was told if we work hard we could be tops in our fields and that is what I intend to do." This goal also motivates some high school students who find their present classes dull and boring, as for example, the youngster who used the pseudonym, Hip O. Potamus: "My main purpose of going to school is to get it over with. But while I am in it, I might as well try my best so some day I will be a success in any field that's fit for me."

As a prerequisite to success in life, many of these students mentioned a college education. They think of a good school record as essential to getting into college and to success in life. The following statement is quite typical of this point of view:

I have come to realize that schooling is most important in life these days. For most skilled jobs you need a college education to even apply. The more education you have the higher the wages. Nowadays the employers go right to the college to get men so I want to keep my marks up high so I'll be able to get into college without too much difficulty.

There are some, however, who have more immediate and personal motivations. "Maybe," said one girl, "I want to do well in school because I want to satisfy myself with the knowledge that I did my best or maybe it's because I want to please my mother." A boy in the same class also mentioned satisfaction in a job well done as a motivating force. "I care what other people think," he wrote, "but also what I think. I get the satisfactions of knowing that I can do the work without anyone helping me—that I can get along on my own." Another boy recognized the central importance of the self-concept when he wrote: "What makes me tick? I do!"

According to their statements, these intellectually gifted students, mostly from well-to-do homes, are motivated in many ways: by everyday happenings that give satisfaction, by external compulsion, by a sense of duty (especially to parents), by desire to make a good impression on people, by a goal in life, by satisfaction in doing a worthwhile job, and by enjoyment of the work itself and of their own competency.

In trying to analyze why some bright students fail in one or more subjects, these ninth-grade youngsters and other gifted groups have mentioned the following possibilities:

"Habitual laziness" originating in elementary school where they did not have work that called forth their best efforts

Being overconfident; they know they are bright and think they don't have to work hard to get through high school

Preoccupation with other things besides their schoolwork—anxieties

at home, extraclass activities at school, involvement in a neighborhood gang

Lack of vocational motivation or conflict over choice of vocation

Specialization of interest in one field, which causes neglect of other
subjects

General lack of purpose or drive

Antagonism toward parents and teachers who are constantly pushing them to achieve

Neglect of parents and teachers who do not seem interested in
them as persons, or who do not care whether they fail or succeed

Motivation is multiple; it fluctuates from time to time as goals
change and school and home conditions vary. But gifted high
school freshmen are frequently consistently motivated by thoughts
of the future and by goals beyond the immediate stimulation
of home and school.

Providing motivation, or rather creating motivation, means
setting up conditions in which school achievement seems desirable
and necessary to the individual. Instead of depending on marks,
prizes, honors, and other extrinsic rewards, the teacher should
help the student to set realistic worthy goals for himself, and
should then provide the materials of instruction, social situations,
and satisfactions that will enable him to make progress toward
these goals.

CONCLUDING STATEMENT

The trend of the times toward reducing the effort needed in any
activity—whether it be using a cake mix or viewing TV in which
the producer has done the work—is reflected in the statements of
many students. They emphasize freedom of choice and put interest in a central position. Others, however, persist in the early
American emphasis on effort. They maintain that if one puts
forth effort, as for example in reading a book in which he was
not initially interested or in completing heavy homework assignments, it will pay off later. He may become interested in the book
and also acquire more efficient reading habits because of the very
pressure of work to be done. There is truth in both points of

view. Interest increases effort, and effort, if it is rewarding rather than frustrating, is likely to build worthwhile interests.

Scholastic success is important to adolescents for various reasons. Some are motivated to study by fear of punishment, loss of privileges, or loss of the love or regard of a person with whom one has identified himself. The fact that so few adolescents express satisfaction in the process of learning or in the knowledge and skills which it imparts indicates serious deficiencies in the curriculum and methods of teaching. Adolescents learn best when they use what they have learned immediately, when they are in good physical condition, when they are free to explore the resources available, when the task is appropriate to them, when they are ready to do it, when they help plan their projects and work individually or in groups on things they want to know, when they have suitable materials of instruction, and when they are taught how to find cues to learning of printed material, motor skills, and attitudes.[11] An adolescent learns best those things that contribute to the development of his most acceptable self. He learns best in a situation where his uniqueness and worth are respected.

Teachers know all this in a general way. Perhaps when they have heard it said in the students' own words, they will be moved to action more than by the pedagogical pronouncements of professors. It is important for adults to take into account adolescents' perception of their study methods and difficulties.

COMPREHENSION QUESTIONS

1. In what different ways is school success interpreted by adolescents, by teachers, and by parents?

2. What range of response is represented in students' feelings about their report cards? What range of response is represented in the actions which parents take as a result of these reports?

[11] William Clark Trow, *What Research Says to the Teacher: The Learning Process.* Washington, D.C.: National Education Association, American Educational Research Association, Department of Classroom Teachers, 1954.

3. What things do adolescents mention as making studying easy or difficult for them?

4. Which of the study factors mentioned by adolescents are the same as those discussed in "How to Study" books? Which do adolescents emphasize more?

5. How may a parent improve home study conditions after reading students' comments?

6. How may a teacher improve school study conditions after reading students' comments?

7. What are the facts about growth in intelligence during adolescence?

STUDY PROJECTS

1. Ask individual adolescents what makes studying easy or hard, or obtain compositions on this topic from a group. Then work with them to improve their study conditions.

2. Obtain anonymous compositions on "How I feel when I get my report card, and what my parents do about it." Use quotations from these compositions in parents' or teachers' meetings.

3. Interest a committee of students in making a survey of study conditions at home and at school with a view to improving them.

4. If you have comparable intelligence-test records covering a period of years, make a study of fluctuations and growth in intelligence by charting a growth curve for each individual.

5. Obtain ideas from compositions or interviews on the subject, "What makes me tick," from less able learners as well as from the gifted. What differences in motivation do you find between the two groups?

FOR FURTHER STUDY

BAYLEY, NANCY, "On the Growth of Intelligence," *The American Psychologist,* vol. 10 (December, 1955), pp. 805–818.

BULLOCK, HARRISON, *Helping the Non-reading Pupil in the Secondary School.* New York: Bureau of Publications, Teachers College, Columbia University, 1956.

DILLON, HAROLD J., *Early School Leavers.* Washington, D.C.: National Child Labor Committee, Publication No. 401, 1949.

ECKERT, RUTH E., and THOMAS O. MARSHALL, *When Youth Leave School* (the Regents' inquiry). New York: McGraw-Hill Book Company, Inc., 1938.

EPHRON, BEULAH KANTER, *Emotional Difficulties in Reading.* New York: The Julian Press, Inc., 1953.

HOFFMAN, HERBERT NATHANIEL, *A Study in an Aspect of Concept Formation, with Subnormal, Average, and Superior Adolescents,* Genetic Psychology Monographs, vol. 52 (November, 1955), pp. 195–239.

HOLLINGWORTH, LETA S., *Children above 180 IQ, Stanford-Binet: Origin and Development.* Yonkers, N.Y.: World Book Company, 1942.

HORROCKS, JOHN E., *The Psychology of Adolescence,* chap. VII. Boston: Houghton Mifflin Company, 1951.

JOHNSON, ELIZABETH S., and C. E. LEGG, "Why Young People Leave School," *Bulletin of the National Association of Secondary-school Principals,* vol. 32 (November, 1948), pp. 14–24.

KUHLEN, RAYMOND G., *The Psychology of Adolescent Development,* chaps. III, X. New York: Harper & Brothers, 1952.

MERRILL, KENNETH GRIGGS, "A Teacher Made the Difference," *NEA Journal,* vol. 43 (October, 1954), pp. 413–414.

NATIONAL SOCIETY FOR THE STUDY OF EDUCATION. "Intelligence: Its Nature and Nurture," *Original Studies and Experiments,* Thirty-ninth Yearbook, part II. Bloomington, Ill.: Public School Publishing Company, 1940.

OJEMANN, RALPH H., and OTHERS, "Effects of a Causal Teacher-training Program and Certain Curricular Changes on Grade-school Children," *Journal of Experimental Education,* vol. 24 (December, 1955), pp. 95–114.

PENTY, RUTH, *Reading Ability and High School Drop-outs.* New York: Bureau of Publications, Teachers College, Columbia University, 1956.

WATTENBERG, WILLIAM W., *The Adolescent Years,* chaps. XII, XXIII. New York: Harcourt, Brace and Company, Inc., 1955.

Popular Articles and Pamphlets

ESCALONA, SIBYLLE, *Understanding Hostility in Children,* Chicago: Science Research Associates, Inc., 1954.

OSBORNE, ERNEST, *How to Teach Your Child about Work,* Public Affairs Pamphlet No. 216. New York: Public Affairs Pamphlets, 22 East 38th Street, New York.

STRANG, RUTH, "What Did You Get on Your Report Card?" *National Parent-Teacher,* vol. 44 (March, 1950), pp. 26–28.

Audio-visual Aids

Problem of Pupil Adjustment—The Drop-out. 19 minutes. Sound. Black and white. McGraw-Hill.

Problem of Pupil Adjustment—The Stay-in. 19 minutes. Sound. Black and white. McGraw-Hill.

CHAPTER 8

Building Desirable Social Relations

Many of the satisfactions and the distresses of adolescence are connected with making friends and winning a place in the peer group. Adolescents have a dominant desire to be popular, to be accepted, to be well thought of by many people, especially by their peers. Their concept of themselves also includes the quality of liking other people. They may realize that liking others and being liked are two sides of the same coin.

The urge to free oneself from strong family ties leads the adolescent to join groups of his own age, either of his own sex or mixed. Much of his dependence on the family for standards and support normally shifts to the peer group. If the peer relations become too absorbing, the adolescent may fail to develop his unique personality and emotional pattern. Three major adolescent tasks are here related: gaining emotional independence from the family, establishing one's masculine or feminine role, and relating oneself to one's own age group.

Some of the compositions written by adolescents show how it feels to be left out; others describe ways of handling such a situation. Compositions on "The kind of person I want to be" highlight young people's desire to have others like them. Many junior and senior high school students repeatedly say they "would want to be well liked by others," "to be the kind of person that everyone can get along with and has a lot of friends," "to be popular with both boys and girls." One thirteen-year-old girl in the eighth grade gave a basis for, in addition to expressing a desire for, popularity: "I would like to be the type of person who never says anything bad or slightly bad about others. This type of person everybody would like to have as a friend." Another girl of the same age gave another point of view about keeping friends: "Of course, I would like to be the idle of all my friends. But sometimes if you are so good that you haven't got faults, people get bored with you and before you know it you haven't got one friend."

One sophisticated college student tried to analyze this common desire for friendship as follows:

There is nothing that upsets me more than to know that I am not wanted or liked by others. When worried over any situation I can always relate it to this one factor. Many a time I admit that I'm "scared to death" over an examination, but this lack of assurance does not compare to my worry over others' feelings toward me.

Not long ago I was placed in a situation where I was forced to a test of my popularity. With the passing of the experience I didn't feel too happy. . . . I was still not sure whether I was liked and desired by this group.

To me, the reason for this lack of assurance in a person with apparent self-confidence is clear. I have never taken a really vital interest in my classmates. To satisfy a certain egotism, I have devoted interest that might have well been spent on others, to myself.

High school offers the adolescent more freedom and a wider choice of friends than he previously had. College broadens the field still more. Making friends is especially difficult for the person who is moving into a new school or neighborhood. To facilitate the formation of friendships, orientation programs in high school and college can be helpful. Personal contacts through the "Big Brother" or "Big Sister" form of organization may lead to permanent friendships. Working together on worthwhile projects increases the opportunity for friendly relations with both sexes.

THE IMPORTANCE OF FRIENDS

Making friends is a major adolescent task. All during childhood and adolescence, friends of one's own sex are important. A sixteen-year-old boy wrote: "There is never a darker moment than the time it seems as if one is without a friend." Such a strong sense of loneliness sometimes overcomes a shy adolescent's anxiety about making any contact with another person. Beginning with preadolescence, both boys and girls increasingly confide in their friends, first in friends of the same sex. The companionship of a friend cheers and comforts them. During adolescence, they shift much of their interest and intimacy to the opposite sex.

Although they still rely on their parents for advice and help, they more and more seek friends who will serve as confidants. This tendency, which is common among preadolescent girls, is expressed by one sixteen-year-old girl as follows:

Some personal matters such as popularity and problems with boys I feel embarrassed to talk about with my parents and usually figure it out in my own mind. A thing I would appreciate would be a friend that I could talk my problems over with and know she wouldn't tell others or be influenced by them in their feeling toward me—a person who I wouldn't see except to talk over things. Often when you're troubled you don't want to keep things to yourself but tell someone all about it and get it off your mind.

Through "talking it out" with friends, many preadolescents and adolescents gain insight into their problems; they see more clearly the kind of person they can become.

Friends can be very helpful in other ways, as a freshman high school girl pointed out: "In my estimation, the one that's been of great help to me was one of my best friends. When school first started I thought I wouldn't be able to pass this year. But Diane has helped me and encouraged me to look ahead, and do my best." The nature of the friend's influence depends on the nature of the friend. The wrong friend may further confuse the bewildered adolescent, or have a detrimental influence on him or her.

Friends may also give prestige. Both boys and girls say, "I'm proud to be seen with my best friend." Some youngsters seem content to bask in the reflected glory of a popular friend; consequently they fail to develop their own individuality and social ability.

Friends seem more important to girls than to boys. Girls are more likely "to feel lost" without their best friend. Boys are more likely to get tired or jealous of their pals, or to envy their success in school or in sports.[1]

STABILITY OF FRIENDSHIP

Children change friends more quickly than adolescents. The child has many personal contacts with other children in the neighborhood; as he grows up, he abandons these casual relationships in favor of more intimate friendships with a few selected persons in his new school or college environment.

These adolescent friendships, too, may prove transitory for various reasons. Interests and values may change, parental pressure may be brought to bear, other persons may prove more attractive, or one's needs for friendship may change. Whatever its cause, one of the deep troubles of adolescence is the instability of friendship. One fourteen-year-old boy took the loss of his best friend very hard. In his composition on "How it feels to grow up" he wrote:

Me, I don't wished to be young again *ever*. My best pal all of a sudden is not my best pal. That is one of my main problems. He just wouldn't speak with me. He's a big boy 2 years older than I am almost and for 4 years we were the best of friends and now because he can drive and I can't I'm a simpleton. I don't quite know the reason for it. If I did I'd do all I could to correct it. He wasn't my only friend; I have other's but we had such good times together.

Some adolescents who are initially insecure and anxious may attribute their lack of friends or inability to hold friends to imaginary or real faults of their own. This was the case with a seventeen-year-old boy in the twelfth grade:

I know other people think that I am rather a dull person. When with other people, I feel self-conscious and ill-at-ease. This makes

[1] Sister M. Lucina, "Sex Differences in Adolescent Attitudes toward Best Friends," *School Review*, vol. 48 (September, 1940), pp. 512–516.

me feel inferior, yet in my mind I know I possess some special abilities, but I never seem to excel in them for lack of ambition. What is worse I have not a chance to air these problems and many others with my mother and I have no father. My mother is unsympathetic and always thinks I have peculiar ideas. These problems accumulate and periodically I wonder if it's worth living.

Friends tend to be similar in personality traits and interests.[2,3] They score alike in tests of dominance, self-sufficiency, self-confidence, security, and sociality. However, there are exceptions: a dominant person may choose a submissive friend, or a cautious person, a reckless one. When one personality supplements the other, or when one friend shares his different interests with the other, their friendship has as stable a basis as it would have if they were alike.

COMPLEXITY OF FRIENDSHIP PROBLEMS

The problems of getting acquainted and making friends are interrelated with other concerns such as parental relations, boy-girl relations, sex education, and the extent to which the school should aid in the solution of such problems. A sixteen-year-old boy in the eleventh grade recognized these complex interrelations:

The field in which I usually have the most trouble is that of friendship. I have a desire to have a few close friends and still maintain a friendship with many people on a more casual basis. . . . Sometimes actions on my part have offended a friend (or so I think), and I am afraid of losing that person's friendship. Other times it seems as if my own friends shun me for no reason at all except for the reason of liking others' company better. These are many times tricks of my own imagination and many times I reason this out for myself. . . . It always is difficult to deal with the opposite sex, I think, be-

[2] Natalie Reader and Horace B. English, "Personality Factors in Adolescent Female Friendships," *Journal of Consulting Psychology,* vol. 11 (July, 1947), pp. 212–220.

[3] E. Virginia Van Dyne, "Personality Traits and Friendship Formation in Adolescent Girls," *Journal of Social Psychology,* vol. 12 (November, 1940), pp. 291–303.

cause one does not really know how they will react to one thing or another, what point of view they have, or what things girls really care for. The personality courses at school have given a great deal of helpful information.

Friendship always involves the interaction of the individual personality with the social environment.

WHAT MAKES ADOLESCENTS POPULAR?

If only they knew! Studies have suggested that the most acceptable adolescents are cheerful and happy, cooperative and helpful, enthusiastic but self-controlled, friendly and considerate of others, honest and unselfish. They enjoy jokes, initiate games and other activities, help others to feel successful and happy. In a summer camp for boys aged twelve to sixteen, those who were most acceptable to others "rarely or never show off, bluff, bully, quarrel, carry grudges, think they are 'picked on,' or make excuses, act superior and domineering, or show over-dependence on others." [4]

The unacceptable youngsters are usually those who show off or are listless, lacking in vitality, disinterested in others and their activities, shy, rebellious, or boastful. Fortunately, most of the characteristics that bring adolescents social acceptability among their peers are likewise socially approved.

The social values of certain characteristics change during adolescence. The most admired seventh-grade boys tended to be fairly expert in organized games, daring, boisterous, restless, aggressive, and unkempt. The peer culture demands one thing; adults demand other kinds of behavior. Popular girls of the same age showed opposite characteristics. Two years later, physical skills, courage, and aggressiveness in boys were still admired but being boisterous, unkempt, and a nuisance in class had acquired negative value. Ninth-grade girls had moved in the opposite direction, becoming a little more boisterous and casual,

[4] Hedley S. Dimock, *Rediscovering the Adolescent*, p. 139. New York: Association Press, 1937.

while boys became more polite and clean. During early adolescence girls tend to be the more sociable; in later adolescence boys "tend to dominate the social scene." Popular twelfth-grade boys tend to be good in athletics, good dancers, active in group activities; they possess social ease and poise, look grown-up and mature. In general, they tend to be extroverts, and able to enjoy a joke. The popular girls engaged mildly in sports for the fun of it. Some popular girls are of the vampire type; others are tactful, supportive rather than exploitive. The "clinging vine" type is generally unacceptable to both boys and girls. Among a group of college men [5] the two traits most frequently given as reasons for rejection were loudness and fancied superiority.

It is frequently suggested that social class and socio-economic status of the adolescent's family are determinants of his acceptance or rejection by his peers. A number of investigators—among them Warner, Merker and Eels, Hollingshead, and Havighurst and Taba—have reported a relation between class status and popularity in school. Class status, family status, and adolescent peer status all are involved in school social relations, but of these three the most influential may be the status an individual adolescent wins in his group because of his personality, social competence, or special athletic or other abilities. McGuire [6] found little relation between peer acceptance and family background.

It may be that young people are not especially aware of social stratification or discrimination unless it is specifically called to their attention by adults. Only a few references to family status and social class were found in hundreds of compositions. If it were uppermost in their minds, we should expect them to make frequent reference to it when writing frankly about themselves and their problems. Perhaps awareness of class distinction, when expressed, is largely a reflection of parental attitudes or it may be functioning on an unconscious level. The tendency for older

[5] John W. Kidd, "Personality Traits as Barriers to Acceptability in a College Men's Residence Hall," *Journal of Social Psychology*, vol. 38 (August, 1953), pp. 127–130.

[6] John Carson McGuire, *Adolescent Society and Social Mobility*, doctoral thesis. Chicago: University of Chicago, 1949.

students to check "middle" or "upper-middle" class when filling out application forms, although a third of them may actually be from the lower-middle or lower socio-economic groups and about a tenth from the upper, may be variously interpreted. It may indicate a desire to be "democratic," a tendency toward class motility in the direction of the average, a manifestation of the desire not to be different from others in the group, or an attempt to conceal a socio-economic status which one feels will be unacceptable.

Adolescent friendships are an important means to social mobility. The best way for a youngster to get in the swim is to have one of the "big wheels" invite him or her to a social activity. In McGuire's study [7] about 40 per cent of the lower-class youth raised their social level by forming friendships with youths from families above their social status. As a result of these friendships, they tended to stay in school longer and to aspire to higher vocations. From their friends they learned new values and different ways of living. Their behavior was no longer so much influenced by their home status and conditions. These friendships became more fixed in later adolescence.

PROBLEMS OF SOCIAL ACCEPTANCE

In one school a new boy, Percy, entered the seventh-grade class six weeks after the beginning of the term. He was a small lad, who slowly walked with downcast eyes to the front of the room to hand the teacher his class card. As he got to the teacher's desk, a tin box in which he carried his pencils, compass, and other things dropped out of his hands and struck the floor with a clatter. While he hurried to retrieve his belongings, Stephen, a class instigator of ill will, laughed and said, "Hey, kid, you dropped your watch." The class laughed. The teacher talked to the boy and then introduced him to the class and assigned him a seat. Later in the week, Percy came to class on the verge of tears. The other boys had been teasing him by calling him "sissy,"

[7] *Ibid.*

"teacher's pet," and "cry-baby." What role should a teacher play in a situation like this? Certainly he should not make the mistake of trying to substitute adult approval for peer approval; it cannot be done. Nor should he give the student unrealistic reassurance or sympathy that might increase his feeling of social inadequacy. It is much better to accept the situation casually and watch for an opportunity in which the shy student may join a very small congenial group working on something that will make a contribution to the class.

The case of Mary Jane illustrates another kind of problem in group acceptance. She was a girl of superior intelligence who had made excellent marks through the seventh grade. She was a quiet girl, but quick and accurate in mathematics; she usually finished her work far in advance of her classmates. During the third six weeks her work fell off sharply in quality and she became a disciplinary problem during the class period. Other teachers noticed the same tendency. Her mathematics teacher thought she might be bored with the work and asked her to see him one afternoon after school. When asked about her work and attitudes in class, she was embarrassed, but finally said, "I just can't help it. I can do the work and all that and I want to make good marks. But the kids I go around with tease me because I get high marks and make the merit roll. You just aren't accepted by the other kids unless you cut up in class. I know I shouldn't do it and I don't want to. I want to get good marks, but what can I do?" This attitude toward superior performance is unfortunately too common in our society as well as in some of our schools. It is part of the problem of not accepting differences. If the attitude of other students cannot be changed, it would be desirable for the very able learners to be in special groups for part of the school day, where they will have materials on their level, challenging methods of instruction, and stimulation from their peers.

Fortunately a certain degree of social acceptance is quite widely distributed. From his study of adolescent groups, Dimock found that

relatively few boys in ordinary group situations are unanimously popular or acceptable. The friendship preferences of all the members of
a group do not converge on a single boy, but are distributed among
a few at least. The second conclusion follows in part from the first.
A substantial number, probably a majority, of the boys enjoy a moderate degree of acceptability or popularity among their associates.
The final conclusion is that a minority, but a highly significant group
of perhaps 15 to 25 per cent of the boys, possesses an acceptability
status that we have arbitrarily judged to be below the minimum needs
for wholesome and satisfying personality.[8]

An individual's acceptance or rejection by his peer group is
usually due to a combination of causes, as, for example, a poor
home background, plus annoying personal characteristics, plus
teachers who are not sensitive to the interpersonal relations in
their classes. Acceptance depends a great deal on an environment
in which there are worthwhile goals and activities to which all
members of the group can contribute through their special
abilities.

EFFORTS TO WIN ACCEPTANCE

Although nothing seems quite so important to teen-agers as
acceptance by their age-mates, they do not know quite how to
bring this about. They seek acceptance by their peer group, i.e.,
youngsters of approximately the same age level, and try to gain
status in various ways.

Many personal and environmental factors enter in. The overage
or early-maturing boy, being bigger than the others, can excel in
athletics and become a leader in sports activities. For example, although Eddie was several years older than the other sixth-grade
pupils and much lower in IQ, he found the things he could
do well and did them. For this he was accepted by the class and
gained satisfaction from learning that was unrelated to books.

Sometimes environmental barriers are insurmountable and a
youngster's efforts to gain acceptance are unsuccessful, as in

[8] Dimock, *op. cit.*, p. 125.

the case of Irwin. When he came back from the reformatory eager to make a new start, he was afraid no one would accept him. The teachers wanted to help him but his age-mates, the most important people in his life, did not. Most of the class shunned him. At first he felt that one teacher was the only person who accepted him and he would do anything for her. However, as the class continued to reject him, he sought to gain their attention and win their admiration by antisocial behavior. He even turned against the teacher. He defied her at every opportunity, even when she attempted to modify his program so as to capitalize on his interests. At first his antics were amusing to the class. But gradually they tired of them. As Irwin became aware of their growing dislike for him, he became even more aggressive. Although only about 5 feet tall, he insisted that anyone who said or did anything to him would be "knocked silly." He was such a wiry individual that he could make good his boast, and usually came out the winner in any fight. He even hit the gym teacher for taking his cigarettes away from him. The more aggressive he became, the more he was rejected.

If this delinquent boy had won the acceptance of his classmates at the beginning, he would probably be a good citizen today. If the teacher, instead of showing Irwin such obvious special consideration, had helped the other members of the class, especially the natural leaders, to understand Irwin's need for their approval, they might have handled his rehabilitation successfully.

Social acceptance may become more difficult for lower-class youngsters during adolescence. Consciousness of social class seems to increase with age. As boys and girls begin to date and look forward to marriage, social distance usually grows wider. About the middle of the eighth grade in some communities, students' awareness of their classmates' socio-economic backgrounds tends to increase. In one eighth-grade class, when certain youngsters were pushing to get a good position in a line, one boy said, "Move back, Polack," and was answered, "Not for you, hillbilly." Such epithets may or may not denote real bitterness, antagonism, or hostility; it all depends on the intents, feelings, and meanings attached to them. In our high schools today, we find many instances in which students of lower socio-economic status and minority races and religions are accepted by their peers. Such students have been elected to important positions in student organizations and have made friends with members of higher social groups.

In an autocratic school atmosphere, it is especially difficult for unprepossessing youngsters to gain acceptance. The other children are likely to be cruel to them, and do not seem to identify themselves with the scapegoats whom they single out. One girl from a poorer than average family was shunned and mocked by a large portion of the class. Only a few defended her. Unfortunately the teacher did not know how to bring her into the group and help her to feel that she counted and belonged.

THE PEER GROUP

Belonging to a group of one's own age means a great deal to young adolescents. It means security, for the group is protective and encouraging. It means growth in independence from the family, for group sanctions often carry more weight than parental authority and the peer group offers the individual adolescent more chance to take responsibility than does a group of adults. For youngsters who are accepted and active in groups, belonging means increasing one's self-esteem through achieving success in human relations. Teen-age groups can be important laboratories for social learning.

Adolescents seek security in the group. The group extends and strengthens their often timorous egos. Many college freshmen are surprisingly lacking in self-confidence. One study showed that 90 per cent were afraid that they would not be successful; 85 per cent were concerned about hurting other people's feelings. Some have long-established feelings of guilt and anxiety stemming from conflicts in their inner world.

To gain security, many college students try to conform to the culture of their peer group. Freshmen exert themselves to learn the current catch phrases, the right places to eat, the proper ways to dress. The popular costume will vary on different college campuses. On an eastern women's college campus the girls' appearance would have to be described as "sloppy." On a western coeducational campus the girls pay a good deal of attention to grooming and wear the newest modes. In another college the girls wear casual clothes such as attractive shorts with blouses and socks to match.

The peer group promotes independence and self-esteem. Young adolescents are capable of conducting successful group experiences. One junior high school class of exceptional ability and maturity decided to have a three weeks' unit which they would conduct themselves, with the teacher serving as consultant to individuals and small groups. At the beginning, the teacher asked them to make up their own rules of conduct for this period if they thought such rules would be needed. Betty, who was inclined to be noisy herself, said, "We have to have rules to go by. If we don't, we'll get so noisy we can't get anything done." The class agreed, and they proceeded to make a list of rules which were much more strict than the teacher could have imposed. As adolescents grow older, they become increasingly competent in group situations. Some know how to handle misunderstandings and problems of human relations in a sensible way; they talk things over and usually come to some agreement with each other.

Progression in Group Experiences

At the beginning of the seventh grade, if left to themselves, boys and girls tend to play apart. Toward the end of the seventh grade the girls often form little cliques. Sociograms show this tendency. These cliques are essentially hierarchies of friends. Teachers often intercept notes from one girl to another asking, "Am I your 1st best friend or your 2nd best friend? You are my 1st best friend"—there are unlimited numerical possibilities. A girl may be extremely jealous if her first best friend should happen to walk to school with someone else. During the seventh grade these close friendships may merge into a group loyalty; best friends or "buddies" may offer to take charge of a bulletin board or some other group project. Chums relate themselves with others to form groups.

During the eighth grade, youngsters become interested in groups with definite purposes. In a central school in an agricultural region, about half of the eighth grade belonged to a church group and another fourth to Scouts, 4-H, or an athletic group. The rest showed an interest in these groups even though they did not participate.

There seems to be quite a wide gap between seventh- and eighth-grade youngsters. Toward the end of the seventh grade some of the youngsters try to become a social part of the eighth-grade group. They are tolerated but not often accepted by the eighth-grade students. The junior high school girls want older boy friends, and the younger boys try to get on the neighborhood athletic teams of the older boys. They will often work hard on any all-school project to show the upperclassmen that they are "not babies any longer."

Adolescents are often kind to the small children in the school. In one instance a little first-grade boy threw a stone through the windshield of the school truck. The junior high school pupils saw him do this, and were extremely curious as to what the

school authorities were going to do about it. Their teacher described to them the child's home situation—how he had been shifted from one home to another and had had no friends or fun. The junior high school pupils took this to their hearts. Several times they invited the little fellow to their room and treated him royally. He rarely left without a gift. When he moved once again, he came down to say goodbye. He was a very different boy than he had been when they first saw him. He had responded to the kindness and affection of these teen-agers, and they had gained a little understanding of the cause and cure of delinquent behavior.

At this age some youngsters show little enthusiasm for activities planned for them by adults.

Those who were most active in reaching out for contacts with their age mates were most antagonistic toward adults. But this was a passing phase, for a year or so later the same boys and girls who had been so distant and almost antagonistic toward teachers and club leaders were the first ones to "warm up" to adults and to "hang around" them as though they needed something from them.[9]

When a group of young adolescents is left to its own devices, the girls may start social dancing; some of the boys who are playing games, listening to the radio, or reading may gradually join in. Many more girls than boys are interested in parties and dancing; a much larger proportion of the boys are interested in the Scouts and in shopwork. As might be expected in view of their earlier physiological maturity, girls become interested in adult social activities while boys are still primarily interested in reading, in pets, and in playing active games. Depending upon environmental opportunities, the emerging interest of prepubescent boys in driving cars and participating in adult sports increases during adolescent years.

In high school, organized groups of many kinds are established. Although their alleged purpose may be to study science

[9] Robert J. Havighurst, "Poised at the Crossroads of Life; Suggestions to Parents and Teachers of Young Adolescents," *School Review*, vol. 61 (September, 1953), pp. 329–336.

or photography or some other field or skill, the "hidden agenda" of most of their members is to make friends and to engage in social activities in mixed groups of boys and girls. One group of youngsters who petitioned to form "a philosophy club," when asked what they wanted to do in the first meeting, said, "Have a party." They wanted an adult sponsor who would serve as a consultant or "a very present help in time of trouble," but would not dictate or dominate.

SORORITIES AND FRATERNITIES

Outside of school, gangs and secret societies are formed. These often evolve from informal neighborhood play groups. Once established, these organizations tend to resist adult interference. Yet there is good in gangs. They have tendencies leading to socialization as well as to antisocial behavior. Some have a constructive influence. Delinquent gangs, which will be described in Chapter 12, have their own value systems to which they demand that their members be loyal.

High school sororities and fraternities cause much concern to school people. Some of these secret organizations have been known to require revolting and harmful initiation ceremonies. Others are congenial but exclusive social groups. In their compositions, students expressed diverse opinions about the sororities and fraternities with which they had had experience, and it is important for adults to know how they feel. A 14½-year-old girl wrote a very significant composition showing the ambivalent feelings, perhaps somewhat rationalized, of a young adolescent who had been left out of her age groups:

It seems to me teen-agers are always forming groups. If you don't fall into any of these groups you feel left out and the crowd considers you queer. It isn't so bad when you stop and think of the others who are also left out, because you feel you have something in common. And when some of them act like a slave to the leaders, then you are glad you aren't one of their group.

Teen-agers are always saying sharp little things that burn and hurt like when you're hit by pebbles from a passing car. It stings for a minute but you can usually think of it later without the hurt.

Sometimes after calling all your friends only to find they're all busy, you wish desperately you were one of them. When you're sitting home with nothing to do, then you would give anything to be part of the group. The best thing then is to find something to do, for when you're deeply engrossed, the feeling goes away.

An exceptionally mature point of view was expressed by a socially minded fifteen-year-old girl who had the ability to form opinions on the basis of sound reasoning and to stand up for them:

My problem is that I have been asked repeatedly to join a sorority and have refused all bids. Unfortunately the majority of teenagers in this city are members of a sorority or fraternity and those who do not belong are more or less social outcasts.

Though I have many friends in school I have only three very close friends. I go out every week end with different boys who are not in fraternities but I do not get a chance to meet other boys. I definitely am missing some aspects of social life and I am wondering if my reasons for not joining a sorority are justifiable and wise.

My reasons are that sororities and fraternities are undemocratic and snobbish. The system of "black balling" a member is inexcusable. I have seen girls join sororities and become so dependent on the sorority's name that they loose all individuality.

I am independent and do not want to limit my friendships to one certain group of people. I do not like the idea of being treated like dirt, as you are during the long "goating" period.

I am doing what I think is right but I am not sure whether it is beneficial to me and if I am just trying to be righteous and "different."

To me the only benefits sororities hold are social benefits and these are limited since you only meet one type of person.

In one suburban school the question of sororities became a storm center, as in many other communities. The students had much to say about them.

The following composition expresses the feelings of a seventeen-year-old senior high school girl about her sorority and the way in which she thought the school had handled the situation:

The most serious problem that I have been confronted with has been the sorority question in the High School. I was in one of the best sororities and no adult fully realizes how much it meant to all of us—the meetings, picnics, the yearly dance we gave, the Rummage Sale that we gave for charity and the perfect two weeks we spent at the shore. The latter will be especially missed as it is just heaven to be in a big house with your twenty five "sisters" for two weeks, sharing the work, each others' problems and the fun. To think that all this had to end, even after we tried to cooperate with the school, makes me mad. Last spring when the school complained, we had a special meeting, agreeing not to wear our pins to school and to keep all "dogging" or pledging out of the school. After that decision, we could honestly see no grounds that the school could stand on, as far as being against us. We felt that now that everything had been completely removed from the school, what we did on Friday nights and during our own time, was not any business of the school's.

This fall we found out differently. We were informed that the Office had "the name of every girl in a sorority" and two of my friends were forced by the Office to choose between keeping their important positions in the High School (with good chances for scholarships) or being in a sorority. Of course they had to choose the former and drop out. With things getting worse by the week we finally, after much debate, decided to disband, before it affected more people. This, I'm sorry to say, we did and I think every one of us wishes we hadn't done so. Maybe if the four sororities and the three fraternities had stuck together, we could have held out.

As to the effects—thirty girls greatly miss the closeness and pleasure of being in a sorority. Of course, we are still very good friends, but it isn't quite the same as being a "sister," going through pledging and finally the beautiful ceremony.

As a conclusion, we thought we were doing the right thing at the time, but now I wonder. Does the school have the right to regulate our activities outside of school and let them affect our standing in school?

Another seventeen-year-old girl in the same school situation, who had received a bid from one of the best sororities, joined in the hope of getting her best friend in. She wrote:

My friend never did become a sorority girl. Even though I'm a sorority girl, I hate sororities. I don't think a group of sixteen- and seventeen-year-old girls are qualified to judge whether a girl they have met at an open house or tea is or isn't good sorority material. I realize there are good points about sororities, but I don't think the good ones make up for the bad.

With this personal attitude toward sororities, she went on to say:

The sororities and fraternities went half way with the school by cutting out all public "dogging" and any signs of "dogging" in school. It seems to me that the more the sororities cooperated, the more the schools persecuted them. I think the high school has gone about getting rid of sororities in the worst way possible. I feel that if the school had let the sororities stay out in the open, they would have had a better chance of getting rid of them.

This is the way other high school students analyzed the situation.

They recognized that a number of objections to out-of-school sororities and fraternities are justified:

The worst thing about them is that they hurt a lot of girls' feelings.

They don't give those who are not in them a chance to join. It's not democratic.

It makes some people unhappy; they feel left out.

They make snobs.

In high school you should still be learning how to make friends and what to look for in friends. In a sorority your friends are ready-made.

My father and mother are against them, but I'm dying to get in one.

The school lacks spirit because the students' interests are outside the school.

On the other hand, they thought the outside social clubs have some good points:

They do help to give you social life.

It's something to do with your time, and very helpful to a girl who is backward and shy. You get to meet people. It is silly they aren't allowed in the school.

People would go around with the friends they like whether there were sororities or not.

Even if there were no sororities there would still be outside clubs.

It is not fair to ban members from school activities and other opportunities when the sororities and fraternities are doing their level best to comply with school standards.

In school and in life there are many clubs with limited membership. Teachers belong to them.

According to the state law of New Jersey these organizations are illegal if formed and maintained in the school. They are not! It is strictly outside business over which the school has no jurisdiction.

A few were neutral:

Personally, it doesn't bother me. Everybody has his own crowd, and why not?

I don't belong; but I don't mind. They give dances that are open to anyone. At the school dances, you can't bring people from other towns.

In their compositions seniors expressed frustration and resentment that their social societies were outlawed. They protested vigorously against the way in which the school has handled the sorority-fraternity situation. In the last paragraph one girl wrote: "This problem has made me feel at a loss. I don't want to go against my teachers and school. I believe they are the finest there are and the most understanding, but any methods of solution that we've tried thus far have been completely unsatisfactory." Others expressed very much the same attitude. They wanted to be active in school affairs but they did not think it fair for the school to insist that they drop membership in sororities and fraternities. Some of the students have done this; some sororities and fraternities have been disbanded; some have been reorganized as clubs recognized by the school. But the anger and resentment are still strong.

What to do about sororities and fraternities is a more difficult problem than that of citing their good and bad points. The students were agreed that prohibiting members of the outside groups from holding school offices was *not* the way to handle the situation. They suggested the following positive way of dealing with the problem:

Bring the problem right out in the open: have key persons on the Board of Education talk with sorority and fraternity presidents to get their point of view; invite faculty members to attend the sorority and fraternity meetings. Get the facts about these clubs; be careful not to make false accusations. Play fair; don't threaten idly. Instead of each group making separate recommendations, which the others will not accept, why can't school people, parents, and students all get together and come to some common agreement?

Any of the following specific recommendations may be made:

1. Have the school board and faculty recognize them, give them a meeting place in school, suggest worthwhile projects they can carry on; in short, change them into school clubs, Friday night basketball games, youth canteens, etc.

2. Get rid of them slowly: stop taking in new members; discourage them in junior high school.

3. "Make the school activities more interesting, and encourage participation as in the operetta." Have more interesting activities so everyone can be a member. "Make the high school a center of social activities; then outside groups won't be so important to the kids."

4. "If you can't get rid of them, call them clubs instead of sororities and fraternities and get an older person with good ideas to sponsor them."

5. "Have all the presidents of sororities and fraternities get together with school authorities and thrash it out. That's the only way."

6. Carry out fully and consistently the plans agreed upon in joint conference.

It is important that all parties agree on a course of action and stick by it. Here is an opportunity to test democratic student-parent–teacher-administrator cooperation.

College freshmen look to upperclassmen to establish standards and exemplify college customs. They follow upper-class examples socially and in observing or breaking rules. Establishing good morale in the upper classes is the best way to get freshmen "off to a good start." Sororities and fraternities may aid or prevent good adjustment to college.

One college freshman expressed great enthusiasm for student activities, and indicated excessive participation in them:

> The more activities I have, the more fun I have and the less time I have to get in trouble. . . . The fraternity I belong to is one of the finest in the world. It gives a boy an opportunity to be accustomed to leadership and working with others. Basketball being my favorite sport occupies much of my time also. I am also employed in a drugstore and find the job very beneficial toward chemistry. Whenever I have any other free time I go camping.

One wonders whether this boy by being constantly "on the go" is trying to run away from thoughts and feelings that are troubling him.

The greater the recognized prestige and status of sororities and fraternities, the more detrimental they may be to the persons who are not invited to become members. In fact, any group activity should be judged from the standpoint of its contribution to individuals as well as to the community and to the accomplishment of the group goal.[10] Failure to be chosen as a member of the group has made many college students feel that there must be something wrong with them; it has torn down self-esteem. Another danger is domination by a forceful member of the group, whose intent is to influence others without modifying his own beliefs; this may lead to undesirable social norms in the group as a whole.

Interrelationships within Peer Groups

Some adolescents take active leadership responsibilities in the group. There is the dictator type, who controls the group through fear or force of personality. There are benevolent despots who get their own way in a group through less coercive methods. There are natural leaders, not in positions of leadership, who

[10] Ruth Strang, *Group Activities in College and Secondary School.* New York: Harper & Brothers, 1947.

help the group move cooperatively toward the accomplishment of its goal; these youngsters take the tension out of situations and in other ways help the group to maintain good relationships among its members. They often accomplish these ends by their sense of humor and good nature. Members with good verbal intelligence may also play important roles in a group. They mold opinion and serve as resource persons and facilitate discussion. They are the "idea-men."

There are also members who contribute little or nothing; they play a passive role, content to go along with the crowd. Other members carry responsibilities that certain ones originate and then try to evade. Since they have a low estimate of their personal worth, they seldom take initiative and responsibility themselves. They are often the isolates or "fringe" persons, never wholeheartedly accepted by the others.

There are also the "tearer-downers"—those who have a negative or destructive influence on the group. These are a source of contagion in a group that is easily thrown out of balance. They differ from the persons who may be critical of the group, but for its own good. Sometimes they have a small following who attach a certain prestige to any form of rebellion.

Finally there are the youngsters who are openly rejected for various reasons, some inherent in the values of the group, some, in the personalities and home backgrounds of the members, and some in the youngsters' own personalities and conduct. Adult leaders find it difficult to help these rejected ones find acceptance in any group. The adults cannot command acceptance on the part of the other members. They are usually most success-ful when they work indirectly, creating conditions in which the isolate, the fringe member, the rejected one can make a genuine contribution to the group or participate in a small congenial committee or other subgroup.

Conformity to Peer Culture

It is the rare adolescent who is not afraid to be different from his age-mates. In a panel discussion by gifted children, only one teen-ager resisted the general attitude of the others—"We don't want the kids to think we're different." This youngster spoke up and said, "But we *are* different! And why not accept it?"

Conformity to the peer culture also has its bright side. Ideally, participation in a peer group should lead to self-discovery and thus foster individuality. As the adolescent obtains acceptance and recognition from the group, he becomes sure of himself as a person, of what he can and what he cannot do. When the group favors wholesome activities, the problem of rebellion against parental restrictions is solved. The adolescent enjoys the group experience without forfeiting his parents' approval. For example, one freshman English class was planning, under the supervision of their teacher, to attend a five-o'clock performance of *Julius Caesar*. One mother later related what took place:

> My daughter assured me that all of the girls were going to a restaurant for supper after the performance, and could she please have permission to join them. My husband and I were reluctant to give our consent, for we objected to her coming home from the city after dark unescorted; but the dining out seemed to mean a great deal to her, and we finally agreed.
>
> We were greatly surprised, however, when our child arrived home promptly after the showing of the film and *without* supper. She simply stated that, since most the girls had been refused permission to dine out, and since most of them were going straight home, she decided to do the same thing.

Here the desire not to be different coincided with parental standards, because the decision of the group was in accord with them.

Why conformity? It may be the price one pays for safety. An early-acquired fear of making mistakes may create enough anxiety to prevent an adolescent from being different from the rest of the group. An early-acquired fear of losing the love of one's parents, which in childhood led to model behavior, may also be manifested in conformity to group standards; it may survive as a fear of losing group acceptance. If conformity to the group forces the individual to deny or to conceal his real values and goals in order to "belong," it may result in loss of self. On a different level, conformity may be learned as a technique of getting along with people and being liked by them. Adolescents rated "well-adjusted" by teachers usually express a preference for friends who conform to the wishes of other people and the group. Many youngsters do not know how to say "no" without hurting the other person's feelings. Conformity may also arise from apathy; it is the path of least resistance. When conformity is the price of group acceptance, it may result in loss of individuality, in subservience to the crowd, in harmful practices. On the other hand, when conformity is merely a transitional stage for the individual, it furthers his identification with the peer group and aids in the process of psychological weaning—attainment of a desirable degree of independence from the family.

The Tyranny of the Group

In addition to demanding conformity and loyalty on the part of its members, the peer group may be cruel to individual members. The social group or gang is so important to adolescents that an individual feels crushed when he fails in the struggle for acceptance. The following incident illustrates this: A group of eighth-grade girls was sitting in the room after school discussing plans for a party which Donna was going to give that week end. They were attempting to decide on whom they were going to invite. Nellie was not an accepted member of the clique, but she sought this acceptance at every opportunity. As the names were discussed and either approved or dismissed, Ethel was openly and frankly against inviting Nellie. Nellie sat there looking at a book which she had picked up. Her name was dropped from the list. As the other girls left a short time later, her eyes filled with tears and she left the room alone.

If an adolescent is not accepted by the crowd he really wants to join, he may, on the rebound, take up with another gang. If this gang is unsupervised, he may get involved in smoking, hanging around the corner store, or even in delinquent activities. If he has not learned to resist the tyranny of the crowd, he may be headed down a path he would not have chosen to follow.

Some teen-age gangs have taken on sinister aspects, as newspaper headlines show. The following description of delinquent gangs was given by a high school boy who lived in an urban area where they were prevalent. His account affords insight into their origin, appeal, and tyrannical operation.

You begin to go with certain kids in elementary school. The gangs begin to form then. Once in a gang it's hard to pull out. They meet you on the street or in the movies and say, "Going out with us?" No matter where you go, some of them speak to you and ask, "What are you going to do?"

I knew the gang I was with was going to join with an older gang so I pulled out right after I graduated from grammar school. Sometimes the only way to get out is to move away from the neighborhood, if you don't want to get beat up. About 5 per cent of the gang members, perhaps, want to get out; but most of them want to stay in the gang.

The gang is like a little city in itself. A territory may be eight blocks square. The gang has a regular organization with persons in charge to see that no one gets into trouble. One gang had a membership of about 125. They decided to run socials every Friday night. Sometimes they steal, just for the experience, not for the money. They have places to hide stolen goods. They have zip guns that they make themselves. They use different words in the gang. In school they sit at the same tables in the cafeteria. Anyone else coming by would not know what they are talking about. It makes you feel good in a way to belong to a special group.

The gang leaders are all ages. As soon as the pressure is on them they get forced out, like Stalin. Older men run their own gangs. All they do about the teen-age gangs is to tell them to lay off sometimes when the police are active in the neighborhood.

There are gangs among well-to-do teen-agers outside the city. They pay $20 dues instead of $3. They let their chauffeurs do their dirty work.

My mother couldn't do anything about the gangs. If she went to the police, they'd raid the club house but what would they get? No evidence. It's all in the gang members' minds.

Parents don't know where their children are. I could come home from school and be away for two hours. I might be 10 miles away if I had a car, or robbing a store. My mother wouldn't know. Three-fourths of the time parents *could* know what their child is doing. But the mothers go off and play bridge and chew the rag. When the children are little, they take good care of them, but they don't pay much attention to their teen-agers. The mothers neglect their homes; the fathers are busy.

The church can't help much. The priest has his hands full. He wants them to continue with their education, but they do what the other kids do, not what the priest wants them to do.

The appeal of the gang is strong. The kids want someone who will listen to them. A lot of these boys want to be strong arms. Older members give the younger ones cigarettes free. Then there's the big wonder world, marajana. Some recognize the danger and pull out. Some start going steady with a nice girl and pull out.

The best way to break up a gang is to isolate the members—grab one member at a time. If you get them by themselves, they turn yellow. In a way, you've got to use psychology as well as force.

They go to school as long as they have to. Everyone of the gang has something else on his mind when he's sitting in class. They bring to school the unrest of what is going on in their neighborhood gangs and think about what they'll be doing that night.

If boys like these could begin at an early stage to get satisfactions from their school groups, delinquent gangs would not have such a strong appeal for them.

During adolescence the "peer culture" tends to exert a greater influence than the family or school. This influence may be beneficial to adolescent development; or, as in the case of delinquent gangs, it may be extremely harmful. Much attention has been given to helping adolescents gain status in their group. More attention should be given to teaching them how to resist group pressures whose direction is undesirable.

Cliques in the Adolescent Culture

Within a school, a class, a club, subgroups form. The bases for their formation may be (1) personal likes, dislikes, and interests, (2) similarities in socio-economic background, or (3) proximity of residence. Certainly it is not undemocratic for congenial people to want to be together. What, then, distinguishes a clique from an interest group? A clique excludes others from membership on the basis of some irrelevant factor. An example of this is the belittling remarks often made about some "rushee" during a sorority "hash" session. One girl may say, "Oh, I don't think she'd make a good XYZ—she's not our kind," or "We can't take her—she's too fat; the other sororities will think we're pretty hard up." Other members nod in agreement. Perhaps they do not know the girl in question at all, or not well enough to pass judgment on her, yet they feel they are agreeing in the best interests of the sorority.

Adolescents frequently speak of cliques. In their compositions, reference to cliques is usually associated with a feeling of being "left out" and not "belonging." In group discussions of sororities and fraternities, many youngsters defend the closed group, but some recognize how those who are not invited to join may feel.

Cliques constitute more than half the population of many high schools. One-fourth or more of the students, who are on the fringes of these cliques, are not getting the social experience and the feeling of "belonging" which they need. Their isolation often becomes more intense as they go through high school. They ascribe their loneliness to difficulty in making friends and to having no place to go and nothing to do. Some of the older pupils recognize personality difficulties as a cause of loneliness.

The ideal peer group would assure an adolescent of his present social acceptability, and still leave him free to be himself later on. When the time comes for him to assert his independence, he must learn how to extricate himself from group domination and gain recognition for himself as an individual. There is a danger of "over-extending the group approach"—of permitting youngsters to "get so used to being in groups that they can't stand being by themselves." Both "the solace that comes from nature and the stimulus that comes from man" are needed for the best balance.

Study of Group Interaction

As an aid to understanding the patterns of attraction and rejection in a group, the sociometric technique is of great value.

In its simplest form it consists in asking members of a group to list in order of preference the three persons with whom they would like to serve on a committee, sit with in the cafeteria, or participate with in some other real-life situation. These choices are then charted in the form of a sociogram which shows clusters of relationships, pairs, and isolates; it reveals which members are chosen by few or none. Sometimes the question is also asked in its negative form: "With whom would you *not* like to serve on a committee, etc.?" In general, it is better not to direct the students' attention to their dislikes, but to emphasize their positive relations. As Jennings [11] has shown, the sociogram is a starting point. It describes the present group structure, suggests further considerations, and raises questions about the "motives underlying the choices" and the "values that affect the children's interaction."

The sociometric technique is employed in conjunction with other means of understanding children and adolescents—observation, group discussion, and casual conversation. All these techniques, if employed systematically, show how the members of a group are relating themselves to each other. The sociometric test shows which persons an individual would like to associate with, and whether or not the others feel the same way toward that person. Skillful interviews may throw light on the basis for a given pattern of choices; case studies indicate the characteristics of individuals who are chosen by many, and of those who are not chosen or are rejected.

The Socially Rejected Adolescent

It is difficult to help a socially rejected or lonely adolescent. A "pep talk," superficial reassurance urging him to join a club or go to a party, may intensify his feeling of social inadequacy. Nothing can be accomplished without some understanding of the causes of his isolation. These may reside in certain unpleasant physical characteristics or personality traits that make people shun him. Or the causes may be found in his early childhood

[11] Helen H. Jennings, *Sociometry in Group Relations: A Work Guide for Teachers*, p. 11. Washington, D.C.: American Council on Education, 1948.

and preadolescent experiences, which have made him overdependent, anxious, and unable to relate to others. Occasionally, an adolescent withdraws from social groups because he has other interests he wants to pursue.

Sometimes, when the cause is quite obvious, the adolescent can be tactfully helped to make desirable changes in his appearance and acquire some of the social techniques that will make him more acceptable. Often learning some skill that is popular at the time will give him entree to a group and increase his self-esteem. Association in a very small congenial subgroup within a class or a club will provide a social identity for him and an opportunity to find a friend.

For more deep-seated personality problems, expert counseling or group psychotherapy are means by which lonely adolescents and those who have never learned to relate themselves to other persons may be helped to form closer ties. If their feeling of loneliness is intense, they may break through even a strong feeling of anxiety and venture to form a new friendship or learn to participate in a group. In group-therapy sessions individuals have an opportunity to put into immediate practice the new insights they have gained, to test their competency in the group situation, to realize that others have similar problems, and to help other members of the group become more spontaneous and creative.[12]

FAVORABLE RECREATIONAL CONDITIONS

The need for a school recreational program that will meet individual needs is less widely recognized than the need for an individualized curriculum. Too often clubs and social activities are recommended without regard to the individual's capacities, personality, and background of experience. A youngster will gain nothing but an increased sense of inadequacy if he attempts to "make the team" when he lacks the physique for it, to join a music group when he does not have the necessary ability, to

[12] Paul Eiserer, "Group Psychotherapy," *Journal of the National Association of Deans of Women*, vol. 19 (March, 1956), pp. 113–122.

participate in social events when he lacks both desire and know-how.

Many individuals are not naturally "group happy"; it is a strain for them to keep up with the more extrovert teen-agers. They should not be made to feel inferior if they prefer to engage in more individual types of activities.

A common complaint of adolescents is that they "have nothing to do and no place to go." A seventeen-year-old girl described this problem in a typical way:

My one big problem is having no place to go to at night so I can dance, meet boys and also eat. Children here at Central don't come from people who have money. So they cannot be always giving partys so that you can get to meet other children.

I live in a small place just two rooms and when I come home I do my homework, eat and then look at four walls. And nothing can make someone so sick as doing that night as well as day.

I have a boy I wented with most all the time and he came over

about three times a week. We either wented for a walk or to the movies—where else could we go? He went to school like me and couldn't pay to be going to dances all the time.

I am in two clubs at school and also one out of school, but I don't get to meet boys at school clubs—not the boys I like to know.

Now you know why children live on the streets—*No places to go.*

This complaint about having "no place to go" is realistic. In many communities many teen-agers do not have homes to which they feel they can invite friends. There may be no youth recreation centers where they can have fun together; the school building is usually closed afternoons and evenings. Adults should become aware of this need, and help to provide recreational facilities.

It is still better if the young people themselves take the initiative. Some have done this successfully. A rural youth council [13] recognized a need for recreation, presented a plan to the adult community council, obtained a grant of land near the school, and built a recreation shelter and equipped it themselves. They went further: they discussed with the high school principal and members of the faculty the possibility of including an activity period within the school day. This would give the students who had to leave immediately after school on "the impatient bus" a chance to have the social experiences they needed. Other groups have obtained permission to use some old building as a recreation center and have worked very hard in renovating it.

Even without a special recreation center, there are untapped opportunities for wholesome recreation in every community. In a rural community, the boys may have good adventures and acquire many outdoor skills. In their compositions rural youngsters mentioned the following experiences:

A canoe trip with my father in the spring when the river was on its annual rampage. . . . As we neared home I had a feeling of the thrill we had just gone through.

[13] Amber Warburton, *Guidance in a Rural Community, Green Sea, South Carolina.* Washington, D.C.: Alliance for Guidance of Rural Youth and National Education Association, Department of Rural Education, 1952.

Hunting and fishing.

Watching the two large male deer fighting in the woods, with their horns locked together.

Getting a car of my own. It was a Dodge convertible. I worked a few summers for the money for it, in a knitting mill and in a grocery store. I was the only high school girl to drive, much less my own car. I'll never forget all the good times we had with it. I never drove to school without a full load of classmates in it. We were always going to football games with the top down. My car brought many exciting times to me.

Camping trips with family and friends.

Bicycling—the most exciting experience I had during the past year was when I bought my new English bike.

School sports are the big recreational events in the lives of the large majority, whether they play on the team, go to the games as spectators, or act as cheer leaders.

One composition by a sixteen-year-old boy described a recreational interest that should be further developed:

When I first came to this town there was little for me to do. So I spent my spare time listening to the radio. I also had a close friend who owned a phonograph. We didn't have very many records at first, only a few popular ones. So my friend and I decided to try a classic record to see if we might like it, and the next thing we knew we were "classic crazy." One day we saw a sign stating how to join a music association, so we signed up. At Christmas I got a brand new symphonic three-speed automatic portable phonograph. I could have passed out! I've already gotten a few records. One of my favorites is "Chopin Etude Op. 10 No. 3." If you have ever heard it you know how beautiful music can really be. I only wish I had enough patience to learn to play the piano.

This account is a good example of the way a recreational impulse may grow into a permanent leisure interest.

On quite a different level is the "hacking around" described by another sixteen-year-old boy in the same rural community:

Quite a few of us "teen-agers" were sitting on the front step of our local "hang-out" (the restaurant where we can do just about what we please, within reason). The restaurant was closed but with

nothing else to do we just sat there. We have one "comedian" in
the crowd and he (who doesn't smoke) was putting on a real show
for us, chewing and trying to smoke a cigar. He'd put nearly half
in his mouth and light it, chew one end and still trying to smoke
the other, would attempt to spit out the horrible-tasting juice in his
mouth.

This episode alone, would be quite vulgar but with his witty remarks and hilarious facial expressions, he was an unmatched "riot."
Being in a silly mood at the time, of course I was laughing so—my
stomach began to ache; everyone gets a "big kick" out of the way
I laugh so it wasn't long before everyone was laughing so at me that
no one was doing a thing but laughing at nothing.

This type of "cavorting around" we usually consider quite juvenile
and really it is, but we have all remarked about that evening, many
times.

Teachers should know more about the harmless activities that
teen-agers find most interesting and amusing, and start where
they are, instead of condemning them.

Even in the city it is not necessary for teen-agers to hang
around on street corners. The flat roofs of apartment houses can
be equipped with "deck games"—shuffleboard, ring toss, and the
like. In every large city there is a wealth of free recreational
facilities—parks, museums, beaches, and many others. One class
made a directory of the recreation available to groups of high
school students. This helped to divert their attention from disreputable commercialized amusement to creative social experiences.

In the effort to provide recreation that will attract young people, some church and other community groups have set up "milk
bars" and "imitation night clubs." There is need to study what
effect this kind of recreation may have on adolescents. Does it,
in some cases, arouse an interest in real night clubs? Does it
serve as a stepping stone to undesirable commercial recreation?
Instead of introducing activities that resemble demoralizing types
of adult recreation, it would be much better to build on the
present wholesome interests of the large majority of young people. In planning sessions with adults, they can determine what

these interests are and how they can be developed. In a teen-age canteen initiated by a social club in one town, everything went smoothly as long as the young people themselves took in-itiative in planning and carrying out the program. Interest lapsed and problems arose when the adults began to assume too much responsibility.

CONCLUDING STATEMENT

There is a reciprocal relationship between the kind and qual-ity of the recreation and the quality of interpersonal relations which it develops. New friends are made through common in-terests. Worthwhile group experiences strengthen friendship. Friends grow in stature as they engage in constructive activi-ties together. Service activities develop initiative and responsi-bility.

The peer group meets basic adolescent needs. It helps mem-bers to learn to relate themselves warmly to others. It helps them to relinquish childish dependence on the family. It gives them an opportunity to know themselves through comparison with others.

On the negative side, the group may suppress individuality if the emphasis on conformity is too strong. An anti-social group may influence the individual's standards in the wrong direction and lead to activities that may be permanently detrimental to him.

The plus values of group activities may be realized by skillful adult leadership that recognizes the needs of individuals, the interaction taking place in the group, and the dynamics of the group process. Adults need skill in utilizing the potentialities of youth and in helping young people to think through the problems of living and learn that there are many different points of view.

COMPREHENSION QUESTIONS

1. Why are friends of their own age so important to adolescents?
2. What are some of the characteristics associated with popularity among adolescents?
3. How does participation in student activities vary with age?
4. What are the advantages and the dangers of conformity to the peer culture? What are some of the reasons why group members agree to group decisions?
5. Explain what is meant by "the tyranny of the group."
6. What are some ways of studying interaction in a group?
7. How may wholesome recreational facilities be developed and used in different types of communities? What kinds of recreation can be provided for family groups?

STUDY PROJECTS

1. Make a sociometric study of a group of adolescents, and consider what role you can best play in helping some of the isolates to win acceptance from their classmates.
2. Help a shy adolescent to learn some skill or develop an interest which he can share with others.

3. Recall some successful group experiences which you have observed or in which you have participated. What made them successful?

4. Talk with student leaders—those who hold positions of leadership, and those who are natural leaders but do not hold positions in organized activities—to find out their attitude toward leadership.

5. Experiment with ways of helping adolescents resist group pressures to do things that might lead to trouble.

6. Plan to become friendly over a period of time with a neighborhood clique or gang, and gain some understanding of the dynamics of these groups.

FOR FURTHER STUDY

AUSUBEL, DAVID P., *Theory and Problems of Adolescent Development,* chap. 12. New York: Grune & Stratton, Inc., 1954.

CARTWRIGHT, DORWIN, and ALVIN ZANDER, *Group Dynamics, Research and Theory.* Evanston, Ill.: Row, Peterson & Company, 1953.

CUNNINGHAM, RUTH, and ASSOCIATES, *Understanding the Group Behavior of Boys and Girls.* New York: Bureau of Publications, Teachers College, Columbia University, 1951.

FURFEY, PAUL HANLY, *The Gang Age: a Study of the Preadolescent Boy and His Recreational Needs.* New York: The Macmillan Company, 1926.

GESELL, ARNOLD, FRANCES L. ILG, and LOUISE BATES AMES, *Youth, the Years from Ten to Sixteen,* chap. XV. New York: Harper & Brothers, 1956.

KUHLEN, RAYMOND G., *The Psychology of Adolescent Development,* chap. VII. New York: Harper & Brothers, 1952.

MEEK, LOIS H. (ed.), *Personal-Social Development of Boys and Girls with Implications for Secondary Education.* New York: Progressive Education Association, Committee on Workshops, 1940.

STOLZ, HERBERT R., MARY COVER JONES, and JUDITH CHAFFEY, "The Junior High School Age," *University High School Journal,* vol. 15 (January, 1937), pp. 63–72.

SYMONDS, PERCIVAL M., *Adolescent Fantasy.* New York: Columbia University Press, 1949.

TRYON, CAROLINE M., "The Adolescent Peer Culture," in *Adolescence,* Forty-third Yearbook of the National Society for the Study of Education, part I. Chicago: University of Chicago Press, 1944.

WATTENBERG, WILLIAM W., *The Adolescent Years,* chaps. XI, XV,

XXV. New York: Harcourt, Brace and Company, Inc., 1955.

WHYTE, W. F., *Street Corner Society.* Chicago: University of Chicago Press, 1943.

WITTENBERG, RUDOLPH M., and JANICE BERG, "The Stranger in the Group," *American Journal of Orthopsychiatry,* vol. 22 (January, 1952), pp. 89–97.

Fiction and Popular Articles

BECK, BERTRUM M., "Delinquents in the Classroom," *NEA Journal,* vol. 45 (November, 1956), pp. 485–487.

* HERBERT, F. H., *Meet Corliss Archer.* New York: Random House, Inc., 1944.

OJEMANN, RALPH H., *The Child's Society—Club Gangs and Cliques,* Chicago: Science Research Associates, Inc., 1953.

* PLAGEMANN, BENTZ, *This Is Goggle.* New York: McGraw-Hill Book Company, Inc., 1955.

Audio-visual Aids

Are You Popular? 10 minutes. Sound. Coronet.

Belonging to the Group. 16 minutes. Sound. Encyclopaedia Britannica Films.

The Eye of the Beholder. 25 minutes. Sound. Sovereign Productions.

The Outsider. 10 minutes. Sound. Young America Films.

Self-conscious Guy. 10 minutes. Sound. Coronet.

Shy Guy. 13 minutes. Sound. Coronet.

Plays

The Ins and Outs. National Association for Mental Health.

* Fiction.

CHAPTER 9

Making a Good Adjustment
to the Opposite Sex

Two main goals of adolescence are to relate oneself to age-mates of both sexes and to establish clearly one's masculine or feminine sex role. When youngsters have achieved these tasks, by the age of about sixteen years, they are easier to teach and more pleasant to have around. They choose activities that offer opportunities for relations with both sexes. Through these relations they achieve status in their adolescent world.

Boy-girl relations loom large in teen-agers' thoughts about growing up. Previous studies [1,2] of large numbers of adolescents have revealed their concern about sex talk, about their sexual development, about acceptance of an appropriate sex role, and about their strong feelings of attachment to the opposite sex. They express these same concerns in unstructured compositions (see Chapter 3).

In these compositions they frequently mention their relations to the opposite sex and their feeling of responsibility in situations involving both sexes. Quotations from these personal documents will show the range and individuality of their experiences in establishing heterosexual relations.

[1] Melvin J. Williams, "Personal and Familial Problems of High School Youths and Their Bearing on Family-life Education Needs," *Social Forces,* vol. 27 (March, 1949), pp. 279–285.

[2] H. H. Remmers and Benjamin Shimberg, *Examiner Manual for the SRA Youth Inventory.* Chicago: Science Research Associates, Inc., 1949.

DEVELOPMENT OF SEX INTEREST

Adolescent problems of establishing satisfying relations with the opposite sex should be seen in a developmental perspective. In infancy, interest centers in oneself, then moves to interest in persons of the same sex, and eventually to heterosexual relations.

Sex interest does not suddenly appear at puberty. There is actually no true "latency period" during the elementary school years, although at certain stages interest in sex is more strongly suppressed than at others. This interest mounts with the child's developmental curve. It may be stimulated by promiscuous parents, by parents who make a fuss over masturbation or other expression of sex interest on the part of the child, or by the common sex play among children in the home or neighborhood.

Sex interest often takes the form of masturbation, which, according to one study,[3] is almost universally practiced, especially by males, at one time or another. It represents an infantile stage of sexual development and an attempt to satisfy the sex drive without incurring the risk involved in heterosexual relations. It is more common among the educated group than among those of lower socio-economic status, who move more rapidly toward sexual intercourse. Masturbation is also more common in boys' or girls' schools than in coeducational institutions, and among insecure children who have been deprived of affection than among children who are relatively secure in their parents' love. When the practice persists into the teens, it should be regarded as representing retarded rather than abnormal sexual development. Much anxiety and guilt have been aroused by erroneous statements about the dire consequences of masturbation. The occasional practice should be accepted at the time, with the knowledge that it can be overcome, and with the expectation that it will be replaced by more mature sex interests. If, however, masturbation is used as the exclusive method by which an adoles-

---

[3] Robert T. Ross, "Measures of Sex Behavior in College Males Compared with Kinsey's Results," *Journal of Abnormal and Social Psychology*, vol. 45 (October, 1950), pp. 753–755.

cent expresses the sex drive, he may never achieve intimacy with the opposite sex. Thus he fails to achieve his most important adolescent task.

The next stage of development centers upon interest in the same sex. For most children, sex play with members of their own sex is transitory; they pass through this stage to normal heterosexual relations. During preadolescence it is very important that youngsters achieve intimacy with members of the same sex before the strong sex drive of early adolescence sets in. If unwisely handled, so-called homosexual experiences during preadolescence may leave a residue of feelings of guilt and inferiority.

Quite usual is the emotional attachment to someone of the same sex, commonly called a "crush." It results from a fusion of dependency, intimacy, and sexual needs; usually the sexual element is of minor importance. Adolescents often form such attachments with age-mates of the same sex and with teachers and counselors. If wisely handled, this experience can meet an adolescent's real need for acceptance, for help in understanding and dealing with his upsurging impulses, and for an ideal to imitate. If unwisely handled by a person who is frightened by the relation and breaks it off suddenly or by a person who has a neurotic need for the adolescent's devotion, the experience may result in a withdrawal from any close relationship in the future, or in a permanent homosexual orientation.

Persistent homosexual relations may arise out of deep-seated emotional needs. Such relations give rise to feelings of guilt, or they may be openly flaunted as a cult. This type of homosexuality makes normal marriage and family life exceedingly difficult unless it is successfully treated by psychotherapy.

In a mature heterosexual relation, each member feels respect as well as affection for the other. They recognize that love has a spiritual as well as a physical basis. "Love is a many-splendored thing" that cannot be understood by anyone who ignores its moral, spiritual, and psychological aspects.

In its most mature form, love may transcend family boundaries and reach out in compassion to all mankind. This is the kind of love which Paul described in the thirteenth chapter of First Corinthians, and which other writers have designated as *loving kindness.*

THE SEX DRIVE IN ADOLESCENCE

It has become the habit of our Freudian era to represent the infant mind as oppressed by a heavy burden of sex. It may be that the curiosity of modern children is more advanced on such subjects. For myself, I cannot recall that I speculated about sex, or singled out this instinct as a special province of wonder.[4]

Many modern psychiatrists and psychologists, while recognizing the importance of the sex drive, object to the view that personality development is dominated by sex. They would not single out sex as the sole or even chief determinant of character. They think of sex behavior more as an expression of the total personality than as a separate kind of behavior. They recognize its biological basis, but also take into account the complex personal, family, and environmental conditions that influence its various manifestations.

With boys, a sharp increase in sexual excitement may be expected between the ages of about fourteen and eighteen. Thus boys of these ages usually want to go as far as they can with a girl. However, because of the values and standards still prevalent in many parts of our country, they may expect to be refused. They are even likely to feel contempt for the girl who permits them to take too great liberties. Boys who fear to indulge their sex impulses frequently feel more secure with girls who practice restraint. If a boy has a strong desire for social approval in a society that does not sanction premarital or extramarital relations, he will appreciate the girl who keeps the situation from going too far. "The problem for the boy is not to repress sexual impulses completely, simply to depress the inten-

[4] Ellen Glasgow, *The Woman Within,* p. 54. New York: Harcourt, Brace and Company, Inc., 1954.

sity with which they enter his consciousness." [5] He should direct these impulses into constructive work and into vigorous play activities with other boys. Through the peer society he will be learning "new forms of behavior, trying out new feelings, expressing ideas, and formulating the self that is to become an adult." [6] If the adolescent boy makes a clear-cut distinction between girls with whom he can satisfy his sex drive and girls with whom he can satisfy his need for intimacy, he will have a corresponding cleavage in his sexual behavior. He will not, as Sullivan pointed out, "really be capable of integrating sex into his life, simply and with self-respect." [7]

It is significant that girls of these ages are, in general, more restrained sexually than boys. For girls, the physical changes at puberty are relatively abrupt. To cope with them, girls tend to repress their impulses. By not thinking of themselves in a sex role, they may even restrict their awareness of these impulses. During the subsequent years of dating, they likewise tend to exercise restraint. For some, this restraint may become a habit which may later inhibit their marital relations. They may also channel their emotions into social activities. Girls handle their sex impulses in accord with social expectations to a greater extent than do boys. The earlier-maturing girl may date even though she lacks emotional readiness for it, just because her age-mates are dating or her mother expects her to.

The socially successful girl seems to be the one who can act as if she were sexually mature, yet not allow herself to feel the emotions that would normally accompany such behavior. [8] She may indulge in petting more because the boy wants it than because she is driven by her own desires. The situation changes, however, once the sexual barriers have been penetrated. Sexual

[5] Douglas M. More, *Developmental Concordance and Discordance during Puberty and Early Adolescence*, pp. 119–120, monograph of the Society for Research in Child Development, ser. 56, vol. 18, no. 1, 1954, Champaign, Ill.: University of Illinois, Child Development Publications, 1955.

[6] *Ibid.*, p. 121.

[7] Harry Stack Sullivan, *The Interpersonal Theory of Psychiatry*, p. 270. New York: W. W. Norton & Company, Inc., 1953.

[8] More, *op. cit.*, p. 117.

activity is somewhat like a habit-forming drug—one becomes addicted to it. Heavy petting overstimulates the sex drive and tends to supplant other methods of showing affection and understanding.

Overemphasis on sex is characteristic of "the neurotic personality of our times." Sex appeal is everywhere—in posters, in magazines and paper-covered books conveniently available in drugstores and newsstands, in movies and plays, on radio and television. This overstimulation of sex interest makes it difficult for young people to channel their emotions into more wholesome avenues such as active participation in sports, creative activities, and service projects.

There is some convincing evidence that premarital sex repression does not necessarily cause frustration or emotional conflict. It is not true, as some college students have been told, that one becomes neurotic if the sex impulse is not gratified. Margaret Mead's studies [9] have shown that girls in the Manus tribe who practice complete sexual repression and the Arapesh adolescents who can choose between chastity and indulgence apparently experience as little storm and stress during adolescence as do the Samoans, where no social restrictions are placed upon childhood sex activities. There is difficulty in all the periods of life in which the individual has to modify his previous status; sex is only one of a number of sources of conflict.

Girls have relatively little difficulty in broadening their manifestations of affection to include more than the act of intercourse. They associate love with having a home and children. It is sound to "accentuate the positive" in helping adolescents handle their feelings about sex; they need help in finding healthy outlets for their emotions, as well as guidance in controlling their behavior.

The intensity of the sex drive varies with individuals. The early-maturing boys and girls are likely to have the most difficulty and need the most help; they are approaching biological maturity with relatively little social and intellectual experience.

---

[9] Margaret Mead, *From the South Seas*. New York: William Morrow & Company, Inc., 1939.

If they have never learned self-discipline, if they have always got what they wanted, if they have never learned to show consideration for others, and if, in addition, they are highly sexed, they may get into serious difficulty themselves, and may stimulate sex talk and practices among their peers. These youngsters need to be identified early. The physical education teacher can easily recognize these early maturers among the girls and call them to the counselor's attention. They need frank, positive, inspirational guidance. They need to know that contraceptives do not always work, and that some may injure the body tissue. But facts about sex are not enough; feelings must be recognized. For early maturers who have creative outlets, adequate self-control, and confidence in their ability to handle social situations, organized discussion of sex problems is unnecessary; in fact, it may overemphasize sex and thus create problems. It is the early maturers who have not built satisfying interests and self-control who especially need guidance and sex education. This can best be done individually, before problems arise.

The late-maturing girl and boy have the advantage of greater intellectual maturity, social experience, and emotional control. If they have established social outlets and wholesome interests, they are not likely to have serious sex problems.

Sex education of the right kind is helpful.[10] It should begin early because attitudes toward sex develop early. It should be

more than sex *information*. It should emphasize positive aspects, and should be introduced as part of education as a whole. It should be given in a setting in which the individual feels free to discuss his problems and can expect sincere and accurate answers to his questions.

PROGRESSION IN HETEROSEXUAL RELATIONS

Preschool children progress from solitary play to parallel play to cooperative activities. Elementary school children progress from individualism in groups to the two-group or chum relationship. Having achieved intimacy with a friend of the same sex, the groups of two enter into a larger social relationship. In these preadolescent gangs, youngsters appraise themselves and gain experience in social organization. After a period of avoid-

[10] Lester A. Kirkendall, *Sex Education as Human Relations*. New York: Inor Publishing Company, 1950.

ance of the opposite sex, there comes a turning point; considerable boy-girl interest begins to emerge, temporarily at least.

Transition Period

Like the course of true love, interest in heterosexual relations does not run smooth. On the whole, however, it increases from about the sixth to the twelfth grade. Youngsters recognize this change in their attitudes toward the opposite sex. Girls frequently say: "And you start getting interested in boys and going on dates, instead of playing hiding-seek, rope, and other games. And then you think back and remember when you use to say you would never bother with boys."

In this "in-between" period a variety of boy-girl attitudes and relations can be observed. Some boys talk about girls, but do nothing about them. They may discuss quite enthusiastically the personalities of their girl classmates. But the attitude they generally present to the world in the seventh, and sometimes in the eighth, grade is "Nuts to girls." Socially they seem to avoid girls. At school dances they are likely to let the girls dance with one another while they discuss things like baseball scores. They sometimes resent it if anyone tries to get them to mix, though when the announcer calls, "Ladies' choice," the floor fills with dancing partners, self-conscious, but laughing. The highlight of the evening for the boys is when they can pull down the decorations and break the balloons which have been used to give the school gym "atmosphere." On leaving the dance, most of them go off in groups that are exclusively masculine. Their attitude toward girls begins to change about the end of the eighth grade or sooner.

Many girls, on the other hand, show interest in boys early in the seventh grade—usually in older boys. Girls who are becoming "boy-conscious" have many problems in getting the right boy to notice them. If they succeed, then they have trouble in getting their parents to let them go out with him. Their Monday morning discussions become concerned with whom they dated, where they went, whether they had a good time, and which boys they like. One seventh-grade girl described the following ways of entertaining a boy friend: "For instance you can go to parties with a boy, have a soda with him. Ask the boy to your house and entertain him like this: play some games, put records on the phonegraph, go out and eat hot dogs."

The age for beginning to have dates and go to formal dances is being constantly lowered. The effect of this tendency on these younger children should be considered. When a twelve-year-old girl goes to a formal dance with a thirteen-year-old boy and has a miserable time, is the hurt deeper than that of a similar experience at sixteen or seventeen? What should parents do about this tendency to lower the age at which formal "dating" begins? The best answer is: Provide group activities that are fun.

There are a number of reasons why formal dating is undesirable for children in the sixth and seventh grades:

1. Youngsters of this age are already faced with all the problems of adjustment which they can handle.

2. The difference in maturity between boys and girls of this age is especially wide.

3. The initiative for early dating seems to come chiefly from a few socially aggressive girls and from adults who think it is "cute"; most of the children of this age do not have the "emotional readiness" for it. They should not be forced into a social pattern that is premature for them.

4. Many children of this age prefer other activities such as games, taffy pulls, square dancing, eating, talking together. A successful party meets these individual differences in maturity by offering a variety of activities.

A fourteen-year-old girl presented a point of view about dating that is exceptional in its psychological soundness:

The way I feel now is that I'm not going to rush into things, but take each year as it is and be satisfied. I'm not allowed to date yet and if I were, I doubt if I'd go anyway. I feel dating is for older teenagers, and if you start acting and thinking like an older girl, chances are you'll look old before your time. Older teenagers have many problems dating and I don't feel it's necessary for a fourteen-year-old to have the same problems. Growing up is a trying period, but I feel you should live and love every year as it comes.

Individual Differences in Junior High School

During the junior high school years youngsters report many varieties of boy-girl relations. One extreme is represented by this opening sentence from the composition of a ninth-grade girl, "I found my self falling in love with a married man." At the other extreme, an eighth-grade girl apparently had not been able to choose between her boy friend and her dog: "Well this boy [of whom she was as fond as her dog] said that I better leave dogs to dogs and people to people, and I didn't, so he stopped coming to my house and I was very sad." Other eighth-grade girls admit that they would like to have boy friends but do not know how to get them: "At my age of twelve I have begun to think about boys but I can't seem to attract them. They tell me to wait until I am older. I would like very much to have one boy-friend."

More Success in Senior High School

Establishing heterosexual relations is a most important task during the senior high school years. Schools in which subject matter is the chief concern do not provide adequate opportunities for boys and girls to work together and play together whole-heartedly. If there are no opportunities for casual contacts, no clubs in which boys and girls can get acquainted, wholesome heterosexual relations do not flourish.

Dating normally increases during senior high school years. In one investigation [11] over half of the high school freshman boys and girls in twelve high schools in nine states reported having no dates at all; about one-tenth said they had more than ten dates a month. Of the seniors, only about one-fifth of the boys and one-eighth of the girls reported having no dates, and one-fifth of the boys and one-third of the girls reported ten dates or more a month.

However, in some situations heterosexual relations are far from the rule even in the twelfth grade. In a sociometric test of one

[11] Harold H. Punke, "Dating Practices of High School Youth," *NEA Bulletin of Secondary-school Principals,* vol. 28 (January, 1944), p. 48.

twelfth grade, about one-third were not chosen by the opposite sex and one-fourth made no choices of the opposite sex. In the twelfth grade of a private school, except in a couple of the sophisticated cliques, the boys and girls were often shy of one another in groups. Informal dances were occasionally held at an outdoor pavilion; usually the boys and girls came separately. The boys would line up on one side of the room and the girls on the other. Scarcely anyone would be on the dance floor. The chaperones would try to persuade a couple of student leaders to start things off. After all verbal suggestions had failed, they would arrange to have a group dance such as the Virginia Reel to encourage the boys to ask the girls for the next round dance. After a few fox trots, another group dance would get a few more on the floor. At the end of the evening there would be more people dancing than sitting down, but the chaperones would be exhausted. At the next informal dance the whole procedure would have to be repeated. If these boys and girls had had more frequent informal opportunities to get together, they would have developed more ease with one another.

In recent years dating procedures have changed. According to a nation-wide survey,[12] of the girls 14–16 years old, 70 per cent reported dating; 90 per cent over 16 said that they dated regularly. They were not enthusiastic, however, about "going steady," seeing more disadvantages than advantages in this practice.

Senior high school girls who date usually prefer older boys —graduates, seniors, or the older boys in their own class. It makes them feel important to date a boy who is socially or athletically prominent in the school. Few, if any, are interested in younger boys. They often look on boys of their own age as mere children. Some senior girls date boys at a near-by college or university.

Problems Encountered in College

Adolescents of college age also face problems in establishing heterosexual relationships. Girls who have not dated before com-

[12] *Adolescent Girls,* Survey Research Center, Institute for Social Research, University of Michigan, 1956.

ing to college get such a thrill out of being "rushed" that they go out with almost any boy who invites them. Others, more sophisticated, set their minds on getting a "steady," and they are usually successful. "Going steady" affects students in different ways. At the beginning it may cause inattention and daydreaming; an intense romance may lower marks. In a girls' residence college, only one of the freshmen who were popular with boys made the dean's honor list. Older adolescents who are going steady sometimes become more ambitious and stable.

Those who long to have dates but are unsuccessful may seek compensation in their studies or in recreational reading. Girls who are unsuccessful socially may criticize the "parlor conduct" of their fortunate classmates, or withdraw into themselves to avoid being hurt.

The intellectually gifted girl who has entered college at an early age may also have problems: "Evidently boys of my own age or slightly older feel out of place with a younger girl who is in college while they are still in high school. The college boys find me too juvenile, unsophisticated and 'kid-sister type.' Shall I forget how old I am; or that I go to college?"

Statistics on divorce rates should cause many college students to think seriously about marriage. One group of college students agreed that matrimony should not be entered into lightly, and that divorce represents failure. They were critical of adults who "didn't take their responsibilities seriously," and felt sorry for children who were the victims of broken homes. They were of the opinion that intellectual and spiritual compatibility were as important as physical attraction, if not more so. According to Bossard,[13] many young people, in increasing numbers, marry too young. However, chronological age per se may not be of primary importance. A combination of conditions, some of them associated with immaturity, is more likely to explain failure in marital adjustment. Bossard goes on to say that many unsuccessful married couples have not revealed their important attitudes and qualities during courtship. They enter thoughtlessly

[13] James H. S. Bossard, "Eight Reasons Why Marriages Go Wrong," *New York Times Magazine* (June 24, 1956), pp. 5, 20–23.

Pulling together with one's peers and at the same time maintaining one's individuality is a highly satisfying and important adolescent experience. (*Courtesy of H. Armstrong Roberts.*)

Physical and social development are fused when boy meets girl for outdoor recreation. (*Courtesy of H. Armstrong Roberts.*)

Adolescents stay home when a family plays together. (*Courtesy of H. Armstrong Roberts.*)

Carol singing gives pleasure to both the shut-ins who listen and to the young people who carry out this service project. (*Courtesy of the National Council of the Protestant Episcopal Church.*)

into mixed marriages, accept the romantic and the sexual aspects as the primary bases for marriage, seek personality development for themselves as the main value in marriage, underestimate the influence of parenthood, strain to maintain or upgrade their social status, and fail to consider marriage as a project in group living. As a result; some 12 million of the 45 million children in the United States have been subjected to the consequences of divorce.

CONFLICT BETWEEN TEEN-AGE AND ADULT VIEWS

Adolescents' efforts to establish heterosexual relations are often hindered by well-meaning parents. For example, a seventeen-year-old high school girl who gets along with other boys and girls and enjoys her many friends has parents who do not think she should date while in high school. It is often easier for young adolescents to get along with their age-mates than with their parents. A great many home problems and conflicts arise as a result of parental objections to children's attempts to establish heterosexual relations. (See Chapter 13 for more detail.)

However, some youngsters report favorable results from parental interference, as in the following case:

Not long ago I was dating a soldier that my mother disapproved of. She said he was too loud and that I knew nothing of his family or friends. She didn't forbid me to date him, however, and I kept seeing him. Yet because my mother didn't like him I was always uncertain about my liking for him. I found myself troubled over this matter and began seeing him less. Much to my surprise I was relieved when I stopped seeing him altogether.

Beneath their "slap-happy" exterior, young adolescents are really concerned about what they *should* or *should not* do, say, and feel. They desperately desire to do the "right thing," but are uncertain what it is. They ask teachers such questions as, "If a boy asks you to the prom and you want to go with someone else, what should you do? What should you tell him?" One older adolescent boy employed King-Solomon-like strategy to help him decide between two girls, one whom he had known for two years, the other a new acquaintance. He described his tactics as follows:

On Saturday night there was to be a hay-ride so I invited both girls (one at a time) to go with me. That afternoon I had my sister call up the girls telling them I was sick in bed and would not be able to go. I knew both girls could get other dates so I sat home and waited until about 7.00 P.M. Then there was a knock at the door and one of the girls showed up saying that she wanted to see me and did not feel like going to the hay-ride with another boy as she liked me. The other girl (I found out later) went on the hay-ride with the first person who called her. Who was the girl that came to see me? You were right—the first girl, the one I had known for two years.

Although many adolescents handle their problems of social relations quite competently, they sometimes gain much help from talking their problems over with some older person. As one sixteen-year-old girl said, "When you're troubled you don't want to keep things to yourself but tell someone all about it and get it off your mind—someone who knows what to do." Their most serious indictment of adults, perhaps, is that adults will not, or cannot, understand their point of view—in fact, will not take the trouble to listen to them.

DATING PROBLEMS AND PRACTICES

Many of the problems mentioned by teen-agers involve dating. The first question that concerns many girls is how to get a date. The next question is how to have a good time on a date. This question involves many others: What about kissing, necking, and petting? How far can you go? How can you protect yourself against pregnancy? At what time and age is it best to get married? Girls at a vocational high school summarized their dating problems as follows: how to get a man, how to hold him, how to find out what makes him act as he does, how to stop thinking about him, and how to modify their parents' attitude toward boy-girl relations. The junior high school problems centered around how to make a date and what to talk about and do on a date. Senior high school students were more concerned about "whether to go steady," whether they were really in love, and whether they would find a suitable mate. They also felt the need for information about sex matters.

How to Get a Date

For girls this is the basic problem. Boys are scarce in some communities. Consequently, competition is keen, and a state of war exists; the more aggressive personalities show little mercy. As one girl said, "I've had to suffer, so if I get my date, let the other girl suffer."

Many girls are uncertain as to what approach to use. Here is the way one seventeen-year-old girl described her perplexity:

One of the problems that I've had is concerned with the Girls' Club dance which is November 28th. I asked a boy in the latter part of October and he said he'd let me know in the early part of the following week whether he could go or not. The telephone didn't ring the first night. Well, I thought, he'll call me up tomorrow night. The next night I proceeded to wait again. Ah, there goes the telephone, but it wasn't for me. I waited all week and finally called up a mutual friend to see if she'd heard from him. She had and he'd told her he didn't think he could go, but I still wanted to hear from him. I didn't know whether to call him or not. I decided that he'd let me know as soon as possible and that it would be less embarrassing if he called me up. After about 3 weeks he finally called up and said he couldn't go. The result certainly wasn't satisfactory but it was better than having me call him.

The anguish of not getting a date for an important school event is expressed in the following composition by a sixteen-year-old girl:

In the girls' locker room the topic of discussion is the prom.

"Gee, just think one more week and I'm going to the Jr. Prom with Tom," remarked Jane.

I did think. I thought how lonely and miserable I would feel that night, when all my friends, including my best friend, Dorothy, would be having a wonderful time at the prom. No one had asked me to go; and today was the last day. I felt horrible, I waited for the dreaded moment when they would ask me with whom I was going. What would I say? What would I do?

In the peer culture, failing to get a date not only deprives the adolescent of the pleasure of the event itself, but isolates the youngster from the group, and, in the present culture, is one of the most ego-deflating experiences of adolescence.

The trepidation with which some teen-agers approach asking for a date is described by an eighteen-year-old high school senior:

My most exciting experience was when I was a junior in high school. That made me eligible to ask a boy to our annual League Ball. My mind was full of ideas of how to ask a boy, but my biggest problem was, did I have enough courage to ask one boy in particular, whom I had known all my life.

One Friday night in May of that year, I had gone to a dance at the Central School. Toward the end of the dance was the time my dreamboat came and cut-in on me. We danced all the dances together after that, and at the end, he asked me to go home with him. I was very happy and accepted the offer after careful consideration. Coming home we stopped at a restaurant for something to eat and we talked about each other, and the things that we had been doing. Then I came right home and when the time came for him to say goodnight, I thought it would be a perfect time for asking him about our League Ball and if he would like to go with me. I asked him and he said that he really would like to go, and was very pleased. After this, we saw each other very regularly and we had wonderful times together.

What to Do on a Date

If adolescents have wholesome and thoroughly enjoyable experiences early, they will develop standards and satisfactions that may be strong enough to keep them from indulging in necking and the kind of petting parties that arouse sex impulses and cause anxiety, guilt, and self-depreciation. A seventeen-year-old girl described a Christmas dance which was an exciting and completely happy experience for her:

Bill, the boy I went with, called for me at 6:30 P.M. After a half hour drive we drove into the drive-way of one of his classmates' home, where we had cocktails (no liquor).

About a half hour later we were in the car again heading for another home. At this destination we were treated to a turkey and ham dinner. Everything was just beautiful here. After filling-up on all the food we could eat we headed for another home that belonged to another classmate of Bill. Here we had dessert.

Although I was very excited and worried that I wouldn't make a good impression, like most girls do, I wondered why Bill hadn't given me flowers. Well, at the last home we stopped at before the dance, I found out the answer. The boys had sent all of their flowers to this one home so that the girls could put their flowers on all at the same time. To my astonishment I received a beautiful orchid.

Finally we were on our way to the dance. The dance hall was beautifully decorated. There was an exceptionally good orchestra playing soft music. We danced and danced. . . .

After the dance we met at the last home to talk and just sit for awhile.

Although it was late, and I should have been sleeping long ago, I was wide awake. I was so happy that the evening had turned out to be just right. I couldn't have asked for a better evening.

We should have more accounts of parties and other social experiences that have proved thoroughly enjoyable and desirable for adolescents of different ages.

Quite a different kind of evening was described by a fifteen-year-old girl living in a small town:

One afternoon my girl friend asked me if I would stay overnight with her. It was New Year's Eve. She had to baby sit, so I went along with her. We had planned to have two boys come over to be with us during the evening. About 10:30 my boy friend and two of his friends came over drunk and wanted to come in. We wouldn't let them. Finally after banging on the door and almost waking up the kids, we let them in. They started drinking right there in front of us. We told them to leave but they wouldn't. My boy friend started to argue and finally started fighting with my new boy friend. My girl friend broke it up by stepping in between them. Finally the three of them left.

Petting, or whatever it is currently called, may have many meanings to different individuals. For some, it is the price of popularity. For others it is an activity about which they later feel guilty and anxious. For some boys it may be an expression of hostility or a means of building self-esteem through making a conquest. An eighteen-year-old girl of low socio-economic status recognized that "you meet some very bad boys, and never know whether or not to go out with a fellow who asks for a date." But when she does go out with one, her methods of dealing with him are rough and ready:

If you think he is trying to get fresh with you. Well that is the time to tell him off. Slap him in the face. But sometimes a fellow is very persistent. The saying is that a fellow will go as far as a girl will let him. But the way I see it is for the girl to go and find out for herself.

Other Questions about Dating

The opinions of high school pupils about dating were collected by teen-age reporters, most of them serving in some capacity on their school newspaper.[14] They dealt with the following questions:

1. *When to start dating?* That's an individual matter; some teen-agers are ready for dates sooner than others; perhaps fifteen is a good age at which to start. The first few dates should be double dates or group dates. One seventeen-year-old girl wrote, "My mother says that I may not go out on dates until I am eighteen, but many of my girl friends go out on dates earlier than that."

2. *What time should we have to come home?* Except for special occasions, between eleven and twelve o'clock seemed to them a reasonable hour. They thought that agreeing on a certain hour with friends and parents would avoid the thing they most dislike—breaking up the fun because they have to come home earlier than the rest.

3. *What about going steady?* Strictly speaking, going steady means having no dates with anyone else. Most girls thought it better not

[14] "The Mirror of Youth," *Better Homes and Gardens,* vol. 30 (October, 1952), pp. 764, 767, 769.

to be "tied down"; some boys asked, "Why not go steady if you like the girl?"

The practice of going steady is prevalent among high school youngsters. It has been estimated that from 25 to 50 per cent of the high school population engages in this form of "guaranteed dating." For girls, it represents "Saturday night social security"; in fact, it insures a faithful escort for all social events. For boys, it saves one the trouble of stalking new girl friends.

Going steady usually involves being together a great deal during

the day as well as going together to special affairs. The couple may sit together in classes, eat lunch together, walk home together, study and watch television together, and do a moderate amount of what they call "parking" or "necking." In this way parents get a chance to know their child's boy or girl friend, and the youngsters get to know each other's faults and learn how to handle their differences and misunderstandings. Parents, some adolescents say, take going steady more seriously than they do themselves.

On the negative side, going steady shuts the couple out of a wider circle of acquaintances; it may distract them from other adolescent tasks and precipitate a too-early marriage. Some of the boys thought they should "get to know as many kids as possible."

"In the majority of cases, going steady lasts only a few months," according to one student reporter. "Going steady," said another, "should be on a full-of-fun, not-too-serious basis." Some, however, take "going steady" very seriously. They look forward to early marriage. Some also learn that "going steady" is not always "steady going."

To overcome some of the difficulties and disadvantages of going steady, teen-agers have hit upon a refinement, "going semi-steady," as the following comment shows: "Then last Sunday Teddy asked me to go semi-steady, which means that every Saturday night we would have a date. Neither of us intend to get serious."

4. *What are some of the pitfalls of dating?* These were mentioned: "being alone with one person too much," "chumming with the wrong set," going to night clubs, insisting that the girl stay out later than her parents approve, drinking, petting in cars, getting "picked up," and "secret dates." These are problems with some teen-agers because, while they want to do what is right, they also dislike being called "chicken," and fear being snubbed by the gang or losing a date. They need courage to live up to their convictions.

5. *What makes a successful date?* Some think "conversation either makes or breaks a date." To be a good conversationalist, they suggest, one must have common interests, willingness to talk about the other person's interest, willingness to listen as well as talk, and a desire to understand the other person. One girl's recipe was, "Have fun, smile, and laugh sincerely. Get home at a reasonable hour. Say, 'Thanks for a lovely evening.'"

VARIETIES OF ADOLESCENT LOVE EXPERIENCES

Preadolescents' ideas of marriage are amusingly romantic; early adolescents' ideas are exploratory; later adolescents are thinking seriously of marriage, sometimes as an escape from loneliness, maladjustment, or a difficult home situation. Many adolescents of all ages take their first love affair seriously. The following accounts suggest the wide range of adolescent love experiences, which vary with the values and the biological and emotional make-up of the individual as well as with family attitudes and community standards.

However trivial a youngster's heartache may seem to be, it is very real and very trying to him or her at the time. One sixteen-year-old described the feelings she experienced while waiting for a letter from her boy friend: "The next two weeks were tormenting. I didn't eat much, I couldn't study for my exams, and I couldn't sleep at night. In fact, I believe I lost four pounds during those weeks and I don't lose weight easily either. My friends kept reassuring me that he would write. But I didn't know what to think." It turned out in the end that he had written, but to the wrong address. She continued: "When I heard this I felt so relieved that he had written and that he still liked me that I had to sit down because my knees just buckled under me. I immediately called him up and we straightened everything out."

Teen-age love is quite different from mature love; it is more intense, more absorbing. But mature love is built on the childhood and adolescent experiences of loving and being loved.

Being in love may involve all the areas of an adolescent's life—his family relations, his educational and vocational plans, and his future success and happiness. An eleventh-grade boy, eighteen years old, shows in the following excerpt a keen awareness of the realities he is facing:

When I was in junior high I met a nice girl and went with her for a while, and then didn't see her for several years. During the early part of the summer I met her again; we started going steady and now she wants to get engaged. I love her very much. I have lost all interest in school and do hardly any studying whatsoever. You see during the summer I had a job as mechanic in a garage and I was making $55 per week, five days. I want to quit school and go back to work. But I hate to hurt my mom and pop by quitting school. I have not told them that I love this girl. I know it would hurt them because they do not care much for this girl and both of these things would hurt them. I have not made any decision yet, but when I make it, I hope I take the right road to happiness and success.

This boy needs to be encouraged to take a long-distance view. His desire to make the wisest possible decision would make him accessible to counseling.

A seventeen-year-old boy described an adolescent "triangle" which was as serious to the youngsters involved as similar situations are to their elders. His problem was threefold: trying to be loyal to his best friend, wanting the girl, and wanting to have a good time himself:

During the summer my best friend met a very cute girl. They immediately liked each other and they were soon going steady. At the end of the summer I met this girl and I soon realized that I liked her an awful lot. I guess she liked me too because whenever the three of us went around together, as we did most of the time, I found that my best friend was left a little high and dry. I know the girl still liked him a lot.

I went out with this girl a number of times but I was always afraid to get too chummy with her, because I kept remembering my loyalty to my friend with whom I had gone around for almost 13 years. So now I am right back where I started. She happens to be a very bright individual and seemed to understand my problems. Lately she has gone back to the other fellow with whom she probably has a better time because he feels no barrier.

Some teen-age love affairs are complicated by religious differences. A seventeen-year-old senior in a rural community described the problem in this way:

The problem we have is religion. He is a catholic and I am a protestant. My parents seem to think that I might become too serious with him and things just wouldn't work out for us. I haven't told them how we feel about each other. I told him I couldn't change but he said he thought he could, but when the time actually comes, it might be different. We have been planning for the future and hoping things will work out. I don't know whether I should tell my parents how we feel. I'm afraid if I do, they will make us break up, because we are so serious. I don't know what we would do, if we had to break up. After school he plans to go in the service for two years and then come home and get a job, because he is only 17. I plan to go to a business college for a year or two and then find a job. We feel as if we can wait for each other because I know I love him very much and he feels the same.

Most adolescent love affairs involve mixed emotions. These arise from conflicts between the adolescent's feeling of attraction to the particular boy or girl and his own values and standards, parental attitudes, and the advice of friends. A sixteen-year-old girl described her mixed-up feelings about boys and lamented her inability to confide in her parents. Speaking of a boy, she wrote:

At school he appeared to be *so* nice but alone he was exactly opposite. Several times he tried to get intimate. Of course I refused. I liked him so much and he always talked about marriage and that spoiled everything. People warned me I would get a bad reputation and my sorority advised me not to go out with him. He has not called me up recently. This hurts because I really like him, except for his one fault. As a result I have tried liking other boys and going out with them. One of these boys is shy and keeps me worried all the time. I don't know what to do with boys! They're the worst problem I know!

My parents don't know anything about the first boy. My sorority sisters and the maid are the only ones. My mother isn't the type to whom you can talk about problems or anything you would like. She is so old-fashioned about "hours" that I am resentful. My children are going to be able to do everything I couldn't do when I was growing up.

Some high school girls are thinking seriously and happily about marriage in the immediate future. One junior, aged seventeen, described the night when her boy friend gave her an engagement ring:

When I first got even a small hint as to what my Christmas present would be, I had a long discussion with my parents as to whether or not I would be allowed to keep it. Being so young, I didn't know if my mother and father would let me accept it or not.

I'll remember the night as long as I live. We sat there on the couch talking, and he pulled the little box out of his pocket, and handed it to me. As the custom goes, he made a wish and put the ring on my finger. To this very day I'm glad and also very thrilled that I accepted the ring. In the near future (about a year), it will be even more thrilling to add a wedding band to the little ring already there!

With each passing decade, according to the Midcentury White House Conference report, adolescents are marrying earlier and choosing mates their own age. Other statistics show that there is a greater chance of divorce for early marriages than for those which take place after the age of twenty.

The dark side of adolescent love affairs is illustrated by a rural girl. When she was eleven years old, her mother warned her to stay away from one of the men in the lumber camp, who was attentive to her. In the winter the child was sent to board with a woman in town. The woman arranged the incident which the girl described:

We told her husband we wanted to go to the movies . . . and we got in the car with the two men and went off to park. She was in the front seat and I was in the back. While we were parking I'll admit he tryed to get fresh many of times. But I never lost my head. I always could control myself even at that age.

Well, her husband caught us . . . and my mother found out about what I had done. Oh, I cried for hours and since then I've had so many problems. I wish someone could help.

Mom and Dad wouldn't even speak to me when they came and got us that Friday night. They thought something diffrent in that car happened that awfull night. But I keep trying to tell Mom that, nothing did. And nothing did happen never and never and that's the truth.

The prevalence of premarital relations varies with the situation. The effect on the individual also varies. Some get enough satisfaction from the experience to indulge in it excessively. For these individuals, it may become so casual that marriage and family life have no significance and evoke no depth of feeling. For others, a single incident may serve as a prelude to marriage. Some young people turn to alcohol to relieve their anxiety over the first sex experience. But being only a prop, affording temporary relief, alcohol does not in any way solve the problem. Moreover, alcohol "definitely poisons the self-system progressively . . .

[and] practically all the anxiety is experienced later, retrospectively." [15] For many, the anxieties arising from social and religious disapproval and the necessity for secrecy outweigh any immediate satisfaction. For still others, the experience is associated with intense fear of discovery, and of venereal disease or pregnancy. The consequences of premarital sex relations are described by two older boys:

She told me the most shocking thing that I had ever heard; she said that she was two weeks late in her period. I must admit that we had had relationship before but I thought I had prevented that thing from happening as it appeared to have had. I was so scared that I couldn't do anything; I couldn't study, sleep, eat or consintrate on anything but her, and this terrible situation.

After tests had proved that the girl was not pregnant, the boy was reassured; his closing comments are: "I never have told anyone anything about this and I don't intend to. I never did confess this situation to anyone because I did not feel that I had anyone I could tell, that is except my Mom and Dad and I did not want them to know it until I was sure she was not going to have the child."

In the second case the consequences were still more serious; the college boy who was involved became so confused and the whole affair so complicated that expert assistance was needed:

I have gone with a girl for five months last year. We were good friends and that's all. She had other dates with other boys and sometimes let things go too far. She has called me twice since and has told me that I am the father of her unborn child. I am certain that I am not because during our affair I took certain well-known precautions such as condoms and germ killing drugs. I do like her still, but I will not marry her and take care of somebody else's child. I don't think our marriage would be a success because I would deeply mistrust her. But I don't know how I can prevent it, the marriage. She can say the kid is mine, and what court jury will accept my answers of denial? I am now going with another girl, C. She is quite different than M. But if news of M's pregnancy ever reached C's

---

[15] Harry Stack Sullivan, *op. cit.*, pp. 273–274.

ears, she would never forgive me. If I have to marry M, I will lose everything which I now have. I will lose C, my new friend, and my career, and probably my education.

This boy feels resentment rather than remorse. He realizes that his affair with M may seriously affect his future success and happiness. His exclusive concern for himself may reveal his general attitude toward sex relations. At such a point, guidance is "too little and too late"; it must begin much earlier if fundamental values of respect and consideration for others are to be developed.

These varied examples of adolescent love experience suggest the wide range of involvement and intensity that may occur in this period. Some love interests are transient. It is fairly typical for adolescents, who are not very discriminating at first, to fall in and out of love three or four times. As one girl said of a boy with whom she had considered herself in love: "I knew then that I would never go out with him again and that what I had felt for him was just another infatuation."

However, "puppy love" can be a serious matter: a fourteen-year-old boy and girl committed suicide when their parents tried to keep them apart. These love affairs may last only a few months, but the way the youngsters handle them may indicate how they will handle other love affairs in the future. Instead of ridiculing or discouraging young love, teachers and parents should recognize and sympathize with young people's ardent feelings. They should try to understand what love means to the individual adolescent. Is it associated with pride in making a conquest or the prestige it gives in their peer group? Is love an inspiration or does it result in a withdrawal of effort from long-term educational plans? Does the experience teach them that love means mutual trust and concern for the welfare of the other?

THE ROLE OF TEACHERS AND PARENTS

Teachers should take the attitude described so well by one teacher:

Unless we are careful, we tend to minimize the love affairs of teen-agers and to laugh them off. If we are going to be of help, we must look at these affairs through their eyes and not laugh at them. I think I can be of aid to these youngsters by picturing them as rapidly maturing adults with many adolescent traits, and by lending them a sympathetic ear.

Parents often react to these usually transient love affairs with anger or ridicule because they themselves are immature, jealous, or fearful. The first love affair is the most serious threat to the continued dependence of the child on the parent, who may be jealous when the child shifts his affection to another person. Then, too, parents often fear that the first affair will result in a permanent relationship with a person whom they consider undesirable. Parental opposition or ridicule may have either of two harmful results: (1) it may associate a perfectly healthy, normal emotion with feelings of anger, fear, or guilt; (2) it may transform a transient love affair into a more intense experience, resulting sometimes in an elopement and a too early marriage.

Even without parental interference these early love affairs sometimes become too serious. This is probably happening if the youngsters completely withdraw from their other friends— no longer double-date or spend time with their crowd. Those who become involved in such exclusive sexual relations are usually youngsters who are unhappy, lonely, unsuccessful in social adjustment. They find solace in this close relationship with each other; they do not care to share their happiness with others.

Parents would be less concerned about normal early love affairs if they recognized the positive values in them and treated them with respect. The fact that their child can love another person is evidence that they have been successful in providing the affectionate atmosphere in which the child has learned to love, has acquired the capacity to love. The experience of being in love also has the value of teaching youngsters how to handle this normal and desirable emotion. They learn to give affection wholeheartedly. They learn to accept another person as he is. They learn what loyalty and devotion mean, and discover that these emotions are not inspired only by parents. Successive infatuations, often the result of increased ability to discriminate, may lead to recognition of the characteristics desirable for a permanent relationship. Last but not least, improvement in cleanliness, grooming, and courtesy is often stimulated by the desire to appear as attractive as possible to the boy friend or girl friend, or to his or her parents.

Parents who are tolerant toward ordinary teen-age love affairs at times have to set limits. They may have to make it clear that they will not allow the child to make a serious mistake. Young people often welcome parental intervention when a love affair is getting out of control and they know it.

Adolescent love, based on affection, is a very different thing from the preoccupation with sex that confronts young people in many magazines, radio and television programs, records, theaters, and motion pictures. This demoralizing overemphasis on sex has been vigorously opposed by Sorokin.[16]

The most constructive approach is to help youngsters see the difference between the spiritual and social aspects of the sex relation and mere physical gratification, which is sometimes an attempt to compensate for inability to establish intimacy or psychological closeness. The older adolescent should realize that the only way to build a happy and lasting marriage is to use the sex impulse as "a language of expression" between two people, under conditions of security and peace of mind.

COMPREHENSION QUESTIONS

1. Trace the development of heterosexual relations from early childhood. At what periods do marked changes in boy-girl relations occur?

2. What are the most common sources of conflict between child and parent with respect to boy-girl relations?

3. Show how dating practices are related to heterosexual development during adolescence.

4. How might a group of adolescents be encouraged to raise their standards with respect to boy-girl relations?

[16] Pitirim A. Sorokin, *The American Sex Revolution*. Boston: Porter Sargent, 1957.

5. How do adolescents feel about their first love experiences? How may parents cause harm by lack of sympathy and understanding?

6. What evidence do you have that the sex drive is overstimulated in our present-day society?

7. Why should sex be considered part of a total pattern which has been developing since early childhood?

STUDY PROJECTS

1. Select an adolescent boy and girl who seem to have made an especially good adjustment to the opposite sex. How do they behave? What are their attitudes toward boy-girl relations—dating, petting, and the like? What are their home backgrounds?

2. Plan a panel discussion of parents and adolescents on "Teen-Age Problems." What are some of the special problems for adolescents in low socio-economic groups?

3. Encourage a group of teen-agers to write an attractive booklet on recommended dating practices. One group of college students recommended "moderation in petting, not total abstinence."

4. Talk with parents to learn more about why they are concerned about adolescents' behavior and about how they can create more favorable conditions for adolescents' social development. In some communities this would involve cleaning up disreputable "hang-outs."

5. Plan a way of helping a "boy-crazy" girl to express the sex drive in other affectionate and creative ways.

6. Make a study of the sex stimuli presented to adolescents in drugstores, via radio and TV, and in magazines.

7. Read a number of stories about adolescents in current magazines and analyze the attitudes toward sex expressed in these stories.

8. Analyze also the content of several current popular magazines. What percentage of the illustrations in the stories and in the advertisements have sex appeal?

FOR FURTHER STUDY

BIBBY, HAROLD CYRIL, *Sex Education: A Guide for Parents, Teachers and Youth Leaders.* New York: Emerson Books, Inc., 1946.

FISHBEIN, MORRIS, and ERNEST W. BURGESS, *Successful Marriage: A Modern Guide to Love, Sex and Family Life,* rev. ed. New York: Doubleday & Company, Inc., 1955.

HENRY, GEORGE WILLIAM, *All the Sexes: A Study of Masculinity and Femininity,* foreword by David E. Roberts. New York: Rinehart & Company, Inc., 1955.

HURLOCK, ELIZABETH B., *Adolescent Development,* chaps. V, VI, XII, XIII. New York: McGraw-Hill Book Company, Inc., 1955.

JOSSELYN, IRENE M., *The Adolescent and His World,* chaps. VI, X. New York: Family Service Association of America, 1952.

KIRKENDALL, LESTER ALLEN, *Helping Children Understand Sex.* Chicago: Science Research Associates, Inc., 1952.

———, *Sex Education as Human Relations.* New York: Inor Publishing Company, 1950.

LERRIGO, MARION O., and HELEN SOUTHARD, *The Dutton Series on Sex Education.* New York: E. P. Dutton & Co., Inc., 1956.

LOWRIE, SAMUEL, "Sex Differences and Age of Initial Dating," *Social Forces,* vol. 30 (1952), pp. 456–461.

MEAD, MARGARET, *Male and Female: A Study of the Sexes in a Changing World.* New York: William Morrow & Company, Inc., 1949.

SOROKIN, PITIRIM, *The American Sex Revolution,* Boston: Porter Sargent, 1956.

SULLIVAN, HARRY STACK, *The Interpersonal Theory of Psychiatry,* chaps. XVI, XVII. New York: W. W. Norton & Company, Inc., 1953.

Fiction and Popular Articles

* BENSON, SALLY, *Junior Miss.* New York: Random House, Inc., 1941.

BOWMAN, HENRY, "Boy Meets Girl—Then What?" *National Parent-Teacher,* vol. 51 (November, 1956), pp. 12–14.

* DALY, MAUREEN, *Seventeenth Summer.* New York: Dodd, Mead & Company, Inc., 1942.

DUVALL, EVELYN MILLIS, "Are They Too Young for Love?" *National Parent-Teacher,* vol. 48 (March, 1954), pp. 4–6.

* TARKINGTON, BOOTH, *Seventeen.* New York: Harper & Brothers, 1916.

WHITMAN, HOWARD, "Youth and 'the Natural Urge.'" *Better Homes and Gardens,* vol. 35 (July, 1957), pp. 43–102, 112, 114–115, 120.

Audio-visual Aids

How Do You Know It's Love. 13½ minutes. Sound. Coronet.
Human Growth. 19 minutes. Sound. E. C. Brown Trust.

* Fiction.

Marriage Series: *This Charming Couple*. 19 minutes. Sound.
Marriage Today. 22 minutes. Sound.
Choosing for Happiness. 14 minutes. Sound.
It Takes All Kinds. 20 minutes. Sound.
Who's Boss? 16 minutes. Sound.
Who's Right? 18 minutes. Sound.
Jealousy. 16 minutes. Sound.
In Time of Trouble. 14 minutes. Sound. McGraw-Hill.
Social Sex Attitudes in Adolescence. 22 minutes. Sound. Mc-Graw-Hill.

CHAPTER 10

Family Factors in Achieving
Independence without Antagonism

The adolescent's goal of emancipation from the family, or "psychological weaning," as Leta S. Hollingworth called it, is, perhaps, the most pervasive developmental task. According to Ausubel,

This process of desatellization begins in middle childhood and preadolescence; and what is accomplished during this period in the way of learning responsibility and independence predetermines in large measure the later success or failure of emancipation. . . .

The surprising thing about emancipation is that it is largely the outcome of positive changes in the relationships between the adolescent and non-parents rather than the result of any positive modification of the parent-child relationship itself. Seldom is there any planned or deliberate determination of policy. There is merely the deterioration of a relationship as it is replaced by new loyalties, new standards, and new sources of status.[1]

This positive point of view emphasizes the forming of new relations with one's peers rather than the breaking of family ties. Ideally, a new and positive relationship with parents should be developing parallel with the emerging peer relations. Adolescents still need parents. They want someone to whom they can turn in times of trouble, someone who will stand by them through

[1] David P. Ausubel, *Ego Development and the Personality Disorders*, p. 98. New York: Grune & Stratton, Inc., 1952.

thick and thin and will give them genuine help *when they ask for it*. One teen-ager said: "Today's parents are too concerned with their teen-agers. If they would give them a little more freedom, it would help."

The following progression of attitudes is frequently observed in young people between the ages of twelve and eighteen: antagonism and negative behavior toward adults; renewed feelings of confidence and respect, minus the earlier dependence; and eventually, emotional independence. We should also recognize that adolescents cling to behavior appropriate to an earlier stage of development only as long as they have need for it; they can be expected to fluctuate between dependency and independence. Older adolescents often experience a phase of antagonism, or at least estrangement, which is more bitter though less impetuous than that of early adolescence.

ECONOMIC INDEPENDENCE

Emancipation from the family is frequently associated with money problems. High school and college students think of money as a symbol of independence. Parents sometimes use it as a means of controlling adolescent behavior. To be completely dependent on the family for spending money is irksome to teenagers; to earn money themselves increases their self-esteem. For these reasons a large proportion of high school students get part-time jobs as soon as the law allows. The adolescent's dependence on his family is often prolonged by his need for financial help in getting an education and by restricted opportunities for employment.

Money is frequently a bone of contention in the family.[2] There are squabbles over how much the child should receive as an allowance, how much of the child's earnings should be contributed to the family, whether or not the adolescent should get a part-time job, or how he should spend the money he earns for recreation or for other purposes, such as paying tuition, buying

---

[2] L. J. Elias, *High School Youth Look at Their Problems.* Pullman, Washington: State College of Washington, 1947.

clothes and school supplies, financing a car, or whether he should save it toward college expenses.

For many boys, the purpose of earning money is to buy a car. Often the car stands as a symbol of other desires and needs: greater independence, a wider choice of friends and social opportunities, and the more frequent assertion of adult status. Hav-

ing a convertible roadster practically ensures popularity. To adolescents, then, an automobile represents much more than transportation. And because so many of the boys now possess an automobile of their own or hope soon to have one, conflicts over the use of the family car have in some cases become less troublesome. Despite their fear of accidents from reckless teen-age driving, parents often yield to pressure. One family even decided to turn back an expensive automobile for two less expensive ones.

Other adolescent money problems are usually tied up with social relations and obligations. One seventeen-year-old boy specifically described his money problems:

Earlier in the week, I was confronted with the situation of having too little money. I had to buy two tickets to a play, which cost 75 cents apiece, one 70 cent ticket to a football game, and a 35 cent student ticket to the same game. I had asked my girl friend to go to the senior play and to the football game. This all adds up to $2.55, but I had only 98 cents. So I had to buy $2.55 worth of tickets with only 98 cents.

All day Monday and Tuesday, I worried about it, and wondered how I could raise the money. On Tuesday nite, my girl friend called up and asked if I had bought the tickets to the play or the game yet. I shamefully told her that I hadn't. I was very much surprised when she told me that she was glad that I hadn't bought them. It seems that her parents had made some plans on short notice and so she couldn't go. I was very much relieved. Instead of spending $2.25, I only had to spend 35 cents to buy my own ticket to the game.

There is still a little catch in the situation yet. The play is also going to be given on the following Friday and Saturday nites, so I'll probably have to buy the play tickets anyway—out of next week's allowance.

Some adolescents have more serious money problems which reflect the family's financial condition. In one case a seventeen-year-old boy was worried not only about financing his own college education, but also about the welfare of his family. His attitude toward the problem showed his keen sense of responsibility:

When I was attending grammar school and the other primary grades, I was under the impression that my father would be able to assist me through college. I believed this because he was holding a job which paid a good salary. I realized that I would also have to work; however, I thought he would be able to help me through the first two or three years of college. Unfortunately, after I had entered high school, I discovered that he, through faults which I would rather not deal with at the present moment, did not have any money either to assist me through college or for the family if an urgent need should arise. This was the problem which would not only affect me, but what is more important, might have a serious effect upon our home someday.

I am now working after school and week ends to earn money for college. I have saved enough so I'll not have to worry about college. As for my dad, he has recently begun to save. The amount is not tremendous, but thank God he has done this. Although some arguments still arise, the problem is slowly being solved and may be completely solved when I have completed college.

The pressure of home responsibilities likewise weighed heavily on a teen-age girl:

My father is quite sick and cannot work. My mother works at night and I take care of my little brother. Mother doesn't make enough money to support us, so we live with my grandmother. It is quite unpleasant, because she is always fussing. I sometimes take care of other children in the neighborhood, making one or two dollars each time.

The effect of financial problems on the adolescent depends on many factors: the intensity of the need for money, the family relationships involved, the change in social status resulting from financial reverses, the loss of opportunities for heterosexual experiences, the standards and values of associates. In the play *I Remember Mama,* the mother creates a sense of security despite the family's low-income status. The family-council plan is ideal; all the children participate and thus become familiar with the family's financial condition, and understand why their allowances are not larger. The best preparation for economic independence probably involves a combination of approaches—a regular allowance, supplemented as necessary by special grants when crises arise, and by remunerative work suitable to the age and ability of the individual.

HOME INFLUENCES

"Home is where we start from." Despite the desire of preadolescents and early adolescents to be rid of home restrictions, lack of home ties may have a detrimental influence, especially around the ages of twelve and thirteen. Where there is no father, where the mother is employed outside the home, where there are dislocations due to war or divorce, the children are more likely to become involved in truancy, lying, stealing, and other delinquent behavior. A home base seems to be a psychological as well as a biological necessity.

The family influences the adolescent's development in many ways. From the attitudes which members of the family adopt toward him he derives a concept of himself. If his parents give him as much responsibility as he is able to assume at each stage of his development, he will begin to think of himself as a competent, reliable person. If they are genuinely affectionate, he learns to love and to be loved. If they do not thwart his periodic thrusts toward independence, he is able during adolescence to achieve the necessary degree of emancipation from home and parents, and to relinquish more and more his childish dependency.

Parental Attitudes and Behavior

Parental attitudes and behavior may either hinder or facilitate the child's achievement of maturity. The possessive and overprotective parent makes emancipation extremely difficult. The girl who is excessively attached to her father may identify with him even if his behavior is disapproved socially. The boy who fears his mother's attachment and his own response to it often has to use explosive methods to free himself. The dominating parent may prevent an adolescent from benefiting from the new positive relations with his peers which are so important in achieving emancipation. The understanding, accepting parent is a source of solace and security to the worried adolescent; such a parent will give help on problems the adolescent cannot solve himself but will also encourage him to be independent and to assume responsibilities he can carry.

Parents' values are of crucial importance. The parent who has high standards and values and lives by them is a reservoir of strength to the adolescent confronted with conflicting standards and practices. In the world today, we see on all sides parents who are irresponsible, who do exactly as they please, who are thoroughly materialistic, who have no moral answers in their own lives for the problems of their children. By many means other than words, they convey to their impressionable children their values, standards, and outlooks on life.

Many parents feel inadequate at times when the adolescent needs some good practical information and advice that works. Too often parents themselves have no sound solutions; they give their child "a dusty answer . . . when pressed for certainty in this our life." Instead of giving support, they create more uncertainty and confusion. Instead of offering constructive suggestions and encouragement, they find fault and criticize.

Why do parents indulge in excessive criticism and repression of their adolescent children? Do they hate to see them growing up? Are they afraid of losing their jobs as parents which kept them so occupied when the children were small? Are they subconsciously jealous of the vitality and attractiveness of their teenagers, and annoyed when the youngsters surpass them physically and sometimes mentally? Do they fear the harm that may come to the adolescent when he is on his own? Are they afraid he may do something to disgrace the family?

Probably any of these reasons may motivate a particular parent. Some parents, realizing the possible dangers to which their teen-age children may be exposed, become more anxious and repressive than they were earlier. New restrictions are particularly irksome when they coincide with an upsurge in the youngster's striving for independence. Still other parents may withdraw affection from a child who has not turned out to be as much of a credit to them as they hoped. According to Mary Ellen Chase,[3] many of the strained relationships between parents and older adolescents are owing to fear: parents fear that they may be unable to adjust to the new ideas, new speech, new manners and morals that their young people bring back from college or work; the young people fear that they may not be accepted again—may not be able to get back into the old friendly relationship.

Parents' attitudes toward a given child should change as he

[3] Mary Ellen Chase, "When You Go Home," *Coronet*, vol. 33 (December, 1952), pp. 23–27.

grows older. They can be glad that their children are gaining independence, and that they are being surpassed in many ways. They can be proud rather than resentful.

Home Atmosphere

Similarly, the home atmosphere may advance or hinder adolescents' aspirations to achieve adulthood. A home in which members of the family work together, play together, and make important decisions together is likely to produce self-confident adolescents who want to establish similar homes of their own. On the other hand, adolescents growing up in homes where there is continual dissension, suspicion, and fault-finding have difficulty in finding themselves and establishing themselves in desirable peer groups. Adolescents often escape from such homes to walk the streets or join a gang. Occasionally, however, a child from such a home who has remarkable ego strength will resolve not to be like his parents, and will achieve a premature emancipation from his home in order to lead a different kind of life.

Financial Status of Family

Economic deprivation may affect adolescents' growth toward maturity in several ways. In financially handicapped families, the older child often has to sacrifice his education to help support the family or send younger brothers or sisters to college. Membership in a family whose socio-economic level is low sometimes prevents an adolescent's acceptance in a socially acceptable peer group. Thus he is deprived of the status and support outside the family that are so important. Poverty may also make it necessary for a family to live in a delinquent area where antisocial acts are the badge of maturity. In a poor family, the adolescent often has to leave school as soon as the law allows, and go to work. If he is intellectually able, he is likely to feel dissatisfaction at not having realized his potentialities. The public school has helped many such children to make the most of themselves, and opportunities for part-time and summer work have given them a sense of independence and control over circumstances.

Multiple Deprivations

When poverty is combined with lack of parental affection and defects of parental character, the adolescent's basic need for security and support in the family circle is not met. This need was tragically illustrated in the case of Sally, who told her story in her own words at the age of sixteen to a social worker. She had lived in three rooms in a slum section of a large city. Every night her father would come home drunk. He spent most of his pay for liquor. Her mother used to "'yell at him for money but he wouldn't give her any, only when he was sober." One night when Sally was six and her sister eight, her mother told them she was pregnant again. A few minutes later her father came in as drunk as ever. Her mother told him to get out because she couldn't put up with it any more. But he didn't get out; he swung his hand at the mother's face and started beating her. The children screamed so loudly that a neighbor came running upstairs. The father left the house that night after beating the children with a strap that left welts on their backs and faces. The next day the father came home sober and said he was sorry. They forgave him but knew it would happen again. And it did. That same day Sally and her sister ran away from school.

They went into stores and took cookies, bread, and butter, then sat down in an empty building and ate the food. That night they wandered around until one o'clock in the morning, just walking the streets, freezing and ready to drop. A policeman picked them up, took them to a warm room, covered them with blankets, and fed them rolls and milk. They were brought home, and the father beat them until they said they were sorry and would not run away again. The children just lay there and cried after he left for work. They were so sore they couldn't go to school that day. They planned how they could run away again.

This pattern of living continued—the severe punishment, the running away, the stealing, the periodic increase in the size of the family. When Sally was nine, she was placed in a foster home. The woman there made her work like a dog, and her delinquency increased. She ran away again with her sister, and they stole from people's pocketbooks in churches and theaters. During the next few years she was in a succession of foster homes and institutions; intermittently she returned to her own home. The four younger children were placed in an orphanage. Sally wrote at the end of her autobiography: "Maybe some day I'll leave here and go home to my family. I know I am still being bad, but maybe some day God will give me strength and courage to be good. I know it's going to be hard to; I know it because I've tried a lot of times and couldn't be good."

Soon after writing this, Sally was permitted to make a one-day visit to her home. There she came face to face with her parents' rejection: they told her they could not take care of her. This was more than she could accept. Her mental condition became much worse. She wanted to die and attempted to injure herself. She was transferred to a mental hospital.

It is impossible to know all the complex hereditary and environmental factors that contributed to this adolescent's breakdown. She was coping, in the only way she knew, with cruelty, hunger, fear, rejection. Despite it all, she repeatedly returned to the only place she knew as "home."

In contrast, another child brought up in what on the surface seemed to be comparable family conditions has become a prominent professional person. He says that his dominant motivation became "not to be like his parents." This motivation was strengthened by teachers who gave him the support he needed at critical times. They recognized his ability. They built up his self-esteem by providing conditions in which he could succeed. Gradually he acquired a sense of worth and direction.

Surely family life must have a core of mutual respect, trust, loyalty, and morality. There is some place, too, for sacrifice, not as self-denial but as self-fulfillment. The remarkable thing is that so many American youngsters are mature, idealistic, balanced, and responsible despite unfavorable home conditions and the tawdry values reiterated in many radio and television programs, movies, and popular magazines.

PROBLEMS OF FAMILY RELATIONS
AS ADOLESCENTS SEE THEM

In a ninth-grade English class, one day a week was set aside for panel discussions on topics of common interest to the class. On one day the topic was "Getting Along with Parents." Excerpts from this discussion illustrate these youngsters' skill in working together as a group, as well as common attitudes toward parental regulation under favorable home conditions. Burt was the chairman and began the discussion as follows:

BURT: Well, the first question I'd like to ask the panel is what kinds of problems they have at home—in getting along with their parents.

TEACHER (*after a short pause*): Can you think of ways in which you don't always agree with your parents—ways in which you think they might be too strict perhaps?

TED: Well, sometimes I have trouble with my folks about staying out late at night.

BURT: What do you mean by late?

TED: Oh, usually after ten o'clock—sometimes earlier than that when I have to go to school the next day.

BURT: You mean then that your parents usually expect you to be home by ten o'clock or earlier.

TED: Yeah, that's about it. My mother worries about it more than my father does. She says the streets are no place for a *child* after ten or eleven at night. But . . .

BURT: Do you think of yourself as a child?

TED: No, I was just going to say that I think I'm old enough to take care of myself. Kids down the block from me, even younger than I am, stay out till eleven or later every night.

BURT: How do some of the others feel about this?

SALLY: I agree with Ted. I think that lots of times mothers and fathers forget that their children *are* growing up. They think we're still in the cradle and naturally we don't like it.

BURT: Being in the cradle?

SALLY (*laughing*): No. We don't like being treated like little children. At fourteen I think we should be given *some* privileges.

TED: What time are you supposed to be home?

SALLY: Oh, ten or ten:thirty during the week. Sometimes—if I'm at a friend's house—later. It all depends on whether I've got school the next day or not.

BURT: How about you, Jack? I'm sure you've got something to say.

JACK: Well, my folks don't bother me much about the hours I keep unless I stay out awfully late.

BURT: Which is?

JACK: Well, I don't know. I guess around midnight. And what about *you?*

BURT (*who obviously hadn't expected the question*): Oh, I generally stay out as long as I want to.

SALLY: Now, Burt, do you mean that your parents don't mind at all *how* long you stay out?

BURT: Oh, well, if I stay out *terribly* late, of course! I wonder if we aren't forgetting that there might be two sides to this question.

TED: You mean that parents have rights, too! (*laughter*)

BURT: Something like that. What does the panel think?

JACK: I think it's a pretty good point. After all, parents naturally feel responsible for their kids.

SALLY: That's all true, but still, if I was a parent, I'd try to see my children's point of view, too.

BURT: I think that most parents try to be fair about it. After all, they've been around longer than we have and you can't blame them for getting worried sometimes.

SALLY: Well, sometimes maybe, but my parents seem to be that way all the time. My younger brother can stay out later than I can because he's a boy.

BURT: Brothers usually are. (*laughter*)

SALLY: Yes, but I can't help it if I'm a girl!

JACK: Have you ever tried talking it over with your parents?

SALLY: Yes, well . . . ever since I stayed at my friend's house till real late one night without calling home. . . .

JACK: Well, there you are! You really scared them, so naturally they're afraid to let you go out.

BURT: I think that's a good point. Perhaps we have to let our parents see that we *can* be trusted.

TED: That's true. I know my folks are much easier on me when they know who I'm going out with.

BURT: I wonder do any of you have different kinds of problems with your parents—other than staying out late at night?

TED: Well, I have trouble talking my old man into giving me a decent allowance.

TEACHER: Your *what*, Ted?

TED: I mean my father.

TEACHER: That's better.

BURT: Do any of the others have the same problem?

JACK: I used to. But then I went out and got a part-time job at the soda fountain and made my own money. I still get a small allowance but with what I make at the store I can buy the things I want.

SALLY: I earn my allowance by doing chores at home.

TED: Like what?

SALLY: Oh, doing the dishes, shopping, things like that. A little housework once in a while. I think it's good to work for your allowance. It makes you appreciate the money. If it's just given to you, you spend it on foolish things.

BURT: What do you other panel members think of that?

JACK: I agree. I know money means a lot more to me since I went out and earned it. I'm careful now in spending it, because I had to work for it. (*To Ted*) Do you work for your allowance?

TED: Well. . . . Sometimes I *do* help around the house. (*pause*) I suppose I could do more.

JACK: I know a problem I have at home is having friends in. My mother says they make too much noise, but, heck, I go over to their houses and their mothers don't complain.

ELEANOR: I have that problem, too.

BURT: Would you like to tell us about it, Eleanor?

ELEANOR: Well, my mother doesn't want me to have any of the neighborhood girls in. (*pause*)

JACK: Well, does she think they're too noisy—like my mother does?

ELEANOR: No, it's not that. She says they mess things up after she's cleaned.

SALLY: Sometimes, if you promise to help clean up after you have friends in or have a party, your parents don't mind your having them in.

TED: Maybe you could do what we did at home. I got permission from my folks to use part of the cellar for parties and as a sort of den. My old—my father helped me to partition it off from the boiler room and fix it up.

Transition from chums to double dating. Through association in small mixed groups, young adolescents may achieve intimacy with the opposite sex, as they have with chums of the same sex. (*Courtesy of H. Armstrong Roberts.*)

Happy memories of friendships, beauty, creative work help adolescents like these, attending the Denton Lake Conferences of the Reformed Church in America, to cope with life's problems and disappointments and to realize their potentialities for growth. (*Courtesy of Ewing Galloway.*)

High school and college interests in outdoor sports may be continued in community centers for out-of-school youth, such as the Bayway Community Center, Elizabeth, New Jersey. (*Courtesy of the Standard Oil Co., N.J.*)

BURT: Maybe some of those who have this problem at home could do something like that. Sometimes just talking these things over with parents helps, especially if they know that other parents let their children's friends have the full run of the house.

Much conflict between parents and their teen-age children would be avoided if parents listened more and tried to view things through their children's eyes. The anonymous compositions give glimpses of the ways children in different family situations are thinking and feeling. From their statements one senses how resolutely some adolescents have to struggle in order to gain a reasonable degree of emancipation from their families.

An eighteen-year-old boy arrived at the following solution to the problem of gaining independence:

As I tried to gain more freedom my parents immediately tried to hold me tighter. The more you hold someone, the more they struggle to be free. Gradually things became worse. I couldn't go certain places, there were more and more restrictions, until I felt hemmed in. Then like a mule I balked . . . and things shifted to the other extreme. They were, of course, no better than before. Suddenly a thought struck me. I was living under their roof, eating their food; I should be expected to obey them. And I found that as I proved myself to them by my actions, then I gained my independence.

This boy, instead of resorting to violent rebellion or regressing to childish dependency, apparently found a way of handling the situation with a minimum of conflict.

Among the problems of family relations most frequently mentioned by junior high school students were conflict with brothers or sisters and resentment at parental restrictions and demands, especially with respect to dating, choice of friends, going out on school nights, getting home at a certain hour, and attending certain kinds of social functions. At the same time, these students were concerned about parents who were ill or overworking, and many expressed bitter resentment of divorce.

Senior high school students were in general more resentful of parental criticism than were the younger adolescents. They mentioned "talking back" to parents and being unable to discuss certain problems at home. Their areas of conflict frequently involved boy-girl relations, money matters, economic independence, and the desire for more freedom in the family situation.

Relations with Brothers and Sisters

The younger adolescent frequently mentions troublesome relationships with brothers and sisters. Sometimes his complaint is just that the young child is a nuisance to have around. The younger child bothers him by taking and breaking his possessions, tagging along after him, making work for him, getting him blamed for things he doesn't do. Many younger adolescents say something like this: "My brother is only seven years old and every time I go to play with boys my age he cries because he can't play with us." That is annoying but not too serious. When the family relationship is good, the teen-ager may call his little brother a "pest," "a little monster," or "a brat," but also admit that he's "kind of cute." Older brothers and sisters sometimes cause resentment by bossing, teasing, and fighting with the younger teen-ager.

It is more serious when parents prefer one child to another. Parental favoritism toward another child may decrease the adolescent's self-esteem and generate hostility. The presence of more brilliant and successful siblings may prevent him from perceiving himself as a competent person.

A sixteen-year-old girl perceives her family relations as a complex situation involving rejection by her mother, which has made her hostile and desperate, attachment to her father, and resentment of a favored sister. She can see no way of coping with the situation except eventually to withdraw from it. This is the way she described it:

I feel very left out in my family affairs. I have a sister 13 who gets everything she wants. If she and I want to go out the same night I must stay home with my baby brother. My mother never gives her any responsibilities, always putting them on me. She is allowed to stay out later than I am.

Any time my mother can find something to pick on me for, she does it. I sometimes wonder if it wouldn't be better if I were dead. My father is hardly ever home, though when he is he tries to stick up for me. I'm not really bad looking but my sister is beautiful and my mother is always mocking me. She never buys me clothes, my father's sister sometimes buys me some. Some day I probably will leave home but I hope it is because I have found a nice boy who wishes to make me a nice home. When I have my children I will surely know how to treat them.

The older child frequently complains of having to take the blame for any trouble that arises. Comments like the following were common among junior high school youngsters:

When my little sister or brother does something, my mother blames it on me because I'm the oldest. I don't think that's right.

My brother seven is the one that gets his own way all the time. He is my father's boy, my father thinks he is so cute and the best boy in the family.

I have a brother and a sister both younger than I am and to my mother they're perfect angels. Every time something happens my parents always needle me—"Philip, did you do that?" And it annoys me very much. I think it isn't fair. They should figure it out before they start accuseing people.

Some of these compositions support the findings of some psychological studies which have shown that it is the oldest or middle, not the youngest, child who is most likely to be maladjusted. Adolescents' own accounts help us to see why this may be so. Sometimes, however, it's the other way round—the oldest boy is favored. Other factors such as relative intelligence, differences in age, appearance, and personality, and the parents' attitudes, emotional needs, and personal preferences are more important than position in the family per se.

When each child is valued for himself and has his own rightful place in the family pattern, relationships among brothers and sisters may be very beneficial. Sometimes an older brother or sister serves as a confidant or even as a counselor to a troubled adolescent.

Parental Demands and Restrictions

Many adolescents are upset by parents who dominate them, forbid them to engage in normal adolescent activities, or make unreasonable demands on them. A certain amount of the ensuing conflict arises from inconsistency in community practices. Parents do not agree about evening hours and suitable activities. Consequently, some youngsters are sure to complain, "Why can't I do what the other kids do?" or "Everybody's doing it except me." Often parents do not understand how important it is for the teen-ager to establish status with his peer group.

The most pervasive source of conflict reported by junior high school students is with regard to dates. One eighth-grade girl viewed it in this way: "My mother does not allow me to go out with boys because she says I am not cabble of taking care of myself. But what I think about it is if she would only give me a chance I am sure I would learn."

Restrictions that teen-agers consider unnecessary can also be embarrassing to them, as this fourteen-year-old girl indicates:

All the other girls in my club go to the meetings on the bus, but I am not allowed to do this as mother thinks it unsafe. Every Friday the question comes up as to who will drive me to the meeting. Someone always gives in, in a martyr-like fashion, so that I feel it is my fault for making them drive me. Then after the meeting I have to call home and tell them I'm ready. This is very embarrassing because usually the rest of the girls go to the Hot Shoppe or some similar place, and many times the hostess goes too. However, she feels obliged to wait until I am called for. I would like very much to go with the other girls as I am the only one who doesn't go. The other girls ask why, and as it sounds childish to say I have to go home to bed, I usually say I don't enjoy going with the rest of the crowd, which isn't true.

Although to adults this may seem a minor matter, to the girl, it is of the utmost importance. That she is not giving up the struggle to gain independence from her mother and status in her group is indicated by her last sentence: "Every time I speak to my mother about this she disagrees, but I still keep working on her!"

Parental restrictions on girls' activities are likely to be more severe in certain homes where the parents are foreign born or have been brought up in a different culture. A tenth-grade girl described this conflict as follows:

Most of the time everything seems to be going along all right but now and then I think no one could be unhappier. My parents are very old-fashioned. They came from Europe and don't seem to realize that times have changed. For instance, I want to go on a hay-ride soon and they won't let me because they don't like the idea. I'm not allowed to go out with boys and mother nearly has a fit when a boy telephones me. The only reason I get for this is because I'm too young to think about boys, and she didn't go out with them until she was twenty-one. Another thing that bothers me is that my parents expect me to bring home straight A's on my report card because my father always did. He skipped a lot of grades and has many degrees and when I get a C they tell me I should do better and that *I* shouldn't get a C. I can't imagine what they think I am. I was on

the honor roll all through junior high school, and did my best but still they weren't pleased.

Persistent parental supervision is irksome to young adolescents. Many mention this problem, expressed as follows by a sixteen-year-old boy: "The main thing I detest is my mother keeps telling me that I should do this and that. And when I don't do a certain thing perfectly she punishes me by not letting me do something I like. I feel like I'm in a prison cell. Sometimes I even look forward to school, and that's unusual for me."

A seventeen-year-old girl had the same complaint: "My main problem is trying to influence the family to recognize that I am no longer a baby. Every time I want to go some place the whole family wants to know where I am going, who I am going with, and if I want anyone to come for me. No one in the family wants me to work because I'm the youngest girl."

That parents interfere unnecessarily with their activities is one of the most common complaints of young teen-agers. Most teen-agers will do their share of household chores. What they object to is unequal sharing of responsibility in an autocratic home where duties are arbitrarily assigned. They like to share in planning the work; they want to feel that they are part of a going concern.

Lack of Home Supervision

In contrast with these protests against parental restrictions, some adolescents recognize their need for a certain amount of adult support and protection. Consequently, they complain about lack of home supervision. This neglect is understandable when we reflect that one mother out of five works outside the home. Research [4] showed that girls in their middle teens whose mothers worked had more conflicts with their parents, felt more unloved, and were more often ashamed of their parents than a comparable group of daughters of nonworking mothers. This does not mean that being employed outside the home per se is the cause

[4] Mary Essig and D. H. Morgan, "Adjustment of Adolescent Daughters of Employed Women to Family Life," *Journal of Educational Psychology,* vol. 37 (April, 1946), pp. 219–233.

of adolescent difficulties. Understanding, affectionate parents may still meet adolescents' needs even though they are away from home during the day. If they plan together and play together, the family is more likely to stay together.

In some families children are neglected by over-social mothers, some of whom have no real affection for their children and are glad to send them off to school, camp, or recreation center. Other parents seem to get involved in too many "extra-home" activities. This was recognized by Donald, aged twelve, who said: "I think I would get along much better with my family if Mother did not go to so many organization meetings, because she's usually at a meeting and can't help me with my problems."

In other homes the parents are so burdened with their own problems that they cannot give much attention to their older children. Some parents are physically ill; others are worried about financial matters; still others may never have learned to love because they were deprived of affection or treated cruelly as children.

When a child is neglected or ignored, he often interprets this as rejection. Adolescents want their parents to understand them and to be interested in them. For some, being ignored is worse than being scolded; a scolding by a basically affectionate parent may mean to the child that the parent really cares what becomes of him.

Similar kinds of responses were reported in a survey made by the Gilbert Youth Research Company [5] by using trained teen-age interviewers to ask over two hundred questions of 5,065 representative teen-agers in thirty-five cities. The proportions of the various responses, however, were different; the teen-agers in the Stewart and Gilbert study indicated greater dissatisfaction with family relations. The main complaint of almost all of them was that parents do not understand them. More than half said they do not do things with their family. These two factors together with the repeatedly expressed desire for independence may account for the fact that 42 per cent said "they would prefer to

[5] Jack Stewart and Eugene Gilbert, "What's Wrong at Home?" *This Week Magazine* (December 11, 1955), pp. 7, 64–67.

live away from home." In contrast with their criticism of parents, more than eight out of ten considered teachers as helpful and generous.

Criticism of parents seems to be highest around fifteen and sixteen years. Those younger and older tend to be more favorably disposed toward parents.

The adolescent's resentments, whether true or false, whether justified or not, are related to his drive toward independence. The adolescent has

to combat ambivalent tendencies in both himself and his parents. If he is too submissive and dependent he loses face in his own eyes and in the eyes of his peers; he might alternately feel inadequate for failing to maintain developmental progress, and resentful or hostile toward his parents for thwarting his growth. Carried too far, dependence raises the threat of a perpetually immature and inadequate personality. But if he is too independent and aggressive, he feels guilty for excessive repudiation of his parents. . . . In the constantly shifting equilibrium between dependence and independence, therefore, the preadolescent child must "steer a precarious course." [6]

Some adolescents seem able to achieve a middle-of-the-road, tolerant point of view. They give parents credit for having profited by their years of experience, and seek their help in situations that they cannot handle alone. In other situations they try to demonstrate their competency. They learn to set goals for themselves, plan ways to realize these goals, make decisions and assume responsibility for them. All these characteristics the young people themselves mention in writing about "How it feels to be growing up."

Personality Defects in Parents

Problems of family relations often stem from personality faults in the parents. Adolescents are quick to note faults of character in adults. There is no substitute for being a real person. What adults say is not so important as what they do and what they are. The values they verbalize do not impress adolescents nearly

[6] David P. Ausubel, *Ego Development and the Personality Disorders,* pp. 81–82. New York: Grune & Stratton, Inc., 1952.

so much as the philosophy by which they live. A bright senior said: "Our greatest problem is being told what to do by adults, without ever being shown 'how' in most instances. We can follow a good example better than a good lecture."

Some adolescents come from delinquent homes. They have had firsthand experience with promiscuity, with various kinds of crime, and with drunkenness. Others are from fairly well-to-do homes where there is misfortune, maladjustment, and little real affection. A sixteen-year-old girl wrote as follows:

My problem is that of many others in this mixed-up world today —my home life! My brother was killed in action in 1945. My mother nearly died from the shock of it, while my father took to drinking. This situation has become worse until it has got to the point where I want to leave home. . . . After these miserable week ends I can't put my mind on my schoolwork or homework.

Another girl, fifteen, described her plight in these words:

My personal problem is my home. I have a drunken father. He does not do harm to me but continually is drunk. We have a fine home and dress very well. He supplies us with money and food but still there is no happiness. I am slowly losing my love for my dad, because besides making a home for us he should give us love and be kind toward us, which he is not. I have to stay up late at night to listen to see that he does not harm mother as he has threatened to do. This affects my schoolwork, my health, and my activities. I cannot explain this to teachers as I would like to, but whoever reads this, I hope your home is better than mine.

In such a disturbed family relation, emancipation and normal heterosexual relations would be extremely difficult. Lacking the normal relation with a father, being in a protective position toward the mother, being too disturbed at home to get the most out of school life, this adolescent is struggling alone against almost insurmountable odds.

Adolescent adjustment reflects the parents' personality. A study by Handford [7] showed that mothers of emotionally disturbed ad-

[7] Nora Prudence Handford, "Mothers of Adolescent Girls," *Smith College Studies of Social Work,* vol. 24 (February, 1954), pp. 9–34.

olescent girls were distinguished from mothers of normal girls of the same age in the following respects:

They imposed their plans upon their daughters.
They were neurotically possessive.
They were not frank with their daughters.
Their relations with the father were strained.
They were overanxious.

Many parents think that if they give their children all the comforts and material things they need, they are doing all that is necessary. They do not realize that children need love more than anything else—a feeling that they are wanted and count for something. To be loved, parents must be lovable; to be respected, they must be respectable.

Broken Homes

The total number of broken homes is very large. According to the 1950 census [8] and other reports, between one-quarter and one-third of all adolescents live in homes broken by death, divorce, desertion, or by other causes. The proportion of adolescents in homes broken by separation, divorce, or death is larger than the proportion of younger children so situated. Adolescents from broken homes have much to contend with.

The effect which a broken home may have upon a child depends on many interrelated factors, such as the child's age at the time of separation, the cause of the dissolution, the child's own personality, and his relation with the adults with whom he subsequently lives. Studies have shown that the proportion of delinquents from broken homes is more than twice as great as the proportion from unbroken homes. This does not mean that a child from a broken home will necessarily become delinquent or maladjusted. In fact, many such children have been able, with the help of understanding adults, to accept the situation and move toward adult maturity.

However, broken homes present special problems. Some of

[8] U.S. Bureau of the Census, *Current Population Reports, Population Characteristics*, ser. P-20, no. 32, December 4, 1950.

these are poignantly described in the compositions. One is the problem of a girl's relations with her stepmother. Many a stepmother sincerely desires to do right by her stepdaughter, and may even deprive her own children of their rightful share of attention and affection. But she may not recognize the deep-seated psychological bases of her stepdaughter's antagonism to her. This antagonism may arise from the fact that the child had a very close, affectionate relation with her own mother. Or it may stem from the daughter's deep attachment to her father, causing jealousy toward the stepmother.

On the other hand, the stepdaughter may have to cope with jealousy and hostility on the part of the stepmother. According to her own account, a seventeen-year-old girl was making every effort to get along well with her stepmother. She was generous in her appreciation of the privileges her parents gave her, cleaned the house on Saturday, and usually inquired when she went out if there was anything needed from the store. But the girl became aware of a growing estrangement. She wrote: "It seemed to me as though every time I came in the door Mother had something to find fault with. Many times I've walked away with my heart heavy and the words only too eager to come out, but I'd keep them in for fear of antagonizing her all the more. Well, things had to come to a head sooner or later." They did, one Sunday morning. It was about the cleaning of the stepmother's room. "Well," the girl said, "that sort of lit the match that started the fire. Mother flared up and I flared up, only I can remember her telling me to get out and stay out, as I walked out the door. Where I walked to and how long I walked that day, I still don't know."

We have no way of knowing, except from the composition itself, whether the stepmother actually behaved in the way the girl described, and if she did, what caused her to do so. The composition as a whole presents the girl as reasonable, cooperative, and anxious to think well of her stepmother. It may be that the stepmother's action was due to increasing jealousy of the girl's place in her husband's affection.

The home broken by divorce presents special problems. In recent years the number of divorces has ranged from between one-fourth to one-third of the total marriages.[9] In addition are the large numbers of married persons who are separated because of family discord and those who are living together unhappily. Adolescents express poignant feelings about the separation of their parents, as in the following composition:

When I was sixteen, I had a problem of having to face the fact that my mother and father were going to separate. This was something I couldn't do a thing about. The fact of my loving them both and having to be separated from my father hurt me more than anything in this world.

Well, I couldn't help but feel bad. When I went to school, the girls were always talking of going this place and the other with Mother and Dad; it made me feel sort of out of place. At meetings in school my mother and father used to go together. But now my mother is the only one that goes to the PTA meetings. Those were some of the things I had to face.

This was the way I met this problem: I had a long talk with my mother and she explained why she and my dad couldn't make a go of the marriage. I also had a talk with my father and heard his side of the story. Then I said to them that I was more than sorry that they had waited until I was able to take the thing so to heart. Then I decided, since the thing was not going to work out, that I'd do things to stop me from thinking of my home life. So I joined clubs, went to dances and movies. I soon (not completely, of course, for I never will) forgot the unhappiness of the situation, but I have the same affection as always in my heart for them both.

This is a fine example of a young person's ability to meet a severe adjustment in her family relations without getting into trouble and without apparent emotional disorganization. She tried to understand both parents. She began to live her life more independently, as all teen-agers eventually have to learn to do. Most important of all, she went through the experience without apparent bitterness.

Too often one parent tries to influence the child to dislike or blame the other parent. One girl wrote bitterly about this:

[9] James H. S. Bossard, "Eight Reasons Why Marriages Go Wrong," *New York Times Magazine* (June 24, 1956), p. 5.

My problem is a very common one. My mother was divorced from my father last year. I love my father very much, as is only natural. My mother hates him, which is probably natural too. My grandmother (Mother's mother) and all of her relations are constantly telling me what a terrible man he is and how horribly he treated Mother. . . . The only solution (and this would be perfect) is that I go to live with my father. This idea was quickly stopped by my Mother's statement that she would surely die if I went to live with Daddy.

The result is that through lots of things piling up I am learning to hate my mother through and through.

Divorce may create still another kind of problem for adolescents—the problem of the mother's having to support the family. Under such circumstances, another member of the family will often play an important role in an adolescent's adjustment to the separation of her parents. Without this help, the mother who has to go out to work would have to leave her child with little or no supervision during the day. A sixteen-year-old girl described her situation as follows:

My greatest worry is my grandmother. I love her dearly, and I fear the day she might die.

When I was six months old, my mother and father were divorced. My mother went to work, so we lived with my grandmother that someone might care for me. I grew very fond of my grandmother and love her more dearly than my mother, though my mother is very good to me, and we are great pals. We lived a very happy, wonderful life with my "Bigma," until the fateful day when my stepfather married my mother. That broke my heart, as it ruined our home. When I was seven we moved to another city, leaving "Bigma" behind. I cried for several weeks and was, needless to say, heartbroken. I visit my grandmother every summer, and I love her more and more as time goes by, if possible.

About three years ago my "Bigma" fell and broke her hip. No one expected her to live. My mother and I rushed to her home to be by her side. By God alone, she lived. If she had died, I fear, I'd have lost the only person I really call "my own."

I hate my stepfather very much. Not because he is my stepfather, but because he took me from my "Bigma," from my California home, and took my mother from me. I hated him even more when my

"Bigma" fell, because I feel if we'd been there, we could have prevented it. My "Bigma" is up and around, but she has very poor health as a result of the fall. She used to be beautiful, very spry and always on the go, now she seems to be old all of a sudden.

My stepfather can be a pretty nice guy and I'd probably like him, *if* he wasn't my stepfather.

When the breakup of the home coincides with the adolescent's own most difficult period of adjustment, the young person may undergo serious emotional disturbance. If teachers only knew what tragedies are taking place in the homes of some of their students, they would not be surprised at their behavior in school. One sixteen-year-old girl wrote the following account of her home conditions:

My problem is a common one today. It is a home that is breaking up. My mother and father had been married twenty-five years when trouble first began to rear its head three years ago. My father held an important position and began to have to work late. Mother was not in good health and was often ill on the nights he was working, which left me to take care of her till midnight or later. These late hours and worrying made me very nervous, which in turn affected my schoolwork.

Then came the shock: several of mothers' friends told her that they had seen my father many times with another woman. I couldn't believe it. At that time I worshipped my father. The world seemed to be tumbling around my ears.

When mother asked him if it were true, he admitted it, but mother refused to give him a divorce. There were many nights that I didn't get to sleep, listening to the cruel words Mother and Dad were saying to each other. Mother was a nervous wreck from then on and I began to hate him for what he was doing to us.

Then came the most awful day of my life. It was a Sunday. Daddy had told Mother he wouldn't be home for dinner and she seemed to reach her breaking point. She went in the bathroom and when she came out she told us she had swallowed a box of sleeping pills. I was petrified with fear. Daddy called the hospital and mother was taken away. Of course she recovered and she went away for a rest. When she returned she was much better and although my father hasn't improved, things are more peaceful. Mother tells me that I mustn't bear hard feelings for my father, but after all that, how can I help it? I don't believe it was entirely my father's fault, for he was always easily led, and some women seem to have no qualms about breaking up a happy home. But he has lost all respect I ever felt for him. I try not to show it, but sometimes I can't help it. This may ruin my chances for college, and so I am still uncertain as to what I am going to do.

However, broken homes are not invariably bad for adolescents. Adolescents may achieve what appears to be normal development in a broken home. Frank, for example, except for his close attachment to his mother, seemed to have made a good surface adjustment. His father, who at one time had held a position of local prominence, had deserted his family and was living in another state. Frank worked all summer and part-time during the school year to defray expenses. His IQ on a group intelligence test was 120. He was a handsome lad of eighteen, six feet tall, weighed 165 pounds, and was in excellent health. He played on a high school football team which won the state championship.

His scholastic record was excellent and his attitude toward teachers and schoolwork was all that could be desired. He cooperated willingly in all class activities and displayed much enthusiasm for those he enjoyed, especially the undertakings that afforded him opportunities to lead. He participated quite actively in discussions, at times to the point of monopolizing them. His questions and comments, however, seemed mature and purposeful, rather than irrelevant or distracting. He took a special delight in debating, oratory, and in using the public address system. He had won honors for these performances, and was well aware of his accomplishments. He showed great satisfaction when others remarked favorably on his achievements. On one occasion when the teacher had listened to one of his orations without comment, he said, with an air of disappointment, "Mr. P, the speech coach I formerly had always bragged about us when we did good work. That made us feel better."

Generally, Frank was able to maintain favorable relationships with his classmates including both boys and girls; however, he never dated girls outside of school or singled them out at the school's social events. Many of the students were eager to be Frank's colleagues in debating, since his team usually won. Though at times there seemed to be some evidence of jealousy on the part of a few students who also aspired to make superior grades and exert leadership, many of the students accepted him as a leader who excelled in speech activities. He is now majoring in speech at a state university, where he is making an excellent record.

This boy was fortunate in being able to identify with and gain status in his peer groups. This experience reduced his emotional dependence on his mother, and helped him to speed up the process of gaining adult independence. As part of this process, it might be expected that his friendly relations with girls subsequently led him to establish more definite heterosexual interests.

Homes that were broken by the late war created other kinds of problems. Most obvious was the change in the status of young men which resulted from the country's need for manpower. Instead of being held back in the accomplishment of their adolescent tasks, they were encouraged to accelerate the process of growing up. However, enforced absence of the father could intensify the adolescent boy's relationship with his mother. Then, later, after he had temporarily been the "man of the family," the boy sometimes found it difficult to adjust to his father's return home. A seventeen-year-old boy described with clarity a situation which many youngsters must have had to face when their fathers came back from the war. Many a counselor might well admire the skill of the boy's older sister:

I have seen my father only about four years out of seventeen. Recently he retired from the Coast Guard and came to live with us permanently. My reactions to him, I am ashamed to say, were very bad. My life had been wrapped up with that of my mother and sister, and then my father came into my life. I felt that he was intruding and I began to feel moody and became very cross. Fortunately I have a very wise sister who saw what was troubling me. One night we had a very serious talk and I opened up and told her why I felt resentful to my father. After I finished telling her, I felt better because now it was in the open and not hidden deep inside me. I was afraid, though, that she would be shocked, but she wasn't at all. She then asked me if I thought I was being fair to my father. It was just as hard if maybe not harder on him. He was having to adjust himself to a new way of life and become acquainted again with his family. Instead of trying to help him, I was hostile to him.

His coming home should make no difference. It didn't mean that I was being ignored or that mother loved me any less. Here was my father who wanted very much to become a part of the family. Why didn't I try to talk to him more, and get him to help me with homework? Give both my father and I a chance to become acquainted? Think more of helping my father to find his place in civilian life? I started talking to him more and getting him to help me. Now I find he isn't an intruder at all and it was all in my mind. I was too wrapped up in myself to want to help someone else. Now my family makes the best foursome I know of.

Complexity of Home Influences

In complex ways the home affects the adolescent's journey toward independence. Of basic importance is his relationship with each parent. At times he makes a strategic alliance with his parents; at other times he moves ahead on his own as his new powers develop; thus he steers a zigzag course toward increasing self-direction. By successfully handling his emotional relations with each parent, he achieves the masculine or feminine identification so essential to mature functioning. He recognizes that freedom from childish dependence on one's parents is essential to growing up, and looks forward to being on his own. Yet he would like to achieve this independence with a minimum of pain to his parents.

Parental demands and restrictions often make the process of growing up difficult for adolescents. Parents may be too strict or too permissive for their children's best development. The effect of parental behavior depends largely on the way in which the child perceives the parents—the meaning which their behavior has for him. Adolescents who have a good basic relation with their parents usually approve their parents' supervisory

methods, while those who have negative attitudes toward their
parents tend to object to almost any supervision.

The whole family atmosphere, including the relation of the
parents to each other and of the children to one another, may

encourage or discourage self-reliance and independence. In
homes broken by death, divorce, or other causes, adolescents
may make accelerated progress toward emancipation from the
family, though often at the expense of considerable emotional
stress and strain.

WHAT KIND OF PARENTS DO ADOLESCENTS WANT?

What do teen-agers want from the grown-ups in their lives?
Comments by adolescents on their parents' behavior, as expressed
in anonymous compositions, should be helpful to parents.

Someone in Whom They Can Confide

They want adults who will listen, who will be sure to understand them, and in whom they can confide. Sometimes these are parents, sometimes teachers. They will not confide in an adult if he does not show that he understands how they feel. One girl expressed this need in the following words: "I feel that I have lost a great deal of companionship. I don't feel close to my family; I feel cheated of their affection. It is true I have all the material things I could possibly need, but I don't feel it can make up for the companionship I feel I will never have."

"In times of despair," one seventeen-year-old girl wrote, "I can always get advice from my family. . . . They know it's my life that I have to live."

Perhaps we have overemphasized the disagreements between adolescents and their parents, and have tended to minimize their agreements. Remmers and Weltman [10] found a high commonality of attitudes between children and their parents. Parents and their children seemed to be more similar in their attitudes than were teachers and their pupils. Adolescents in grades eleven and twelve, however, tended to be less like their parents in attitude patterns than were those in grades nine and ten.

Someone They Can Trust

Before they confide in an adult, they want to be sure that they can trust him. This is the way one fortunate young person described this kind of trust:

I think my mother has been my best influence, she has been more of an understanding friend than a mother. I can tell her anything, and I tell her everything that happens (good or bad). I tell her my school problems, and we discuss them and work them out.

Since my mother and I trust each other, I don't have a reason to lie to her anytime.

[10] H. H. Remmers and Naomi Weltman, "Attitude Inter-relationships of Youth, Their Parents, and Their Teachers," *Journal of Social Psychology,* vol. 26 (August, 1947), pp. 61–68.

When they have done something their parents consider wrong, they want a chance to explain. As one girl said, "My father yells at us before we can explain." There is nothing more comforting to a troubled adolescent than a parent to whom he can talk freely.

Freedom of Decision

They want to solve their own problems—to be free to make their own decisions on the basis of the best help a parent or teacher can give them. If a parent steps in when it is not necessary, he deprives the adolescent both of confidence in his own ability to handle the situation, and of the excitement of arriving at his own solution. Moreover, it is impossible for an adult to *give* a young person the resolution of his conflicts; that must be achieved by the individual. They need to be helped to see a problem from all sides, rather than to be told what to do. One sixteen-year-old boy thought that "parents should realize that teen-agers can more or less take care of themselves and they should not try to run their lives completely." He added, "It is easy to get along with one's family if you follow a wise pattern and live on a give-and-take basis."

Unobtrusive Concern

Adolescents, even college students, like to have a responsible adult in the offing; it gives them a sense of security to know they can call on him. The adolescent who cannot count on adult reinforcement for his still inadequate inner controls may feel defenseless and panicky. Although adolescents want parents on the sidelines for consultation and protection, most of them do not want parents to mingle with their friends. One popular fourteen-year-old extrovert wrote: "It's a bother to have parents driving you to a dance or something of the kind. They try to make fake conversations and it's awful. They make everybody in the car shy and there are quiet spells. Ugh!" And they certainly do not want parents sitting in the room with them and their friends.

However, they do not want parents to absolve themselves of all responsibility for their children. Quite a few said they thought parents ought to know where their children go at night. Some would like their parents to provide entertainment occasionally for their friends, and to reserve time when they may talk to them alone. This is about all adolescents ask. They only object if parents are so absorbed in their work and social activities that they neglect their children's welfare.

Consistency

Adolescents want a reasonable degree of consistency in their parents' behavior. But parents are sometimes unpredictable. They have their moods and their own problems. Mothers are sometimes tired and jumpy. Fathers have their special worries about the high cost of living, and changing economic and political conditions. Instead of asking, "What's wrong with our teen-agers?" parents might well ask, "Why does their behavior annoy *us?*"

Disagreements between parents are another source of inconsistency in the treatment of the child. These may involve fairly trivial matters such as the way their daughter should wear her hair, or they may represent fundamental differences in points of view. Many youngsters are seriously disturbed by the conflicting wishes of their parents. One sixteen-year-old girl in the eleventh grade wrote: "I love my parents very deeply but, somehow, I just can't tell them why I've been so miserable. If I could only tell them that my brother and I would be much happier and do better if we didn't always have to take 'sides' with my parents."

The inconsistencies of adults are vexatious to adolescents. Some parents fluctuate between leniency and strictness. Adolescents, as well as younger children, want the security that comes from knowing exactly what they can do and what they cannot do. They do not like to live in an uncertain world, in which the same act is punished one day and ignored the next. Moreover, families have different standards as to the use of the family car and the hour for returning from parties. If some definite standards were set by parents and children together in a family council or in adult-youth community councils or committees, there would be less conflict between children and adults. A parent council in the Philadelphia area has done this.

Adolescents become increasingly aware of inconsistencies between what parents say and what they do, between the social world that has been described to them and the social world which they now begin to see for themselves. They need help in handling conflicting values and standards. They want their parents to take a consistent stand. They accept strictness, if it grows out of love, better than they accept inconsistency. Havighurst [11] has reported evidence that character is related to parental consistency. Either extreme permissiveness or extreme severity seems to be less detrimental to character formation than inconsistency of discipline.

Encouragement

Adolescents want to be encouraged, and to receive praise when they deserve it. They usually get an overdose of criticism. "When parents show no interest," one rural boy wrote, "who cares about growing up. No one likes to have to grow up by himself without even a little encouragement from his family."

Positive Expectancy

Adolescents want adults to expect the best of them. They want to have something to live up to. If they have established an affectionate relationship with an adult, they will try hard not to "let him down."

As the volume of unfavorable publicity about teen-agers increases, adolescents become more and more resentful at being blamed for everything that happens. They want us to remember that the vast majority of teen-agers never get into serious trouble. They want their parents to trust them more and not worry so much about them.

Respect for Reticence

They want privacy. They speak feelingly of having a room of their own, a door on which they can put up a sign, "Please don't disturb." They do not want counselors who probe.

[11] Robert Havighurst, "Poised at the Crossroads of Life; Suggestions to Parents and Teachers of Young Adolescents," *School Review*, vol. 61 (September, 1953), pp. 329–336.

Understanding Modern Youth

Adolescents want parents who keep abreast of the times, who especially are aware of the various currents and moods of today's youth. So many teen-agers describe their parents as "old-fashioned."

Some adolescents have been helped to gain more sympathy and understanding of their parents. They feel less antagonistic

toward parents if they realize that much of the conflict they describe stems from the parents' insecurity and unfulfilled ambitions. Josselyn [12] explained the attitude of parents in the following quotation:

Parents of an adolescent are often frightened people. They see their child as an extension of themselves, growing, they hope, into a more nearly adequate adult than either of them is. Their wish derives not only from pride in their own child but also from an honest desire that their child should have a happier adult life than they themselves have had. They sense the confusion of the adolescent and are frightened by it. They also sense the impact of biological urges. They recognize that the adolescent as yet does not have the tools with which to deal constructively with these internal impulses. They look back upon their own adolescence and recall it as a time of stress in which

[12] Irene M. Josselyn, *The Adolescent and His World.* New York: Family Service Association of America, 1952.

they were apparently in grave danger of ruining their lives. By some miracle they were saved from destroying their potentialities, a destruction that seems, in retrospect, to have been imminent. They fear that the same fortuitous circumstances that saved them may not be present to save their child. They do not wish to trust to the fate by which their past was protected as the instrument for safeguarding their own child. They want their child to develop into a heterosexual adult, yet they are fearful that he cannot avoid the pitfalls of that development. They wish him to be independent but they are fearful that he cannot handle independence without their guidance. Most parents, consciously at least, wish their child to grow up to be a happy adult. They are frightened by their own roles in this process.

It is equally true that many parents, while they consciously wish their child to grow up, actually are resistant to this process. Perhaps they cannot face the vacuum that will exist when the child is no longer dependent upon them. Sometimes they are jealous of the child entering early adulthood with all its apparent glamor when their own adulthood seems tarnished. Many of them express their own neuroses in handling their adolescent son or daughter. The father may unconsciously fear to compete with his mature son because his son may experience greater success than he and thus point up the father's inadequacy. In other instances the father may fear that his boy will be as inadequate as he himself is. The son's failure will be his own failure and thus he tries to delay the evil day when he will be doubly exposed. The father may be so emotionally tied to his daughter that he cannot give her up to another man. He may strive to keep her a child to avoid the implications of his love for her if she becomes a mature woman. Whatever may be the hidden conflict in the relationship with the child, the unconscious motivation of parental behavior toward the child is often in contrast to the conscious motivation. Regardless of what produced the conflict, parents as well as adolescents are confused, and the confusion of each adds to the confusion of the other.[13]

A happy home does not "just happen." Everybody has to help to make it so. A well-balanced, alert mother, able to adapt herself to the different needs and interests of a large family, makes the greatest contribution to the personal happiness and good

[13] *Ibid.*, pp. 28–29.

adjustment of all its members, including the temperamental teen-ager. Time, love, and companionship are the essentials.

HOW HOME AND SCHOOL CAN COOPERATE

Neither parents nor teachers stand alone in their efforts to help adolescents attain their developmental goals. Both groups belong to a team which has at its command more or less specialized services, depending upon the community. The school has the best chance to work with both adolescents and parents. Theoretically at least, it reaches all the children of all the people.

A course in family life education offers in its content special opportunities for personal and social development, in addition to the values of a good group experience per se. Such a course was developed in a number of high schools in Illinois.[14] The main features of this group experience as developed in Hinsdale, Illinois, are as follows:

The superintendent selected a teacher well qualified by personality to give this course "after she had had ample opportunity to prepare herself and after the public had been fully educated to what was being planned."[15] She attended conferences and workshops, studied books and pamphlets, and brought together references and films needed for the students. During the same period the parent-teacher association helped the community to understand the new course, which was called "Sociology of the Family." It was first offered as an elective one-semester course for seniors. Later the course was extended to juniors.

Each semester the course has been built around the problems of the group. Many of these were problems of family relations and personality such as the following:

How to make a marriage work. Youngsters from broken homes had no one to teach them or demonstrate a happy married life; consequently they were afraid of marriage.

[14] Ruth Farnham Osborne and Lester A. Kirkendall, "Family-life Education in Illinois High Schools," *School Review,* vol. 58 (December, 1950), pp. 516–526.

[15] *Ibid.,* p. 517.

How to be better parents than their parents had been to them.

What it means to grow up and become more mature.

How to recognize and correct, if possible, some of their personality faults.

How to deal with failure.

How to see other people's point of view.

How to accept the fact that one cannot always have "what he wants when he wants it."

Problems of mental hygiene came up in connection with other problems, and with the study of birth, infancy, and early childhood. Sex education was introduced in connection with the question of how to teach children about sex. In this connection Frances Bruce Strain's *Being Born* and the film, *Human Reproduction* (McGraw-Hill), were used.

When specialized information was needed, questions were prepared and sent to the speaker ahead of time.

Compositions written by the students on such topics as "How I have been disciplined" and "What I can't understand about girls [or boys]" were used as a springboard for discussion. The teacher was careful to change any identifying detail in these papers, and to keep confidences.

Students took part in panel discussions of certain topics near the end of the semester, and several meetings were held with parents. Student panels also presented their points of view at parent-teacher association meetings and before other school and community groups.

Students mentioned many values of the course: "a better attitude toward sex and more understanding of what marriage means," better understanding of people and how to bring up children, and more cooperation with parents. The course helped some individuals to find meaning in school, and to become contributing members of the group.

Through school visitations, parent-teacher associations, parent study groups, parent-teacher conferences, and home visits, parents and teachers may become more understanding of adolescents and more skillful in helping them make the crucial transition from childhood to adulthood.

By visiting the school either during the day or on parents' open-school night, mothers and fathers will gain some understanding of the modern school program. A popular type of evening is one in which the parents go through a regular, though abbreviated, school program of classes, along with their children.

Parent-teacher associations and parent child-study groups can help parents understand their adolescent sons and daughters. Popular types of parent-teacher meetings feature panel discussions by children and parents, parent-planned programs, showings and discussions of some of the excellent films on adolescence now available, use of guidance or mental hygiene plays as a springboard for discussion (see bibliography), and sociodrama. All of these kinds of programs require a leader skilled in conducting discussions and using the other specialized techniques just mentioned. Adult education programs associated with public school systems offer courses in understanding adolescence, as well as in creative activities that enrich the parents' own lives.

Parent-teacher conferences are growing in popularity with both teachers and parents, as a cooperative effort to assess a student's progress. There are ways of providing time for them, and methods of helping parents and teachers acquire skill in conducting them. Parent-teacher conferences may accomplish several purposes: (1) establish a friendly relation between parents and teachers, (2) help the parents understand their child, (3) help the parents understand what the school is trying to do for the child, (4) acquaint the teacher with home conditions that may be affecting the child's behavior in school, and (5) enable parents and teachers to plan together how they can make the home, school, and neighborhood environment more conducive to the child's best development.

To accomplish these purposes, the teacher usually encourages the parents to talk freely. They often begin by pouring forth all their complaints about the child. When they have finished, the teacher may share the factual information she has about the child, as she has observed him in school. Then together they try to think of best next steps to take. If the teacher is quite highly skilled in counseling, she may make an occasional interpretation which helps the parents to see the child's behavior in a different light and leads them to think of some of the child's good qualities. Eventually the parents may gain some insight into the relation between their attitudes and the child's behavior. This insight may lead them to make some simple changes in their behavior toward the child. In such an interview the role of the counselor is to listen and feel with the parents, make interpretations when the opportunity is offered, and reinforce the parents' positive suggestions.

CONCLUDING STATEMENT

In the process of gaining emancipation, some conflict is to be expected. But antagonism and emotional upsets can be reduced for both parents and children if both parents and youngsters realize that gaining independence is desirable and necessary, that they can do this without losing their parents' love, and that they can develop skills which will enable them to take on the responsibilities their parents now think are impossible for them. They need experiences in which they can develop self-direction. Group experiences adolescents especially need in order to make the transfer of dependence from their parents to the peer group. To the teen-ager, the importance of the peer group waxes as parental influence wanes. Parents assume another role: they serve as consultants, as a resource, as "a very present help in time of trouble." Adolescents can be helped to develop more understanding and sympathy for their parents. They should realize that dependency and independence can be coexistent—dependency in time of stress, independence when they can master a given task alone. They will never be entirely independent "for we are members one of another" (Ephesians 4:25). Family values and beliefs should not be ruthlessly overthrown; rather, they and parental ties should be reconstructed on a more mature and understanding level.

COMPREHENSION QUESTIONS

1. How do you account for the fact that so many children and adolescents seem attached to their homes even though the conditions there are apparently exceedingly poor?

2. What factors complicate the struggle of many adolescents for emancipation from the family?

3. What kinds of conflicts and home problems do adolescents mention most frequently in their compositions?

4. What is the relation between earning money and gaining adolescent independence?

5. How do adolescents feel about broken homes? What adjustments do they make to divorce and to the quarreling of parents?

6. Which of the causes of antagonism toward parents mentioned by adolescents could be avoided?

7. What do adolescents want in parents and other grown-ups?

STUDY PROJECTS

1. If you know an adolescent who is living under the shadow of a more successful or attractive brother or sister, try to help his parents change their attitude toward him, or to help him change his attitude toward them.

2. After reading the youngsters' statements about what annoys them, plan to avoid some of these sources of annoyance in your own dealings with them.

3. Work out the best possible financial program for a particular adolescent.

4. Observe how broken homes affect adolescents.

5. Obtain anonymous compositions on "How to get along with one's family" or a similar topic. Use common situations as a basis for class discussion and role-playing, using no names, of course.

FOR FURTHER STUDY

AUSUBEL, DAVID P., *Theory and Problems of Adolescent Develop-ment*, chap. VIII. New York: Grune & Stratton, Inc., 1954.

BARUCH, DOROTHY W., *How to Live with Your Teen-ager*. New York: McGraw-Hill Book Company, Inc., 1953.

BOSSARD, JAMES H. S., and ELEANOR STOKER BOLL, *The Large Family System*. Philadelphia: University of Pennsylvania Press, 1957.

FAEGRE, MARION E., *The Adolescent in Your Family*. Washington, D.C.: U.S. Department of Health, Education, and Welfare, Social Security Administration, Children's Bureau, 1954.

GESELL, ARNOLD, FRANCES L. ILG, and LOUISE BATES AMES, *Youth, the Years from Ten to Sixteen*, chap. XV. New York: Harper & Brothers, 1956.

JOSSELYN, IRENE M., *The Adolescent and His World*, chap. V. New York: Family Service Association of America, 1952.

KUHLEN, RAYMOND G., *The Psychology of Adolescent Development*, chap. XII. New York: Harper & Brothers, 1952.

LANDIS, PAUL H., *The Broken Home in Teen-age Adjustments*. Washington Agricultural Experiment Station, Institute of Agricultural Science, Bulletin 542, 1953.

———, *Teen-age Adjustments in Large and Small Families*. Washington Agricultural Experiment Station, Bulletin 549, 1954.

WATTENBERG, WILLIAM W., *The Adolescent Years*, chaps. VIII, IX, X, XXII. New York: Harcourt, Brace and Company, Inc., 1955.

Fiction and Popular Articles

* FARREL, JAMES T., *Father and Son*. New York: Vanguard Press, Inc., 1940.

* FISHER, DOROTHY CANFIELD, *The Deepening Stream*. New York: Harcourt, Brace and Company, Inc., 1930.

FRANK, LAWRENCE K., and MARY, *Your Adolescent at Home and in School*. New York: The Viking Press, Inc., 1956.

GALLAGHER, JAMES ROSWELL, *Understanding Your Son's Adolescence*. Boston: Little, Brown & Company, 1951.

OSBORNE, ERNEST G., *Understanding Your Parents*. New York: Association Press, 1956.

* RAWLINGS, MARJORIE K., *The Yearling*. New York: Charles Scribner's Sons, 1938.

* SMITH, BETTY, *A Tree Grows in Brooklyn*. New York: Harper & Brothers, 1943.

* ———, *Tomorrow Will Be Better*. New York: Harper & Brothers, 1948.

TAYLOR, KATHERINE WHITESIDE, "Journey toward Freedom," *National Parent-Teacher*, vol. 49 (November, 1954), pp. 7–9.

* Fiction.

Audio-visual Aids

A Family Affair. 30 minutes. Sound. Film Images.
Farewell to Childhood. 23 minutes. Sound. International Film Bureau.
Feelings of Depression. 30 minutes. Sound. McGraw-Hill.
Meeting the Needs of Adolescents. 19 minutes. Sound. McGraw-Hill.
The Quiet One. 1 hour, 7 minutes. Sound. Athena Films.
Roots of Happiness. 24 minutes. Sound. International Film Bureau.

Plays

High Pressure Area. And You Never Know. American Theatre Wing
    Community Plays. New York: National Association for Mental
    Health, Inc.

CHAPTER 11

Progressing toward Educational and Vocational Goals

Educational programs and vocational plans are complex components of an individual's total development. Among the factors which help to determine the best educational and vocational pattern for a given person are his mental ability, home background, personality traits, and previous experiences; current employment conditions must also be considered. Appropriate educational and vocational development stems from a realistic self-concept. If vocational opportunities are available, the individual expresses his personality and his values through his work. To help an adolescent make appropriate educational and vocational plans, it is important to know him as a person, and to be acquainted with the history of his development.

Educational guidance is concerned with learning the potentialities of an individual, helping him to obtain a realistic picture of his abilities and motivations, acquainting him with educational opportunities, helping to make suitable educational plans and to progress in them. Thus viewed, educational guidance precedes vocational guidance. At some point, however, educational plans begin to involve a consideration of the vocational field toward which the student will be moving. Later, when the curriculum becomes more differentiated, he may have to make a choice between college preparatory, commercial, shopwork, vocational home economics or agriculture, and the general curricula. Then he needs more factual information about different kinds of work,

A changing world is a challenge to adolescents. (*Courtesy of H. Armstrong Roberts.*)

The adolescent needs religion: for faith in life, for a feeling of security, for ethical clarity and moral conviction; religion gives meaning to life. (*Courtesy of the National Council of the Protestant Episcopal Church.*)

why he is attracted to a certain type of job, and what preparation is needed for it. Still later, when he is ready to enter the world of work, he needs information about specific jobs available, how to apply for them, and how to succeed in them.

Obviously, educational and vocational guidance cannot be concentrated at a certain grade. The interest which a person shows at any one time may be out of line with his basic personality and his main trend of development. More important, abilities unfold from the earliest years if the individual has opportunities to develop them. Accordingly, a continuity of guidance is necessary to ensure continuity of development.

There are several reasons why educational guidance during the school years may be considered more basic than guidance that is concerned with specific vocations. If, during these years, the individual discovers his potentialities and has the experiences necessary for their development, he will be ready to undertake any requisite specialized education at the appropriate time. It has been estimated that only 8 per cent of the vocations can be specifically chosen in advance. This means that information about specific occupations is not so important as self-understanding, knowledge of one's educational capacities, and opportunities to develop them as fully as possible at each stage of life.

It would seem that many adolescents have not been helped to develop realistic self-concepts, nor been given opportunities to reach their immediate goals; on the contrary, they have been pushed into premature choice of a specific vocation. Consequently they have become anxious and confused, like the sixteen-year-old boy who wrote the following composition on "Difficulties in choosing my life work":

I have a lot of trouble choosing my work. I really mean I don't exactly know what I want to be when I grow up. It seems very hard just to pick one thing that you may have the ability to do out of all the rest for the rest of your life. Maybe after you decide what you want to be and you don't like it so much. Then you think back to all the other things you could have been and made a success out of it and also enjoy it. It's very hard for me to decide just yet what I want to be because I don't know what I enjoy most working at school. But I know I have to decide sooner or later what I want to be when I grow up. I hope whatever I pick, I make a success out of it and enjoy working with the people. I feel kind of scared knowing that I'll be getting out of school next year and that I will have to work. I figure I might not know what I want to be by then, or maybe I won't get along with the people where I work if I do decide what I want to be. Every day I wonder what lies ahead for me, I also wonder if it's good or bad.

If, during his elementary and high school years, this boy had been helped to explore his interests, recognize his strengths and weaknesses, and test this self-knowledge in part-time jobs, he might have developed a vocational maturity that would have enabled him to make a sound choice of full-time work experience at the appropriate time.

EVALUATION OF EDUCATIONAL AND VOCATIONAL PLANS

As has already been suggested, educational and vocational development and adjustment continue throughout the school years and, in fact, throughout life. Ginzberg,[1] Super,[2] and others have suggested stages in vocational development: fantasy; orientation and exploration; and thoughtful consideration of personal qualifications and job opportunities which makes possible a wise, realistic, and flexible choice of a vocational field and eventual development of a life plan. As in other aspects of development, some individuals will be precocious and others will be retarded in evolving a life plan.

Compositions written by adolescents often illustrate this view of the development of vocational interests. The following account written by a high school sophomore boy also illustrates variability of choice, and the special difficulties which a generally gifted student may experience in deciding among the many lines of endeavor in which he might succeed:

[1] Eli Ginzberg et al., *Occupational Choice.* New York: Columbia University Press, 1951.

[2] Donald E. Super, "Dimensions and Measurement of Vocational Maturity," *Teachers College Record,* vol. 57 (December, 1955), pp. 151–162.

When I was three or four years old, my choice was unequivocally fixed in my mind: I would be President of the U.S. At about the age of five, however, medicine appealed to me and for several years I persisted in this idea. But, as the years passed, doubt began to shroud my mind. I wasn't so sure. I never gave much thought to it; the future seemed so far away.

In the higher grades and in high school I have discovered that I derive pleasure from writing. I can say, with no intention to brag or with conceit that I have done fairly well in it. Then again, I have always had an abiding interest in science, especially chemistry. In my daydreams, I have seen myself the world-famous novelist or a great chemist working unselfishly for humanity.

A verbally gifted ninth-grade girl also chose the Presidency as her early vocational goal! But in her case this ambition has persisted and she has tried to relate it to reality. She says that by the time she grows up, people will have accepted the idea of a woman president. She has mapped out her educational and vocational plans in accordance with this goal: completing high school; graduating from college with a major in sociology, politics, and economics; gaining experience in local politics, and gradually working up to more important posts.

Children often begin to show a naïve concern with vocations early in life. In the fantasy stage, they associate vocational interests with play activities, and look forward to careers as G-men or cowboys, railroad engineers or airplane pilots, teachers, nurses, or dancers. Although some of these early choices are fantastic, others are sufficiently realistic to persist. In some instances, these early choices seem to be related to later job satisfaction.

During the period of orientation and exploration, young adolescents show a real interest in vocations. The fourteen- or fifteen-year-old may ask a teacher such questions as, "What is your salary? I bet you don't earn as much as my father does. Teachers are underpaid, aren't they? Do you really vacation for the whole summer? My father can take only two weeks off." Their interest in vocations is stimulated by their desire to be independent, by social pressures and expectations, and by the courses in occupations which are offered in many junior high schools. Quite a few youngsters of this age feel that their minds are definitely made up about their life's work. During early adolescence, girls often reach a peak of interest in being actresses, musicians, or nurses. At the same age, boys may want to become professional ball players, engineers, pilots, or doctors.

Boys' choices may be complicated either by identification with or hostility toward their fathers. Some feel that they want to follow in their fathers' footsteps, while others are determined not to. Identification with the father may lead a boy to choose a certain vocation even though it is inappropriate for him; hostility toward the father may lead him to reject an appropriate vocation simply because it is associated with the father.

In studies of vocational interest, fantasy may have been encouraged by the wording of the question: "What would you like to be?" When another question is asked—"What do you *really* expect to be?"—the replies are more in line with the individual's abilities and the available job opportunities.

Whether the young adolescent needs at this stage to make more than a general choice corresponding to the elective programs offered in high school is a question that might well be considered. For boys who plan to go to work as soon as they leave high school, there is more justification for the study of possible vocations. This kind of study may increase their motivation to succeed in related schoolwork.

The next stage begins at about the age of sixteen; according to Ginzberg, adolescents at this stage are concerned with making a realistic life plan. Actually, fantasy may enter into vocational planning at all ages. The plans of many senior high school students are also vague and are based on inadequate information. To face reality and make conscious choices, students need facts.

Some teen-agers are primarily concerned with obtaining an acceptable job right away, a job which they can handle and which will provide money for their present needs. They make a compromise between reality and fantasy, between future goals and immediate desires. They do not see any connection between their first full-time job and their subsequent employment. The large degree of job dissatisfaction prevalent among adults results from not finding appropriate outlets for their interests, abilities, and values; it indicates the need for more careful consideration of the development of an adolescent's vocational interests with reference both to his self-image—who he is, what he can and cannot do, what kind of person he hopes to become—and to the realities of the world of work.

Too many students are bewildered because they feel they must act, and yet realize that their information is incomplete. Too many fail to get perspective on the problem of planning for the future; they do not view it as a process of development. Their bewilderment increases as time seems to run short; many of them believe that their first decision is eternally binding. Information about the nature of interests and the way in which they expand or contract with experience and age would be reassuring to them.

In fact, educational and vocational planning should continue after a young person has prepared for and entered a vocation. Many business firms and industries have excellent personnel programs that enable their employees to obtain further training and to achieve corresponding advancement. Thousands take advantage of evening schools and other formal and informal adult programs in order to grow educationally and vocationally.

CONSISTENCY OF CHOICE

We expect children to abandon their fantastic vocational choices as they advance through school; we have more or less assumed that they are consistent in their choices during the high school years. Schmidt and Rothney [3] obtained evidence on this important question from a carefully planned developmental study of 347 sophomore students in four representative Wisconsin high schools. These students had received "fairly intensive counseling" during their last three years in high school and were followed up six months after graduation. Approximately two-thirds of this group changed their vocational plans at least once

[3] John L. Schmidt and John W. M. Rothney, "Variability of Vocational Choices of High School Students," *Personnel and Guidance Journal,* vol. 34 (November, 1955), pp. 142–146.

during the three high school years; only a little more than a third expressed the same choice each year all the way through high school; and another third were inconsistent over the three-year period. "The assumption that vocational choices are consistent enough to warrant long-range planning of high school programs is thus applicable in less than half the cases." [4] Those students who had been most consistent all through school had followed up their choices either by entering the desired occupation or getting suitable training for it. Whether consistency is desirable or undesirable depends on the wisdom of the choice.

Consistency of choice may begin to manifest itself in the elementary school years; it is sometimes related to the vocation which the person actually enters. A number of high school seniors, writing on why they wanted or did not want to become teachers, [5] mentioned their early interest in teaching:

As far back as I can remember I have wanted to be a school teacher.

The idea of becoming a teacher first entered my mind in my junior year of high school when I was asked to be a student teacher in Latin in the absence of the regular instructor. I enjoyed this so much that, from that moment on, I watched my teachers constantly and tried to discover their methods of teaching their classes, controlling their classes, etc. Then I became a sort of critic, observing in my own mind their mistakes and ways of correcting them. From then on, I knew what I wanted in life and for a year and a half my mind has not changed one bit. I only hope that several years from now, I will find myself teaching in a good high school like the one I am about to leave now. [6]

A teacher traced in retrospect the early origin of his interest in the teaching profession: "I recall as I sat in the second row,

---

[4] *Ibid.*, p. 144.

[5] Edwin Dukes Reese, "Delaware Teacher Recruitment Study—Implications for Teacher Recruitment Drawn from a Study of Factors Which High School Students Report Influence Them in the Selection of a Career," unpublished doctoral project, Teachers College, Columbia University, New York, 1954.

[6] *Ibid.*, pp. 38–39.

third desk, how fleeting notions of being a teacher flashed through my mind; even in elementary school children are forming conclusions as to life occupations. When I disagreed with the teacher's procedures I remember I decided the way I would handle the situation."

Vocational choices become more consistent with age. After the age of twenty-five, vocational interests usually change very little.

BASES FOR CHOICE OF VOCATION

Many adolescents are making specific vocational choices on the basis of very meager information about the nature of different jobs and about their ability to do them. Sixth-grade youngsters were choosing nursing because "the nurses of today are doing a great job," and because "I saw some nurses walking down the street in their white uniforms and they looked so nice, I wanted to be a nurse." They were choosing teaching because "I like to learn people," or because "I have always loved little children." One boy gave the following reasons for becoming a farmer: "I will be a farmer because then I will get more outdoor air. And because I like to work around farm animals and take care of the gardens. And I like to live in the country and all the other reasons." He also added: "I'd treat my wife as well as I treat the farm animals."

Older adolescents with specialized interests have more adequate bases for vocational choice. For example, a group of bright boys with IQs from 109 to 145 in a large city high school where science is emphasized wrote compositions on "What I want to be or become and why." Most of them chose engineering, medicine, dentistry, or pharmacy; three chose business. The reasons they most frequently gave were:

1. Interest, and belief in one's ability
2. Monetary rewards, financial gains
3. Influence of parents and other relatives
4. The prestige and community acceptance of the vocation

These reasons did not occur singly; a combination of them was mentioned in most instances, as in the following statement by a boy with an IQ of 145 and a high scholastic record:

It is my ambition to become an electronics engineer because I feel that I have natural ability in the line. Not the natural ability of an artist or musician, but the ability to grasp electrical data. I enjoy working in electronics and feel relaxed and at ease while studying electronics. Electronics is a budding field open for much improvement. I feel that by going into electronics I will be able to apply my maximum effort. This way I will be able to accomplish the most for my country and eventually my family.

Studies of why young people choose teaching indicate that they commonly give the following reasons:

1. Good working conditions: security, good chance of getting a job, good pay, pleasant associations
2. Interest in children and young people; interest in a subject; enjoyment of school; admiration for some teacher
3. Opportunity for service; important job
4. Encouragement of friends, relatives, and teachers
5. The general usefulness of the education one gets in preparing for teaching

The reasons young people give for not choosing teaching as a vocation are equally interesting—and more emphatic. Among the personal reasons most frequently mentioned were lack of patience and lack of interest. Some felt they were not suited to teaching, and some frankly said they did not like children. A few quotations from high school seniors give more specific and colorful reasons:

I am too kind-hearted to teach.

I do not want to become a school teacher because children practically drive me crazy now. I don't know what I can do to change my attitude toward them, but I don't think I should enter teaching feeling as I do.

Teaching is a profession that requires a lot of your time; therefore teachers usually remain single. I want to live a full-rounded life containing a career, marriage, etc., and I do not feel that I could become a teacher and do all the other things I want to do.

The mechanic's pay is equal to that of a teacher, so I can't see spending the money for college and giving up the money I could be making during that time just to be a teacher.

Vocational choices are sometimes made, as it were, by default —through lack of any positive interests. One eighteen-year-old boy described his lack of interest in school and indicated the bearing of this situation on his vocational choice:

When I graduate from high school I plan to enter into the service, and when I come out of the service I plan to become a state trooper. The subjects which I have taken through my years of high school have had no bearing on my career and therefore I felt that school was not really doing me any good. My grades have not been very good, in fact they have been barely passing. I have never really put my mind to work in anything I have ever done in school, and I probably never will. For as I said before, I have little or no interest in my subjects.

In conducting surveys of guidance in a number of large cities the author has asked thousands of high school students, "Have you chosen a vocation or life work?" and "If so, why did you choose it?" The replies have almost always been inadequate. Only rarely did the students mention any systematic attempt to obtain accurate information about their own abilities or about the characteristic patterns of abilities, interests, and personality required for different jobs: the preparation needed, the salary that might be expected, the working conditions, the opportunities for advancement, the advantages and disadvantages of various vocations, or their social usefulness.

Owing to inadequate information, educational and vocational plans often miscarry. A seventeen-year-old girl wrote:

Recently I have been faced with a problem which seemed of great importance to me. I will graduate in February and have every hope of entering nursing school the same month. When I obtained information from the hospital where I hope to train, I discovered that I was lacking one credit in social studies. This came as a blow to me because I wanted so much to start in February instead of putting it off for a whole semester.

I don't believe that the lack of credit was my fault and I don't wish to put the blame on my adviser, but I had stated when I first came to this school that I wished to enter either medical school or nursing school. Since my adviser knew this, it seems to me that she should have made provisions for it in my long-range program.

When I spoke to the director of nurses about it, she told me that if my marks were high enough, I would be able to enter the school and make up the credit during my training. I hope I will be able to do this. If not, I must wait until September.

I believe that the school should have persons well equipped to advise the pupils as to the subjects they should take. They should know the requirements for the different schools and their courses. If they are not sure, they should have the information at hand where it could be found easily, before giving the wrong advice.[7]

It is better to give no information than to give misinformation. Effective educational and vocational guidance requires accurate, up-to-date information and skilled teachers and counselors who help students interpret and apply it.

Reasons for Inadequacy

The fact that so many high school students lack pertinent vocational information can be explained in several ways. Some youngsters are hurried into premature decisions or make a choice just to relieve their own anxiety. Others, blinded by the prestige value of certain jobs, refuse to face the facts about the qualifications for and the nature of the work. Moreover, collecting pertinent, up-to-date information about the thousands of available jobs is a tremendous task, and even the best job description does not give the young person the kind of firsthand information that an actual tryout experience would impart. We need to know much more about the way various occupations affect the health, physical and social development, and mental outlook of the young person who begins work at fourteen to eighteen years of

[7] Ruth Strang, "Manifestations of Maturity in Adolescents," *Mental Hygiene,* vol. 30 (October, 1949), p. 567.

age. We should also help young people to consider the motivations which underlie their choice of vocation.[8]

PREMATURE PRESSURE TO MAKE CHOICES

Are young adolescents ready to choose a vocation? Too often they are subjected to premature pressure to decide upon a specific vocation. If they are urged to choose a vocation too early, they may become overanxious about their adult responsibilities and make a hasty and inappropriate choice. They may feel guilty because their wishes run counter to those of their parents. Parents often expect an adolescent to make a choice before he is ready to do so. In the following interview with a high school boy [9] we find an instance of this:

"Gosh, I'm just an ordinary boy—I don't know what I should be, but my folks keep after me all the time. They look at me and say, 'You're big enough to be deciding what you want to do—do you want to be a doctor or an engineer or what?'" With this, he straightened up his big frame, looked a bit sheepish, and said, "I guess I am big enough, but I still don't know."

As the worker smiled sympathetically, he got a bit red and said: "I wish I did know, for it sure would be easier. You see, in this school they teach for the bright students—and I'm only average or less, I guess. Anyway, I don't want to be a doctor or engineer or any of those things."

WORKER: And you feel that it's one of those things that your folks would like you to be.

LAWRENCE: That's it, I guess. I'd like to please them, but if you're not made that way, you just aren't. My father keeps saying to me: "Why don't you have a hobby? Other boys have, and a hobby's a good idea because then you have something to interest you besides your work." He's right, I guess; but I go in for sports all the time, and when I get home I guess I don't do much but eat and sleep; but I'm tired by then.

WORKER: Then, in a way, sports are your hobby.

[8] David P. Ausubel, *Theory and Problems of Adolescent Development*, p. 457. New York: Grune & Stratton, Inc., 1954.

[9] Helen Williams, "The Case-study Method of Evaluation of Guidance," pp. 133–134, unpublished doctoral project, Teachers College, Columbia University, New York, 1945.

LAWRENCE: That's it (*beaming*). Sure wish my father could see it that way. You know, I do know what I'd like to be (*pause, as he eyed the counselor anxiously*). I've always wanted to be a parachute jumper. But I never tell anyone because they'd likely laugh at it. See, I tried my father out on what he thought of it as a profession, and he just laughed and said it wasn't worth the risk—that it took a long time to get good in it, and that maybe then you made a lot of money—but that you didn't need college for it or anything. But I've always read everything I could get my hands on about it, and the more I read the more I know I want to do it. So I figured it this way—I wouldn't say much about it; and I'd try as many things as I could before I get out of school.

WORKER: Like your work last summer?

LAWRENCE: Yeah, see—I took a job summer before last—sort of clerical; but didn't think I'd like being inside much; but I did it all summer and got along all right. Then last year I took a job in the open; and I liked it a lot better. At least it was outside even though it wasn't very fancy. So, I thought, seeing that I like sports, I'd go on to college and maybe try to be a coach—only I guess I should know absolutely what I want to be in college.

WORKER: You feel that the other students will have made up their minds before they get to college?

LAWRENCE: Well, a lot of them here in high school—the ones that will amount to anything—have; anyway, the bright ones.

WORKER (*explained that a great many boys and girls didn't make up their minds definitely even by the time they had finished college—that it didn't mean a student wouldn't amount to anything if he were undecided—that colleges were so set up that the first year or the first two years were more or less general for everyone and that you then specialized more in the subjects in which you were most interested*).

LAWRENCE: Phew—why didn't someone tell me that before—I wouldn't have been worrying so much. (*Smiled sheepishly again*) I guess I don't look like I have enough sense to worry much, but it gets you down to have your folks always asking you to make up your mind. You begin to wonder if you've got even part of one to make up. . . . Then I could take college work and do the sports and maybe by the time I finished I'd know whether I should go in for the jumping or whether there's something else I maybe haven't even heard of yet that would be the thing for me.

On the Wechsler-Bellevue Intelligence Scale this boy rated as a "superior adult." Like many adolescents, he needed to be encouraged to take time to make a wise choice, instead of being hurried or pressured. Since he was well developed physically, his parents expected him to behave like an adult. Since he was eager to attain adult status, he was naturally concerned about achieving the independence and prestige associated with choosing, preparing for, and succeeding in an occupation. He needed first to consider what he really wanted from a vocation and to appraise himself—the kind of person he was, the kind of person he hoped to become. By going over his records and interpreting them to him, the counselor helped him to begin to see himself as a very likeable young man, physically and socially competent, with plenty of ability to succeed in college and in a wide range of possible vocations which he could continue to explore and test out by further study and part-time and summer work experiences.

An eighteen-year-old girl, writing on the same problem, showed how her uncertainty had been increased by unnecessary pressures from the outside:

Trying to decide on a permanent goal in life has caused me more serious mental distress than anything else I know of. To make things worse, my sister, who is fifteen months younger than I, decided once and for all that she wanted to enter nurse's training. My mother thought there was something lacking in me as I would change from one plan to another, with no apparent reason or sense. I am inclined to think that something could be wrong with me because I want to do too many things in life.

This girl, who should have been encouraged in her interests, was actually beginning to fear them and to doubt herself. Modern society itself often expects young people to make choices before they are ready to do so; there is pressure on them to take advantage of the rich vocational opportunities immediately open to them. The very multiplicity of opportunities increases their bewilderment.

FACTORS INFLUENCING VOCATIONAL DEVELOPMENT

Some of the factors influencing an adolescent's vocational development are personal; some stem from family attitudes and relations; others reside in the culture and in current social and economic conditions.

Personality

Many aspects of the adolescent's personality influence his vocational development. Level of intelligence is one selective factor. Different vocations require somewhat different ranges of intelligence, although there is much overlapping in the intelligence-ranges of persons actually employed in various vocational fields. An individual may be barred from many vocations by low mental ability, by physical defects, by emotional disturbances. Adolescents with mental ages of only three or four can successfully handle certain jobs, such as boxing Christmas tree ornaments. But the adolescent with both low mentality and emotional disturbance is very hard to place.

Special abilities and aptitudes in a certain line often develop into vocational proficiency if opportunity is offered. However, the correlation that we might expect between interest and ability may be lowered by many environmental and personality factors that thwart the development of the ability.

Girls are more likely to choose certain vocations than others, although theoretically few doors are closed to women today. However, the social pressure to attain vocational success is still less for girls than for boys; this doubtless depresses the vocational aspirations of many, as does also the intent to marry.

Other motivations may influence an individual's vocational development—his desire for prestige, his temperament and philosophy of life. Vocational decisions are sometimes difficult for an adolescent because they involve his still unformulated philosophy of life.

Social ability is often a factor in choosing and succeeding in a vocation. Success on a job depends a great deal on ability to get along with people—customers, employers, supervisors, and fellow workers. Many more people lose their jobs because of personality and character faults than because of insufficient skill.

Influence of Parents

Conflicts with parents over vocational choice are often very disturbing to the adolescent. A youngster who is fond of his parents may suffer more if he senses their silent disappointment in him, than he would if there were open conflict. The following composition written by a seventeen-year-old senior girl illustrates this feeling of guilt:

For the past two or more years I have been extremely interested in music. My parents recognized in me a definite aptitude for the piano. I was quickly mastering skills and techniques to an extent that even my instructor was a little amazed. My father, being quick to follow up any artistic flare found in either my brother or myself, arranged for several auditions in New York City. Having received advice from all sides, we decided that it would be best if I was sent to a music school. We selected a school of music with fine reputation. Our old upright piano was sold and a new Steinway grand was purchased.

My interest was keenly aroused; I practiced three or more hours every day, in addition to attending public school. I well realized the sacrifice that my parents were making and I tried to work even harder. On the other hand, I was forfeiting all the pleasures which are coherent to adolescence.

This curriculum continued without relent for two years. I believed that I was willing to sacrifice pleasure to attain virtuosity at the keyboard. However, I suddenly began finding myself drawn away from music. I took part in school activities, sought other amusements. Practicing became a chore. I paid less attention to the piano and my parents noticed it. I knew how bad they felt and I was torn between persuing an interest I no longer desired and engaging in school activities.

I didn't return to music school this year. I convinced my parents that my time was too occupied with schoolwork and trying to gain admission to college. I know I have disappointed my parents and believe I've disappointed myself.

In this case ambitious parents exerted a major influence on the child's interests throughout her childhood. It was only when normal adolescent interests began to compete with music that the girl was no longer moved by the motivation supplied by her parents.

Many adolescents fight against the vocational ambitions which their parents try to impose on them. A younger adolescent, also interested in music, expressed her growing resentment at her mother's insistence that she choose teaching as a vocation:

I feel sick and miserable when thinking of my future. . . . My mother believes teaching is a respectable and needed occupation. Sometimes she tries to drive me into it. I don't want a restricted life. I want to be a musician. But I'm scared to tell her. She always laughs when I am serious. I hate her for trying to force me into her plans. I don't want to hate her; she's really good and I love her honestly. . . . She made me quit my piano lessons because I did not practice enough. I cried until I was so sick inside I wished I could die. . . . My father consoled me and two weeks later I was again at my piano. . . . While I am playing I do not think of the future for there is only one future for me—music.

This youngster expressed a common ambivalent attitude toward her mother. Her vocational problem involved her relations with both father and mother, as well as her mother's insistence that she make an uncongenial vocational choice at the age of thirteen.

Parental influence is often much more pervasive and subtle than in the illustrations just given. The child may not even be aware of it. The vocation that the parents choose for the child may be accepted by the child as his own choice. Beginning in the early years, the child may "catch" his parents' attitudes toward different vocations. But if an individual submits while deeply resenting the submission, his health and stability and school achievement may be seriously affected.

Later on, economic difficulties may prematurely precipitate the adolescent into the world of work, or determine his choice by limiting the training that the parents can or will supply. However, dependence upon the family's financial support in certain vocations is becoming less necessary as scholarships and other sources of financial aid increase.

Perception of Various Vocations

Success and satisfaction in a vocation may also depend a great deal on the way in which the individual perceives the vocation. In our culture some vocations are considered high in social prestige; others, low. This is an important factor in determining how parents and young people perceive a given vocation; many youngsters choose a vocation because it is in line with their social-class level or their aspirations to move upward in the social scale. It has been estimated that about two-thirds of young people today aspire to jobs higher than their fathers' in prestige and income. There are, of course, individual differences in the need for prestige and social recognition among members of the same social group.

A sense of the social value of one's work motivates some young people. To feel that one is doing something socially useful helps to make even mechanical work seem worthwhile. During the last war, new employees who had some specialized job such as tightening a certain nut on an airplane were shown how their work was related to the making of the plane, and thus to the whole war effort. An idealistic adolescent may choose an occupation for its social value. He wants to serve society as well as to utilize and further develop his potentialities. The following idealistic expression by a junior high school girl was apparently crystallized by her reading of a biography of Madame Curie:

I should like to be a scientist like Madame Curie. I would like to practice medical science. I want to be a scientist because science is necessary to help our nation grow strong. Our nation must have strong and healthy people free from sickness. There must be scientists to find the necessary things to keep sickness away from our nation . . . to find new discoveries and to improve on the discoveries of others.

If the individual has a concept of himself as a socially acceptable person, he is likely to choose a socially useful vocation.

In their compositions, adolescents seldom mention the prestige value of an occupation as the reason for choosing it. Adults likewise seldom admit their lack of genuine respect for the "lower level" occupations, probably because they feel this is not in accord with their profession of democratic principles. But if people in general had a real respect for any socially useful occupation that is suitable to the individual, many adolescents would make more realistic vocational choices.

By knowing how adolescents perceive various occupations, we can gain a better understanding of their vocational choices. Grunes [10] made a study of how American high school students view the world of work. They made the clearest distinction between white-collar jobs and work done with the hands. This common view has been responsible in the past for the frequent oversupply of applicants for white-collar jobs and the undersupply of manual workers (whom automation is now making less necessary). Too often young people persist in seeking office or sales work even when no jobs in these fields are available. Grunes also noted misconceptions about the average incomes of certain groups of workers. The students greatly overestimated the amount of money earned by actors and actresses, and also by farmers; they underestimated the salaries of aviators, stewardesses, and teachers.

General Economic and Social Conditions

Both depression and prosperity exert characteristic influences on the general occupational outlook of adolescents. In times of depression adolescents are seriously hampered in their vocational adjustments. There are no jobs for them. They do not have a chance to achieve economic independence or test the wisdom of their vocational plans. In times of prosperity the appeal of available jobs is so strong that teen-agers may leave school to go to work. In times of war the same adults who have been saying that older boys are too young to work now expect them to fight like men.

[10] Willa Freeman Grunes, "On Perception of Occupations," *Personnel and Guidance Journal,* vol. 34 (January, 1956), pp. 276–279.

War—past, present, and pending—influences the thinking and the behavior of teen-agers, both boys and girls. Some take a fatalistic attitude: "There's sure to be a war, so why think of the future? Better have a good time now." For others, the possibility of military service stimulates scholarship: the only way to avoid the draft is to continue making a good record in school or college. Deferment of students who can profit by further college study in technical fields seems to be in line with sound policy for the most effective use of human resources. Certainly it is better for able learners to continue their college programs than to mark time in relatively inactive and inappropriate military service. On the other hand, they may thus be discouraged from choosing esthetic or social-service careers in favor of engineering or other vocations more directly useful in war. The idea that war is inevitable influences some boys to make military service their career so that the compulsory period will be part of their total life plan, not an interruption in it. Other boys, remembering stories about the sordid side of war which their older brothers have told them, feel the horror of it and resent being forced into military service.

College students are concerned about the interruption of their vocational plans. They raise questions as to the advantages and disadvantages of getting their military service over with before entering their chosen fields. Some veterans who went on to college seemed to feel that there was a definite advantage in having this service behind them. They said they could settle down better since they "knew where they stood." Some felt that the service experience had helped them to mature, and that they were able to do a better job in college than if they had entered directly from high school. Others had observed the demoralizing effects of military service on some younger boys who had entered it while still emotionally and morally immature. These boys needed time to strengthen their inner controls in a more favorable setting of home, school, or college.

Girls also feel the impact of their boy friends' impending or immediate military service. A sixteen-year-old high school girl described the problem as follows:

One of the major problems of a teen-age girl is the army. I don't know what it is, but the armed forces seem to interfere with all of a girl's plans. Just when you begin to see a fellow and you really think you like him, Uncle Sam steps in and breaks up the beginning of a big romance. There is the little matter of being away from each other for long periods of time and the possibility of one or the other meeting someone new. . . .

Also, having someone far across the sea makes a girl put her mind to thinking about him all the time. Then things start to happen. Schoolwork becomes unimportant and marks are inevitably lowered. The family relations are also impaired because the girl spends most of her time brooding about her far off companion and is very touchy when people speak about him.

There is also the matter of letter writing. As much as a fellow and girl like each other it is often hard to find things to write in letters and after a while writing becomes a chore instead of a pleasure and it is very nerve-wracking.

Both men and women in college weigh the advantages and disadvantages of marrying before military duty has been finished. Many feel it is better to wait. They often decide that the prospective bride should be working and saving money while the man is in service.

Other Factors Mentioned by Students

An original study which the author made of 550 compositions on the subject, "Difficulties in choosing my life work," by students ranging from sixth-grade pupils to college seniors throws further light on factors affecting vocational choice. The factors most frequently mentioned by these students were as follows:

Desire for immediate cash, financial security, or prestige. . 19%
Satisfaction in summer or part-time work experiences. 15%
Desire to be helpful to others. 11%
Identification with or influence of significant adults. 7%
Availability of job opportunities in the chosen field. 6%

The money aspect was mentioned more frequently by the junior high school youngsters than by any other group. However, this may not be due to an age difference but to the nature of the sampling, or to differences in the ways in which occupations had been presented in their classes. The senior high school students were the ones who most frequently mentioned the value of work experience. Humanitarian motives were most often mentioned by female college students, high school girls, and junior high school youngsters—probably not too seriously by the latter group.

Patterns of Influences

A unique pattern of influences enters into each adolescent's vocational development. Beginning with his inherited capacities, his interests, motivations, and personality are influenced by his family relations, early childhood experiences, school success or failure, and the ways in which people respond to him. All of these factors bear upon his vocational interests and choices; they often generate unrealistic vocational choices—choices that are out of line with the jobs actually available to the individual. Social and economic conditions may also prevent individuals from carrying out appropriate educational and vocational plans. Ausubel concluded that "under these circumstances, a large number of individuals are inevitably doomed to chronic frustration, job disillusionment, and general dissatisfaction with what life has to offer them." [11]

PROBLEMS IN MAKING EDUCATIONAL AND VOCATIONAL PLANS

In the 550 compositions on this subject, not all mentioned difficulties. More than a third expressed satisfaction with their choices. Junior high school youngsters seemed most certain that they had made a satisfying, lasting vocational choice; senior high school and college students were less confident. The satisfaction which the junior high school students expressed with respect to their vocational choices may be due to the nature of the vocational guidance they had received, and also to the fact that they had not had much opportunity to test the reality of their choices.

The following difficulties occurred most frequently:

[11] Ausubel, *op. cit.,* p. 453.

Indecision as to choice of vocation 42%
Concern over military service 39%
Concern about financing the necessary education for the
    vocation 21%
Concern over marriage-vocation relationships 17%
Feeling of scholastic inadequacy to undertake the prepara-
    tion needed for the desired vocation 12%
Problem of selecting a specific vocation in the chosen field
    of interest 11%
Having to pursue a second choice or otherwise unsatisfac-
    tory vocational goal 10%
Indecision about entering college 8%
Problems of selecting and succeeding in a proper secondary
    program of studies 8%
Uncertainty and fear about vocational failure and financial
    insecurity 8%

Although the difficulty most frequently mentioned was indecision as to choice of vocation, there was also an undercurrent
of anxiety expressed or implied. Many of these students were
apparently worried about financing their vocational education,
as well as succeeding in the educational program and in the vocation selected. Their own adequacy as a person was at stake,
and earlier feelings of security or insecurity would reappear in
modified form.

The individual who has had a series of experiences during the
elementary and high school years in which he gradually discovered his abilities, aptitudes, values, and aspirations is best prepared to make further educational and vocational decisions. He
should be helped to understand why he feels as he does about
his own educational plans and vocational goals, or those which
his parents would like him to adopt. He should consider which
curricular experiences, extraclass activities, and part-time jobs
will contribute most to his evolving realistic self-concept. This
self-concept, in turn, will further develop as he thoughtfully considers his life work. Such pervasive guidance requires the cooperation and coordinated efforts of all the student's teachers and
counselors.

DECISIONS ABOUT FURTHER EDUCATION

Early adolescence is a time when important choices have to be made. In junior high school the student may have to decide whether to take algebra or general mathematics, whether to take a foreign language or a shop, whether to begin a college-preparatory, a commercial, or an agricultural course. To make a wise choice one must have a realistic idea of the kind of person he is and can become.

Making such a decision at this developmental stage seems very serious. One ninth-grade boy wrote of his dilemma as follows:

One of the toughest situations that I ever encountered was in trying to find out to what high school I should attend. My reason for so much trouble was that I didn't know what I wanted to become in later life.

In trying to find my answers I asked myself the following: what interests me the most; what is my favorite hobby; what am I good in?

After having asked myself these questions I found out that my chief interests were chemistry and engineering.

The answer to my second question was rather simple. Chemistry, my favorite hobby, coincided with my interest.

After another bit of careful thinking I came to the conclusion that I was best in chemistry because I had a chemistry set, and I had read many books on the subject.

My main problems were now over, my only one was to find out which high school would be best for a start in Chemical Engineering. Again I went to my guidance counselor and she said there were several schools that would give me a beginning in it. So I chose one of these and am now attending it.

This boy is only one of a considerable number of adolescents who are trying to solve problems of this kind in an intelligent, deliberative manner. They consult with parents, with school advisers, with college representatives, and sometimes with various persons engaged in the particular vocation in which they are interested.

Many high school seniors, especially those of high or average intelligence, mention choice of college as the major problem they now face. Some are uncertain as to whether they really want to attend college; some feel doubtful of their ability to do college work; a considerable number are aware that they may not be admitted. Some have problems of financing a college education. An immediate problem is to keep their marks high enough to gain admittance to the college of their choice.

Many report that they are able to get little help: "I have been to the college committee here in school, but they have not given me much satisfaction. I have also written to several colleges for information but I still have no idea what college I want to attend."

A girl in the twelfth grade relates this experience:

Later I went to the college committee of our school and asked if I could obtain any help in choosing a college. The teacher in charge pointed to some stacks of catalogues and said I could look through them. I did this and found I didn't know any more than I did before. When I was finally able to talk with an adviser, she named any number of colleges which I could not afford or which did not offer the courses in the field I wanted to enter. I gave up in disgust.

This girl's response to her experience may be interpreted in several ways, of course. Yet it seems difficult to avoid the conclusion that, at least for her, the college committee did not operate satisfactorily. Moreover, although college catalogues contain a great deal of information, they apparently do not tell the teenager what he wants to know in a way that he can understand. Many students who are really concerned about going to college are uncertain about the purposes of higher education, about college requirements and their ability to meet them, about the total cost, the availability of scholarships, and the feasibility of working one's way through college.[12] Only about one-fourth had learned about widely publicized college scholarship programs.

[12] Vernon E. Anderson and Arthur Goldberg, "Schools for Adolescents: Curriculum Content and Organization," *Review of Educational Research,* vol. 24 (February, 1954), pp. 30–38.

Social and family background influences adolescents' ideas about going to college. Children of professional parents—those from homes with a tradition of higher education—think of themselves as destined to go to college; they take it for granted. Those with different family backgrounds may not even consider going to college unless they are stimulated by teachers, counselors, or friends. Of the students now in college, about four times as many come from homes with a professional background as from farmers' and laborers' homes. Many adolescents who are "college material" do not continue their education beyond high school. Some of these students resent the fact that they did not receive guidance that would have led them to consider the possibility of a college education before it was too late. It was reported in 1950 that only one in three of the most intelligent graduates of Minnesota high schools went on to earn a college degree. Other studies have shown that percentages varying from 40 to 50 per cent of high school graduates in the top quarter of ability failed to attend college.[13] In view of the increase in the number of families able to pay for a college education and the increased availability of scholarships and other financial aid, desire to go to college has become more important than financial ability. According to several studies, only half of the bright high school graduates who were not planning to go to college thought that their decisions would have been changed if they had had more money. "Unless a high school graduate wants to go to college, the existence of other favorable circumstances is unlikely to get him there." [14]

The total percentage of high school students going on to college, however, has been increasing rapidly. For example, in one suburban high school the figures were 17 per cent in 1952, 28 per cent in 1953, and 31 per cent in 1954. During these same years an almost constant proportion—about 18 per cent—were at-

[13] Byron S. Hollinshead, *Who Should Go to College.* New York: Columbia University Press, 1952.

[14] Joseph G. Smith and Dael L. Wolfle, "Some General Problems of Educating Post-high-school Youth," *Review of Educational Research,* vol. 24 (October, 1954), p. 272.

tending higher institutions other than four-year colleges. It has been predicted that there will be about twice as many college students in 1970 as in 1954.[15]

Young people's reasons for going or not going to college are often superficial. They plan to go to a certain college because a friend is going there or because they do not know what else to do. One high school senior wrote: "The only reason I am going to college is because I am not prepared to work."

For others the decision about college is only part of a more important adolescent task—determining one's goal in life. This point of view was expressed by an intelligent senior girl:

> My problem is one that is facing many high school pupils of today. The simple, yet all-important problem of college. Many people want to rush you into an occupation that you do not care for and they tell you that a college degree is simply all that can help you.
>
> Also they tell you early in your high school, and even in the latter part of junior high, that you must hurry and decide what your future work will be, that you must hurry and prepare yourself, that you should strive toward your all-important goal. Then I sit down to wonder—What is my goal? I have not found one yet, I have come across none that I feel I should put my whole life on. I also get to wondering if this feeling is unnatural; suppose I am the only one who has not planned his future to the exact detail. And it worries me.
>
> I hope that in time I will make up my mind as to my future, without people pushing me.
>
> But instead of looking forward to the future, I find myself trying to lag behind so I will not have to face the decision.

Parents' wishes and ambitions also have much to do with an adolescent's decision about college. A seventeen-year-old girl was torn between her own appraisal of her ability and her parents' desire to have her go to college:

> My mother and father have saved all their life to send me to college, but I thought I wouldn't go and did not take the right subjects. It has made me a very sad and unhappy person, because the

[15] *Ibid.*, p. 270.

least I could do for all they have done for me, is to fulfill their one big wish. Even though I have told them it may be impossible to go to college on account of taking a general course instead of an ackedemic course, they still have hoped. They think maybe I could major in home economics. But I think it is impossible. They just don't seem to understand and won't take no for an answer.

Sometimes we are not aware of the conflicts and anxieties aroused by these educational decisions. A seventeen-year-old boy expressed a multiplicity of fears which were mentioned singly by many other students:

To me, the problem of a college education and its aftermath is most depressing. The very idea of the red tape I must go through to get into a college frightens me. At times I feel I am not worthy to go to college. I feel that if I go to college, I might burden my father with an unnecessary pecuniary debt. I am fearful of what will happen if I go to college and fail. If that were to happen there would be no outlet for me. I would have to go to work, ever feeling that I had wasted my father's hard-earned money and had misused his confidence.

However, after a long period of thought and careful consideration I realized that these problems are not only my own. They are faced by almost every student entering college.

A college senior looking back over his college years, expressed an intelligent point of view:

The most important thing in the way of preparation for college is to have a fairly definite idea of one's goal in life. The college should be selected upon the basis of how well it is equipped to prepare the particular student for that goal. The personality of the student should also be taken into consideration. Some students get along splendidly in a small college and would be miserable in a large university. Others might thrive on university life. Whether to go to a co-ed or a segregated college is also a problem. Most students have been used to co-education in high school and usually it is more desirable and wholesome, but there are a few students who because of too much interest in the opposite sex find studying in a man's or woman's college easier. Also very timid people or those not interested or not attractive to the other sex can get along better with their own sex and are happier, but they do not get the social experience they need.

If a student is not sure or at least does not have a general idea of what he wants in the way of a life work, he would be wiser to postpone college and go to work for a year or two until he is more sure of himself.

Educational plans, like vocational development, depend on the adolescent's self-concept, which is a product of the interaction between his environment and all that he is at a given time. The expectations of his parents and the values and goals of his peers are among the most important environmental factors.

DECISION ABOUT LEAVING SCHOOL

Dissatisfaction with school is often balanced against the advantages of having a high school diploma. The following was written by a nineteen-year-old boy whose education had been interrupted:

Should I finish school? . . . The time I have spent on the first part of my education was to a good advantage. The latter part of my education seems to be a lot of wasted time. Oh I know a lot of this wastefulness is due to personal reasons, and I also know that with conditions as they are today, if I don't obtain my diploma, I'll end up washing dishes for life at $35 per week. True, some slide on to fame and fortune without a diploma, but these are very few.

Should I be attending school solely for this purpose—I don't believe so. Let's try and install some type of education that comes with experience. I want to be so educated, that once I'm insated with knowledge I shall never forget it. With the present education system, it is extremely easy to forget.

Many—at least one-third—of those who drop out of school have the ability to complete high school.[16] Why do they leave school before graduating? Some of the reasons they give on questionnaires and in interviews are probably rationalizations. This is especially true when the person collecting the information fails to gain the confidence and cooperation of the youngsters. The chief

[16] Harold J. Dillon, *Early School Leavers,* National Child Labor Committee Publication No. 491, 1949.

reason, given by about half of the students in the admirable study of school leavers made by Johnson and Legg,[17] is dissatisfaction with the program and the methods of teaching; they disliked the teachers; they felt unable to learn the subjects required of them and did not want to repeat a grade. Many lost interest when they fell behind in their schoolwork. One cannot blame students for rebelling when they are expected to meet standards that are beyond their capacity. Some of these blamed their failure on the teacher: "I go's and talks with her and she said 'you don't work hard enough,' which is wrong." A number of pupils complained about lack of praise and encouragement: "I try to did my work and the teacher did not gave me any complement." School records show that the majority of those who drop out of high school score low on group intelligence tests and are doing poor work in school.

About a fifth of the students surveyed by Johnson and Legg [18] said that they left for economic reasons, and another fifth left to get married or for other miscellaneous reasons. Some responded to the "lure of the job" and the desire to be independent. Half of the students in this study were sure they had done the right thing in leaving school, but the older ones expressed an increasing degree of regret at having dropped out before graduating.

Part of students' dissatisfaction with school is caused by unhappiness in their social relations. Penty [19] found that among a group of poor readers, those who dropped out had found the other students less friendly and the teachers more difficult to get along with than did the poor readers who graduated. A much larger number of the graduates than of the dropouts participated in group activities. In fact, the number of dropouts who participated in school or out-of-school clubs was very small—only nine, as compared with forty-four of the graduates. Their main rea-

---

[17] Elizabeth S. Johnson and C. E. Legg, "Why Young People Leave School," *Bulletin of the National Association of Secondary-school Principals,* vol. 32 (November, 1948), pp. 14–24.

[18] *Ibid.*

[19] Ruth Penty, *Reading Ability and High School Drop-outs.* New York: Bureau of Publications, Teachers College, Columbia University, 1956.

sons for not joining clubs were as follows: they had to work; they felt that they did not belong; they were not interested; they were new to the school or community; or they did not know how to make friends. Some of these youngsters said, "The other kids were all right, but I was shy in meeting them."

The reasons which dropouts gave at the time of leaving school, in the exit interview, were often different from those which they gave to their counselors. In the exit interview the students most frequently mentioned obvious reasons such as having to work, lack of interest, dislike of school, planning to join the armed services, and marriage. To the counselors they more often attributed their leaving to the school's failure to meet their needs, discouragement over schoolwork, greater appeal of outside work, and lack of support and interest at home.

The reasons given by dropouts one to six years after they had left school were still more enlightening: "I was discouraged. I was not getting any place in school. I thought the Marines was a better place to be. I had difficulty with reading. I couldn't remember what I read. I was often embarrassed in class." [20] This was the explanation given by a boy with an IQ of 92 and a reading grade level of 6.1. A girl with an IQ of 94 and a reading grade level of 5.2 made a somewhat similar statement: "I didn't like school too well. I wanted to get married. I couldn't remember what I read. I didn't like to go to classes and be around other kids who seemed to learn easier than I did."

Another girl with practically the same IQ and reading level expressed a depth of feeling in the following words:

I wasn't interested in school because I had no friends. No one cared whether I came to school or not. I liked typing, but I wasn't a good speller, so I made too many mistakes. I couldn't find anything interesting to read in school. I read some things now; I couldn't remember what I read in school. I was afraid to recite in class. I got a job at a drive-in when I left school. I felt all right out of school. I felt sick a lot of the time when I was going to school; guess part of it was that I didn't like school.[21]

20 *Ibid.*, pp. 42–43.
21 *Ibid.*, pp. 43–44.

In some cases school leaving was associated with family relations. A number of these students thought that their parents did not care whether they stayed in school or not. For example, a girl with an Otis IQ of 89 and a reading grade of 6.5 gave the following explanation of why she left school: "We were always quarreling at home; I wasn't getting along in subjects at school either. English and history are hard for me. I didn't know some of the words, so I couldn't understand what I was reading. I wanted to get married. I think now that marriage isn't always rosy. It is better for kids to finish school first." [22]

It is significant that some students with below-average IQs and reading scores two or more years below their grade level do stay in school. Following are the main reasons they give for remaining to graduate from senior high school:

They feel it is expected of them. One said, "My mother very much wanted me to graduate. My brother quit and she felt very bad about it."

They have always expected to graduate—"never thought of quitting."

They have "made up their minds" to graduate.

Their parents, teachers, or counselors encourage them.

They think a high school education will help them get a better job.

Last, but far from least, they are getting some satisfactions from school—in class discussions, athletics, extraclass activities, school dances, and the like. They are doing fairly well in their subjects and "like the kids."

Students drop out of college for various reasons, among them inability to budget time and lack of purpose. More specific explanations were given by some eighteen-year-old college students who dropped out after six months:

I couldn't concentrate on my work. Too many other things came into my mind. College is too much for me. I know now I will not go far by trying.

College is different from high school—a lot of courses, no friends to ask for help, no hopes to improve my work.

[22] *Ibid.,* p. 46.

I can't get into groups. To join those groups you have to have time and also be in the clicks and have plenty of money. Many of us feel left out with no opportunity to participate in college activities.

I came to realize that I couldn't stay 3 or 4 years in college always being dependent on my father. If you pay your own expenses, you don't have to worry; you don't have to care about someone expecting or waiting for results.

We must not conclude, however, that leaving school is always detrimental to a young person; it may facilitate progress toward a new and more rewarding goal.[23] Certainly if we require adolescents to stay in school, we must offer them something besides frustrating experiences. We need not blame the young person who said: "When youth want to quit school, let them quit and don't force them to go. It drives me nuts to sit in school when you are not learning anything." [24]

THE ROLE OF WORK EXPERIENCE

During the last war a large proportion of adolescents was encouraged to work in war industries. Some of them worked full time and also continued their school programs. An English teacher, who had her class keep daily schedules, discovered that one sixteen-year-old boy was working in a factory on an eight-hour night shift and coming to school during the day.

Part-time work still plays a most important part in the lives of many adolescents, and increasing numbers are holding jobs. In a typical town high school in 1953 to 1954, about one-fourth of the freshmen and one-half of the seniors were holding part-time jobs. They were doing work as clerks, salesmen, typists, apprentice cooks, electricians, garage assistants, laborers, servants in homes or clubs, stock boys, waitresses, machine operators, nurse's aides. In 1956 some two million young people aged four-

[23] David Segel, *Frustration in Adolescent Youth*, U.S. Office of Education Bulletin 1951, no. 1, 1951.

[24] Howard M. Bell, *Youth Tell Their Story*, p. 252. Washington, D.C.: American Council on Education, 1938.

High school students build a house; at the same time they are learning skills and building a sense of competence and self-esteem. (*Courtesy of Wide World Photos.*)

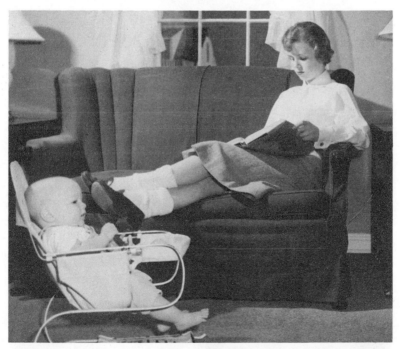

Baby sitting may benefit both baby and adolescent, if the sitter is fond of little children and knows some sound child psychology. (*Courtesy of H. Armstrong Roberts.*)

This sixteen-year-old high school boy's ambitions have expanded so he turns over his paper route to a younger boy. (*Courtesy of Wide World Photos.*)

A girl scout, volunteering her services as a hospital aide, is giving the "tender loving care" that babies need so much. (*Courtesy of the Girl Scouts of the U.S.A.*)

teen to seventeen had some kind of employment during the school year. During the summer three million were employed. According to another survey, 10 per cent of the high school pupils were enrolled in work experience programs as one phase of vocational education.

The work experience program enables the high school student to do part-time work under supervision, and thus to extract the maximum value from it. The "four-four plan" developed in the Oakland, California, school system during wartime [25] made it possible for students to spend four hours in school and four hours on a job. The work experience was treated like an elective subject and was supervised jointly by the school and by the employers. In Philadelphia the wartime school-work program

[25] Marion Brown, "The Work-experience Program in the Oakland Public Schools," *Journal of the National Association of Deans of Women,* vol. 8 (October, 1944), pp. 4–26.

has been continued; it contributes to the students' self-esteem and to the reduction of discipline problems.

Another form of work experience is the productive enterprises and improvement projects carried on in connection with agricultural and home economics courses. These projects have a close relation to community and home-life situations. In one study carried on in Oklahoma, the students who participated in the largest number of projects tended to be the ones who entered college or became farm owners.

Well-selected, carefully supervised part-time work may contribute to the attainment of major adolescent goals. The Negro boys, fourteen to seventeen years old, interviewed by Scales and Hutson,[26] put the most emphasis on the value of part-time employment in establishing economic self-sufficiency and achieving emotional independence from parents and other adults. "No work —no money—no further education—no good times"—this is the way one unemployed youth summed up the effect of unemployment. On the positive side, gainful employment often assists adolescents in achieving independence, feeling more grown up, gaining status with their peers, and getting along better with their families. The students in Scales and Hutson's survey expressed their satisfactions as follows:

Feelings of Independence

I feel like I'm on my own. I can buy my own clothes and spend money for what I want and have the money to do it with.

I don't have to depend on my parents and be a leech.

Working makes you independent.

Feelings of Growing Up

If you work, you're treated better—not like a kid.

You feel a lot bigger with your own money and things you have bought.

I feel bigger. I can help my dad with bills and expenses.

[26] Eldridge E. Scales and Percival W. Hutson, "How Gainful Employment Affects the Accomplishment of Developmental Tasks of Adolescent Boys," *School Review,* vol. 43 (January, 1955), pp. 31–37.

Improved Relations with Parents

It helped me and my mother get along.

She says "Yes" mostly; before it was "No" all the time.

I'm not my own boss, but it's better now.

Status with Peers

I can get things the other kids get, like these boots.

I feel eighteen, nineteen, or twenty—most of the boys I go around with are.

I can be as sharp as the other boys.[27]

Part-time work often helps to change parental attitudes; it makes some parents realize that their children are really growing up. Consequently they become more permissive and appreciative. One mother said that through participation in a work experience program her son had become more mature and had also been able to save money for a college education. Work experience in connection with the school program had also given him the incentive to save more by working during the summer.

Part-time work and the desire for spending money are closely related. Students in both junior and senior high school prefer earning money themselves to having an allowance. They are embarrassed by having less money than their friends have. The solution most of them see to this problem is to earn some money of their own. To this rural high school boy, work was important for this and other reasons: "The best thing that happened to me was when I turned 16, and I was able to work, get my hunting license and learn to drive. Now that I am able to work I can earn and save my own money. I can by my own clothes and save up money for a car."

Part-time work may also enhance the adolescent's ability to choose and prepare for his life work. A senior high school boy expressed this point of view as follows:

The work experience program has helped me greatly. My first contact with it was in my junior year when I got a job as an apprentice machinist. Upon taking advantage of this I received special

---

[27] *Ibid.*, p. 34.

instruction which otherwise might not have been offered. The next year they secured a job for me as an X-ray technician. This job also has guaranteed me a chance for specialization.

The problem is to find suitable jobs for young people still in school and for those aged sixteen to eighteen who have left school but have not yet become established in a regular position. Dorothy Barclay [28] mentioned a number of agencies that are concerned with this problem: the National Child Labor Committee is interested in finding sound and realistic work experience for young people; its youth employment committee locates jobs for teen-agers during the Christmas and Easter vacations. In another situation, teen-agers themselves made a survey of summer-job opportunities. In Mason City, Iowa, teachers took the initiative in finding jobs for students. A parent-teachers association council in Michigan and the Police Athletic League in New York City have lined up part-time jobs for students. In Berkeley, California, several agencies organized a "workreation" project for boys fourteen to seventeen during five weeks of the summer vacation. It included four hours of paid employment and two hours of supervised recreation, five days a week. The jobs contributed to community betterment. A film for parent groups entitled "Beyond the Classroom" illustrates the work plan in Millbrook School, Millbrook, New York. These are all efforts to find suitable work experience for young people.

CONCLUDING STATEMENT

Progression toward educational and vocational goals means evolving one's own long-range goals and making one's own important decisions. The anxiety so many adolescents feel concerning their inability to make educational and vocational choices arises from their general struggle to become psychologically independent. This anxiety is augmented by their parents' conflicts, insecurity, and unfulfilled ambitions, and by social and economic

[28] Dorothy Barclay, "Wanted: Jobs for Teen-agers," *New York Times Magazine* (February 5, 1956), p. 48.

conditions which limit their choice or make it impossible for them to carry out appropriate plans. Added to these causes of anxiety are the earlier feelings of insecurity and inadequacy many adolescents bring with them into the teens. Fortunate is the young person who has a realistic, hopeful concept of himself. For him, educational opportunities, work experience outside of school, evolving educational and vocational plans for the future —all are guided by and contribute to his self-image and his self-esteem.

COMPREHENSION QUESTIONS

1. What is the relationship between educational and vocational guidance? How are they related to the adolescent's total pattern of development?

2. How may educational and vocational plans be influenced by the individual's concept of himself and the way in which he and his parents perceive different vocations?

3. Describe the development of educational and vocational goals.

4. What are the common reasons given by adolescents for not becoming teachers? How could these objections be minimized or overcome?

5. Why should many young adolescents not be urged to choose a specific vocation?

6. What are some of the difficulties adolescents meet in making educational and vocational plans? What can adults do to help them overcome each of these difficulties?

7. On what do job satisfactions and life satisfactions depend? To what extent can one's vocation contribute to one's preferred way of life?

STUDY PROJECTS

1. Ask a number of adolescents to try to give you the history of their vocational choices, and to state the bases for the choices they have now made.

2. Collect information about available scholarship aid.

3. Study the effect of part-time work on a number of adolescents.

4. What knowledge and skills would you need to counsel high school students with respect to college plans?

5. Make a plan for educational guidance which recognizes the needs of high school students who are not going to college.

6. Plan a career conference that includes all the best features of such conferences.

7. Help some adolescent apply for a job by role-playing an interview with an employer.

8. Are the following materials on colleges and scholarships available to high school students whom you know?

Directories of scholarships:

U.S. Department of Health, Education and Welfare, Office of Education. Washington, D.C.: Government Printing Office.

Feingold, S. Norman, *Scholarships, Fellowships, Loans,* vol. 3. Cambridge, Mass.: Bellman Publishing Company, 1955.

Jones, Theodore S. (ed.), *Your Opportunities to Help Yourself and to Help Others.* Milton, Mass.: Published by the author, 1952.

FOR FURTHER STUDY

Davis, Junius Ayers, "Returns Sought from Adult Work by Early Adolescents in Relation to Sociometric Status among Peers," doctoral thesis, Teachers College, Columbia University, New York, 1956.

Fine, Benjamin, "Jobs that Keep Students in College," *New York Times* (February 21, 1954), p. E9.

Jahoda, G., "Adolescent Attitudes to Starting Work," *Occupational Psychology* (London), vol. 23 (July, 1949), pp. 184–188.

Kuhlen, Raymond G., *The Psychology of Adolescent Development,* chap. XI. New York: Harper & Brothers, 1952.

Norton, J. L., "Patterns of Vocational Interest Development and Actual Job Choice," *Journal of Genetic Psychology,* vol. 82 (second half, 1953), pp. 235–262.

———, "General Motives and Influences in Vocational Development," *Journal of Genetic Psychology,* vol. 82 (second half, 1953), pp. 263–278.

Reilly, William J., *Career Planning for High School Students.* New York: Harper & Brothers, 1953.

Schmidt, John L., and John W. M. Rothney, "Variability of Vocational Choices of High School Students," *Personnel and Guidance Journal,* vol. 34 (November, 1955), pp. 142–146.

STRANG, RUTH, "Social Aspects of Vocational Guidance," *School Review,* vol. 58 (September, 1950), pp. 326–334.

STRONG, E. K., *Changes in Interests with Age.* Stanford, Calif.: Stanford University Press, 1931.

SUPER, DONALD E., "Dimensions and Measurement of Vocational Maturity," *Teachers College Record,* vol. 57 (December, 1955), pp. 151–162.

THOMAS, LAWRENCE G., *Occupational Structure and Education.* Englewood Cliffs, N.J.: Prentice-Hall, Inc., 1956.

THOMPSON, ALBERT S., "Rationale for Vocational Guidance," *Personnel and Guidance Journal,* vol. 32 (May, 1954), pp. 533–535.

WATTENBERG, WILLIAM W., *The Adolescent Years,* chap. XIX. New York: Harcourt, Brace and Company, Inc., 1955.

Fiction and Popular Articles

BARCLAY, DOROTHY, "Wanted: Jobs for Teen-agers," *New York Times Magazine* (February 5, 1956), p. 48.

* FAULKNER, WILLIAM, *The Unvanquished.* New York: Random House, Inc., 1938.

FERGUSON, CHARLES W., "What Enterprising Youth Can Do," *National Parent-Teacher,* vol. 50 (January, 1956), pp. 4–7.

LONG, WILLIAM G., "Let's Put Our Teen-agers to Work," *American Magazine,* vol. 160 (October, 1955), p. 17.

SPENCER, LYLE M., "What Job for Junior?" *National Parent-Teacher,* vol. 49 (January, 1955), pp. 25–27.

Audio-visual Aids

Feelings of Hostility. 27 minutes. Sound. National Film Board of Canada.

Careers for Girls. 18 minutes. Sound. March of Time Forum Films.

* Fiction.

CHAPTER 12

Achieving Socially Responsible Behavior

Stated positively, this developmental task is to desire and achieve socially responsible behavior and to contribute to the life of the community. Good citizenship requires both personal independence and interdependence, common goals and loyalities as well as individuality. If we would "accentuate the positive" instead of publicizing the negative, we might make better progress in checking the rising tide of juvenile delinquency.

Headlines, sensational news stories, magazine articles, books, movies, and TV programs that exaggerate teen-age delinquency are, in several ways, likely to intensify the problem. Some adolescents, reading and listening to accounts of "kid bandits," teen-

440

age immorality or loose conduct, school-age drinking, wild driving, reckless spending, and dope addiction, may get the impression that these kinds of behavior are "normal" for their age—that "it's the thing to do." Teachers in New York City noted an increase in school behavior problems following a series of newspaper articles describing delinquent behavior in the schools. Moreover, this publicity gives the members of juvenile gangs the very kind of attention they crave. Some gangs delight in notoriety. They are annoyed if a rival gang is written up in the newspaper; they outdo themselves to get their delinquency reported in a subsequent issue. Other youngsters, reading these newspaper accounts, may want to share in these exciting experiences. There is a serious defect in the approach that emphasizes only faults, and thus shows young people how bad they can be.

All this emphasis on juvenile delinquency tends to make adults forget that at least 95 per cent of teen-agers are not juvenile delinquents by any legal definition of the term.[1] Of the 5 per cent who are thus classified, about half have committed no serious crime, but have run afoul of the law because of parental neglect, unsuitable home conditions, and association with older delinquents.

WHAT'S RIGHT ABOUT TEEN-AGERS?

Even juvenile delinquents have many fine qualities. They are often loyal, brave, ingenious, energetic. Some of the most troublesome are the smartest. The good things teen-agers do do not make the headlines.

The large majority of teen-agers want to do what is right. They sincerely want to conform to acceptable social and moral standards. They seem willing to accept essential restraints, if

---

[1] Any individual between seven and seventeen years of age who commits even a single act in violation of the law is technically a *delinquent*. A person in this same age group who habitually associates with vicious or immoral persons, is stubborn, runs away from home, etc., is called a wayward child.

adults will help them understand what they are and why they exist. Too much emphasis has been placed on "staying out of trouble," rather than on doing the right thing for the satisfaction it brings. Many youngsters are extraordinarily capable; they finance their own education, contribute to the support of their family, do creative work, engage in service projects. They may well be indignant at the tendency of some adults to generalize about all teen-agers from the lurid accounts of delinquent gangs.

A high school senior named Betsy Evans wrote an article titled "In Defense of My Generation," from which the following excerpts are quoted:

I am 17. Have you raised your eyebrows? Relax. I've never set a fire, robbed a gas station, or beaten a defenseless old man. In fact, I don't even know anyone who has.

But every year a million American teenagers just like me—oh, some a few years younger and some a few years older, some from families a little larger or a little smaller than mine, many from cities bigger than the city I live in and some from towns smaller than mine, but, basically, a million American kids *just like me*—are in trouble with the police.

All this makes very good newspaper and magazine copy. You know the kind of story I mean: "Teenagers Arrested in Riots," "Boy Mob Attacks Beach Party," "Youths Rob, Beat Motorist."

Sure, it's a problem. It's one of the biggest problems facing America today.

But sometimes I wish someone would think of the 95% of us who *aren't* delinquents. Because we're here, too. And we're the ones who will be the scientists and the editors and the clergymen and the statesmen 10 and 20 and 30 years from now. We're the ones who'll be pushing most of the nation's baby carriages and growing its food and selling its shoes and making its automobiles. We're the ones who'll be electing its leaders and filling its churches and, if necessary, fighting its wars.

Our job is to stay on the right track until we reach maturity. . . .

A gang of teenage vandals breaks into a school and destroys books and smashes desks. An average adult reads about it in the newspaper, shakes his head, and says, "What's the younger generation coming to?"

Well, *I* belong to this younger generation. So do my friends. But we didn't break into that school!

Should the vandals who did it be punished? Of course! But why should we be punished with them?

And injustice isn't the only danger. There's that tantalizing power of suggestion.

A boy has a new driver's license. Because he is 16, he figures he must be a reckless driver! What gives him that idea? Why, he has heard the same glib statement over and over again: *all* teenagers are reckless drivers!

Several boys go to a football game together on Friday night. Afterwards they run into a gang from another school, and there's a fight, and someone calls the police. Did those boys want to get in trouble? No, but they felt that teenage fellows are expected to be tough; you see it in the paper every day!

It's a vicious circle. The more that is said about juvenile delinquency, the more it becomes the expected pattern of behavior.

I'm wondering if it would work backwards. I'm wondering whether, if the process were reversed and *good* behavior came to be considered normal, it would become so.

But always there'll be those willing to try. Always there'll be those who go on believing there *can* be a better world, and working to make it come true. We may fail. But maybe we'll succeed.

Well, I haven't taken any surveys or written any books or formed any committees.

But I am 17. I know what our generation needs, what we need more than laws or courts or recreation centers, more than better schools or better entertainment or better discipline—no matter how much we may need all of those.

We need someone to believe in us.[2]

Sensational accounts of teen-age crimes also have an effect on parents; they may disrupt a good parent-child relationship. This lurid publicity may change the parents' attitude toward the child: they may begin to expect the worst of him. Children and adolescents are greatly influenced by the expectations of the people who count most in their lives. A negative parental attitude may evoke anxiety or rebellion on the part of the child.

A comparison of the attitudes of today's teachers with those reported by Wickman in 1928 showed that teachers are still most concerned with the aggressive child, though they are not as oblivious to social and emotional maladjustment as they seemed to be more than twenty-five years ago. They still think of behavior problems as what children do rather than what they fail to do.[3]

FACING THE FACTS ABOUT JUVENILE DELINQUENCY

While taking a positive approach, we still must face the facts of juvenile delinquency. Crimes committed by young people are on the increase. J. Edgar Hoover, Director of the Federal Bureau of Investigation, stated that in a recent year persons under eighteen years of age committed 53.6 per cent of all car thefts,

[2] Elizabeth Evans, "In Defense of My Generation," *National Education Association Journal,* vol. 44 (March, 1955), pp. 139–140.

[3] G. Stauffer and J. Owens, "Behavior Problems of Children as Identified by Today's Teachers and Compared with Those Reported by E. K. Wickman," *Journal of Educational Research,* vol. 48 (January, 1955), pp. 321–331.

49.3 per cent of all burglaries, 18 per cent of all robberies, and 16.2 per cent of all rapes. Increasing numbers of these crimes were committed by children under sixteen years. Why is the number of juvenile delinquents constantly increasing? What does this alarming fact mean? It may mean that young people are becoming immune or accustomed to brutality. It may mean that they have abandoned traditional standards and values, or that they lack examples of considerate conduct and concern for the welfare of others. It certainly means that many young people are "growing up without inner controls on their behavior." Such controls should stem from "a social imagination" that sees "how one's own acts affect others." According to Bertram M. Beck, "It is the failure to produce in the individual youngster a sense of belonging to family and community, and through belonging to the community, to the larger world of which he is a part that is, in essence, the cause of delinquency." [4] His perception of himself and his environment to a great extent determines his behavior.

Sex Delinquency

There are a number of reasons why teen-agers get mixed up about sex. To begin with, many of their elders are perplexed. There is a constant conflict between what adults preach and what they practice. They say one thing and do the opposite. Consequently teen-agers have too few well-adjusted men and women to guide them.

Then, too, youngsters are subjected to erotic stimulation on all sides. Advertisements of all sorts of products employ pictures of women suggestively clothed. TV and movie programs present love songs and love scenes more frequently than any other feature. Juke boxes croon interminably in drugstores and lunch counters. At the same time, young people have too few approved opportunities for expressing affection in nonphysical ways, or for sublimating normal sex impulses.

[4] Bertram M. Beck, "The Nature of the Problem of Delinquency," *Religious Education*, vol. 50 (March–April, 1955), p. 84.

Drinking and Drugs

Drinking is a double-edged problem for many teen-agers. Many of them suffer physically, socially, and psychologically because their parents drink. Two young teen-age girls described home conditions as follows:

My mother is a heavy drinker. When I bring friends to my home she often embarrasses me by using vulgar language. . . .

It seems my parents can't get along very well. This misunderstanding occurs only when both become intoxicated. It starts off with an argument, leads to profane language, then to fighting.

The other side of the problem is the drinking that goes on within the teen-age group. A fifteen-year-old girl described a typical situation: "On the way back from the party some of the gang wanted to go to a roadhouse just to dance, but there was alcoholic beverages being sold there. The gang called me a 'fraidy cat,' so I finally went in. The music wasn't anything but filth which anyone with any culture wouldn't want to waste time listening to."

A gifted sixteen-year-old girl made this mature analysis of the situation:

Then I started observing the other people in my crowd. The more I thought about it, the surer I was that they drink, not because they really like to, but because it gave them a thrill to indulge in something which was thought wrong for teen-agers, and because they didn't want to feel different from the group, as I had felt. I found that teen-agers who drink were not the ones who were respected. I talked it over with several of the other kids in our crowd and I was glad to hear that they shared my views on the subject. . . . I really believe that if every person who drinks would analyze his views on the subject and find out why he does and what he gets out of it, there would be fewer cases of teen-age drinking in America today.

Some adolescents begin by drinking alcoholic beverages and then turn to narcotic drugs to get a bigger kick. "The wild ones are wilder" than they used to be, and it is hard to tell them anything after they have started using drugs. Preaching does not do much good. Sometimes, as in the case of Alcoholics Anonymous, they can help one another conquer a habit.

The attitude of the natural leaders toward this problem is very important. If a popular girl or boy takes a mature point of view such as the one last quoted, he or she may markedly influence the behavior of the group.

Reckless Driving

Teen-age drivers should not all be lumped together. Some are expert mechanics and highly skillful drivers. A bona fide "hot-rodder" takes no chances on a collision that might damage the synthetic model on which he has spent hundreds of dollars and thousands of hours of work. Others are not real "hot-rodders." They are "screwballs," not engineers. They drive junk heaps recklessly and are a menace on the road.

Delinquent Adults

Much juvenile delinquency may be attributed to adult models. We cannot expect adolescents to be more moral than we are. They are watching us. In their behavior they are reflecting us, in exaggerated form perhaps. They do as we do, not as we say.

Adolescents need to have many contacts with people of integrity and kindness. However, radio and television programs, movies, magazines, newspapers, and comic books introduce them to a steady stream of sex-centered men and women, crooks, hypocrites, swindlers, and killers. In many of the mass media of communication the world is presented as full of malice and violence. The impulse to kill is receiving far more stimulation than the desire to be kind. No wonder violence in thoughts and acts is on the increase.

EARLY ORIGINS OF DELINQUENT BEHAVIOR

The roots of delinquency have often been traced to early childhood experiences, especially to parental attitudes and behavior in the early years. In one instance, a panel of experts and teachers were able to predict, with more than 75 per cent accuracy, which second-grade children would later become seriously delinquent.[5] Sheldon and Eleanor Glueck [6] have experimentally established early manifestations of delinquent behavior. The most important positive factors seemed to relate to wholesome identification of the boy with the father, alert supervision of the home by the mother, affection of both parents for the boy, and cohesiveness of the family. They studied 500 persistently delinquent boys, ranging in age from eleven to seventeen. Nearly half of them showed evidence of maladaptation before their eighth year. Their average age at the onset of antisocial behavior was 8.3 years, although their average age on first appearing in court was 12.4. These persistent juvenile delinquents were maladjusted and delinquent children long before they joined gangs.

However, attempts to predict delinquent behavior present many difficulties.[7] Some young people who have court records may have committed less serious acts than others who have escaped detection. Delinquent behavior may be placed on a continuum representing varying degrees of seriousness, persistence, or pervasiveness. Those who end up in a state training school may not be very different from those on probation or those referred to child guidance clinics; it all depends on differences in the intake policies of the institutions and the point of view of the juvenile court judge. Moreover, the causation of delinquency is so complex that a check list or scale fails to capture the dynamic interplay of forces which affect behavior. Many forms of "problem behavior" are normal for children at different stages of their development. Rebellion at fifteen might have been preceded in childhood by extreme and fear-motivated submission at six years of age.

During the elementary and high school years many adoles-

[5] Edwin Powers, "The School's Responsibility for the Early Detection of Delinquency-prone Children," Harvard Educational Review, vol. 19 (March, 1949), pp. 80–86.

[6] Sheldon Glueck and Eleanor Glueck, Delinquents in the Making. New York: Harper & Brothers, 1952.

[7] William C. Kvaraceus, "Prediction Studies of Delinquent Behavior," Personnel and Guidance Journal, vol. 34 (November, 1955), pp. 147–149.

cents do not learn to use their energies and emotions constructively. Adolescents go "haywire" when they let their feelings run
away with them. They have not learned that although they cannot at times help feeling anger, hostility, and sexual impulses,
they do not have to do what their feelings dictate. They need
to learn how to impose limits on their acts and to express their
feelings in socially acceptable ways.

Some uncontrolled behavior may be traced to a misunderstanding of the "permissiveness" of well-meaning parents and
teachers. To some parents, and youngsters too, "permissiveness"
seems to mean "passivity"—never interfering with anything the
child does. In a completely laissez-faire atmosphere, we cannot
expect the child to grow in inner control and self-discipline.

CONDITIONS AND CHARACTERISTICS CONDUCIVE TO JUVENILE DELINQUENCY

By comparing 500 delinquents with 500 nondelinquents
matched as to age, ethnic derivation, general intelligence, and
residence in underprivileged urban neighborhoods, the Gluecks [8]
were able to describe the environmental conditions and personal
characteristics that differentiated the two groups. Their findings
correspond closely with the results of other studies,[9] and the
factors thus discovered will now be discussed.

Neighborhood Conditions

It is well known that the percentage of juvenile delinquency
is much higher in some neighborhoods than in others. In large
cities, delinquency is high in certain slum sections, but there may
also be delinquent areas in towns and in rural communities. The
underlying factor seems to be not geographical location per se,
but economic level, which in turn is associated with overcrowd-

[8] Glueck and Glueck, *op. cit.*
[9] William Healy and Augusta F. Bronner, "What Makes a Child Delinquent?" *Juvenile Delinquency and the Schools*, Forty-seventh Yearbook of
the National Society for the Study of Education, part I, chap. II, pp. 39–
47. Chicago: University of Chicago Press, 1948.

ing, poor family relations, below-average intelligence, and anti-social values and standards.

Home Conditions

The families of delinquents were more frequently character-ized by mental retardation, emotional disturbance, drunkenness, and criminality than were the families of nondelinquents. The father was likely to need financial aid because of failure to as-sume responsibility as the breadwinner, rather than because of economic depression or seasonal unemployment. A much lower proportion of fathers of delinquents had good work habits. The home was marked by poor management and inefficient routine. The parents were less self-respecting and less ambitious to im-prove their social and economic status. They had lower stand-ards of conduct. They had poor relationships with their children, maintained little supervision of them, and made meager pro-visions for their recreation. The delinquents received little warmth and affection from their parents, brothers, and sisters; the delinquent boys did not develop a wholesome identification with their fathers. The delinquents received more severe physical punishment from their parents, especially from their fathers. The families were slightly larger, and the homes more likely to be unstable or broken. It is clear, the Gluecks stated, that the most vital roots of character development are in the home and in the parent-child relation.

School Conditions

Delinquents shifted from one school to another more fre-quently than nondelinquents. Twice as many were two or more years retarded, and showed more dislike of subjects that involved logic, reasoning, and persistency. Their educational attainments were far below those of the nondelinquents; they had less desire to continue school and had given less thought to plans for the future. The delinquents had a poor relationship with their school-mates, and persistently misbehaved, often seriously, before pu-berty. No one, with the exception of parents, has a better opportunity to stem the rising tide of delinquency than elementary and high school administrators, teachers, and counselors.

Students often discipline themselves. One aggressive senior high school student was excessively argumentative in class. He would often disagree with the instructor, who took a permissive attitude toward him. This approach enabled the class to become more aware of the boy's aggressiveness, and they firmly but kindly corrected his errors. They did this consistently in class until his aggressiveness was modified. One day he started to make an exaggerated claim; then he stopped suddenly, apparently catching sight of himself as others viewed him, and said humorously, "Famous last words!"

Work Experience

Both delinquent and nondelinquent groups had after-school jobs, but the delinquents more often did jobs like peddling and bootblacking that exposed them to the influences of the street. Fewer of the delinquents were required to help their families financially.

Leisure Activities and Companions

A much higher percentage of the delinquents expressed a desire for adventurous activities. They were generally restless. They wanted excitement. They attended the movies three or more times weekly, as compared with the once-a-week attendance of the nondelinquents. More of the delinquents were in the habit of stealing rides, roaming the streets after dark, staying up late. Ninety per cent of the delinquents, as compared with 23 per cent of the nondelinquents, began to smoke at an early age; 29 per cent as against 0.4 per cent began to drink in their early teens. Many more of the delinquents sneaked into movies, engaged in destructive mischief, ran away from home, "bunked out," gambled, and set fires. A much larger percentage of the nondelinquents spent leisure time at home and on playgrounds.

The majority of both groups were not "girl-minded," but a higher percentage of the delinquents sought the companionship of girls and had engaged in various forms of sex delinquency.

Nine out of ten youngsters of both groups had at some time participated in settlement house or other supervised recreational programs, but the delinquents attended less regularly and twice as many expressed dislike or contempt for organized recreation. Fewer delinquents (four in ten) attended church once a week.

Physical Appearance and Health

In half of the body measurements, the delinquents showed superiority. They were more stocky in build; nondelinquents were more slender. Delinquents were more harmonious in physique, and were as healthy as nondelinquents. They also had a lower proportion of neurological handicaps.

Mental Ability

The average intelligence of 5,925 institutionalized juvenile delinquents was 82.4 IQ; [10] their IQs ranged from 30 to 150. The delinquents showed more deficiency on the vocabulary, information, and comprehension sections of intelligence tests. Their generalizations were more likely to be closely related to concrete realities, though they were often unrealistic thinkers and unmethodical in their approach to the mastery of mental problems. Intellectually competent adolescents may become delinquent. These youngsters are often expressing hostile feelings toward themselves or their environment. In their histories we often find parental "neglect, inconsistency and/or cruelty, with evidence that they could neither feel secure within that early environment nor place their trust in any future relationship. Their consistent emotional detachment from parent figures distinguishes their behavior from that of other groups." [11] If church, school, or other community agencies had even partially met their needs for ac-

[10] Mary B. Owen, "The Intelligence of the Institutionalized Juvenile Delinquent," *Journal of Juvenile Research,* vol. 21 (October, 1937), pp. 199–204.

[11] Irwin M. Marcus, "The Problem of Evaluation," *The Adolescent Exceptional Child,* Proceedings of the 1954 Spring Conference of the Woods Schools, p. 13. Langhorne, Pa.: The Woods Schools, 1954.

ceptance, affection, and a sense of belonging they might have overcome their early emotional handicaps.

Personality Traits

Delinquents, though less stable emotionally than nondelinquents, are more dynamic and energetic, more aggressive, adventurous, suggestible, and stubborn. They are more inclined to be impulsive—to act out emotional tensions and difficulties rather than think them out. They are far more defiant of social custom, far less submissive to authority. They are markedly less cooperative, more suspicious of the motives of others, more on the defensive, less dependent on others. On the positive side, the delinquents seem to have fewer feelings of anxiety, insecurity, helplessness, fear of failure or defeat.

Those who violate the law are more self-centered, and more destructively sadistic. Their traits and tendencies in general are those which are unfavorable to wholesome social adjustment. Their pattern is consistently that of the uninhibited, unreflective, undisciplined child.

Social development is not a simple problem. It is tied up with the individual's concept of himself and his feelings of adequacy as a person. When the emotionally disturbed adolescent tries to cope with his environment by means of anti-social behavior, he is seldom understood. People consider him "willfully bad." He usually does not understand why he behaves as he does; it is the only way he has learned to deal with a threatening or frustrating situation. By limiting his behavior to these self-damaging defensive responses, he blocks "further emotional, intellectual, and social maturation. In other words, the neurotic adolescent limits his adaptability and flexibility for growth." [12]

There are few educational provisions for the disturbed adolescent. "We are willing to pay fifteen billion dollars annually to correct the delinquency of adolescents and young adults, but only spend one quarter of this sum on public education." [13]

[12] *Ibid.,* p. 12.
[13] *Loc. cit.*

Some juvenile delinquents are psychopathic personalities who use any methods to get what they want, who do not learn from experience, who know no loyalty, and who show no genuine remorse for their acts.

Perception of Their Environment

Much less information has been obtained as to how adolescents perceive their relationships and environmental conditions. A home that looks "bad" to the outsider may seem "good" to a child; it may embody some relationship which he cherishes, some person whom he loves. Moreover, different children will respond in different ways to the same kind of pressure. How they respond depends not only on the way in which they perceive the home situation, but also on their goals and purposes, and on their "emotional tensile strength"—the degree to which they can tolerate frustration.

ADOLESCENTS' VIEWS OF JUVENILE DELINQUENCY AND DISCIPLINE

What are adolescents' views of juvenile delinquency? What do they think are the reasons why children and young people "go wrong"? The reasons they give are similar to those turned up by extensive studies of juvenile delinquents: they mention faulty family relationships much more frequently than housing conditions, being on relief, or other physical and economic conditions. They point to parents who do not seem to care what becomes of their children, who do not know where they go at night, who quarrel and fight, who are unreasonably strict, who expect the worst of them. Sometimes they make allowances for parents; one said, "We should try to understand our parents, too." If we look at the problem through their eyes, we see it more vividly and intimately than in the reports of adults.

Various Viewpoints

They recognize individual differences among adolescents—differences in conduct ranging from serious delinquency to constructive civic-mindedness. This is the view expressed by a senior high school girl:

Some would act like adults. They reach a state where they defy authority. They act according to their beliefs. I guess that that's why we have so much Juvenile Delinquency. They wouldn't listen to their parents or guardians, they just do what they think is right. I'm sure they all have the same crazy thoughts.

On the other hand there are kids that at the age of fifteen act more like grown ups than a person of twenty-five. They have great ideas to help their community and instead of joining gangs they join clubs, school activities, and other activities that are worthwhile.

They vividly describe parental neglect and its consequences. The following analysis was made by a high school girl from a delinquent area of a large city where teen-age crime had been given much publicity:

Some times a parent neglect his or her child, by going to work and having just enough time to fix dinner. Maybe the child asks the mother a question and she would reply "Don't bother me I am to busy for you." That is what I mean by neglecting your child. By not telling him or her right from wrong. Well of couse the child doesn't know. He will get his knowledge from the street, and that's no place to get knowledge from. Because in the street you meet all kinds of people. For all we know he might meet some bad fellow and he will start staying out late probably, he will start drinking or he might go in for drugs, because there is so much dope going around now-a-days, and being under the influence of it he won't be able to help him-self, and this may lead to stealing and a lot of other things. He will stop going to school or when he does go to school he would cut his classes or if asked a question, he would frighten his teacher. Well the best way to stop Juvenile Delinquency is to work with the child, help him to the best of your ability; be a pal to your child, if he or she has troubles try to work them out with the children. Another cause of Juvenile delinquency is that the boy and girl have a lot of time on their hands and they do not know what to do with it. Make sure your child goes to church regularly, so that he can get on the side of God. It is very good to have faith in God, and you will never go wrong. I feel that each and every parent should observe the child's behavior and should know how to approach her child. They should take part in the parent-teacher meetings and go to them regularly.

This girl attributed juvenile delinquency to parents who neither knew nor cared about their child's activities. She wanted understanding parents in whom she could confide, who would encourage and supervise her social contacts.

In the same family, one boy may become delinquent and another not. Delinquency in the family is hard on the other members. We seldom get the picture from the nondelinquent's point of view, as in the following composition written by a seventeen-year-old boy:

I have seen many boys and girls my age with difficult problems both at home and at school. Some are very brokenhearted or ashamed at social events because a brother or sister or even the parent has become drunk and is making a fool of himself. I for one have a brother, whom I am not ashamed of or worried about, but I feel that I am responsible to a certain extent for his actions because I am his older brother. I have talked to him on the subject of drinking but he thinks it is smart and has become very popular because he has a "hot roadster."

I know that when he becomes intoxicated he is a madman at the wheel of a car, no matter whose car it may be, because I happned to be in his "hot rod" one night coming home from a party. We were doing a good fifty through a very winding rough road. He was drunk and driving with three other boys in the car. We hit a tree after going into a side spin a couple of times. He nearly killed all of us plus mashing the side of the car in. I was thrown about ten feet out of the car and down into a raveen. If the tree hadn't been there, we would have gone down the raveen and the car on top of us.

He also has quit school and is hanging around with the wrong crowd. My parents have tried about everything and are sick with worry.

They perceive gangs as a means of gaining independence. Once in a gang, they accept its standards and values, even though doing so gets them into trouble. The following account was written by a member of a street gang:

One night I was with a gang of fellows, fooling around and making a lot of noise. A lady yelled out of a window of a house across the street from where we were standing, that she was going to phone the police if we didn't move. We didn't; she did. In about ten minutes we saw the cop car coming up the street, and we ran. One of the officers got out of the car and was hot on our trail. Boy, he was fast. Finally he caught up to us and got two of the fellows by the back of the neck and threw them into the back of the car. Another fellow and myself who thought we had eluded them, cut through a lot to the next block, and were caught just as the patrol car was turning the corner. We were obliged to go to the police station. The worst of it was that we were kept there till one o'clock at night. The next week we had to go to court and were put on probation for six weeks.

Even though they know the consequences of the gang's wild behavior, they feel honor-bound to do what the gang decides. In adult-sponsored groups, their behavior would be in accord rather than in conflict with ethical standards. We might say it is a delinquent town that provides no wholesome work and recreation for its young people, and a delinquent school that does not provide work suitable for adolescents, and help its students develop standards and values as to the best use of their free time.

Attitudes toward Adult Control

Adolescents have significant ideas as to how behavior problems should be handled. Looking at adult control now from their viewpoint, we realize that various kinds of punishment have different meanings to different individuals with different backgrounds. Preadolescents from lower socio-economic levels are inclined to accept corporal punishment as a means of "teaching one a lesson." One twelve-year-old girl wrote: "The perfect punishment for me is to give me a good licking." In her environment, a licking was the accepted means of punishing disobedience, and the child apparently perceived it as a parent's way of helping her to do what is right. Older adolescents tend to resent both scolding and physical punishment. One seventeen-year-old girl of foreign background and very low socio-economic status analyzed the discipline situation in this way:

To start with, as I said before, I have always been a bad girl. The more my mother spanked and scolded me, the more bad things I would do. That is the worst thing to do, spank or scold a child. If my mother would have sat down and told me "Don't do that for this or that reason," I am sure I would not have done it. Even worse than a spanking is scolding. I don't know why a scolding makes me just go ahead and do the wrong thing again. I realize that grown-ups say, "Well, why should I sit down and explain?" Well, people are wrong. If they only knew that having a heart to heart talk with a child is far better than scolding or spanking us! [14]

Older adolescents prefer to "talk with" parents or teachers; they want to discuss why certain behavior is not socially acceptable. This method was described by a seventeen-year-old girl from a socially superior home background:

I can remember the time I went to a party. It was a Saturday night. I was supposed to be home by 12 P.M. But as the time went by very fast, I stayed later. When I arrived home my father was waiting for me. He wasn't angry, but quite upset, because I didn't call him and let him know I would be home later. Then he would have met me. My father didn't punish me by beating or by making me stay home the rest of the week. He talked with me and explained why he was worried about my arriving home late at night and un-escorted at that time. I felt very much ashamed of myself for worry-ing him and not having enough sense to know my father should be notified first before I myself make a decision to stay later than agreed. If I had asked to stay longer, my father most likely would have granted my wish. I'll never worry my father again as I am engaged now and have an escort to take me home, one whom my father trusts completely. And on school nights, I am home early. [15]

Adolescents do not expect complete permissiveness. Neither do they want to be dominated by adults. They are positive about these two extremes. Moreover, they do not want to be entirely

[14] Ruth Strang, "What Discipline Means to Adolescents," *The Nervous Child,* vol. 9 (March, 1951), p. 142.

[15] *Ibid.,* p. 143.

on their own. In times of crisis they need parents or other adults in whom they can confide. What they want is a middle ground of reasonableness. They want to experiment sometimes; they want a chance to work out their problems by themselves. They want to be treated mostly as adults, but not entirely. If they make mistakes or change their minds, they feel that they should be allowed some consideration on account of their age.

Young adolescents need limits. Firm, reasonable limits help them to feel secure. They feel free to venture because they know they will not go too far. The limits will vary with the environment. Staying out after dark may be permitted in a safe community, but forbidden in a dangerous section of a city. Limitations like this may be broadened as adults work together to make the community a wholesome place for young people to grow up.

If an adult is too strict, if he insists upon dominating the young adolescent, regulating his time, selecting his friends, he may get submission now, and violent rebellion later. Or, in some cases, the youngster, who is struggling within himself to be independent, may relinquish the struggle and relapse into the submissiveness of childhood.

On the other hand, if parents are overpermissive, the young adolescent may make mistakes that are irreparable. He may also get the impression that his parents do not care enough about him to help him make the best of himself. We find this feeling expressed in many adolescent compositions.

DELINQUENT TEEN-AGE GANGS

The adolescent population has its rougher side. You meet this side in the teen-age gangs that deal in dope, sex delinquency, and violence. Some of these teen-age gangs are unbelievably brutal and callous. They are cruel to one another as well as to members of rival gangs. To these boys, girls mean only one thing—sex. Most of them drink; some are drug addicts. An excellent description by Kramer and Karr [16] of teen-age gangs and

[16] Dale Kramer and Madeline Karr, *Teen-age Gangs*. New York: Henry Holt and Company, Inc., 1953.

their leaders is a composite picture based on sociological study and observation by settlement house workers who mingled with street gangs in an effort to bring their natural leaders into constructive leadership activities. Members of the limited number of gangs of this kind include drug addicts, adolescents who have become embittered by childhood experiences, vicious characters who are tough and proud of it. There are also weak characters who are subservient to the will of the gang. Once one is a member, it is difficult to pull out; the member fears that he will get beaten up if he tries to withdraw. The leaders, likewise, hesitate to leave their followers in the lurch.

The arguments of youth workers against gang warfare are of little avail against the members' fear of being called either of two names—"chicken," meaning coward, or still worse, "punk," which indicates both worthlessness and cowardice. Yet the worker knows that the gang may be reluctant to fight for a number of reasons: they may be taken in by the police; they may be beaten severely at home; they may have to go back to school; they may be compelled to stay home at night; or they may be put on probation. If they are already on probation, they may be sent straight to jail or to a reform school. The gang leader may agree that these are possible consequences of gang warfare. But his answer is, "If we don't fight, we're 'chicken.' It's just as simple as that."

The only thing the youth worker can do is to suggest a fair fight instead of a *rumble*—an all-out gang war. If he has a chance to talk with the leader, and if the leader has considerable influence with his gang, the worker may succeed in keeping it a fair fight. But since there are no controls, and since the members may be keyed up with dope, anything may happen.

Gangs have natural leaders who have some admirable qualities. There is a chance of reaching them, of channeling their energy in the right direction. Youth leaders try. But they often fail because the pull of the gang is stronger than what they have to offer in their organized groups.

The following is an account of a settlement-house worker's

success with the leader of a street gang, some of whose members had become interested in an art class:

Blackie came to the House simply to recover his gang. The gang consisted of seven ragged urchins who were busy pounding clay into rocket ships. He slouched his way into the room, took a big piece of clay from the can, and began clawing it to pieces without speaking to anyone and without looking at the clay. After five minutes or so he slammed the clay back into the box and then walked up to me.

"My brother's in the State Pen! I'm gonna meet *you* in the alley by the factory up there when you get outa here, an' ya better be there! Come on, you jerks."

Blackie turned from his ultimatum and walked *out the window.* Five boys followed him. I watched them run to the end of each fire ladder and ride it down to the next level. Finally they reached the last one and jumped to the street. As they ran I thought to myself: What should I do? If I didn't meet Blackie I would lose my whole group. If I did meet him and there was any real trouble I would lose my job as well as the group. I decided to meet him and shock him out of his purpose to beat me up. It seemed to me there was only this one way to do this job because of the immediate nature of his action.

I came to the end of the alley on my way to the streetcar and saw him standing slouched against the wall chewing on an old cigarette butt. Before he could get set to fight I spoke to him.

"Blackie, shut up and listen a minute. Did you know that I wrestled here for the north side championship?"

"No."

His eyes narrowed, but his sureness faded perceptibly.

"Well, I did. I wrestled in the Army, too. Blackie, you wouldn't have a chance with me. I could break your fingers and leave you lying in this alley while your gang watched from that fence over there. But if you're smart you'll walk down the alley with me, and *we'll be friends.*"

He hesitated, with a limpness showing all over him.

"Come on, Blackie, I'll walk you home. Where do you live?"

Blackie didn't say anything. He turned slowly with a sidelong glance at the fence and walked with me down the darkening alley.

We took other walks after that. He would wait for me to come out after the classes and we would walk to the streetcar. He wanted to know all about wrestling. He came to the class a lot, too. The gang came with him. Blackie kept his place with the gang, and I kept my place with the class.

This "gang" had a show of drawings and clay work in the library a few months later. A lot of the parents came who had never been inside the settlement house before.

Delinquent gangs of teen-age girls, while relatively few in number, are becoming a cause for concern. In recent years, some adolescent girls twelve to fifteen years old, even as young as ten, have resorted to fist fighting, kicking, and using knives. Among delinquent girls there seems to be "a new and growing minority dedicated to violence." Their reason for fighting is that it's the thing to do—"You're supposed to settle an argument with a fight." If you don't, you are called "chicken." Their pent-up emotions flare up at the slightest provocation. A small group can terrorize a school.

Instead of gaining the independence he desires, an adolescent or preadolescent who joins a gang may become overdependent on the gang. He is unable to assert his own values, unable to rebel against group standards which threaten his own integrity. Individual standards vanish under the influence of group psychology. As one of a gang, he does destructive things which he would never do as an individual. His good judgment is washed away by a wave of mass violence. He seems to be totally unable to resist it.

Sometimes group opinion decrees that everyone shall turn against a particular member; then, no one in the group, not even his former friends, dares to be friendly with him. They find they must do what is popular at all costs. We have no techniques for helping children "see that identification [with the group] cannot be carried to the point where it means giving up all their own values and judgments under the stress of mass excitement." [17]

[17] Fritz Redl, "Are Parents Worrying about the Wrong Things," *Child Study,* vol. 30 (Summer, 1953), p. 47.

Nevertheless, the gang meets many of an adolescent's needs—the need for friends, approval of his peers, outlets for his expendable energy, and ways to use his leisure time. "Because our boys and girls have so much free time . . . and because they are thrown so much on their own, they have increasing opportunities and increasing needs to form play groups, cliques, and gangs. Indeed, these groups probably represent the most meaningful part of the child's social world." [18]

The problem is "to channel children's energy into constructive activities." The alternative to calling the police to break up teenage gangs is for adult neighbors to form organizations to keep their boys and girls out of trouble. Such neighborhood committees have been formed in Chicago (the Chicago Area Project), in Quincy, Illinois, and in other cities. The members of a committee make casual, friendly contacts with a gang; they may appoint a part-time worker for a "hard-to-reach" group. For example, in one situation the young worker hung around street corners with the group, played games with them, took them to see baseball and football games, encouraged them to form a club. He involved parents and other interested adults. Gradually the youngsters came to participate in the activities of the recreation center and the church groups in the neighborhood. Public parks and other agencies cooperated in providing leisure-time activities. Other citizen groups have built summer camps and youth centers. The central idea of this approach is that of neighbors working together to build better people in better communities, appealing to young people's pride in neighborhood life, to their sense of responsibility and self-respect, and to their need for approval and friendly association.

A FEW WAYS OF COMBATING JUVENILE DELINQUENCY

Some minor delinquent episodes may, as Fritz Redl and James S. Plant have pointed out, be a blessing in disguise. They tell us

[18] Clifford R. Shaw and Anthony Sorrentino, "Is 'Gang-busting' Wise?" *National Parent-Teacher*, vol. 50 (January, 1956), p. 19.

that changes in adults' attitudes or in environmental conditions need to be made, before it is too late.

In addition, much general preventive work can be done. During the preadolescent and adolescent years, the experience of enjoying wholesome teen-age recreation is most important. If young people get sufficient satisfaction from this, it will be easier for them to resist the lure of delinquent activities later on. In addition to attempts to make fundamental improvements in home and community life, in adult standards and values, and in educational offerings, there have been many special efforts to prevent and treat juvenile delinquency which have proved effective.

Youth Referral Boards

Many organizations help children and young adolescents before they get into real trouble. One worried mother went to a youth referral board for help with her early-maturing daughter. She said:

I feel as though I am a complete failure as a parent, as far as Marian is concerned. She has been a problem both at school and at home. She is tall and has an exceptionally winning personality. She smokes, is a truant at school, disobedient, and worst of all dishonest. My husband (Marian's stepfather) and I are stymied as to what to try next to come up with a solution. She takes both guitar and piano lessons, and although she is interested, she does not practice. Two weeks before summer camp closed we were requested to take her home because of smoking. All this was climaxed last October when Marian, who had turned twelve that week, and a thirteen-year-old ran away from home. They were gone three days and although the Missing Persons Bureau had issued a thirteen-state alarm, it was the cold weather that drove them home. They had camped in a deserted house in a near-by state.

The worker at the Youth Referral Board tried to find out the cause of Marian's behavior. Marian told her that she loved her mother and was lucky to have a good stepfather and father. She said she was unhappy because she did things she didn't want to do and made us unhappy. The worker at the Youth Referral Board has referred the case to a social agency to obtain further assistance from a psychiatric social worker.

The case history of Marian illustrates the early origin of adolescent behavior problems. From the preschool years on, she had
shown behavior problems which were intensified by her early
physiological maturity and by her parents' divorce. Since the
mother wrote the above letter, the family has moved from the
city to the suburbs. This change in residence, plus the counseling
service of the social work agency, seems to have helped Marian
to make a much better adjustment. It is exceedingly important
for a potential delinquent to have a warm, constructive relationship with some adult. When there are no parents to play this
role, a counselor, social worker, Scout leader, or other person
outside the family can often help.

The Youth Board in New York City employs trained social
workers to join gangs and try to divert their activities into socially useful channels.

"Big Brother" and "Big Sister" Movements

The "Big Brother" movement is well known. More recent in
origin are the "Big Sisters." A branch of this organization can
easily be established in any city, town, or county. Certain women
in the community volunteer to become Big Sisters. They are then
given training by a professional social worker. After this orientation to the work, they may be called on by a parent or relative,
school principal, or judge to help some young girl. Girls are referred for petty thievery, for running away, for going with bad
companions and gangs of delinquents, and for sexual and other
serious offenses. The Big Sister meets the Little Sister once a
week for some shared activity in which the youngster is interested—cooking, having lunch together, going to the circus, visiting a museum. During these activities, there is opportunity for
conversation. This may be the first time the girl has had a friend
she can trust and respect. Two girls in the same family may be
referred together. This is often desirable because giving special
attention to one sister may arouse rivalry in the other.

The aim of the Big Sisters is to establish a constructive relation
with a girl before she has gone far on the path to delinquency.
This organization also plans group activities that will help chil-

dren make friends in a better neighborhood than that in which they live.

The Youth Authority

Another sound approach to juvenile delinquency has been made by the California Youth Authority. Its emphasis is on gaining an understanding of each serious problem case committed to the Center. This is done by means of a thorough psychological, psychiatric, medical, social, and educational study of each youth. On the basis of this study a program is planned specifically for the individual. Thus he gets off to a good start by being successful in work he is able to do. The many youngsters who need remedial instruction are given this service. Other avenues of learning are provided for those who cannot profit by the usual school curriculum. Youth Authority forest camps provide healthful work experience for nonacademic youth. Guidance is provided through the small-unit cottage organization. The goal of the program is to help young people adjust to community life; in a period of four weeks, problems of adjustment to home and work are considered realistically.

The "Task-force Approach"

An experiment in a "high delinquency area" of New York City combined the efforts of landlords, tenants, the Departments of Buildings, Health and Welfare, Police, and other city departments, a very fine settlement house, and the public school in the neighborhood. The settlement house workers coordinated the project, made personal visits and interpreted the project to all the families involved. The landlords made necessary repairs; the tenants kept the building clean; jobs for the unemployed were found; and help was obtained from the city's health clinics. The community spirit engendered led to a new way of life, conducive to good citizenship rather than to delinquency.

The Public School Teacher

No agency has so great a potential for developing civic competence and preventing delinquency as does the public school teacher. In the early years of elementary school, the teacher can recognize behavior trends that may later lead to delinquency. More important, he can help each pupil to develop a positive self-concept through tasks in which he can discover his abilities and find satisfaction in service and friendship.

To help a boy or girl who has already started on the road to delinquency is more difficult. The process by which one school teacher accomplished this task is effectively presented in the film "Passion for Life." In this film the teacher's philosophy was expressed in the words, "to find the soul behind each face."

Finding children at the crossroads, many teachers, by skillful teaching, by an attitude of positive expectancy, and by warm constructive relationships, have deflected delinquent tendencies into good citizenship. In delinquency, as the Gluecks so well expressed it, "We are dealing not with predestination but with destination." In many cases these children may be helped to take a different road of life if they have effective guidance early enough. With preadolescents and adolescents this would involve knowing the potentialities of each individual and providing the experiences he needs—experiences in which he can succeed and through which he can win the approval of the persons who count most in his life. In some cases this may require group therapy and work with the parents.

Real Work to Do

"Satan finds mischief for idle hands to do" is a more pertinent saying today than it was several generations ago when adolescents had much more real work to do. A Superior Court judge observed that much of the serious delinquency he had seen was associated with idleness.[19]

Young people want real jobs, not "busy work" or "made jobs." Is it not possible for parents and adolescents, teachers and adolescents, to be partners in worthwhile undertakings? What can young people do today that will seem worthwhile to them? They have abundant energy; they are "rarin' to go." When there is an

---

[19] William G. Long, "Let's Put Our Teen-agers to Work," *American Magazine*, vol. 160 (October, 1955), p. 17.

emergency, they rise to the occasion. In fact, as one youngster said, "I *like* emergencies."

The daily home duties of grass to be cut, snow to be shoveled, beds to be made, and marketing to be done are less appealing and seem less urgent than farm chores—cows to be milked and fruit to be harvested. Cars to be washed and kept in good running order and radios to be repaired hold more appeal for mechanically minded boys. Their attitude depends on the significance the task holds for them and the satisfaction and fellowship associated with it.

Ferguson [20] described a number of work projects in which young people have engaged. Five Middle Western youngsters successfully took over the running of a home and farm after the death of their parents. A juvenile court judge sentenced three boys "to plant a thousand trees each as a punishment for starting a forest fire." Following are some constructive projects that have been carried on by adolescents:

Landscaping the schoolgrounds

Doing odd jobs that need to be done in a neighborhood—painting, cleaning out basements, distributing leaflets, etc.

Planting trees where young trees are needed

[20] Charles W. Ferguson, "What Enterprising Youth Can Do," *National Parent-Teacher*, vol. 50 (January, 1956), pp. 4–7.

Helping neighbors who are blind or sick

Completing a high school building

Making a city directory

Canning surplus foods during the summer for the school-lunch program

Raising money for a children's home, recreation center, or other community need

Sponsoring classes or groups in other parts of our country or other lands, exchanging ideas with them, and sending needed supplies

The 4-H Clubs and Future Farmers of America are well known for their constructive projects that bring parents and their children closer to each other. Another organization, Junior Achievement, is sponsored by businessmen. The members learn simple business plans and procedures as they work together in miniature corporations.

The "marginal youth"—those who have left school in their middle teens—are more difficult to contact than those still in school and college. Most of the existing school programs are unsuitable for them, and employment opportunities for those who have not acquired marketable vocational skills are meager. Their interests, attitudes, and activities during periods of depression have been quite extensively studied. The picture is one of "no place to go, nothing to do," and a general inertia or inability to find constructive ways of using their time. These young people have potentialities which could be developed through suitable education and work experiences.

Counseling and Psychotherapy

Some juvenile delinquents are so emotionally disturbed that it is not enough to give them work in which they can succeed, recreation that is enjoyable and meets their developmental needs, and counseling that promotes the discovery and development of their best selves. All these are most important, but the individual needs more expert help in directing his unacceptable drives "into socially acceptable, psychologically constructive paths." [21]

[21] Irene M. Josselyn, *The Adolescent and His World*, p. 96. New York: Family Service Association of America, 1952.

EMOTIONAL PROBLEMS OF GROWING UP

Delinquent behavior is only one way in which adolescents cope with situations in which their basic needs are not being met. Instead of meeting frustration by hurting people or destroying property, they may withdraw from people, give up trying, escape into daydreaming, rationalize by saying that they do not want the things they have been unsuccessfully striving for, develop physical symptoms, or relapse into childish behavior which brought satisfaction in the past. They may also turn their feelings of hostility inward against themselves.

Or, they may face the frustrating situation constructively by changing conditions that can be changed, accepting conditions that are unalterable at present, and working toward more attainable goals. Instead of acting impulsively, they may learn to more often "act on thinking." Thus when they are confronted with a difficulty, they try harder to overcome it, find other ways to accomplish the same purpose, or turn their attention to things they can do successfully. The emotionally stable adolescent meets the demands of a fairly favorable environment without excessive anxiety and tension. He accepts his feelings, and realizes, for example, that intelligent rebellion against an overpossessive or overprotective adult is a necessary part of growing up. He is not afraid of his emotions and realizes that mild emotion has a tonic effect; it has the positive value of stimulating constructive effort.

Apathy may be more difficult to deal with than rebellion. A thorough study of eighteen-year-old men in England found them to be physically fit but emotionally insecure. They were apathetic, and seemed to get little satisfaction from either work or leisure. This picture contrasts vividly with the prevalent notion of restless youth eager to explore and experiment. "These 18-year-olds, however, must be seen against a background of war and threat of war, anxiety and confusion in moral standards." [22]

[22] R. F. L. Logan and E. M. Goldberg, "Rising Eighteen in a London Suburb. A Study of Some Aspects of the Life and Health of Young Men," *British Journal of Sociology*, vol. 4 (December, 1953), pp. 323–345.

How They View Their Emotions

It has been reported in various studies that adolescents emphasize the difficulty of controlling their emotions, especially the emotion of anger. High school freshmen mentioned most frequently physical fears such as darkness, high places, water, and cars as causes of accidents; second, personal inadequacy. Girls still admit having many fears—of snakes and other animals, of being followed on the street, of going down a dark street, of reciting in class. Although many boys have overcome some of their worries by the time they enter college, they admit being increasingly concerned about money, personal appearance, self-consciousness, and getting a job. College girls mention the same worries, except for concern over appearance, which in their case reached a peak during the high school years. From about fifteen to eighteen years of age, girls report more emotional symptoms than boys. Commitments to mental hospitals in one state were almost ten times as numerous for the age period from fifteen to nineteen as for the years from ten to fourteen.[23]

In their compositions, adolescents are more likely to describe their feelings than to analyze their situation and discuss how they might handle it. In some instances they express considerable hostility toward their parents, but they seldom describe the instability and emotional disorganization so often attributed to adolescence. Either they are not aware of experiencing an emotional upheaval, or they cannot verbalize about it, or they take it for granted, or it does not actually exist in the degree which adults assume. However, some youngsters do feel it in all its alleged intensity. This is how one teen-age girl described her feeling of not being loved and accepted:

I am a person who has a constant desire to be loved and respected. The probable cause of this, in my opinion, is that everyone has always held such high hopes for me and I feel compelled to live up to them. To me, it is a serious problem that I cannot be the genius

[23] Lawrence K. Frank, "Introduction: Adolescence as a Period of Transition," *Adolescence,* Forty-third Yearbook of the National Society for the Study of Education, part I, p. 5. Chicago: University of Chicago Press, 1944.

my father wants or the beauty that would give a great deal of pleasure to my mother. They love me, naturally, but I have a great desire to prove to them that even if I'm not ravishingly beautiful or brilliant, I am admired for my rather passable intelligence, my mannerisms, and that I am *loved* and *respected*.

No one realizes my imperfections more clearly than I. But a remark like "Why don't you understand the chemistry? It's so simple" or even a slight criticism from my mother about the way I look is not received well. I'm very fortunate in that I have developed surface poise. Outwardly very few people (only those who know me well) notice any signs of being ill at ease; at a party, where no one is dancing with me, it causes me mental anguish in itself but I also worry about what people are thinking. The combination of the two makes me very ill at ease; I don't know what to do with myself, my inner poise vanishes completely. I am thinking, "This is awful, I am not loved and respected." The things I do in this situation are eating, leaning over the piano, walking around—anything not to look like a forlorn puppy.

There are many causes for turmoil in this "in-between" stage. The struggle for independence becomes intensified as changes in bodily form imply adult status. All kinds of opportunities are opening up at the same time that all sorts of restrictions are being imposed. A certain amount of "transitional anxiety" is inevitable and not entirely undesirable. If not too intense, it may motivate adolescents' personality development.

In many instances adolescents behave in an emotional manner because they have learned no other way of coping with the overpowering problems which confront them. In some environments this is the only way they can get the experiences they need. One teen-age girl, who came from a neurotic family, said, "I know it's childish to have temper tantrums but that's the only way I can get any normal social life." Extensive observation of adolescents led Fritz Redl to remark, "In adolescence there is a good deal of behavior that looks as though it were plain disorganization, but which is largely just emancipation acrobatics." [24] Behavior which seems unpredictable or unreasonable may have an underlying consistency. For example, a girl may one day ob-

[24] Redl, *op. cit.*, p. 8.

ject to any suggestion her mother may make, and the next day become just as angry when her mother tells her to decide for herself. The underlying motivation in both instances may be a desire to show her independence by disagreeing with anything that her mother proposed.

Responses to Frustration

In their compositions, many adolescents describe their responses to frustrating situations such as those mentioned at the beginning of this section. Some youngsters move against people and destroy things; they react with aggressive behavior directed outward. Such behavior seldom solves the problem, although it may temporarily relieve the tension. If the aggressive impulse can be channeled in some positive direction, then remorse at having harmed someone or something is not added to the original frustration.

Sometimes the aggressive impulse is turned inward against oneself. One may assume the role of the suffering hero, or feel worthless and of no account. In its extreme form this leads to thoughts of suicide. Some students' responses to low marks on report cards are of this kind.

Another way of responding to frustrating situations is to withdraw from people into a world of fantasy, often a demoralizing kind of response. It does not solve the problem; it lowers the emotional tone of the individual. It may masquerade as resignation, but it is not true resignation, which comes from recognizing that nothing can be done about the situation at present. Merely evading a difficulty is also different from abandoning an unattainable goal in favor of a goal which one can attain.

Another way of responding to frustration is to revert to behavior that once brought satisfaction but is now inappropriate. This response precludes any fresh analysis of the present situation; it does not lead to a solution of the problem. Stereotyped behavior can afford only the slight relief that activity per se sometimes gives.

The emotional stresses to which adolescents are subjected may produce physical manifestations of illness. Sometimes these stresses result from efforts to adjust to a society that is itself full of conflicts and discontinuities (see Chapter 5).

Perception plays an important part in determining whether or not a situation will be frustrating. If the situation is perceived as detrimental to the self, or as blocking progress toward one's goal, frustration will ensue. However, if the individual can perceive the situation both accurately and creatively, he may be able to decide upon an appropriate course of action. If the action is successful, if it leads toward the attainment of the goal, frustration has been avoided. Much may be done through education to help children and young people become skillful in stating a problem, analyzing a situation, suggesting and evaluating possible solutions, and taking action which will lead to the attainment of the goal.

Adequate perception is limited by physical defects, by absence of analytical ability, by lack of time to analyze the situation, by the persistence of lower-level ways of coping with situations, by emotional blind spots or preoccupation with a particular aspect of the problem. Some adolescents may be hampered by lack of opportunities to develop this perceptive ability through trial and error or through instruction. Accurate perception of the situation should lead to perception of ways to handle it effectively.

If changing conditions is impossible, the person may be helped to change his perception of a situation that cannot be improved at present. Instead of beating his head against a blank wall, he can learn to accept the inevitable, and to turn his attention to activities which will contribute to the attainment of the kind of self he wants.

Dealing with Adolescent Emotion

The first essential is to understand the individual. His emotion is a reaction to some stimulus situation. This may be some recognized environmental condition that is causing frustration, that is interfering with his need for security, recognition, affection, and new experience. Even this cause is difficult to identify because individuals perceive their basic needs in different ways;

what constitutes security for one person is not security for another. Approval by a teacher may be just the thing an adolescent does not want; parental affection may make it more difficult for him to gain adult independence. The underlying pervasive need to make oneself as "good" and complete as possible—in accord with one's self-concept—may account for apparently capricious emotional responses. Each individual copes with the environment as he perceives it and as he experiences it at a given instant. Failure to cope with the environment as perceived causes emotional stress or tension. Even anticipation of such a failure may arouse fear and anxiety. Fear may underlie certain youngsters' lack of hostility toward someone in authority. Other children may not accept an adult for fear that they will be rejected by their age-mates. Fear may also affect school achievement, as one fifteen-year-old girl explained: "I failed in typing; not because I was too dumb to catch on, but because I felt inferior to the kids in my typing class. The real trouble was this: I had lost all faith, given up all hope that I was like the rest of the kids."

It takes a long time and careful observation to know even partially what is going on within and outside an adolescent. For this reason it is risky for adults to meddle with adolescents' emotional responses. It is better to accept their emotions. This attitude of acceptance will help young persons to tolerate a certain amount of frustration and stress and strain as a normal part of life. It is still better to help them learn techniques of living with their emotions, of handling stress and tension as positively as possible. "More studies [should] be made on the dynamics of influencing behavior. To know *why* things happen is only half the job. The next step is to *know how to deal with* behavior." [25]

Adolescents should be helped to choose the methods most appropriate to the situations with which they have to deal. For example, one boy described how he solved the problem of a lack of self-confidence:

Working in the school bank, I was making all kinds of mistakes. What a miserable failure I was! The teacher was quite surprised and

[25] *Ibid.,* p. 7.

disgusted with me for not catching on right away. Usually things of that sort came easy for me to learn but somehow this didn't sink into my brain. I made many mistakes and each time I had to start all over again. I kept saying to myself, "I'll never learn."

Then I started thinking over my problem, and began to say to myself, "I can do it." I realized that the reason I was making so many mistakes was because I didn't have enough confidence in myself. Going at it with confidence, I was soon able not to make even one mistake.

The way in which this boy perceived himself in relation to the work made a difference in his performance on the job. Strong emotion inhibits, mild pleasant emotion facilitates performance.

Daily life is a laboratory for solving emotional problems. It offers opportunities to learn to master or tolerate inevitable tension. Some unnecessary tensions can be reduced—for example, those arising from overemphasis on competition in schools. In offering high rewards and then restricting the number of winners competitively, schools occasion bitter disappointment. Although it may be argued that disappointment is characteristic of life, schools should certainly be urged to examine with their students the bases on which rewards are given, in order to mitigate as far as possible the effects of this kind of disappointment. One of the important lessons to be learned in school is that success is relative.

Schools should take advantage of the many opportunities for fostering mental health. The classroom atmosphere, the pupil-teacher relations, the pupil-pupil relations, and the teaching-learning process—all can be made conducive to the improvement of emotional health. To prevent certain kinds of frustration, it is important to build wholesome acceptant attitudes toward the reasonable regulations of the home, school, and society. When he perceives these restrictions as cooperatively determined and necessary, the adolescent no longer rebels against them. Schools, and other community agencies, should offer more skillfully supervised social activities and more opportunities for service to others. If children and young adolescents engage in such activities with joy and satisfaction, they are not likely to be enticed into undesirable types of commercialized recreation.

Guidance in emotional development should help a teen-ager understand his often tumultuous feelings and channel them into constructive outlets. If they are allowed to commit destructive or unfriendly acts, then their hostility is complicated by the consequent feelings of guilt. Sulking wastes time. Daydreaming about "what might have been" is no preparation for meeting the future situation. "Lighting out" in dangerous ways often gives rise to more serious causes for concern.

It is important for adolescents to learn constructive, or at least harmless, ways of channeling their feelings. They need to express their anger or worry to an adult who understands and accepts their feelings. They can sometimes draw or write about the troublesome things, and thus objectify them. They can find things to do that use up emotional energy, without hurting people or destroying property. If they find these acceptable ways of expressing their feelings, they will grow in self-respect and self-confidence.

CONCLUDING STATEMENT

If we emphasize socially responsible behavior rather than delinquency, we shall be more likely to have a larger proportion of good citizens in the future. The Citizenship Education Project at Teachers College, Columbia University, is sound in its focus on socially useful and constructive activities initiated and carried out by children and adolescents.

This does not mean that we ignore the present delinquency problem or are blind to the complex causation of juvenile delinquency. It does mean that we try to develop a genuine, affectionate relation with adolescents. True affection is not conditioned by the adolescent's achievement or social success. One does not express it by indulging his every whim, permitting him to do exactly as he pleases, or ignoring faults that he can and should correct. True affection helps the adolescent to attain the self that is most acceptable to him and useful to society. We should also try to understand what adolescents are telling us through their behavior, look for their good qualities and build on them. We should be less concerned with a specific change in behavior than with a more fundamental but gradual change in the individual's concept of himself and his environment.

COMPREHENSION QUESTIONS

1. Why is it important for adults to "accentuate the positive" in adolescent behavior?

2. Justify the strong general emphasis on the home as a crucial factor in character development.

3. How is the adolescent's concept of himself related to juvenile delinquency?

4. What is the middle-of-the-road point of view with respect to parental authority and control?

5. Why is it so difficult for youth-serving organizations and settlement houses to attract teen-age delinquent gangs to their programs?

6. What are the positive aspects of adolescent emotion?

7. Point out the wide range of individual differences in delinquent behavior and emotional development.

8. Progress has been made in identifying potential delinquents in the elementary school years. How might this knowledge be used to help prevent juvenile delinquency in the future?

9. Which teacher would you expect to have the best influence on his students—the teacher who makes only general remarks to the whole class, the teacher who directs criticism and sarcasm at individual students, or the teacher who makes many comments on what the students can do and are doing well? Discuss why you think as you do about this.

10. What kind of adolescent behavior gives teachers the most concern? Has their attitude changed in the past twenty-five years?

11. What is the relation between an adolescent's interest and his personality pattern?

12. In what respect are delinquents most different from nondelinquents?

STUDY PROJECTS

1. After reading about the conditions and characteristics conducive to delinquency, translate these negative items into positive factors conducive to good citizenship.

2. From a group of adolescents, obtain compositions in which they express their views of juvenile delinquency.

3. Collect articles on adolescents in newspapers and magazines for a given period. What proportion of them is on "What's wrong with teen-agers"? What proportion is on "What's right with teen-agers"?

4. Read the case histories of several juvenile delinquents.

5. Begin a developmental record of one or more children from birth, with the intent of continuing through adolescence. Read several developmental studies of this kind. (See bibliography.)

6. Make a survey of agencies in your community that could contribute to the goal of good citizenship. Suggest ways in which the public school could prevent children and adolescents from getting into trouble.

7. Study the ways in which you meet frustrating situations.

8. If you are faced with a problem of discipline, first try to find out how the young person himself feels about the situation.

FOR FURTHER STUDY

BARRON, MILTON L., *The Juvenile in Delinquent Society.* New York: Alfred A. Knopf, Inc., 1954.

COLUMBIA UNIVERSITY, TEACHERS COLLEGE, *Improving Citizenship Education.* Citizenship Education Project, Publication No. 29. New York: Teachers College, Columbia University, 1952.

FRANK, LAWRENCE K., *Feelings and Emotions.* New York: Doubleday & Company, Inc., 1954.

GERSTEN, CHARLES, "An Experimental Evaluation of Group Therapy with Juvenile Delinquents," *International Journal of Group Psychotherapy,* vol. 1 (1951), pp. 311–318.

GESELL, ARNOLD, FRANCES L. ILG, and LOUISE BATES AMES, *Youth, the Years from Ten to Sixteen,* chap. XIII. New York: Harper & Brothers, 1956.

GLUECK, SHELDON, and ELEANOR GLUECK, *Delinquents in the Making.* New York: Harper & Brothers, 1952.

HEALY, WILLIAM, and AUGUSTA F. BRONNER, *New Light on Delinquency and Its Treatment.* New Haven, Conn.: Yale University Press, 1936.

IVES, VIRGINIA, MARGUERITE GRANT, and JANE H. RANZONI, "The 'Neurotic' Rorschachs of Normal Adolescents," *Journal of Genetic Psychology,* vol. 83 (September, 1953), pp. 31–61.

JOSSELYN, IRENE M., *The Adolescent and His World,* chap. VII. New York: Family Service Association of America, 1952.

KUHLEN, RAYMOND G., *The Psychology of Adolescent Development,* chap. VIII. New York: Harper & Brothers, 1952.

NATIONAL SOCIETY FOR THE STUDY OF EDUCATION, *Juvenile Delinquency and the Schools,* Forty-seventh Yearbook, part I. Chicago: University of Chicago Press, 1948.

———, *Mental Health in Modern Education,* Fifty-fourth Yearbook, part II. Chicago: University of Chicago Press, 1955.

NEWMAN, RUTH G., "The 'Acting-out' Boy," *Journal of the International Council for Exceptional Children,* vol. 22 (February, 1956), pp. 186–190.

SANFORD, NEVITT, "Personality Development during the College Years," *Personnel and Guidance Journal,* vol. 35 (October, 1956), pp. 74–80.

SEGEL, DAVID, *Frustration in Adolescent Youth,* U.S. Office of Education Bulletin 1951, no. 1, 1951.

SHAFFER, LAWRENCE F., and EDWARD J. SHOBEN, JR., *The Psychology of Adjustment.* Boston: Houghton Mifflin, 1956.

SHEVIAKOV, GEORGE V., and FRITZ REDL, *Discipline for Today's Children and Youth.* Revision by Sybil K. Richardson, Washington, D.C.: National Education Association, Association for Supervision and Curriculum Development, 1956.

STRANG, RUTH, "Young People's Views on Juvenile Delinquency," *Journal of Child Psychiatry,* vol. 1 (section 3, 1948), pp. 273–281.

THRASHER, FREDERIC M., *The Gang.* Chicago: University of Chicago Press, 1936.

TRYON, CAROLINE (ed.), *Fostering Mental Health in Our Schools.* 1950 Yearbook of the Association for Supervision and Curriculum Development. Washington, D.C.: National Education Association, 1950.

WATTENBERG, WILLIAM W., *The Adolescent Years,* chaps. XX, XXVII. New York: Harcourt, Brace and Company, Inc., 1955.

ZACHRY, CAROLINE B., and M. LIGHTY, *Emotion and Conduct in Adolescence.* New York: Appleton-Century-Crofts, Inc., 1940.

Popular Articles and Books

BECK, BERTRAM M., "Delinquents in the Classroom," *NEA Journal,* vol. 45 (November, 1956), pp. 485–487.

ESCALONA, SIBYLLE, *Understanding Hostility in Children.* Chicago: Science Research Associates, Inc., 1954.

GRAZIANO, ROCKY, and ROWLAND BARBER, *Somebody Up There Likes Me.* New York: Simon and Schuster, Inc., 1955.

HYMES, JAMES L., *Behavior and Misbehavior: A Teacher's Guide to Action.* Englewood Cliffs, N.J.: Prentice-Hall, Inc., 1955.

KRAMER, DALE, and MADELINE KARR, *Teen-age Gangs.* New York: Henry Holt and Company, Inc., 1953.

O'NEILL, EUGENE, *Long Day's Journey into Night.* New Haven, Conn.: Yale University Press, 1956.

REDL, FRITZ, "Who Is Delinquent?" *National Parent-Teacher,* vol. 50 (December, 1955), pp. 4–7.

SAMUELS, GERTRUDE, "Plans to Salvage the 'Problem Family,'" *New York Times Magazine* (May 12, 1957), pp. 17, 36, 38, 42, 44.

SHAW, CLIFFORD R., and ANTHONY SORRENTINO, "Is 'Gang-busting' Wise?" *National Parent-Teacher,* vol. 50 (January, 1956), pp. 18–20.

STRANG, RUTH, *Facts about Juvenile Delinquency.* Chicago: Science Research Associates, Inc., 1952.

WALSH, KARIN, "What Is the Press Doing to Teen-agers?" *National Parent-Teacher,* vol. 51 (September, 1956), pp. 4–6.

Audio-visual Aids

Hard Brought Up. 40 minutes. Sound. Black and white. Mental Health Materials Center.

Maintaining Classroom Discipline. 18 minutes. Sound. Black and white. McGraw-Hill.

Make Way for Youth. 22 minutes. Sound. Youth Division of the National Welfare Assembly.

Passion for Life. 85 minutes. Sound. Black and white. Brandon Films, Inc.

Preface to a Life. 90 minutes. Sound. Brandon Films, Inc.

Who's Delinquent? 16 minutes. Sound. RKO Radio Pictures.

Why Vandalism? 17 minutes. Sound. Black and white. Encyclopaedia Britannica Films.

Selected Articles and Books

PART THREE

Favorable Conditions

CHAPTER 13

Favorable Learning Conditions

If favorable environmental conditions were provided, adolescents could "bring themselves up" with a minimum of admonitions, corrections, and restrictions from adults. Preadolescents need opportunities to make one or two close friends of the same sex. Adolescents need time, social groups, and coeducational experiences in school or out of school, where they can get acquainted with the other sex. To confirm their newly achieved feeling of independence, they need real jobs and responsibilities suited to their individual abilities. Since these conditions are described to some extent in other chapters, attention will be focused here on creating favorable conditions for learning at home and at school.

In Chapter 7 it was suggested that we may attack study problems indirectly by creating a more favorable environment, physical and psychological. Parents who are disappointed at the low marks which a child brings home can help him to study more efficiently if they know specifically what makes studying easy, or difficult, for him. Teachers can make studying more difficult or easier for their students. Effective teachers set the stage for efficient learning. Teachers may provide either stimulating or dull books. The nature of the assignment and the way it is given may arouse interest, apathy, or resentment. If the teacher makes no effort to introduce or explain the homework, the student may find it incomprehensible and hence difficult. In their compositions students suggest many conditions which parents and teachers can do something about.

485

THE PLEA FOR PRIVACY

Many preadolescents and adolescents state vigorously their need for privacy in studying. A few fairly typical excerpts from their compositions will show the various conditions uppermost in their minds at different ages:

I find it hard to study when my little brother is crying and my father is shouting. (girl, 10 years)

It's hard for me to study in school because children come to me and talk . . . then I get interested in what they're saying and forget about my work. (girl, 10 years)

It is hard for me to study when someone is nagging me. It is hard for me to study at home because I'm always distracted. (girl, 11 years)

I share a room with two younger sisters which is a horrible predicament. (girl, 16 years)

There are seven in my family, my mother, father, three sisters and a brother. I don't think there is a time when one of the rooms is empty. I don't think it is possible for anyone to study with cowboys and Indians running all around. (boy, 16 years)

Studying is hard for me because of the constant visitors that always "pop up" when they are least expected. Our house is not large so I have to do my homework in the same room where the visitors are. (girl, 18 years)

If you are the only child and have a room for yourself, you can study, but if you're among a large family you have no place for yourself. (boy, 18 years)

The privacy of many students is invaded by friends of their own age, younger brothers and sisters, older sisters who come in with their boy friends or girl friends, parents, company, and other people who keep walking in and out of the room. They complain most frequently about little children who cry, ask questions, want the older brother or sister to do things, or are just Number One nuisances. They also resent being interrupted to perform household tasks and run errands. The feeling tone of their comments varies from good-natured acceptance of distractions to bitter resentment at what they can only regard as inter-

ferences. On the whole, however, they seem to accept conditions which they cannot change at present.

On the positive side, many students of different ages made comments similar to these:

At home it is very easy to study because I can go up in my own room with the door closed where no one will disturb me.

I find that whenever my parents are out, and my sister too, I can work much easier.

When I am alone it is much easier to concentrate on the homework and as a result I finish it much faster.

Parents and teachers can do more to provide adolescents with a quiet place for study and freedom from unnecessary distractions while they are studying. Recognizing this problem, some schools and libraries have provided quiet study rooms for students who are subjected to many distractions at home in the afternoon and evening. Another thing parents can do is schedule definite times for home duties and errands so that they will not have to interrupt their children when they are studying. If we know how adolescents feel about privacy and independence, we will be more considerate in these respects.

PERSONAL FACTORS AFFECTING CONCENTRATION

Another category of conditions affecting study is the one relating to personal worries and competing interests. More things bother adolescents and prevent them from concentrating than most adults realize. Many youngsters say, "Studying is easy when I have my mind on my work." But alas, their minds wander off in many directions: they think of other things they'd rather do, like playing baseball; they picture their friends out having fun; they think about their boy friend or girl friend; they think about a play or dance or party that is coming up, about going on a trip later on, or about things that have happened in the past; or they want to see a TV show or listen to a radio program. For many teen-agers, "the world is so full of a number of things . . ."; their daily schedule is too crowded. A boy in the sixth grade expressed it in this way: "The things that make my homework harder are the things that lure me away from it." These "things that lure them away from study" might be arranged on a continuum from the pull of external conditions, mentioned more frequently by the younger students, to deep-seated inner conflicts revealed by older adolescents:

It is easy for me to study when it isn't a nice day and when my friends aren't home. (girl, 10 years)

Studying is easy when there is nothing to bother me—such as wanting to play baseball. (boy, 11 years)

I enjoy studying—but when a good TV or Radio show is on . . . I can't concentrate because I want to do the other thing. (girl, 13 years)

I also cannot consentrate when something exciting is going to happen. (girl, 15 years)

And of course like other girls my age, I'm very interested in boys and sometimes put them before my schoolwork. (girl, 13 years)

The things that make it hard for me to study is "GIRLS." (boy, 13 years)

The times homework is easy for me is when there is nothing I would like to do much better. (boy, 11 years)

If I know that my friends have not gone out but are also studying, it's easier for me to study. (girl, 17½ years)

Studying is easy when your mind is clear and you have no worries or troubles. (girl, 17 years)

Sometimes I am thinking about things that have happened previously and can't concentrate. (girl, 13 years)

Worrying about whether or not I will pass interfers with studying.
(girl, 14 years)

Sometimes a bad situation at home that results in constant quar-
relling and tension decreases concentration greatly. (girl, 16 years)

When I'm excited about something or when anything is bothering
me emotionally, that is the most hopeless time for me to try to study.
Almost nothing gets through. (girl, 17 years)

I always seem to have something on my mind that is worrying
me or something I like to dream about so my thoughts always start
wandering. (girl, 18 years)

A sixteen-year-old girl summed up the problem of concentration in these words: "If your family life is happy and there are
no major problems bothering you, then it is easy to keep your
mind on your work."

The commonality of personal factors is shown by their frequency of mention in Table 9, Chapter 7. The individuality of
these responses is best shown by the direct quotations from many
compositions. The repeated reference to personal factors indicates the ineffectiveness of sets of study rules that relate only
to time and place and methods of study. It also suggests the
need for counseling on an individual basis, and for frequently
focusing attention on social and emotional factors related to
learning.

Many adolescents are aware of the relation between health
and effective study; practically all the responses in this category
mention fatigue, often attributed to being up too late the night
before. A college sophomore wrote, "One fact is certain, I find
whenever I am well rested I can do much better work and accomplish twice as much as I ordinarily would." Parents often
attribute a slump in academic work to the growth spurt, but
physical growth per se is not an explanation of scholastic dif-

ficulty. No unequivocal general relation between rapid growth and school achievement has been established. Only one student suggested the possibility that "that tired feeling" may have a psychological rather than a physical cause.

"Feeling in the mood for study" seemed very important to a considerable number of youngsters. An eleventh-grade girl felt "just in the mood some nights to do Latin translation." Some said, "If I don't feel like working, I just sit and waste time." Several related their moods to the weather. One seventh-grade girl told how she took advantage of "a working mood" to do in one night all the homework that had been assigned in a week.

Here is a fertile field for guidance by teachers and parents. In addition to understanding, adolescents need help in handling these situations. They can learn ways of orienting themselves to a task and solving personal problems. They can also learn that moods may often be modified or diverted into more profitable channels.

COOPERATION AND ASSISTANCE IN STUDY

There are differences of opinion as to whether studying independently or in groups is more effective. What used to be called "cheating" may now be considered "cooperation." It depends on the kind of homework. A group project initiated by the students certainly calls for cooperation. For the kind of assignment still most prevalent—reading a certain number of assigned pages or writing the answers to certain questions or doing a certain number of problems in mathematics—not much cooperation is possible; some assistance may be necessary.

Judging by the rather low percentage of responses commending parental assistance, it would seem that adolescents do not generally welcome parents' assistance on school subjects. However, a few spoke appreciatively of parental help: "Studying," said a seventh-grade girl, "is made easier for me by having a father and mother who can help me when I get stuck." Occasionally the younger students wrote of mothers who helped with scrapbooks, letter writing, and the like, and fathers and brothers who gave assistance in mathematics. The following unusual instance of parental cooperation was described by a seventeen-year-old girl: "But now, being so near to exam time, my parents are doing everything to help me study in tranquility. They're letting my little brothers remain outdoors a little longer, and not letting them put on television. My father plays card games with them to keep them quiet."

On the other hand, some parents not only fail to help their children; they actually hinder them. Conditions of this kind were described by two twelfth-grade girls. Note the obvious undercurrent of hostility in their comments:

When I was younger and just beginning school I would mention some incident that had happened. My mother (my father and I have never been on speaking terms) would tell me she was too busy to listen, or just simply ignore me. . . . Soon I began to get the feeling, from school and from my mother, that no one was really interested.

Sometimes in the middle of my homework my mother will ask me questions having nothing to do with school, and if I happen to have an idea, I always forget it. Or she may bring up something very unpleasant, which is almost every night. For instance, my failing steno. And then for the rest of the evening I keep thinking about my failure in steno and I sit there with a blank page before me, and no ideas about my homework. My mother doesn't seem to understand that I try my best.

TIME AND PLACE FOR STUDYING

The conditions of time and place mentioned by the students are similar to those found in books on "How to study." Perhaps the students are merely reflecting study rules they have been taught. Or they may be confirming rules that work well for them. The fact that so small a percentage of students mention the importance of having a special time and place suggests either the need for more instruction in the generally accepted "effective study methods," or a reexamination of our recommendations, based on research on the learning process and the recognition of individual differences.

The more mature students welcome help in making a daily schedule. One fifteen-year-old boy in the ninth grade wrote: "Studying is made easier when it is on a time budget. For instance, my budget—3 o'clock I come home and go out to play until 5 o'clock. At five I am up in the house to study and do my homework; in the evening I read for an hour or so."

SUITABLE ASSIGNMENTS

In their denunciation of excessive homework, the students seemed more articulate than in any of the other viewpoints they expressed. Their statements were more extended; they made more of an effort to justify their viewpoints, and used stronger adjectives to describe them. Moreover, the burden of homework assignments was more frequently described by students of the higher IQ groups, although even the lower IQ groups seemed particularly articulate when writing about their dislike of homework.

Part of the resentment against homework is caused by the dull, repetitious nature of the assignments, part by the pull of other things which students want to do or have to do. Among these are work at home, a part-time job, football practice. And one youngster said, "I like to have time of my own at night. When you go out to work, you don't bring work home. I think it should be the same way in school."

In their compositions the students mentioned many important principles underlying effective homework assignments:

1. The study should have meaning, interest, use, and purpose for the students. As they say:

"When I enjoy the topic I am studying, I can always do my best."

"When the subject is interesting, it seems to be easier."

"New angles to the subject make studying easier for me."

"I find it easy to study about things that are happening now or have happened within my lifetime."

"In Spanish sometimes we get a funny story to translate into English. In that way it is interesting to find out what is happening in the story as you go on."

2. The assignment should involve material in which the students have had the necessary preliminary instruction. In their words:

"Studying is easy for me when I understand what I am doing and why."

"I can generally study a lot better if the subject has been reviewed in class by the teacher, instead of having to sit down and learn with a blank mind, not knowing what to expect."

3. The assignment should be of the problem or project type.

4. Ideally, it should be selected on the students' own initiative.

5. It should not be so long as to usurp time that should be used in other ways.

According to the students, the length of the assignment affects the quality of their work; a long assignment is discouraging. They describe various effects of too long assignments:

The amount of homework makes a difference in the quality of studying I do; if I have only a small amount, it usually is done thoroughly and well.

If you have a large amount of homework, you are apt to feel defeated before you start. I become a little disheartened and studying becomes a chore.

When I see a long assignment I'm tired of it before I begin.

Excessive homework may cause dislike of school:

I hate school when teachers are always giving homework. I don't mind when they give a little bit but when they pile it on every night I just don't bother to do it.

School would be allright if there wasn't so much homework. I hardly have time to do anything but eat, go to school, eat, do homework, and go to bed.

The junior high school youngsters are the most rebellious against homework, perhaps because they are in the transition stage from little or no homework required in elementary school to homework required by each of five different teachers. Senior high school students are more likely to feel discouraged than resentful.

Reading difficulty underlies some students' dissatisfaction with homework:

To me studying is very difficult. The main reason for the difficulty is that I have trouble with reading. Ever since my first few years in school I have always seemed to lag behind the others in reading.

I keep reading and I still can't get the important facts.

I came from Puerto Rico three years ago and I don know English so well. I also do not like the hard words.

It would be well for teachers to consider these criticisms of homework. Is it excessive, boring? Does it usurp time that adolescents could use more profitably in voluntary reading, wholesome social activities, or useful work experience? Could school time be used more efficiently so as to make assigned homework unnecessary? Could instruction be made so stimulating that many students would set themselves creative projects to do at home?

Both teachers and parents can contribute to a much more rewarding program of home study than we have at present. Students should be encouraged to initiate projects on which they can work cooperatively and for a social purpose. The teacher can make sure that any assignment given is understood by the students. Assignments should also be differentiated to meet individual needs. At home, parents can create conditions more conducive to study. If home conditions are unfavorable, schools and

librarics may provide places where students can study in peace and quiet.

AN APPROPRIATE CURRICULUM

Critical Comments

A still more basic condition underlying the scholastic achievement of individual students is a curriculum that is suited to their needs and abilities. Students express much dissatisfaction with their school experiences. Criticism such as that made by a non-academic high school boy descrvcs serious consideration:

School made me appreciate being out of school. When I am out of school I feel that I am accomplishing something. When I am working I am building or doing something that will help someone else, or at least I am earning money.

In school all people do is talk. They never accomplish anything. In school they tell how things are done or you read how they are done, but you never do them.

Out of school you have a chance to think things out. Out of school they give you something to do and you do it. If you can't do it they show you how.

In school there's always a teacher watching you. This is a good thing some of the time, but usually they don't show you how to do something if you don't know how to do it they just talk about it.

It is important for teachers to be sensitive to the way students with low IQs and meager reading ability feel in an ordinary classroom situation. They often have a defeatist attitude, like Richard, who said, "It won't do me any good to study. I always fail no matter what I do."

The following quotations show how some youngsters with potential ability but with reading difficulty used to feel in a school situation with which they are unable to cope:

I was afraid of being laughed at if I didn't know the right answers.

I was nervous in school. I had trouble in getting ideas from my reading. The words bothered me, too. I didn't like to recite in class. I would rather write my answers than give them before the class.

I had trouble with reading. Words are hard to understand. I don't know what they are. I can't remember what I read. I got most from films and from the teacher.

I liked athletics but I couldn't keep up my eligibility.

I wasn't interested in school because I had no friends. No one cared whether I came to school or not. I liked typing, but I wasn't a good speller, so I made too many mistakes. I couldn't find anything interesting to read in school. I couldn't remember what I read in school. I was afraid to recite in class. I got a job at a drive-in when I left school. I felt all right out of school. I felt sick a lot of the time when I was going to school; guess part of it was that I didn't like school.

Many slow-learning youngsters leave as soon as the law allows. They dislike school because they do not learn things that are meaningful to them, because they do not like or understand the books they have to read and thus cannot remember what they read, because they feel unhappy in school—embarrassed, insecure, afraid to speak up—and because they get more satisfaction from a job than from school.

Gifted adolescents also have criticisms of the curriculum and teaching methods. They complain that textbooks are dull, subjects are unrelated to their lives, time is wasted in class, there is much needless repetition, and other students dislike them because they excel in schoolwork. They often feel that "grades are given by teachers rather than *earned* by pupils."

Expressions of Satisfaction

On the other hand, some students expressed satisfaction with the curriculum. They like to be given freedom with responsibility. One student wrote enthusiastically about his high school: "This school is the perfect example of democracy. You can do anything you want that's right in a democracy, and you can do anything that's right in this school. It is a very friendly school, too. It is like a second home to me."

A Spanish-speaking student expressed appreciation of the same high school: "I came from Puerto Rico last summer . . . and all the teachers and the students has been very nice with me. This school gives everybody to improve their habilities because here you could learn, for example, how to play an instrument or to make something that you could use in your own house or for yourself."

A girl in a large city senior high school, where the range in IQ on a group test is from 65 to 90, the socio-economic level is low, and about half of the students come from Spanish-speaking homes, found many satisfactions in her school experience. She wrote: "I know a lot of people won't believe this but I really like school. I'd rather be in school than in my house. . . . My favorite subjects are (a) gym, (b) core, (c) study, and last but not least (d) *lunch*. I like lunch very much not only because we eat that period but because I can get together with my friends."

To a rural sixteen-year-old girl, school meant a great deal. She wrote about her class ring as "a symbol—something to give me a goal for the rest of my life. To make me the best person I could be, and to represent my school for all it stood—loyalty, honor, truthfulness, and true friendship." The adolescent's satisfaction with school depends on the social relations and student activities he finds there, as well as on the curriculum in the narrower sense of the word.

Comments on Courses

High school students also request all sorts of courses. Many want more shopwork and other practical courses that will help them get a job. One wrote, "I think they should devise a plan where a student can go out for about six weeks and try the thing he'd like to be." Perhaps he had heard about the Antioch plan, or about distributive education in high school. Although only a few high school courses are specifically designed to prepare young people for jobs, almost any course may contribute to vocational success. For example, boys who have gone into officer-training programs have spoken with appreciation of the good stiff courses in mathematics which they had in high school. A large number of students emphasize the high school's contribution to social development. One wanted "a course in analyzing people's thoughts or the different interpretations that can be derived from conversations."

In compositions on "Why I like or don't like a particular subject," students gave various criticisms of certain subjects and suggestions for improving them. Comments on history by students of lower socio-economic levels, may of whom speak a language other than English at home, are most enlightening. They liked history because:

I have gotten good marks.

History [as it is taught in this school] is just a matter of remembering and memorizing. This is why I liked it.

It gives me a feeling of being more secure around friends when they bring up dates like 1779, etc.

History helps me in my leisure reading for when I read a book of a particular period, I know from history about this period . . . and the book has more meaning.

History classes are very informal. I enjoy sitting down and discussing things that have happened in the past and are happening in the present.

It is like an exciting story, only you know this was true and really has happened. And if people would learn from the faults their ancestors had made, then it helps in the present day.

I like history when it is planned in such an interesting and simple way that even the low-mark girls can grample it sufficiently.

Those who dislike history mentioned three main reasons: (1) it was a required course—they were compelled to take it; (2) they found it dull—"when a teacher stands in front of a class and talks about history the whole period long, I find it boring and my mind turns away from the subject"; and (3) it was hard to understand—"everything seems to happen so fast every week that you cannot make your mind absorb the information you learned last week."

Intellectual understanding may help adolescents, to some extent, to master their anxieties. In addition to the interpersonal relations, the subject matter of every subject can be used, to some extent, to help adolescents meet their emotional problems. Bettelheim [1] mentioned several ways in which the social studies provide a unique tool for this purpose:

1. By helping the adolescent understand the consequences of new sex drives in their social context: how primitive societies made young men live together away from contact with women; how contemporaneous phenomena express adolescent boys' fear of and hostility toward the opposite sex; how they use sex exploits to gain prestige or to overcome their fear by familiarity.

2. By interpreting parent-child relations and the normal critical attitude adolescents take toward parents, the study of the family and the influence of the culture on the child would help adolescents understand their parents.

3. By presenting adolescence as an important phase of social development.

4. By presenting the limitations as well as the opportunities "in finding a job, in making a place for himself in society."

5. By helping the adolescent minimize the importance of material possession as a way of gaining self-respect.

6. By recognizing his fear of competition and some of the reasons for it.

[1] Bruno Bettelheim, "The Social-studies Teacher and the Emotional Needs of Adolescents," *School Review,* vol. 56 (December, 1948), pp. 585–592.

7. In brief, "the greatest service the social-studies teacher can render to his adolescent students is to educate them to a critical understanding of themselves and of the society in which they live." [2] Every teacher, in addition to the unique contribution of the subject matter he teaches, has two general responsibilities: (1) to demonstrate true, satisfying interpersonal relations and (2) "to set an example of the continuous critical examination and intellectual mastery of intellectual and emotional problems." [3] It helps the adolescent to master a problem intellectually even though he is not able to solve it in action.

Student comments on English range from complaints about having to read Shakespeare to complaints about not having to read enough famous plays. The most frequently mentioned value is the poise gained in speech classes and in oral English periods. For example, one tenth-grade girl told how a speech class had helped her to develop an unusual degree of poise:

When I went to speech class, the teacher said, "Remember, you're as good as anyone else." He gave us parts in Shakespeare. Then I was asked to read the Bible in assembly. Later I was to give a speech. The teacher said, "Why don't you use your personality and *ad lib?*" After it was over some of the kids said, "You ought to go into public speaking." They didn't know how scared I was.

Many teachers do not realize what an ordeal speaking in front of the group is to some students. This is the way one eleventh-grade boy described it:

A few weeks ago I was assigned a talk in my English class, which allowed no notes. That night I wrote up the talk which I thought was very good. . . . The next day I would have given anything to have been absent during the English period, but no such luck came. In the middle of the period my name was called and I got up and went to the front of the room. I stood there for a few minutes trying to think of my opening sentence and then it came to me. I started off with my heart beating very loud. I tried to look calm and collected and to speak with ease. As I continued I began to get

2 *Ibid.*, p. 592.
3 *Ibid.*, p. 592.

more confidence and then, before I knew it, I had finished my talk. I walked back to my seat half in a fog. I had become so nervous that I didn't know what I was doing any more.

One student wrote of a teacher who helped him when he felt extremely uncertain and insecure in speaking before an English class: "I think he has done more for me than any other teacher I have ever had, because I am now so accustomed to getting up and talking before class that I really enjoy it and wish other classes furnished such opportunities for expression."

How an English teacher helped a foreign-born student become more self-confident and competent in his use of a second language was as follows: In a conference, the teacher and the student agreed upon two things—that she would not call on him in English class until he felt that he had improved sufficiently in reading and in speaking English, and that she would give him individual help in reading during her free period. The boy showed immediate signs of relief; the cloud of anxiety that had hovered over his brow passed away. As if in appreciation he said, "Just wait and see, Teach, as soon as I can say what I think, I tell you and the students many interesting things about my life." Adolescents who have come from foreign countries feel especially embarrassed about their poor English. They appreciate a teacher like the one just described.

Language should be taught as a social experience, as a means of sharing one's experiences with others through speaking and writing. The teacher should start where the student is in language development, and help him progress from that stage. Many students, like the tenth-grade girl described, have unrealized language potentialities.

The contribution of literature to personality development is being increasingly recognized by English teachers. Literature does "hold the mirror up to nature." It shows how persons may act under the stress of certain feelings, and suggests acceptable outlets for one's own emotions. It helps the individual to interpret his own and others' behavior; it helps him to learn which patterns of behavior are socially acceptable, and stimulates his imagination to evolve the patterns that are most appropriate for him. Literature presents many problems of human relations and shows how they have been solved and with what consequences.

Mathematics is a problem for many. There are students on all educational levels who think of themselves as persons who cannot learn mathematics. The difficulties described in the following composition are probably experienced by many ninth-grade students:

I have a problem in algebra. At first this year it came quite easily to me. But now it seems that it is getting higher and higher above me.

Last year in eighth grade I had trouble in math. I kept on getting C's when I was trying so hard to get a B. I went to see my math teacher and he said that it was my fundamentals. What he ment was I couldn't multiply and divide fast enough.

Of coarse I treid to grasp them, but then a test would come along and I would fail and be right back where I started from.

Such repeated experiences of failure could be avoided, in the first place, if the individual received guidance in the choice of a program suited to his needs and abilities. Second, courses in practical mathematics may be offered for those who do not need the college preparatory type of course. Third, clearer explanations and individual instruction would help all the students to succeed in the subject. When one youngster was asked why the class liked their mathematics teacher so much, he said, "She learns us good." Students should also realize that difficulty in mathematics is cumulative—if they take it too easy in the beginning, difficulties are likely to mount later.

Students generally respond favorably to classes in commercial subjects. They see clearly the vocational value of these subjects. The following comment is typical: "The subjects that have helped me most are typing and shorthand, and general business. By taking these subjects I have prepared myself for a job when I get out of school."

Shopwork, too, is often mentioned as "the thing that has helped me most in school." "One of the most interesting things I've learned in school," wrote one boy, "is the way to take an engine out of a car and how to put it in again." He proceeded to give the technical details. Although this boy was considered retarded, he had no trouble using words or expressing meanings that had come within his firsthand experience.

Home economics including family life education meets many adolescent needs. It aids girls in improving their personal appearance and health, deals with some of their personal and social problems, puts baby-sitting on a sounder psychological basis, and helps prepare them for their most important vocation—marriage and family life.

To adolescents, music offers a variety of opportunities for self-expression and self-development. The young person who cannot perform on any musical instrument can join listening clubs, where students enjoy good records and radio and TV programs, and he can share his enjoyment of music with others. One who participates in musical activities in school is likely to use his leisure time in similar activities after graduation. For those who have some musical skill, the school band, orchestra, mixed chorus, or girls' or boys' glee clubs not only give individual members musical experiences but also help to develop responsibility, self-esteem, cooperation, and social adjustment. For the musically talented, there are opportunities for creative activity: putting original words to a familiar melody, writing an original melody to familiar words, or creating both words and melody. Some of these students decide to make music a career.

Music may play an important part in the individual's total development, as in the case of Steve, who was a somber, unhappy boy who frequently carried a chip on his shoulder. He was troublesome in all his classes except music and band practice. He spent much of his time alone, and would wail "Rhapsody in Blue" on his trumpet and listen to sad music on the radio. In an interview with the guidance worker, Steve's father said he would try to provide more companionship and encouragement for the boy at home. Gradually music became, for Steve, an avenue of self-realization as well as an outlet for his feelings. Later Steve appeared on a local TV program. Now the youngsters call him "the young man with a horn." He has become more cheerful, is interested in a greater variety of music, and plans to make music his career.

Suggested Modifications

Secondary school curricula have been modified on the basis of studies of the needs of youth and of society. The result has been a more functional curriculum. For all-round development adolescents need a broad educational program including experiences in human relations, in selective listening to radio and television, in exploring the world of nature and technology and the world of social forces, and in the creative use of leisure.

To meet the demands of employers, adolescents need to be able to speak and use correct English. Employers list English as the most important course, mathematics as second in importance. They are also aware of the school's responsibility for helping young people learn to get along with fellow workers and supervisors. Keller [4] noted a trend toward including some vocational training in all types of education. Such training widens the student's vocational horizon and increases his repertory of skills, even though specific vocational training is now usually done on the job. The nonacademic student who takes advantage of vocational education, or of a high school or junior college program that combines education with remunerative work, has immediate motivation; his education is meaningful and purposeful to him. The chief criticism by almost five thousand youngsters between seventeen and twenty-two years was that the schools should have given them more vocational training.[5] Public junior colleges provide technical vocational education to young people in many local communities.

To meet the needs for good citizenship and harmonious family life, new courses have been introduced in citizenship education, human relations, life adjustment education, family life education, driver education, conservation and consumer education, and

[4] Franklin J. Keller, *The Double-purpose High School*. New York: Harper & Brothers, 1953.

[5] Jack Stewart, "School Didn't Give Us What We Want," *This Week Magazine* (October 14, 1956), pp. 10, 18, 20–21.

resource use education. Changes along these lines have also been made in the objectives, content, and methods of long-established courses.

A basic-course program, often called a core curriculum, using a block of time for common learnings, has found increasing favor since 1949. The core teacher needs special preparation, equipment, and materials, and a favorable time schedule. Evaluations thus far reported have generally been favorable. The majority of administrators, teachers, and pupils seem to approve of the program; more objective evidence of its success is found in better attendance, fewer dropouts and disciplinary problems, and better pupil-teacher relations. In one controlled experiment,[6] the tenth-grade core classes exceeded the regular classes in all the skills, interests, and attitudes measured except mechanics of expression and analytical thinking.

Modifications in the curriculum to produce a closer relation between school education and reality as students view it should strengthen motivations for learning. As juniors and seniors see more clearly the relation of the school program to their ideal selves and their life goals, they become more interested in school and in further educational plans.

EFFECTIVE TEACHING METHODS

Methods Students Want

Another condition conducive to school achievement mentioned by almost a third of the students (see Chapter 7, Table 9) was effective teaching. It is enlightening to know the teaching methods that adolescents consider effective. According to their statements, effective teaching occurs when the teacher possesses three essentials: interest in the student, interest in the subject, and ability to explain it in a clear and interesting way. More specifically, students would like teachers to:

[6] Bertis E. Capehart, Allen Hodges, and Norman Berdan, "An Objective Evaluation of a Core Program," *School Review*, vol. 60 (February, 1952), pp. 84–89.

Be enthusiastic about their subject and about teaching

Give good reasons for studying their subject

Explain the subject *clearly* and thoroughly

Preview an assignment in class, so that students know what to do when they begin to study

Give two or three nights' assignments in advance

Check the work students hand in

Do not give repetitious, unnecessary drill

Let students discuss the topics, not talk too much themselves

Relate the subject to things of interest to the students

Avoid talking in a mumbling monotonous way

Encourage class discussion

Maintain order—"do not holler all the time; only when they have to"

Introduce humor occasionally

Treat students as adults with respect and consideration; do not "talk down to them"

These comments, if built into a positive program of classroom instruction, would surely result in more effective learning.

Young adolescents need help in channeling their energies. In class they often fidget and break out into chattering. At camp, boys of this age often require more programming than any other age group. If a busy, constructive program is not prepared, they will think of a busy one, not necessarily constructive. One camp, for example, failed to provide such a program. Boys of this age group chased one another with burning brooms, set a ball court on fire, and nailed the lethargic counselor's shoes to the floor. These were only a few of the activities they provided for themselves. Some of the same boys are now at another camp, but are expending their energies in a constructive program.

Young teen-agers will usually be responsive and orderly if (1) they know there are limits on their behavior, (2) they understand the reasons for the limitations, and (3) they have a share in making rules which are enforced fairly and consistently. These youngsters need some form of direction and control. Without it, they feel lost. Classes which lack firm and fair controls are generally described by the pupils as ones in which they "don't learn anything." They interpret a laissez-faire attitude on the part of a teacher as a signal to take over. Unless they have been prepared to do this in a constructive manner, the result is loud talking, shouting, chalk fights, and other disruptive behavior. On the other hand, a group that has learned discussion methods and how to take initiative and work toward a goal will take over in a fairly orderly and effective way.

Problems of Discipline

A group of young adolescents can be mischievous and even cruel to one another and to teachers. Students in one group had been allowed to get into the habit of laughing at others' difficulties. If a student was roundly scolded by a teacher, the class was likely to roar with laughter. Students occasionally take a dislike to a teacher, or find a teacher whom they can easily irritate. For example, an inexperienced young teacher was too permissive and ingratiating at first. Finding this a poor tactic, he became as dictatorial as he had been when a sergeant in the Army. On the last day of the year, his whole class, led by the most intelligent and otherwise cooperative students (seniors too!), upset everything in his room and strewed confetti and other "decorations" all over it. In another school, a middle-aged woman teacher, unfortunately somewhat deaf, had difficulties with study hall. Students would start stomping their feet in various parts of the room. As she tried to sneak quietly to the spot where she thought the noise was, others would start stomping in other parts of the room until the poor woman was almost frantic. The most plausible explanation of such incidents is that there is a kind of "group contagion" which many individuals are unable to withstand. A long series of minor resentments, annoyances, and frustrations may culminate in a sudden outburst of destructive or antagonistic behavior which seems quite disproportionate to the immediate stimulus.

In general, young adolescents are reasonable; they will improve if the reasons are clearly stated, without preaching, and if they see the need for it. One homeroom class was causing the teacher some trouble: they did not pay attention, they talked out of turn, and so on. The teacher devoted a number of home-room discussions to this problem, and had several interviews with the youngsters who were causing the most trouble. Gradually the students' conduct improved. Some teachers need to recognize that youngsters can be talkative in class without meaning to be rude. Teachers should not take this kind of behavior as a personal affront.

Other skillful teachers have found various ways to handle difficult situations. One teacher found it was best to ignore minor incidents so far as possible. Once, while on study-hall duty, he left the room for a moment to locate a student who had gone to the typing room for practice. While he was returning, someone shot off a firecracker. He had no idea who had done it. As a matter of fact, he was new to the school and did not know many of the students. Not knowing what else to do, he did nothing, completely ignoring the incident, saying nothing. To his surprise, the study hall was quiet; no one laughed, and the students seemed to ignore it also.

The best discipline seems to be found in situations where the teacher seldom scolds, where individuals are respected, and where minor incidents are not treated with unnecessary severity. In such situations, the majority are "on the teacher's side": group pressure is against the infrequent unruly act, not against the teacher. It is also important to have some relaxing moments in the classroom. If the teacher laughs with the students at a funny incident, the class seems to get to work much faster. If some situation is bothering the class, such as new rules about conduct in the halls, it is well to let students air their gripes and discuss the problem. Even if half the period is spent in this way, the class may be able to accomplish more work, once these tensions are released. If students feel that a class is worthwhile and that they are learning and accomplishing something, they are likely to show genuine interest and attention. Group pressure will then be exerted, when necessary, in a favorable direction: "We'd better get on with the lesson." These conditions help to create, and are dependent on, the interpersonal relations in the classroom.

CONSTRUCTIVE TEACHER-STUDENT RELATIONS

Some students consider their relationship with the teacher of major importance. A student described his relation with one teacher in this way: "It's like sitting on a park bench chatting with him." Others said it was easier to study when:

You like the teacher and get along well with him.

You know that a teacher has an interest in you and really wants you to pass the course; then you don't want to let him down.

The teacher is a person that you respect and have confidence in.

The teacher has a word of encouragement and helps you develop and express yourself in the work you *did*, rather than criticize you for what you *hadn't* done.

Adolescents' statements are in line with modern theories of education. Both agree that:

1. Learning is a problem-solving process.
2. Cooperative teacher-pupil planning is the most effective way of organizing the learning situation.
3. Student-teacher relationships greatly influence students' learning.

There are probably differences, too, in the effectiveness of a given method with different individuals. Directive methods were preferred by the poorer students who had become accustomed to them. A certain amount of competition is inescapable, and sometimes helps young people discover their potentialities. It becomes harmful when the person continually judges his worth by the extent to which he can surpass others.

Effective methods arouse more student interest, and produce more interaction among students and between students and instructor. Cartwright and Zander,[7] who have applied the theory of group dynamics to the classroom, strongly advocate group-centered teaching. The case study method of teaching and the workshop are likewise presented as building positive atti-

[7] Dorwin Cartwright and Alvin F. Zander, *Group Dynamics, Research and Theory*. Evanston, Ill.: Row, Peterson & Company, 1953.

tudes and personal values. Visual aids also contribute to modern teaching methods, and are especially appreciated by nonacademic students.

TEACHER PERSONALITY

Adolescents are often keen and skillful in understanding their teachers. An intellectually gifted high school sophomore was quite adept at this, as the following quotation shows:

Primarily, it must be accepted that young students are "personality wise"—they see through their teachers. A teacher doesn't need to have a great personality but should have the understanding of children which most of them lack. Second, the teacher should be willing to budget her time to help the slow students catch up and give the quick ones a chance to forge ahead. The most important factor is that the teacher should be willing to take a back seat at times and give everyone a chance to express his or her ideas about subjects pertaining to the lessons.

Another adolescent with a high IQ asked for "bright, interesting teachers for bright, interesting pupils." If a teacher can accept and profit by their critical remarks as well as by their favorable comments, he will obtain a better understanding of himself as a teacher, in addition to insights into the nature of the learning process.

Frequency of Characteristics Mentioned

In writing on the topic, "What I like or dislike about teachers," adolescents described many characteristics and kinds of behavior. The figures in Table 13 give the relative frequency with which certain characteristics were mentioned in 211 compositions by students in a variety of school situations from the sixth through the twelfth grades. This frequency count includes both positive and negative statements about the same category. For example, "willing to give help" and "unwilling to give help" are counted together, since they both belong in the category of helping students with learning difficulties.

TABLE 13

	Frequency of Mention	
Approved Characteristic	Number	Per Cent of Total Compositions
Able to create a genial, informal atmosphere; generally permissive............................	77	36.4
Fair in their treatment of all students............	52	24.6
Friendly in their personal relations with students...	46	21.8
Patient and helpful toward slowness or failure to learn.....................................	43	20.4
Understanding, accepting, and interested in students as persons............................	34	16.1
Not given to scolding or yelling at class..........	33	15.6
Not over-ready to punish or give detentions.......	32	15.2
Not prone to show favoritism...................	28	13.3
Willing to give help with learning difficulties......	26	12.3
Somewhat strict—not too easy.................	24	10.9
Able to "stick to the subject"—doesn't digress to preach, criticize, etc.........................	19	9.0
Not prone to employ personal ridicule or maintain a consistently negative, nagging, destructive attitude toward student efforts...................	15	7.1

Independent Study Stressed by Gifted Students

Teachers expect me to do my best. In return I expect them to have a sense of humor and to be able to explain the lesson so we can understand it.

The teacher I like most was the kind of person who put you very much on your own.

If you had a problem or question, Mr. B would give suggestions that might help you, but he never gave you the answer. He made you do that work yourself!

My best teachers let me do things on my own. They respect my ideas and help me to develop them.

The teacher should be willing to take a back seat at times and give everyone a chance to express his or her ideas on the subject.

Expressions of Dislike

The characteristics of teachers that students dislike are, in general, the reverse of the appealing qualities of teacher personality that have just been mentioned. But the expressions of dislike are usually more vigorous than the expressions of liking. One eighth-grade boy was exceedingly vehement in his remarks about teachers:

I dislike teachers who bore students with lengthy notes, and will yell at the slightest little thing. I *hate* teachers who don't let you say one single word. I *double hate* teachers who pick on one person all the time. I don't like a teacher who will not reason out, as in math; a person who will not let you tell the way you used to work a problem. I don't like a teacher who believes in all work and no play. I hate teachers who are drunk and come to school with a hangover. I hate teachers who almost bust your eardrum hollering.

Dislike was more often expressed by junior than by senior high school students. A large proportion of the junior high school students complained about teachers who "scold and yell" and punish too readily. In other respects, too, age differences in the written responses were quite marked. "Fairness" and "justice" are very important to young teen-agers. "That isn't fair" is a common complaint. Senior high school students emphasized helpfulness, understanding, and friendly acceptance, and expressed dislike of teachers who show favoritism or are "too easy."

Appealing Teacher Personality Patterns

Many studies have been made of the kinds of teachers students like or dislike. In general, they like teachers who have a sense of humor, an understanding of students and willingness to help them, and an ability to explain the subject clearly and to maintain sound standards of conduct and achievement. Youngsters want teachers whom they can respect, who treat them as adults, not as babies, who like them and want them to learn. They want some fun in class and can have fun learning. Witty [8]

[8] Paul Witty, "Some Characteristics of the Effective Teacher," *Educational Administration and Supervision,* vol. 36 (April, 1950), pp. 193–208.

summed up his analysis of 12,000 letters submitted by pupils in the "Quiz Kids" contest by saying, "The teacher most admired was usually a well-adjusted individual who is genuinely responsive in human relations."

An eleventh-grade student summarized the qualities of a good teacher quite comprehensively: "Patience, to me, is the highest quality of a good teacher. A student is much more apt to respond to a patient person, than to one who is constantly going on without making sure the work is understood. The teacher should have the ability to set a standard and stick by it, making the student realize he must fulfill his responsibilities and not get around them by giving excuses. He should evaluate a student's work on the basis of the student's own abilities rather than on those of the class as a whole. He should take an interest in the student's problems, no matter how small they are. He should also be interested in his subject and know how to convey his knowledge and not have to say, 'I can't explain it.' He should be understanding and never be unfair, but be a friend to everyone." Another boy's positive comments were brief and to the point: "I like a teacher who understands and lets you talk but not too loud, who remembers *he* was a boy once."

Other personal qualities infrequently mentioned were sincerity and integrity, willingness to admit mistakes, willingness to accept the student as an adult. A few of the more mature students recognized the role students play in determining teachers' behavior, and pointed out that disobedient and inattentive students are often to blame for unpleasant teachers.

Many students associated teachers' personal qualities with their methods of teaching. When they spoke of wanting "strict" teachers, they did not mean "autocratic," but rather teachers who help them to realize their potentialities. When they complained about teachers who are "too strict," they were usually referring to regimentation and irksome restrictions that arbitrarily limit the freedom they so much desire. They praised teachers who avoid both the anarchy caused by *laissez faire,* and the antagonism created by domination—teachers, that is, who set limits which help the members of the group to control themselves. Adolescents appreciate this reinforcement of their own inadequate controls. It is significant to note how many of the specific teacher qualities mentioned contribute in some way to the adolescent's personality development—to the realization of his most acceptable self.

The following compositions express more concretely and effectively characteristics and procedures mentioned by many adolescents:

One of my favorite teachers was W.A. He never shouted, but always spoke calmly. I always try to follow his example when ever I get mad. He let the class work together on projects most of the time and gave us plenty of time to do them; as a result the work was always better. He let the class take over most of the time in discussions and have many debates. I was always shy when it came to speaking in front of the class, but I had to do it frequently in his class, and got over my shyness. We also had current events every day, from which I learned, and knew many of the current events of the day.

The best teacher I ever had was W.A. He was good, because we got our work done and were interested in it. We did things to learn our social studies by doing other things beside reading and writing. We had projects of all sorts on the Revolution, the Civil, and all other wars. When we were studying the Industrial Revolution we all pretended that we were inventors and picked an inevention. We looked up information on this and gave an oral report explaining how it worked. He not only was interesting but he had a quiet but firm way of conducting the classroom. Unlike most teachers he did not yell when reprimanding someone. He spoke in a quiet tone that made you feel ashamed in a way but also kept you quiet for the rest of the period. He did not have any pets. You could look upon him as a friend and not as one who gives you tests to "catch" or to "trick" you. You could tell in his teaching that he was trying to help you. He used the honor system and stressed the point that if you cheated you were hurting no one but yourself. He tried to get the most learning out of one year, pleasantly. If you had a problem or a question he would give suggestions that might help you, but he never gave you the answer. He made you do that work yourself! As a whole, I think that most students who had him looked upon him as a friend.

Differences in Students' Perception of Teachers

Each student in a class may perceive the same teacher somewhat differently. The way the student views the teacher depends a great deal on the way he perceives himself and the goals toward which he is working.

In general, the way in which adolescents perceive school, teachers, and their classmates is an important factor in their academic achievement. School learning has a personal meaning for each individual. Some "just love school." By many, school is accepted without question as a matter of course, something that "everybody's doing." Others consider it a necessary evil. For a few, conformity to the demands of school may be just another phase of the dependency which they are trying to throw off. Until students perceive school learning as an aid in developing into the kind of persons they want to be, and as a means to achieving important goals, they are likely to do mediocre or failing work.

OTHER FAVORABLE SCHOOL CONDITIONS

Orientation procedures may markedly affect a student's initial attitude toward a new school or college. Superintendent William J. Burkhard, Sacramento City Schools, Sacramento, California, quoted a letter that the principal of the Sacramento High School had received. This is what a former student wrote:

I remember the first day I went to high school. I was two weeks late and I was new to the school. It all looked so big, so many people, so many halls, so many doors, so many things I didn't know. And then someone took me to your desk. You probably won't remember this at all but you asked me where I had been going to school and then if I had ever been fishing in the river there. I often wondered just how you knew just how to ask the right question. And I remember you telling me about fishing in that river, about my family and my school, the things I liked and remembered. When I finished you told me about the school, all the courses and the activities and what they meant in after-school life. And then we went over my reports from the grammar school that I had come from and together we made out my first-year program. You even took me around to the rooms and introduced me personally to the teachers. I remember how important I felt. I remember many of my teachers. Most of them I liked. Some I couldn't understand.[9]

Orientation should be continuous throughout the freshman year; it should enable the student to discover things about himself. Situations should be provided in which the student can test his own powers and thus learn what he can and cannot do. To accomplish this, the orientation course must become an orientation laboratory.

Standardized tests, as part of a self-diagnostic process, should facilitate learning.[10] Administering tests without interpreting their results may increase a student's feeling of inferiority. This is especially true if the student does not know how standardized tests are constructed, and feels that he has failed if he does not complete all the items in the allotted time. The wise use of test results as part of a comprehensive program of appraisal helps the student to choose a suitable curriculum and to profit by effective methods of instruction.

CONCLUDING STATEMENT

Home, school, and community should combine to create a favorable learning environment for adolescents. In school they should have the opportunity to acquire the skills, knowledge, and understanding needed by all students. These common learnings include not only the communication arts and computation but also some understanding of the world in which they live, the world with which they will have to cope, the world which they hope to make better. One teacher may have students in a combined social studies and communication arts class; another, in science and mathematics. A more radical version of the block plan is a core of common problems in the understanding of which the tools of learning and essential facts are acquired.

[9] Pamphlet on counseling, Sacramento City Schools, California.

[10] Arthur E. Traxler, "The Use of Tests in Differentiated Instruction," *Education,* vol. 74 (January, 1954), pp. 272–278.

In addition to the common learning, opportunities to develop individual interests must be provided. This can be done through special classes in art, music, shop, handicrafts, home economics, typing; in regular classes; and in extraclass activities in the school and in community agencies.

A wide range of school activities is needed to meet the manifold needs of young adolescents—basic skills, rigorous college preparatory subjects, exploratory experiences in the arts, practical courses for those preparing to enter a vocation as soon as they leave high school. Certainly, if young people are compelled to stay in school, they should have work to do there in which they can succeed.

Opportunities to make friends of both sexes allow the adolescent to get along with others in groups, to derive from group experiences the values of developing initiative and responsibility for the success of the group; they also assist him in breaking away from too close family ties, and provide the self-confidence that comes with being accepted by one's peers. In this process of learning human-relations skills, the teacher's role is to set and hold firm limits needed to create good working conditions and to reinforce the adolescent's self-control, to serve as a consultant and a resource person, and to guide, not dominate. The urban youngster who lives in an impersonal world needs this acceptance and association in the family, the school classes and clubs, and in community organizations. In literature, especially, there is the personal touch in the interaction between author and reader, in the selections of books suited to individual abilities, in the shared experiences in listening to a story read aloud, and in the personal application many students make to their own lives.[11]

Parents should learn as much as possible about the curriculum and their child's life in school. Most teachers and principals extend a cordial invitation to parents to visit the school, and will take time to confer with them. Effective parent-teacher conferences will clarify the parents' idea of what the school is trying

[11] Dora V. Smith, "Caring for Individual Differences in the Literature Class," *Education*, vol. 74 (January, 1954), pp. 294–299.

to do for the students, and will enlighten the teacher, too. Learning of adolescents' needs for real firmness at times, for association with the opposite sex, for uninterrupted time, parents will try to provide these conditions.

Scholastic success likewise depends on a combination of conditions. Some of these are characteristics and activities of the student: intelligence, regular school attendance, outside-of-school activities, and effective reading and study methods.[12] Emotional factors, complex and often unconscious, often block learning in individual cases.

The administrator has over-all responsibility for creating conditions that make effective learning possible. He employs qualified teachers and other members of the school staff; he is responsible for an effective guidance program and for providing the experiences adolescents need. Much of the good morale of the school emanates from his relations with students, parents, and staff.

Some conditions are the responsibility of the teacher: his attitude of respect for and interest in the student, his skillful teaching methods, the group atmosphere he creates. His skill in individualizing and vitalizing instruction, his personal example, and the values he shares with his students are very important components of an effective pattern. All these conditions constitute the learning environment of the adolescent.

COMPREHENSION QUESTIONS

1. What are some of the personal matters that adolescents say distract them from study? What might be some of the deeper psychological causes of inattention?

2. What individual differences exist with respect to whether or not students want to study with others, or have members of the family help them with their homework?

3. What is the difference between "cooperation in getting one's homework done" and "cheating"?

[12] G. E. Anspaugh, "Qualities Related to High Scholarship in Secondary School," *School Review*, vol. 61 (September, 1953), pp. 337–340.

4. What are the pros and cons of homework?

5. What are some of the reading difficulties that make studying hard for many students?

6. How are the curriculum and methods of teaching related to scholastic success?

7. How are teacher personality and student-teacher relationships related to scholastic success?

STUDY PROJECTS

1. When an adolescent says, "My mind wanders when I begin to study," ask, "Where does it wander to?" In this way you may discover some of the things that are bothering him; you may be able to help him do something about them.

2. Plan an attractive afternoon or evening study place for students who have poor home study conditions. Perhaps you can combine some recreation with the study hours.

3. After reading students' criticisms of assignments, plan some assignments which avoid the faults they mention.

4. After reading students' criticisms of school, what changes would you make in the curriculum and teaching methods?

5. After reading students' comments on what they like or dislike about teachers, what can you as a teacher or parent do to develop some of the favorable characteristics they mention?

FOR FURTHER STUDY

ASSOCIATION FOR SUPERVISION AND CURRICULUM DEVELOPMENT, *Developing Programs for Young Adolescents.* Washington, D.C.: National Education Association, 1954.

———, *What Shall the High Schools Teach?* Washington, D.C.: National Education Association, 1956.

BROOKS, ALICE R., "Integrating Books and Reading with Adolescent Tasks," *School Review,* vol. 58 (April, 1950), pp. 211–219.

BROWN, FREDERICK W., "A Psychotherapeutically Oriented Coeducational Program for Mentally Retarded Adolescents in a Comprehensive High School," *Mental Hygiene,* vol. 39 (April, 1955), pp. 246–270.

DAVIS, ALLISON, *Social-class Influences upon Learning.* Cambridge, Mass.: Harvard University Press, 1950.

"The Educational Program: Adolescence," *Review of Educational Research*, vol. 24 (February, 1954), pp. 4–102.

"The Educational Program: Later Adolescence," *Review of Educational Research*, vol. 24 (October, 1954), pp. 263–350.

KELLER, FRANKLIN J., *The Double-purpose High School*. New York: Harper & Brothers, 1953.

KETTELKAMP, GILBERT C., *Teaching Adolescents*. Boston: D. C. Heath and Company, 1954.

NEA EDUCATIONAL POLICIES COMMISSION, *Education for All American Youth; a Further Look*. Washington, D.C.: National Education Association, 1952.

SMITH, B. O., W. O. STANLEY, and J. H. SHORES, *Fundamentals of Curriculum Development*. Yonkers, N.Y.: World Book Company, 1957.

STRANG, RUTH, "The Counselor's Contribution to the Guidance of the Gifted, the Under-achiever, and the Retarded," *Personnel and Guidance Journal*, vol. 34 (April, 1956), pp. 494–497.

———, "Students' Perception of Factors Affecting Their Studying," *Mental Hygiene*, vol. 41 (January, 1957), pp. 97–102.

WITTY, PAUL, "Answers to Questions about Reading," *National Parent-Teacher*, vol. 50 (September, 1955), pp. 10–13.

Fiction and Popular Articles

BARCLAY, DOROTHY, "Second Big Step—Into High School," *New York Times Magazine* (September 9, 1956), p. 48.

BELLACK, ARNO A., and LELAND B. JACOBS, "Educational Programs for Junior High School Youth," *NEA Journal*, vol. 44 (May, 1955), pp. 267–269.

* HARRIMAN, JOHN, *Winter Term*. New York: Howell, Soskin, Publishers, 1940.

LLOYD, ROBERT C., "I Teach Big City Teen-agers," *NEA Journal*, vol. 45 (October, 1956), pp. 412–413.

MERRILL, KENNETH GRIGGS, "A Teacher Made the Difference," *NEA Journal*, vol. 43 (October, 1954), pp. 413–414.

REDL, FRITZ, *What Do Children Expect of Teachers?* New York: Bank Street College of Education.

SMITH, DORA V., "What Do We Want Johnny to Do—to Pronounce Words or to Read?" *Educational Horizons*, vol. 34 (Winter, 1955), pp. 135–142.

STEWART, JACK, "School Didn't Give Us What We Want," *This Week Magazine* (October 14, 1956), pp. 10, 18, 20–21.

* Fiction.

Audio-visual Aids

Desk for Billie. 57 minutes. Sound. Black and white or color. National Education Association.

Helen Keller in Her Story. 45 minutes. Sound. Black and white. Louis de Rochemont Associates.

The Hot Rod Handicap. 30 minutes. Sound. Color. Richfield Oil Corporation.

A Place for Growing. 15 minutes. Sound. Color. Campus Film Productions, Inc.

School in Centerville. 20 minutes. Sound. Black and white. National Education Association.

Filmstrips

Bringing the World to the Classroom. 45 frames. Silent. Black and white. Wayne University.

A Core Curriculum in Action. 55 frames. Silent. Black and white. Wayne University.

CHAPTER 14

Guidance of Adolescents

In guiding adolescents, we should consider their characteristics and the developmental tasks they hope to accomplish.
Aware of their eagerness to achieve independence, the counselor
will help them to think things through themselves. Knowing their
concern about developing their own philosophy of life, he will
not hesitate to share with them, informally and warmly, his own
philosophy and perspective on life, his own values and standards, if these are true and kind and generous. Understanding
their need for information about boy-girl relations, educational
and vocational plans, moral and religious questions, he will be
able to supply facts and suggest resources.

Since guidance always takes place in a relationship, the counselor realizes that what he is influences the student, even more
than what he says. This relationship affects both counselor and
student; a chain of interactions is set in motion during the interview. Having learned to relate himself to the counselor, the student will be able to bring more social warmth and understanding
to his associations with others.

Instead of focusing his attention on problems, the counselor
will have the more basic aim of helping the student to understand the resources within himself and to create the kind of environment in which he can realize his best self. The counselor
wants the student to grow in self-understanding, in understanding of how other people are feeling when they behave in certain
ways, in capacities and values, and in the techniques of living.

Thus the student will develop "the maturity and flexibility to solve new problems as they are presented." [1]

WHAT KIND OF GUIDANCE DO ADOLESCENTS WANT?

At first, the counselor's goals are seldom clearly recognized by the students, who are more likely to be concerned with their immediate needs. Even though students' and counselor's goals do not entirely agree, nevertheless it is important for the parent, teacher, and counselor to understand what adolescents expect from adults.

One way of ascertaining the kind of guidance which adolescents want and need is to ask them. Accordingly, an analysis was made of 573 compositions on the topic, "What help or guidance do persons of my age want from adults?" These compositions were obtained from five grade levels—eight to twelve inclusive. A variety of schools was represented: a Roman Catholic boys' high school; public high schools in lower-middle class neighborhoods in two cities, in a factory town, in middle class suburbs; a city vocational high school (senior girls with an average IQ of 85); a suburban high school in which three-fourths of the pupils came from wealthy homes; and a private preparatory school.

The youngsters' replies fell into two main groups: (1) those which indicated the problems on which they wanted guidance, and (2) those which indicated the nature of the guidance they desired. The total number of responses tabulated in this set of compositions was 1,522 for all grades. The figures in Table 14 represent the number of responses in each broad category, and the relative frequencies stated as percentages of the total number of responses.

The frequency with which the need for guidance in each kind of problem would be mentioned in a given situation would vary with the students' socio-economic background and intelligence,

[1] Gardner Murphy, "The Cultural Context of Guidance," *Personnel and Guidance Journal*, vol. 34 (September, 1955), p. 8.

TABLE 14

Kind of Problem	Responses in This Category	
	Number	Per Cent of Total Responses
Problems of social relations.....	127	18.5
Educational guidance..........	116	15.1
Moral or religious questions.....	63	6.8
Vocational guidance...........	41	6.7
Money problems..............	12	3.5

the courses they were taking, the guidance they had had, and other conditions.

Social Relations

The problems of social relations on which these students wanted guidance were those connected with meeting people, making friends, knowing points of etiquette and social responsibilities; problems of dating, including adult interference; getting information about the physical facts of sex; selecting clothes, and other matters involving personal appearance; and, for the seniors especially, problems of love, romance, and marriage. Need for general social guidance was felt more strongly by junior high school students; need for marriage counseling was mentioned only by seniors in high school. One thirteen-year-old girl stated her problem frankly: "I want guidance from adults so that I may be the kind of girl all the nice fellows like and want to date a lot. What to say and do on a date so the boy will want to take me out again."

Quite a large order for a counselor! The kind of adult "guidance" youngsters don't want was indicated by a tenth-grade boy in speaking of his mother:

When I get home from school she immediately starts confronting me with questions: Where am I going tonight? Who are you dating? Why don't you date her? You need to get out more! I realize she is doing it for my own good, but I get sick and tired of her constant naging upon that subject. Many times I feel like sitting home at night and watching TV instead of dating.

Instead of getting their information about sex from "smutty conversation," they want to obtain specific facts from adults— "facts of life"; as one boy said, "like on your first night what you are supposed to do and how you are supposed to go about it." A fifteen-year-old girl expressed the viewpoint of many others when she said, "I definitely feel a parent should discuss matters previously depicted as 'secret' with their children (N.B. We no longer live in the Victorian Age)." Information given in an atmosphere in which adolescents feel free to talk about questions that are bothering them tends to promote moral standards and relieve anxieties.

Educational Problems

As we have already noted (see Chapter 11), adolescents want help in choosing elective subjects in high school and meeting college entrance requirements. Many were concerned about education beyond high school. Some wanted help in deciding whether to go to college. One senior boy stated this problem with unusual clarity and comprehensiveness: "Most problems that face a person of my age are: What should I do after I get out of high school? Should I go to college? Would I be or am I a burden to my parents if I decide to go to college? Do I have the aptitude necessary to get a college degree? If I do go to college what subject would I be most adequately fitted for?"

Part of this uncertainty arises from not knowing whether one has the aptitude for college work. This is where the counselor can give students definite help, not only by interpreting their test results, but also by helping them to review their educational history and otherwise explore their interests and abilities. Sound educational guidance presupposes guidance in self-understanding and help in developing appropriate goals and values.

Many felt that the educational guidance they had received was "too little and too late." Counselors should take to heart criticisms such as the following: "I wish I could have been guided correctly in choosing subjects as a freshman. I was just put into a General Math class. In the second year I began to realize I wanted algebra. As a freshman I did not realize my need or ability for math."

Seniors are especially likely to regret that they were not helped early enough to see the value of serious study. The following is a typical regret: "Many students do as I did from the beginning of my high school career. For the first year it was nothing but 'goofing off.' . . . I continued to 'goof off.' Now as a senior I have learned that this was the biggest mistake I ever made."

Counselors could use quotations of this kind in talking with groups of freshmen; such comments made by seniors are more impressive than general admonitions to "get busy."

Many of these students wanted help in progressing in their chosen course. They mentioned wanting help especially when they were behind in their schoolwork, and when they could not understand a subject. "Personally," said a thirteen-year-old girl in the ninth grade, "I want help from my teachers. I want them to help me with my schoolwork. I understand topics much better when I am helped personally. I like a friendly feeling between my teachers and myself." An older student did not want actual help with her homework as much as "to be able to talk to someone about what is troubling me in connection with school." Educational guidance, too, takes place in a relationship.

Problems of Vocational Development

In contrast with the students surveyed in other studies, relatively few of those in this sampling specifically mentioned the need for vocational guidance (see Chapter 11). High school seniors made the largest percentage of references to this item. Of these, a large proportion were concerned with military service: "I would like some advice on whether to join a service or to wait and be drafted." Another stated his vocational guidance problem in this way: "I would like guidance in choosing a field to enter as my life work and encouragement and facts to assure me that this is the right field of work." A few mentioned needing more specific help in applying for a job, or in getting part-time and summer work. One ninth-grade boy suggested that the school should have a "committee of students to find jobs, after and before school, for other students."

Some expressed dissatisfaction with school subjects as preparation for a vocation. "Our schools are not teaching us a trade or something we need to start off on a job," an eighteen-year-old senior boy complained. "They're teaching only what happened in the past, which doesn't pertain to the work we do now." Some felt that parents should not select their children's vocations. "Many parents," said a thirteen-year-old boy, "want their child to be something which the child has no desire to be." An older boy showed insight into his parents' motivation when he said, "I don't think parents should push their kids into certain jobs they want their children to be in. Then it seems as if they are trying to make their children be what they wanted to be but never were."

Only a few mentioned need for guidance in discovering their capabilities. Those who did mention this basic aspect showed a naïve faith in tests, which is all too common: "I want help in choosing my job of the future—they have all kinds of tests to show what field of work you are capable of doing." These students seemed unaware of the broad aspects of vocational development, and of the problem of relating one's capabilities and interests to opportunities in the world of work. Most of the references to vocational guidance in these compositions were concerned with the student's interests and what he *wants* to do. Few showed consideration of what they are capable of doing, what vocational openings are available, or whether the work is socially useful.

Money Problems

Less than 4 per cent of the statements in this sampling referred to the need for guidance in money matters. Curiously enough, most of these references were made by boys in the tenth and twelfth grades of a private preparatory school. They thought a boy should work for most of the money he needs, and have guidance on how his money should be spent. Along this line, one fifteen-year-old boy wrote: "There are many spend-thrift teen-agers today and if there was a way to teach us how to avoid this I'm sure we could have just as much fun on less money." Though youngsters object when adults dictate how they should spend their money, they would probably welcome more opportunity to discuss with adults the question of how to get their money's worth. Such a conversation might lead to a consideration of people's values, as indicated by what they spend money for.

Religious and Moral Guidance

The adolescents in the sample studied were most concerned with questions of "right" and "wrong." Two senior high school students stated the matter as follows:

Sometimes, even if a boy has a good idea of what is right or wrong, he is bound to be confused as to what to do.

I want adults to help me make my decisions, show me where I am wrong, teach me the good things of life, distinguish good from bad, and prevent me from taking the wrong road.

Adolescents on all socio-economic levels want help from adults in this respect. The above comment was made by a senior high school student in a wealthy community. Eighth-grade students in a high-delinquency industrial area stated it in this way: "Older people should teach younger people the right things to do." "The help I want from my parents is to raise me the right way so I won't get mixed up with the wrong people."

These young people indicate clearly that they want some adult controls; sometimes they interpret a wholly permissive attitude as indifference. A fifteen-year-old girl, a junior in a college preparatory course, voiced this opinion: "I think we respect our elders more if they show concern about our affairs, even if we don't think so at the time. I, for one, would hate to be able to go out wherever I wanted and come home as late as I wished. I think we need certain restrictions."

A few mentioned religious matters on which they wanted guidance. These were stated in various ways, as in the following quotations, the first from an eighth-grade student and the second from a girl in the twelfth grade:

I want guidance help in learning about God and His teaching and how to be a better Christian.

I believe that young people my age appreciate the advice of adults which pertains to religious convictions. You may need help in matters of your spiritual life which you cannot tell your roommate. So you ask teachers to help you.

One of the more specific statements was about prayer: "I should like to know what things I should pray for and what I should not pray for. There are many things which I would like to see done, many things I would like to do or have, many things that it seems must be done. I am in doubt about the spirit in which to pray."

On questions of this kind they referred to priests, pastors, Sunday school teachers, and parents as sources of religious guidance.

Some very significant but unique responses emphasized the importance of adult example, as in the following statement by a fifteen-year-old:

As to a guide in religious matters I think that this is one of the greatest ways that a child is influenced by his parents. If a child sees his parents going to church as though it were drudgery he is going to do the same thing, but if he sees his parents going to church as if they had waited all week for it, he is going to think, "Well, if it makes them happy it will probably do the same for me."

Teachers and counselors usually hesitate to share their religious convictions and values with students; they think students are not interested. These compositions suggest that some adolescents welcome guidance on serious moral and religious perplexities.

Discovering Interests and Abilities

Very few of the students in this sample mentioned discovery of one's potentialities as an objective of guidance. This seems to indicate an absence of developmental guidance—guidance that helps an adolescent to understand his capabilities in relation to the opportunities offered for their development. It also suggests that although standardized tests and inventories are administered, their results are not interpreted to the students. A group of high school students, discussing the counseling they had received,[2] objected strenuously to the practice of giving students tests but not letting them use the results in gaining an understanding of themselves. That students can profit by self-appraisal has been demonstrated in a number of schools. This helps students to take an objective, realistic view of themselves.

These general problem areas in which adolescents want guidance are familiar to counselors and teachers; they have been discussed in previous chapters. The youngsters' criticisms and suggestions as to the nature of this guidance are particularly fresh and challenging. In their compositions they vigorously express dissatisfaction with adult guidance or distrust of it. They tell us in no uncertain terms what kind of guidance they desire and describe its quality.

DISSATISFACTION WITH ADULT GUIDANCE

By learning more about young people's dissatisfactions with the guidance they have had and the nature of the guidance they desire, adults can improve the quality of their counseling. Having this knowledge of how the adolescent feels about the guidance offered will enable parents and teachers to avoid many common pitfalls.

Reluctance to Talk with Parents

An increasing number of adolescents from the eighth to the twelfth grade were reluctant to talk with their parents about personal problems; they felt that their parents would not understand them. Part of this reluctance may stem from a desire to be independent: "I don't think I need any help for the simple

[2] Jack R. Matlock, "Counseling as Students See It," *Journal of the National Association of Deans of Women*, vol. 18 (October, 1954), pp. 7–12.

reason I don't want to be dependent on anyone after I leave school. If I get into any difficulties I would want to iron them out for myself." This comment was made by a seventeen-year-old senior boy, who was obviously a nonsatellizer.

Unsatisfactory previous experience with adult guidance is another factor. An eleventh-grade girl wrote:

Speaking for myself, I don't want *any* guidance from adults. I'd like them to leave me alone. My parents, I feel, are not qualified to guide me because if they were, they'd have done a better job of it than they have so far. I've had nothing but bumbling, self-righteous adults to come in contact with. They don't care what happens to me or how I feel, and I know it, and they know it. Of course, I don't expect them to fall all over themselves for love of me, but why must they pretend to be interested in me when they're not?

An eighth-grade boy made a typical comment: "I'm afraid to tell my troubles and problems to my parents. I'm afraid they will get mad and say I shouldn't get into troubles." A fifteen-year-old boy thought that "too much spanking, when younger, will create a feeling of fear toward the father, so that when the boy grows to be fifteen or sixteen, he will not confide in his parents and he should."

A twelfth-grade girl in a city vocational high school expressed her feeling still more poignantly: "I can't go to my mother for advice because she won't listen to me. She never asks me about schools, friends, boy friend, or anything; never asks me if anything is troubling me or what I did in school. I can't even have conversations with her. All my problems whether big or small I have to keep bottled up inside me."

On the other hand, reluctance to confide may indicate maturity. A senior girl from a well-to-do family indicated that she was reluctant, at her age, to seek much help from adults; at the same time she expressed appreciation of her parents' earlier guidance:

I think that if a girl or boy is pampered and protected all his life that he will be lost when he gets out on his own. My parents have always guided me by suggestions but I have always made my own choices. Most of the time after I think it through I usually agreed with them, though.

I feel that by being treated as an adult I have developed a sense of responsibility which I would not have acquired otherwise. It gives me a feeling of self-assurance to know that I don't have to "run home and ask 'Mommy'" every time I have something to decide.

I think my life is my own to live as I choose. I'm not saying that I can "live alone and like it." It's still nice to know that if I ever run into trouble I have two wonderful parents to turn to.

Judging from their comments, these youngsters, however reluctant they may be to show dependence, feel the need of a parent or some adult in whom they can at times confide. Perhaps some of them have not entirely relinquished their childhood dependence on parents. Others have become capable of a more mature relationship; they want to talk with adults as man to man, not as child to a grown-up authority.

Distrust of Adult Knowledge and Values

Fewer of these students expressed distrust of adult values or resentment of adult assumptions of omniscience. In some instances, when they did express this resentment, they were not far wrong. As one twelfth-grade boy said: "Adults will freely give advice on any subject, often incorrect and unsubstantiated. That is my chief criticism of adults—that many of them give advice on those subjects they are not familiar with, thereby misleading the boy or girl."

That this happens too often in educational and vocational guidance is attested by the complaints of students who have taken the wrong courses. In other matters, too, it is important that counselors' ideas about the effects of different courses of action be true and proved by practice. Otherwise young people lose confidence in their advisers. The other thing they object to most is "the air of 'I know it all; just listen to me.'" "Often they say," one boy observed, "'I have lived longer so I should know better.' I don't believe this is true."

If an adult has been wrong, he should admit it. "I don't like people," said a sixteen-year-old girl, "who will not admit a mistake just because they are elders. This often makes you wonder whether it's worth it to admit you're wrong; after all, according to them, all you have to do is wait till you grow old and then you're right all the time."

Dislike of Having Serious Problems Minimized

Another reason why some adolescents hesitate to ask for help from older persons is that adults do not always think the problem important. A senior high school boy expressed the idea this way: "We would like adults to understand our problems which may seem petty to them but are big to us." Adolescents want to be taken seriously when they are serious; they "think parents should let you speak more freely on serious topics as well as joking ones." And certainly when they ask for adult help, they do not want to be laughed at or made fun of. "I expect," a fourteen-year-old girl wrote, "people older than me to help me with problems. Sometimes when I ask my older sister for advice she makes fun of me. Now I hesitate to ask her anything."

Even if parents do not laugh at the problems of their teen-age children, they tend to criticize or scold; these responses are equally distasteful to adolescents. A fourteen-year-old girl in the college preparatory course contrasted two parental attitudes:

I expect from my parents understanding. . . . If I am in any kind of trouble I like my parents to help me so I could change for the better, and not, if I walk in the house with a problem, to start yelling at me without hearing what happened. I would like to be able to sit down and discuss things with my parents. I would like them to have rules about what time I should come home, etc. I would like them to help me a little with schoolwork and to be interested in me.

Resentment of Incessant Gratuitous Advice

Although many adolescents seem to seek advice from adults, they probably make a distinction between advice which they ask for and feel free to take or leave and advice which is forced upon them. "There are times," one of them wrote, "when a person my age will seek help and that is when it should be given." What they object to, and quite rightly, is too much unsolicited help. A senior high school girl expressed mixed feelings about her mother's domination:

Adults seem to feel that it is their duty to guide us. I appreciate it when I feel I can't handle the situation myself. But my mother is constantly showing me the way—*her* way. I feel this attitude is wrong, although I realize that she wants to do the right thing by me. Her assistence is more of a dominating power. If I don't agree with her, she gets very upset. She tells me that I'm deliberately obstinate. This is wrong. I have my own beliefs which I would like to experiment with. If I'm constantly sheltered by my parents, how could I possibly be a well adjusted adult, who could think for herself?

"The adult's help I want," said an eighteen-year-old boy, "is just enough to start my own thinking process in motion." A senior high school boy expressed this same idea briefly but exceedingly well: "I would resent help every step of the way. I feel that doing something yourself and working it through is one of the most satisfying pleasures you can enjoy." The adult who gives young people the solution of a problem deprives them of the joy of discovering it for themselves, and the sense of competence which comes from handling a situation successfully.

These youngsters' remarks on advice should be heeded by overzealous counselors. They should remember that capable adolescents welcome adult help only when they recognize the need for it and are ready for it. They want only enough help to enable them to answer their questions or solve their problems by themselves.

Feeling Misunderstood

One of the most insistent pleas of children and young people is for various kinds of understanding—understanding of the changes they are going through, of their problems, of their developmental need for independence. "There are many parents," a tenth-grade boy remarked with considerable insight, "who say they have heart-to-heart talks, but they just give their opinion and do not let their child give his. If he does, they say he is talking back." Several boys in a school in a lower-class neighborhood complained that people did not understand the harmlessness of their particular gangs. One of them expressed it in this way: "I hang around with a large crowd. When people walk by us they give us dirty looks. They don't understand that we have fun when we are all together."

In this sampling of compositions the relative frequency of this desire for understanding increased between the eighth and twelfth grades from 5.5 per cent to 13 per cent; however, it was a thirteen-year-old girl who wrote, "The most important thing an adult should do before guiding us is understand how we feel." These students leveled their most serious condemnation at those adults who not only do not understand but do not even try to understand. Consequently, the children do not discuss things with their parents, cannot tell them when they go on a date, and are afraid to tell them when they've done something wrong.

Viewpoint that Adults Are to Blame

A few youngsters, especially senior high school students, expressed the viewpoint that adolescent mistakes and juvenile delinquency were due to the indifference of adults or to lack of proper guidance. They mentioned instances of juvenile delinquency and cases of boys who have been sent to reform school; they attributed these occurrences to too much or too little discipline in the home and to lack of adult guidance. Said one eighteen-year-old boy in a private school: "I am sure that if the boys who were asked to leave this school had had the proper guidance and help they would probably be here right now."

All of these are serious sources of dissatisfaction: apparent indifference or neglect, absence of understanding and acceptance, overprotection expressed in continuous unsolicited advice. If we adults were aware of the way adolescents feel about these things, we would meet their needs for guidance more effectively.

Dissatisfactions of College Students

College students expressed many dissatisfactions with the counseling they had had.[3] Among their chief complaints were that counselors:

Wasted their time in irrelevant chit-chat, without apparent goal or purpose

Talked too much

Were "vague, indefinite, unclear, or uncertain"

Treated them as "cases" and showed little real interest in them

Explained all difficulties in accordance with a "pet theory"

Broke appointments, were late

Permitted interruptions, seemed to have their minds on other things

College freshmen work out many problems for themselves; they may talk them over with classmates or roommates, whose happiness and adjustment often influence their state of mind. Many roommates are sympathetic to each other's difficulties, whether these involve homesickness, lack of dates, or other problems. They help each other.

Upperclassmen who serve as freshman advisers are another source of help. They can answer questions about the details of college life—where to cash a check, buy books, get laundry done, etc. If freshmen are having academic problems, they are often more willing to seek the help of an upperclassman who excels in the subject than to reveal their inadequacies to a professor or dean.

College seniors, facing the responsibilities of life after three years in an academic environment, are often confused and less sure of themselves than they were earlier. This instability of later adolescence offers an opportunity to reorganize one's values and goals on a higher level. It requires a mature quality of guidance.

[3] George S. Speer, "Negative Reactions to College Counseling," *Occupations,* vol. 34 (November, 1945), pp. 99–100.

AMOUNT OF GUIDANCE DESIRED

A small percentage of adolescents flaunt their independence by saying that they want no help or guidance whatever. In answer to the question, "What help or guidance do you want from adults?" one senior high school student wrote, "I don't! I have had too much 'help' already." Another explained, "To get along in this world you have to go at it alone. I have done this for a long time now. Since my father died, I have been on my own. So I feel I don't need any help from anybody. . . ." Circumstances may have made this ninth-grade boy unusually independent. Others who stated that they wanted no help or guidance may have been "nonsatellizers"—children who determined in their preschool years to break away violently from the dependency of infancy.

On the positive side, many of these adolescents desired guidance from adults, at home or at school. A thirteen-year-old girl summed up her attitude toward the various adults in her life as follows: "On the whole, I want all my teachers to be personal with me and to know me, not just my school life and marks. I'd like my parents to be less personal so I could go my merry way alone when I want to be alone. I want other adults to be friendly, interested, but not personal, unless very good friends of mine." This girl's attitudes had been conditioned by a happy school experience and a mother "who butts into my social affairs . . . always asks whom I like as a boy-friend. If I tell her (which I seldom do!) she tells all the mothers of my classmates in *friendly* (?) conversation, and the whole school knows within a week."

An older girl, sixteen years of age, expressed a much more favorable attitude toward parental guidance than toward guidance by friends and other people:

If we get in trouble at school or anywhere away from home, our parents will probably be the best persons to ask. Other people may not care about our problems and won't give as good advice as those who love us and want our well-being. If we ask someone else they may also form wrong ideas and bad impressions of us and not care to understand. They may feel that they have a good piece of gossip.

This quotation gives a clue as to why some high school students are so reluctant to talk freely with teachers or school counselors.

About one-fifth of the responses, with by far the largest percentage occurring in the twelfth grade, expressed the viewpoint that adults are qualified by their experience in life to give highly valuable advice, which should be heeded and acted upon. As a seventeen-year-old boy expressed it, "Parents have the perspective of years and as a rule come up with the best decisions." In some, if not all, cases, this favorable attitude toward adult guidance may be the result of past experience. One twelfth-grade girl wrote: "She always gives me the advice I ask for and ten out of eleven times she is right." An eighteen-year-old boy in a private school must also have had good relationships with adults. He wrote: "Many teen-agers hate to have an adult tell them anything. I think this is all wrong because they are really the best friends you have and are giving the advice for one's own good."

Although the young people just quoted may still be somewhat overdependent on their parents, they seem to realize that it is wise to turn to adults for help in situations which they are not able to handle alone. On the whole, they take a sensible attitude toward using adult resources as a means of solving their problems. They realize that a certain amount of dependency is not incompatible with maturity.

There was a small percentage who clung to their close childhood relationship with their parents and seemed reluctant to lose dependence on parental control. Some of this reluctance stems from fear of doing the wrong thing. An eighteen-year-old boy expressed this fear in an extreme form: "I know from experience when my parents let me have some freedom that I don't know enough to get along well by myself. Almost every time I have been told I could do something by myself, it usually ended up in something going wrong."

Detailed study of adolescents' compositions shows clearly that in general they want neither domination nor desertion. They want freedom to make mistakes but "not enough rope to hang themselves." They want advice as a basis for making their own decisions; they want limits that will hold fast against the impetuosity of their impulses. It is significant that so many adolescents want help from parents at the very time when they are struggling to gain psychological emancipation.

Although a few youngsters indicated distrust of adults, a larger number expressed a desire to be trusted and accepted by parents or other adults. A typical statement of this point of view was made by a high school girl from a wealthy community: "I think parents should trust their children and in doing that gain their confidence so that when the child needs advice or guidance she will go to her parents and they can help her." A girl from a poor home environment said wistfully: "I've always wondered what it would be like to have parents that trusted me. All my friends have parents like that, that's why I never stay home." A seventeen-year-old boy summed it up by saying, "I think what most boys want is to be treated like a mature person."

There seems to be nothing more important to adolescents than to have someone who respects and believes in them.

QUALITY OF GUIDANCE DESIRED

Some of the subtler qualities of guidance are also suggested in the compositions. The students' comments imply a sound though unformulated theory or philosophy of counseling. To them, personality counts, and a relationship of confidence and kindness is more important than mere verbal communication.

Client-centered Counseling

In more than one-fifth of this sampling of 305 compositions, youngsters spontaneously expressed the opinion that guidance should permit them to make their own decisions and use their own intelligence in solving problems. They sometimes want advice, but they also want freedom in using it. As one of them put it, one wants "to accept advice and still make some of his own decisions. The adult must learn how and when to give it." Another put the focus on his own initiative: "I want to venture to my own decisions, not have them made for me, although I am always open for suggestions and criticism." And a fifteen-year-old said, "I am just at the age when the more I can do for myself the better it is for me." These adolescents seem to be in accord with the fundamental philosophy of client-centered counseling—respect for the individual, his opinions, his questions, his potentialities.

Perceptive Objectivity

While they desire warmth and friendliness, they abhor sentimentality, which they sometimes interpret as sympathy. One senior high school boy described the objectivity which he desired in teacher counseling: "In school, I look [for guidance] to the person whom I know is the most understanding without being too sympathetic with all problems brought before him."

Perhaps this desirable quality can be most accurately described as perceptive objectivity.

Understanding

Of all the qualities mentioned in compositions, interviews, and group discussions, "understanding" seems to be the most desired. One seventeen-year-old boy expressed the common point of view that

Understanding is what a person of my age needs and wants most. Adults should realize the problems of young people, since they were once young themselves, but I don't think they always do. Our parents should realize that we want to be like other teen-agers and because of that we sometimes do things that they don't approve of but which they probably did themselves when they were younger.

Adolescents want adults to understand how they feel and why they behave as they do, and to be reasonable when they have made a mistake.

More Praise than Criticism

Adolescents respond to praise and approval. A high school girl described the salutary effect of positive expectations and of genuine praise: "When I was in seventh grade I had someone pay me a compliment that I've never forgotten. This person told my mother that he hoped that his two girls would grow up to be like me. My mother told me what he said and I've never forgotten it. All through school right up to today, I've tried to live up to what he said."

Both younger and older adolescents are sensitive to the personality of the counselor. They are keen to detect cool, uninterested, or perfunctory performance of duty. They seek a person who looks for the best in them; who is friendly, honest, and interested in them; and who respects their reticences.

Firmness, When Needed

Adolescents need parents and teachers to set limits. Their firmness on matters that involve health and safety, respect for property, obedience to law and order, and conformity to reasonable social conventions helps the adolescent to resist both his own wayward impulses and the tyranny of the group. An adolescent is less likely to resent restrictions if the adult is honest with him.

Sincerity

A frank approach that does not camouflage the adult's real reasons and feelings about the matter appeals to most adolescents. It helps them to appraise the situation, to recognize that other people sometimes act from motives that are not altogether altruistic, and it relieves them of the burden of "double talk." Such a sincere approach helps to build a sense of trust and a feeling of security in adolescent-adult relations.

This approach means that adults must first of all be honest with themselves and try to understand their own feelings as well as those of adolescents. Before they can share their feelings with young people, they must recognize these feelings for what they are. When the parent cannot share his feelings with a teen-age boy or girl, at least he can admit that his anger or prohibition stemmed from something that was bothering *him*, as much as from the youngster's behavior.

IMPLICATIONS FOR ADULTS

From the comments made by adolescents concerning the kind of guidance they want, parents, teachers, and counselors may obtain the following guidelines:

Listen to what they have to say; don't do all the talking; take them seriously, when they are serious.

Try to understand how they perceive the situation, what it means to them, what is below the surface of their behavior, why they are reluctant to confide.

Accept their feelings; they may not be able to change their feelings, though they can usually control their actions.

Encourage their efforts to solve their own problems; don't give advice or help which they do not want or need.

Respect their reticence.

Be accurate and honest; if you are wrong, admit it.

Help them to develop worthwhile interests and *to discover their capacities* for warm, friendly relations as well as for physical and intellectual accomplishments.

Understand your own feelings; know why certain people please or annoy you.

Set firm, reasonable limits which are necessary to prevent a youngster from getting into serious trouble; your firmness helps to reinforce his own inner controls.

Help to provide an environment in which the adolescent is free to grow.

Build a sound philosophy of life, and share your values and standards with the young person.

GUIDANCE FACILITIES

The aim of guidance is to help the adolescent perceive himself, not as "a crazy mixed-up kid," but as a person with certain abilities that he can develop, certain faults, perhaps, that he can correct, certain tasks of growing up that he must accomplish. He can be helped to see the relation between what he is now doing and the kind of person he wants to, and can, become—a person who has self-respect and is respected by others.

Developmental Guidance

Developmental guidance is accomplished largely through the process of living. In school, this implies guiding-while-teaching. The teacher tries to understand each student and provide the kind of program, the materials of instruction, the service activities, and the group experiences that help him to discover and develop his potentialities. He is concerned with creating life conditions in which the young person can make and remake himself. Discussion of concrete situations helps; role-playing of the situations described is one step nearer guidance in real-life situations. The emphasis in developmental guidance is not on correcting faults or solving problems in the usual sense of the word, but on developing the young person's resources and capacities to establish friendly relations with people, to derive pride and joy from the accomplishment of suitable work, and to become a constructive, contributing member of the community.

Counseling

At some times adolescents need to experience that face-to-face relationship which we call counseling.[4] By creating a permissive, friendly atmosphere, the counselor may help the individual to reevaluate his experience and bring his concept of himself "into closer harmony with experience." Ideally, the individual's feelings of insecurity, inadequacy, and worthlessness are replaced by feelings of security, adequacy, and worth.

Counseling is a learning situation, and various kinds of learning are involved. Usually the adolescent needs information. To make educational and vocational plans, he needs information about his abilities and interests, and about educational and vo-

---

[4] Ralph E. Jenson, "Student Feeling about Counseling Help," *Personnel and Guidance Journal*, vol. 33 (May, 1955), pp. 498–503.

cational opportunities. To make wise choices and decisions about other matters, he needs to know pertinent facts and to see their relations. To make desirable changes in his behavior, he also needs information about the meaning and possible consequences of certain behavior.

Often the adolescent needs to have his misinformation corrected. With respect to sex, for example, he may have acquired a great deal of misinformation. Until these misconceptions are cleared up, he cannot acquire accurate information and take a more constructive attitude toward sex. But it is not enough merely to point out the errors in his thinking; he must understand how he came to get these erroneous ideas. Once he has recognized their source and how he has acquired them, he is better able to modify or discard them.

But underlying his way of thinking are his values. These are still more difficult to change because they are tied in with his self-concept; they are a part of his personality, which is resistant to change. Values cannot be changed merely by talking about them; values are changed by life experiences. However, these life experiences may be interpreted in the counseling situation and may also be "caught" from a counselor who exemplifies sincerity, ability to face reality, warmth of feeling, respect for people, and faith and hope.

Emotions also enter into this learning situation. Emotions experienced in previous situations may be "redintegrated," as Harry L. Hollingworth described it, in a present situation that has some identical elements with the past. In the counseling situation, the individual's perception of these previous emotionally charged situations may very gradually change. As he learns to perceive them more objectively, more hopefully, more constructively, he will respond accordingly.

Since learning takes place in a relationship, the relation between the counselor and the adolescent is basic to successful counseling. In the counseling relationship, the adolescent's sense of trust may be slowly rebuilt. He may gradually learn to relate himself a little more closely to another human being. Having achieved this degree of intimacy with one person, he is better able to feel more warmly toward others.

Counseling a troubled adolescent obviously is a complex and time-consuming process. Changes in his perception of himself and his world are not achieved by a "pep talk," or "tea and sympathy," or admonitions, or threats. But he can be helped, in most cases, by a counselor or a psychotherapist who can establish the degree of intimacy for which the adolescent is ready and use the counseling time to help him gain the understanding he needs to handle his present problems more realistically and hopefully.

Counseling skills enable the adult to establish a warm, human relationship with the young person. In such a relationship, growth takes place in the personality of both the student and the counselor. The counselor changes as a result of the guidance he gives. The adolescent changes as a result of his contact with an understanding, sensitive adult. We need to study the effect on both parties of the interaction in the counseling situation. Through such a study of the counseling process, we shall learn what effect our contacts are having on young people, and how we may make them still more effective. We need to know how young people feel about our guidance.[5]

Psychiatric Treatment

Some adolescents need even more specialized help with their serious emotional problems. This is not a task for amateurs. Theoretically, disturbed adolescents should be helped to understand the motivations of their behavior, to bring hidden relationships to the surface so that they can handle them on a conscious level. The difficulty is that some adolescents are not capable of doing this. Inexpert therapy may remove the psychological barriers but leave the individual with his positive forces unmobilized for growth; in this defenseless state he may become more disturbed than ever. According to Josselyn,

When psychiatric treatment is indicated for the adolescent, the treatment of choice appears to be one that considerably modifies

[5] Murphy, *op. cit.*

both child psychoanalysis and the more classical form of adult psychoanalysis. The individual needs, first of all, to be protected from the external situations that excessively stimulate his internal drives. For example, in the case of the boy who is struggling with his tie to his mother, he needs to be protected from any seductive behavior on her part. In addition, he needs help in redirecting his libidinal drive toward less anxiety-stimulating love objects. He needs an opportunity to sublimate his unacceptable primitive drives into socially acceptable, psychologically constructive paths. Insight therapy should be utilized only when such redirection is impossible.[6]

Self-appraisal

Self-appraisal should be gradual and continuous through the school years. In Delaware, Darling[7] developed a self-appraisal plan in the eighth grade. Pupils obtained information about themselves through a series of interest, ability, and achievement "inventories." The results were explained to the pupils, who were encouraged to take an objective, acceptant attitude toward themselves. They also began to relate their self-concepts to the realities of educational and vocational opportunities.

Adolescents should take initiative; they should define their problem, secure and analyze facts about themselves and about educational and vocational possibilities, consider possible solutions, test their tentative solutions, and make their own decisions.[8]

Valuable as standardized tests and inventories are in guiding adolescents, they should be used with caution. The very process of testing may have a therapeutic effect—or the opposite; it may increase the student's self-confidence or tear it down as he meets increasingly difficult items. Few adolescents understand that standardized tests are built to have plenty of *ceiling*, i.e., items difficult enough to test the brightest members of the class. Moreover, there is considerable misunderstanding of the meaning of

[6] Irene M. Josselyn, *The Adolescent and His World*, p. 96. New York: Family Service Association of America, 1952.

[7] Robert J. Darling, "Student Readiness; Foundation for Student Guidance," *Journal of the National Association of Deans of Women*, vol. 18 (October, 1954), pp. 33–39.

[8] William J. Reilly, *Career Planning for High School Students*. New York: Harper & Brothers, 1953.

intelligence test scores. Some persons feel that a high score on an intelligence test ensures success and a low score predicts failure, not only in school but in life. Those who take intelligence tests should realize that the tests measure only certain aspects of intelligence, that an individual's scores may fluctuate considerably from test to test, and that group intelligence tests depend partly on school achievement, especially on reading ability. Consequently, no important decision should be made on the basis of a single test, and test results should be used in conjunction with all the other available information about the individual.

Even greater caution should be used in interpreting interest and personality inventories. The subject may consciously or unconsciously try to present himself in as favorable a light as possible; he may misinterpret the statements; he may be incapable of the degree of introspection which the inventory demands.

When tests of any kind are given, adolescents should be helped to understand what the test is supposed to measure, the extent to which it may be expected to do so, what the scores mean, and how they are related to the realities of one's life. They should be helped to interpret the resultant profiles, which show that they are better in some things than in others. This procedure should help them to take a positive, objective attitude toward themselves, focusing attention on their strengths rather than on their weaknesses.

Personnel in the Guidance Program

There is no one best program for all schools. A program for a given school should be set up in accordance with the situation —the students' need for guidance, the quantity and quality of the guidance already being provided by the teachers, and the specialized services available in the school system and in the community. In the opinion of the writer, the best general type of program includes four essentials of staff:

1. An administrator who has the guidance point of view as well as ability to establish good human relations and create conditions that make effective guidance possible.

2. Teachers who are well qualified by personality and who guide

as they teach. They play a major role in the developmental guidance of adolescents. If they are friendly in class, students will come to them with personal problems after class. Students, in their compositions, mention the guidance of teachers more often than that of full-time school counselors. One student explained it in this way: "My counselor means well, but she has so many kids to see that I never feel I can stay to talk with her about things that are most important to me."

3. Teacher-counselors who have charge of a small guidance unit such as a homeroom, core curriculum, or extended period; or faculty advisers who serve as counselors of small groups of students, preferably over a period of three or four years for the sake of maintaining continuity of relationship.

4. Guidance specialists who (a) work with and through the teachers, (b) bring their understanding of students to bear on school policies of marking, promotion, discipline, and curriculum, (c) work with individual cases that are too complex and time consuming for the teacher-counselors to handle, and (d) know and use the guidance resources—the educational, psychological, health, and recreational facilities—of the school system and the community.

All of these personnel would profit by reading or listening to what students have to say about the guidance they have had. The important thing is not the form of the program, but the way it is functioning in the lives of the students. Ordinarily it does not function well unless in-service education is provided for all concerned.

The Case Conference

The case conference is one of the best means of helping the members of a school or college staff to understand students and to become aware of their individual opportunities for guidance. In a case conference, information about an individual student is presented by his teacher-counselor or any member of the school staff who knows him well. Other members of the staff— teachers, nurse, guidance specialist, psychologist, administrator —pool their observations of the student. Then they synthesize and interpret the facts and impressions which have been presented, and formulate tentative hypotheses as to the student's developmental needs and the causes of his difficulties.

They then take any immediate steps that may be clearly indicated, each person present assuming responsibility appropriate to him. For example, the dean of girls may take responsibility for contacting a family case work agency, if the difficulty seems to lie in home conditions; the physical education teacher may schedule the student for a rest period instead of an active period in the gymnasium; the nurse may arrange for medical treatment.

At the case conference, everyone learns. By gaining a thorough understanding of one student, staff members are helped to understand many students. Ideally, a case conference should be held for every student, not just for those who are having special difficulties or problems. It is an excellent means both of developmental guidance and of staff education.

GUIDANCE OF MENTALLY RETARDED ADOLESCENTS

Mentally retarded adolescents are not a homogeneous group. The wide individual differences among them must be identified and recognized. Like other adolescents, they need respect, understanding, work which they can do successfully, and wholesome recreation which they can enjoy. They need to develop a realistic, hopeful concept of themselves.

The large majority of mentally handicapped adolescents can get and hold jobs, usually in the mechanical and service fields. Girls with IQs between 60 and 75 have been employed in publishing houses helping in the bindery, inserting folders in envelopes, putting covers on books; in cafeterias and restaurants; in hospitals as nurses' aides, tray attendants, messengers; in the garment trades; and in many other kinds of work. Boys of the same level of mental ability serve as delivery boys, kitchen helpers, porters, mechanics' helpers, packers, factory workers, elevator operators, truck drivers' helpers, and the like.

Personal-social skills and attitudes are most important for their vocational success. They can usually be placed if they have a desire to work, good personal habits, a sense of responsibility, and ability to get along with others. Placement is most difficult when emotional disturbance is added to mental deficiency.

Adolescents with IQs around 50 can work successfully under closely supervised conditions. For these young people, a workshop has been in operation in New York City. They are first given tryout experiences to see what kind of work they can do. As soon as they learn to do productive work of an unskilled or semiskilled type, they are paid for it. During the day, they spend some time in discussions of how to spend money wisely and of other problems as they arise. "Combined consultation-treatment-education centers," serving the child continuously, as he develops, make an important social contribution, both to the young people themselves and to society.

The guidance person who works with mentally retarded adolescents should obtain an accurate early diagnosis of their mental, physical, and emotional ability, know the opportunities for training and employment open to them, and constantly emphasize what they can do rather than what they cannot do. Their placement should be handled by persons who understand exceptional children. After placement, they should continue to receive supportive contacts which will facilitate their adjustment to the job.

Parents often need help in learning to understand and accept an exceptional child, in relieving their own feelings of guilt, and in recognizing the need to cooperate in efforts to secure the best education, treatment, and placement possible for him. The counselor should emphasize what the child can do, not his limitations.

GUIDANCE OF THE GIFTED

Intellectually gifted adolescents have definite opinions as to the kind of guidance they need. If their ability is identified early and suitable experiences are provided for them, their adolescent adjustment becomes much easier. Most of them are particularly sensitive to domination, probably because they are so capable of taking initiative and responsibility and assuming independence of thought and action. On the whole, the gifted adolescent is relatively unlikely to experience emotional disturbance; if he does, he has greater resources within himself to handle the situation.

The comments of a group of ninth-grade private school students, whose IQs covered a range from 103 to 160, with 80 per cent between 118 and 135, are probably quite typical. Their attitudes toward parental guidance range from complete rejection of guidance to overdependence on adults:

Parents drive children to distraction by their questions.

I would like to be let alone and be on my own.

I don't think parents should push their children to do things just because they couldn't do them themselves.

Mother especially butts into my social affairs. I wish she wouldn't always ask me who I like as a boy friend.

I should like to be trusted more.

Why aren't we allowed to use our own judgment more often?

Parents should give reasons why they say "No!"

A parent's guidance can help to prevent very unpleasant experiences.

I have respect for my parents and the way they guide me.

The more mature we are the more we will value and accept help or guidance from people we respect.

My parents have always guided me by suggestions, but I have always made my own choice.

I have never had to question what my parents say, as it has always been the right thing to do.

Here is the whole gamut of attitudes toward adult guidance. What a variety of childhood experiences and home backgrounds underlies these diverse comments!

It is especially important, both for the gifted individual and for society, that such a child develop his concept of himself as an able learner and a socially useful person. Awareness of his ability should motivate him to seek experiences that will develop it. The gifted adolescent especially needs to develop a sense of social responsibility for his good heredity and favorable childhood.

TWO ADOLESCENTS REFERRED FOR GUIDANCE

David, an Anxious Adolescent

David is 14½ years old. He has a younger brother 8 years old, whom the mother favors. In fact, she cannot see anything to commend in David. He says he takes care of the younger brother when his parents are away, but admitted that the brother was not solely in his charge because a grandmother was living with them, "who isn't very well." His older brother, aged twenty, quit college to join the Army. When filling out the application blank for the guidance office, he neglected to mention his father. In his mother's presence David is subdued and cooperative.

His junior high school counselor described him as a quiet, well-behaved boy who had not responded well to instruction, and had been placed in a class for children of retarded mental development for three years. Later they realized he was misplaced, when he obtained an IQ of 110 on the Revised Stanford-Binet Form L. But he had not learned to read well. After graduation from junior high school he entered the ninth grade of a vocational school.

Although apparently subdued at home and at school, David has felt free to express some of his resentment and hostility in the guidance office. One way of gaining his cooperation in reading is to say that if he works quickly and well, there will be a few minutes at the end of the period for him to talk. One day after he had failed, "unfairly" he thought, on a test, he took a piece of paper and cut out a paper doll. This he folded in half, and with a scissors, cut out half a heart-shaped piece so that, when the paper was opened, there was the heart cut out. He said, "If I had a knife, that's what I'd do to her."

He resists the idea of coming to the guidance office for help and expresses his boredom and indifference in word and act. He pushes away reading materials, saunters into the outer office and walks aimlessly around. He glances frequently at his watch. Once seated, he snatches up pencils, plays with any nearby objects.

One of his first remarks was, "Does another dumb guy from

my class come here?" When he talks, his words come rapidly and excitedly. When encouraged to read a suitable selection, his hands were quiet and tense. As the reading teacher jotted down errors, he would struggle with the rest of the sentence, then ask, "What did you write down?" At one point he snatched the paper and said in a loud and almost accusing way, "Did I make all those mistakes?"

He seems to distrust and avoid persons of his own age. He passed by other students without giving any awareness of their presence. Even when introduced to two boys, David said nothing, but walked out of the office without looking back. When playing a reading game with a younger boy who was winning, David picked up a pencil and held it menacingly as one might hold a knife, and with a half smile made excited threats each time a card turned out to be for the other boy. He threw the last few cards on the table, put down his pencil, and walked away without finishing the game. He came back with his pyramid trick with which he challenged the younger boy, Jim. When Jim couldn't do the puzzle, David, with a casual motion, showed him, then pushed his chair back and said, "I'm going now." The two boys with whom he studied for a while asked not to be with him. The younger one now has his reading period before David and whispers in a frightened way, "Here he comes." The older boy said, "He talks so much, I can't learn nuthing." When asked about his friends in school, he quickly answered, "You get to know guys after six months and know the quiet ones, then make friends." Later he said, "You can't trust anyone." He wants the attention of his peers, but dominates others rather than helping them to express their ideas.

The only things he has expressed interest in are "anything about shop" and "fish." There seems to be an undercurrent of hostility in his life that denies any interest a chance to blossom.

There are times, however, when he shows positive behavior. At the end of one period he checked his watch saying, "Forty-five minutes up already?" After his summer vacation he showed delight in his physical growth. "Nothing fits me any more," he said gleefully. When the worker asked him how much he had grown he said, "I was 5 feet, now I'm 5 feet, 1½ inches." Everyone in the office was pleased with his increase in stature. In the same period he looked at the books and said, smiling, "Oh no, you're not getting me to do that," and walked away, but he soon came back to look over the books the reading teacher had put out about how to make and do things. Finally he selected a volume, *Teen-Age Tales,* and commanded, "You read every other paragraph." Later he decided to read his paragraphs first and let the reading teacher finish reading the story to him.

He is beginning to be aware that making friends is up to him: he gave the younger boy some ideas for his composition. When the boy said, "Thanks for helping me," a smile came over David's face though he did not look up.

Recently, about Christmas time, he came in and said, of his own accord, "I want to go on with this till June, then if I can't read well, nobody can help me but myself." When it was suggested later that there was a waiting list, and that if he wanted to continue coming he should let the reading teacher know, he changed his attitude and began to cooperate. One day he even volunteered to read whatever she chose for him.

Here is an adolescent whose performance is far below others' expectations of him and probably below his own level of aspiration. Any situation that threatens him with failure, such as reading, in which he has been failing for so many years, causes intense anxiety. To avoid this anxiety he withdraws from the situation—refusing to read, not finishing a game in which he is losing, etc. It is possible that his mother's pressure on him to read has aroused hostility, especially if he feels that she cares only about his achievement, not for him as a person.

The reading teacher tried to help him begin to understand himself better—to take pride in growing up and to recognize his real ability, as shown by the most recent psychological examination. She encouraged him to express his feelings, and he seems free to do so in her presence, as he does not at home or in school. She also has offered opportunities for him to relate himself to one or two other friendly boys, in the hope of developing a sense of intimacy which he had not achieved in his pre-adolescent period.

Joanne, a Gifted Adolescent

Joanne is fifteen years old and is in the tenth grade of an academic high school. She is attractive in general appearance, has good muscular coordination, and an alert, responsive facial expression.

Her father is a business executive and her mother is also in business. There are two children in the home. Previous teachers have evaluated the home influence as excellent.

On the Otis Self-administering Intelligence Test, Joanne obtained an IQ of 127 when she was in the eighth grade, and 143 two years later. Her grade score on the Stanford Achievement Test administered in the ninth grade was 11.5. Her marks in science and languages, where her major interest lies, are A's, in the other subjects, in the B range.

Joanne is the outstanding student of the biology class. When the instructor asked how the nucleus could be separated from the cytoplasm, she suggested that, since the cytoplasm contains food, starvation might leave only the nucleus. The instructor's correction of this original guess did not bring the slightest trace of any derision toward Joanne on the part of the other members of the class. This attitude is characteristic, despite the common tendency for a peer group to resent or ridicule a gifted individual who takes the lead in class.

Many other evidences have been observed of her interest in formulating her own hypotheses and in problem solving, of her intellectual curiosity, her enjoyment of thinking, and her originality. For example, when the instructor tried to elicit the ring structure of aromatic hydrocarbons from the class, after explaining simpler linear structures, Joanne came closest to the solution, developing the concept of a possible "middle" carbon linked to others. When cancer research was discussed with an emphasis on the hereditary aspect, Joanne referred to recent research that indicates transmission only through the mother's milk. She has a healthy disregard for the complaisant approach, and is satisfied with nothing less than the truth, even when her point of view implies criticism of the instructor's statement. Her genuine interest in the subject causes her frequently to remain after the period ends, eliciting more information from the instructor on whatever problem is bothering her.

She appears to be impelled to examine her religious beliefs also, and may be expected to be tolerant of others' faiths, while working out her own philosophy of life.

Her social adjustment is excellent. She is well balanced in her interests and activities and shows insight and *joie de vivre*. She has been accepted by her peers as an outstanding, likable individual.

Joanne shows most of the characteristics common to gifted adolescents—attractive physical appearance, good social adjustment, intellectual curiosity, delight in thoughtful discussion, creativity, and originality. She has had a lucky combination of good heredity and favorable home and school conditions, which offered opportunities for her to develop physically, intellectually, socially, and spiritually.

A gifted well-adjusted adolescent like Joanne needs guidance in understanding herself—her abilities and potentialities; in finding and using available educational opportunities for developing them; in choosing suitable vocational and avocational goals; and in acquiring a sense of social responsibility for her gifts.

GUIDANCE IN A CHANGING WORLD

All those responsible for the guidance of young people should help them to develop flexibility and adaptability to changing conditions, and patience with conditions that cannot be changed at present. The social aim of guidance is to help every individual change himself so that he can help make the world better.

In a personal letter to the author, Adriaan Smuts, Vocational Adviser, Transvaal Education Department, Johannesburg, South Africa, expressed admirably the social significance of guidance:

Each individual is going to be either a part of the problems of the world or part of the answer. . . . The main goal of guidance is to help the student find the right goal and have the right vision for his or her life. . . . Perspective is of the greatest importance. Young people in a materialistic world tend to think of the immediate gain, the immediate pleasure. Hence the pursuit of thrills, excessive participation in spectator sports, quick pecuniary returns, hasty marriages. . . . The important thing is that the adolescent gets the right slant on life and learns to think and live beyond mere whims and wishful thinking. He must know how to face the challenge of moral issues as they arise.

Each adolescent needs to believe that he has an important place in the world and can carry responsibilities appropriate for him.

COMPREHENSION QUESTIONS

1. On what kinds of problems do adolescents say they want guidance from adults?

2. What are some of their dissatisfactions with adult guidance? From your own experience and reading, do you think these criticisms are justified? In what proportion of cases?

3. After reading adolescents' statements about the kind of guidance they want, make a composite positive approach that you might use with adolescents as a parent, teacher, or friend.

4. Which of the statements quoted seem reasonable to you? Compare these statements with those made by psychologists and psychiatrists.

5. How is developmental guidance related to the self-concept?

6. Give examples of the misuse of standardized tests, and show how this can be avoided.

7. Compare the theory and practice of guidance as applied to the mentally retarded with procedures appropriate to the gifted. Would the same principles and general methods apply to other types of exceptional children—for example, the physically handicapped?

8. Why do you think many counselors in the public schools use a combination of methods rather than a single approach?

9. What relation has been found between the intelligence and the personal adjustment of adolescents?

10. Which so-called "problems" of adolescence are a normal part of growing up?

STUDY PROJECTS

1. From the conversation and unsigned compositions of adolescents with whom you have a good relationship obtain statements on "The kind of guidance adolescents want from adults." Use these to improve the quality of your own guidance.

2. Study the testing program in some school; how could test results there be used more effectively for guidance purposes?

3. Make a study in your community of educational and training opportunities for high school students who are not going to college.

4. Show how essential principles of a guidance program might be applied in the school you know best. What adaptations would be necessary?

5. Observe adolescents reading comics, looking at TV programs, or seeing movies that depict the worst side of adolescents. Try to determine their reactions and find out how these experiences affect them.

6. Discuss with a group of adolescents the comment made by a little girl who put together a jigsaw puzzle with the picture of a man on one side and a map of the world on the other side—"When I got the man right, the world was right." What do they think can be done to raise the level of adolescent values, standards, and goals?

7. Conduct a panel discussion with adolescents and their parents on the kind of home guidance that would be most effective for young people.

FOR FURTHER STUDY

ALLEN, FREDERICK, *Psychotherapy with Children*. New York: W. W. Norton & Company, Inc., 1942.

AUSUBEL, DAVID P., *Theory and Problems of Adolescent Development*, chap. XVII. New York: Grune & Stratton, Inc., 1954.

HALL, ROBERT KING, and J. A. LAUWERYS (eds.), *The Yearbook of Education, 1955: Guidance and Counseling*. Yonkers, N.Y.: World Book Company, 1955.

JOSSELYN, IRENE M., *The Adolescent and His World*, chaps. VIII, IX. New York: Family Service Association of America, 1952.

LANGEVELD, MARTIN J., "Some Considerations of the Ethics of Guidance," in *The Yearbook of Education, 1955: Guidance and Counseling* (Robert King Hall and J. A. Lauwerys, eds.), pp. 31–51. London: Evans Brothers, 1955.

MORRIS, GLYN, *Practical Guidance Methods for Principals and Teachers.* New York: Harper & Brothers, 1952.

NATIONAL SOCIETY FOR THE STUDY OF EDUCATION, *The Exceptional Child,* Forty-ninth Yearbook, part II. Chicago: University of Chicago Press, 1950.

ROGERS, CARL R., *Client-centered Therapy.* Boston: Houghton Mifflin Company, 1951.

———, *Counseling and Psychotherapy: Newer Concepts in Practice.* Boston: Houghton Mifflin Company, 1942.

ROTHNEY, JOHN W. M., and BERT A. ROENS, *Guidance of American Youth.* Cambridge, Mass.: Harvard University Press, 1950.

SANFORD, NEVITT, "The Uncertain Senior," *Journal of the National Association of Deans and Counselors,* vol. 21 (October, 1957), pp. 7–13.

WARBURTON, AMBER, *Guidance in a Rural Community—Green Sea, South Carolina.* Washington, D.C.: National Education Association, Alliance for Guidance of Rural Youth with the Department of Rural Education, 1952.

WATTENBERG, WILLIAM W., *The Adolescent Years,* chap. XXIV. New York: Harcourt, Brace and Company, Inc., 1955.

WILLIAMSON, E. G., *Counseling Adolescents.* New York: McGraw-Hill Book Company, Inc., 1950.

Fiction and Popular Articles

WITTENBERG, RUDOLPH M., *On Call for Youth: How to Understand and Help Young People.* New York: Association Press, 1955.

Audio-visual Aids

Role-playing in Guidance. 14 minutes. Sound. Black and white. University of California.

Family Affair. 31 minutes. Sound. Black and white. Mental Health Film Board.

Filmstrips

A Counselor's Day. 11 minutes. Sound. McGraw-Hill.

Diagnosis and Planning Adjustments in Counseling. 18 minutes. Sound. McGraw-Hill.

Using Analytical Tools. 14 minutes. Sound. McGraw-Hill.

FILM PUBLISHERS

Athena Films, Inc., 165 West 46th St., New York, N.Y.

Brandon Films, Inc., 200 West 57th St., New York, N.Y.

E. C. Brown Trust, Portland, Oregon

Coronet Films, 488 Madison Avenue, New York, N.Y.

Encyclopaedia Britannica Films, Inc., Wilmette, Illinois

Film Images, Inc., 1860 Broadway, New York, N.Y.

International Film Bureau, Chicago, Illinois

March of Time Forum Films, 369 Lexington Avenue, New York 17, N.Y.

McGraw-Hill Book Company, Inc., 330 West 42nd St., New York, N.Y.

Mental Health Film Board, Inc., 166 East 38th St., New York, N.Y.

Mental Health Materials Center, 1790 Broadway, New York 19, N.Y.

National Education Association, Washington, D.C.

National Film Board of Canada, 1270 Avenue of the Americas, New York, N.Y.

National Social Welfare Assembly, Youth Division, 345 East 46th St., New York, N.Y.

Ohio State University, Columbus, Ohio

RKO Radio Pictures, Inc., 1260 Avenue of the Americas, New York 20, N.Y.

Sovereign Productions, Inc., Los Angeles, California

Teaching Film Custodians, Inc., 25 West 43rd St., New York, N.Y.

University of California, Los Angeles, California

Wayne University, Detroit, Michigan

Young America Films, Inc., 18 East 41st St., New York, N.Y.

Name Index

Alcoholics Anonymous, 447
Allen, Frederick, 558
Allen, Lucile, 28
Allport, Gordon W., 7, 12, 34, 42, 70, 75–77, 88, 123, 163
Ames, Louise Bates, 5, 125, 130, 166, 181, 398
Anderson, Vernon E., 424
Arnold, Martha, 121, 130
Association for Supervision and Curriculum Development, 519
Ausubel, David P., 50, 78, 79, 173, 356, 376, 397, 411, 421, 558

Barber, Rowland, 481
Barclay, Dorothy, 6, 436, 439, 520
Barker, A. L., 207
Baron, Milton L., 479
Baruch, Dorothy W., 174, 398
Bayley, Nancy, 242, 246, 274, 275, 283
Beck, Bertram M., 445, 480
Behrman, S. N., 130
Bell, Howard M., 174, 432
Bellack, Arno A., 520
Benedict, Ruth, 33
Benét, Stephen Vincent, 175
Benson, Sally, 354
Berdan, Norman, 505
Berg, Janice, 323
Bettelheim, Bruno, 132, 133, 499, 500
Better Homes and Gardens, 342
Bibby, Harold Cyril, 353
Biddulph, Lowell G., 241
Bills, Robert E., 72, 85

Blair, Arthur Witt, 65, 206
Blos, Peter, 174
Boll, Eleanor Stoker, 398
Bossard, James H. S., 65, 336, 380, 398
Bowman, Henry, 354
Bronner, Augusta F., 449, 480
Brooks, Alice R., 519
Brown, Frederick W., 519
Brown, Marion, 433
Bullock, Harrison, 283
Burgess, Ernest W., 353
Burkhard, William J., 515
Burt, Nathaniel, 207
Burton, William H., 65, 165, 188, 206

Cabot, Hugh, 49
Cantril, Hadley, 33, 50, 130
Capehart, Bertis E., 505
Cartwright, Dorwin, 322, 507, 509
Cather, Willa, 175
Chaffey, Judith, 322
Chapman, A. L., 200
Chase, Mary Ellen, 362
Childs, Marquis W., 66
Clark, Willis W., 85
Cobb, Henry V. Z., 124
Cole, Luella, 207
Combs, Arthur W., 70, 130
Conrad, Herbert S., 275
Coon, Herbert L., 126
Corey, Stephen M., 199
Cowen, Emory, 78
Cronin, A. J., 207
Crow, Alice, 207

Subject Index